Lecture Notes in Computer !

Founding Editors

Gerhard Goos
Juris Hartmanis

The series Lecture Notes in Computer Science (LNCS), including its subseries Lecture Notes in Artificial Intelligence (LNAI) and Lecture Notes in Bioinformatics (LNBI), has established itself as a medium for the publication of new developments in computer science and information technology research, teaching, and education.

LNCS enjoys close cooperation with the computer science R & D community, the series counts many renowned academics among its volume editors and paper authors, and collaborates with prestigious societies. Its mission is to serve this international community by providing an invaluable service, mainly focused on the publication of conference and workshop proceedings and postproceedings. LNCS commenced publication in 1973.

Héctor D. Menéndez · Gema Bello-Orgaz ·
Pepita Barnard · John Robert Bautista ·
Arya Farahi · Santanu Dash · DongGyun Han ·
Sophie Fortz · Victor Rodriguez-Fernandez
Editors

Testing Software and Systems

36th IFIP WG 6.1 International Conference, ICTSS 2024
London, UK, October 30 – November 1, 2024
Proceedings

 Springer

Editors
Héctor D. Menéndez (iD)
King's College London
London, UK

Gema Bello-Orgaz (iD)
Universidad Politécnica de Madrid
Madrid, Spain

Pepita Barnard (iD)
University of Nottingham
Nottingham, UK

John Robert Bautista (iD)
University of Missouri
Columbia, MO, USA

Arya Farahi (iD)
The University of Texas at Austin
Austin, TX, USA

Santanu Dash (iD)
University of Surrey
Guildford, UK

DongGyun Han (iD)
Royal Holloway University of London
Egham, UK

Sophie Fortz (iD)
King's College London
London, UK

Victor Rodriguez-Fernandez (iD)
Universidad Politécnica de Madrid
Madrid, Spain

ISSN 0302-9743   ISSN 1611-3349 (electronic)
Lecture Notes in Computer Science
ISBN 978-3-031-80888-3   ISBN 978-3-031-80889-0 (eBook)
https://doi.org/10.1007/978-3-031-80889-0

This Springer imprint is published by the registered company Springer Nature Switzerland AG
The registered company address is: Gewerbestrasse 11, 6330 Cham, Switzerland

If disposing of this product, please recycle the paper.

Preface

This volume contains the proceedings of the 36th IFIP International Conference on Testing Software Systems (ICTSS 2024). This event is a well-established conference of Working Group 6.1 of the International Federation for Information Processing (IFIP). The conference was organized at King's College London in the UK but conducted at the Royal National Hotel in London. The conference took place during October 30th to November 1st, 2024.

ICTSS addresses multiple topics related to software systems, ranging from theoretical concepts of testing to practical testing frameworks. These include communication protocols, services, distributed computing, embedded systems, cyber-physical systems, security, infrastructure evaluation, applications of artificial intelligence to testing, and more. The conference engages both academic researchers and industrial practitioners, providing a forum for reviews and discussions on new contributions to the testing field in the form of methodologies, theories, tools, and use cases. This year also put extra emphasis on testing applications to Quantum Computing, Large Language Models, and Health.

This year, the conference received a total of 40 submissions consisting of regular papers, short papers, and project reports. From these submissions 17 were accepted as full papers, four as short papers, and one as a journal-first short paper. These papers cover multiple topics including artificial intelligence in testing, security of programs, monitoring and performance, and use cases. In this edition there is a strong emphasis on Large Language Models (LLMs)-based testing. ICTSS 2024 created a forum to share experiences and research works related to the conference topics. Papers from both academia and industry were represented and several aimed to find impact in new applications of testing for artificial intelligence. The papers were submitted following a single-blind peer review process with three reviewers per paper.

We want to thank King's College London for support in organizing the conference, the Trustworthy Autonomous System Hub (EP/V00784X/1) and the Alan Turing Institute (Grant G2027 - MuSE) for funding the conference, the Royal National Hotel for hosting the conference, and the authors who submitted their insightful contributions, the reviewers who provided their time and expertise and helped to ensure the quality of the accepted papers, the session chairs who managed the sessions, the keynote speakers, Cristian Cadar and Robert Hierons, the ICTSS career award, Ana Cavalli, and, finally, the Program Committee for their participation and advice along with the local organization team for running the conference and handling every specific detail. We would like to thank the ICTSS Steering Committee who gave support and advice when decisions were tricky. We especially thank Ma'ayan Armony, Hari Indran, Yazhuo Cao, Aidan Dakhama, Karine Even-Mendoza, and Gunel Jahangirova from the Organizing Committee who underpinned the conference organization and were always available to solve problems, whether of advertising, the webpage, or technical support during the conference. In addition we would like to thank IFIP for their ongoing support for this and earlier conferences in the series, as well as our publishers, Springer.

November 2024

Héctor D. Menéndez
Gema Bello-Orgaz
Pepita Barnard
John Robert Bautista
Arya Farahi
Santanu Dash
DongGyun Han
Sophie Fortz
Victor Rodriguez-Fernandez

Organization

General Chair

Héctor D. Menéndez   King's College London, UK

Program Committee Chairs

Gema Bello-Orgaz	Universidad Politécnica de Madrid, Spain
Pepita Barnard	University of Nottingham, UK
John Robert Bautista	University of Missouri - Columbia, USA
Arya Farahi	University of Texas at Austin, USA
Santanu Dash	University of Surrey, UK
DongGyun Han	Royal Holloway University of London, UK
Sophie Fortz	King's College London, UK
Victor Rodriguez-Fernandez	Universidad Politécnica de Madrid, Spain

Steering Committee

Ana Cavalli	Télécom & Management SudParis, France
Mercedes Merayo	Universidad Complutense de Madrid, Spain
David Clark	University College London, UK
Robert Hierons	University of Sheffield, UK
Angelo Gargantini	University of Bergamo, Italy
Silvia Bonfanti	University of Bergamo, Italy
Héctor D. Menéndez	King's College London, UK

Program Committee

Ricardo Aler	Universidad Carlos III, Spain
Shaukat Ali	Simula Research Laboratory and Oslo Metropolitan University, Norway
Moussa Amrani	University of Namur, Belgium
Kelly Androutsopoulos	Middlesex University London, UK
Paolo Arcaini	National Institute of Informatics, Japan

David Arroyo	Consejo Superior de Investigaciones Científicas, Spain
Martin Balfroid	University of Namur, Belgium
Kamel Barkaoui	CNAM, France
Pepita Barnard	University of Nottingham, UK
John Robert Bautista	University of Missouri - Columbia, USA
Gema Bello-Orgaz	Universidad Politécnica de Madrid, Spain
Matteo Biagiola	Università della Svizzera italiana, Switzerland
Daniel Blackwell	University College London, UK
Szymon Bobek	AGH University of Science and Technology, Poland
Silvia Bonfanti	University of Bergamo, Italy
Jose Campos	University of Porto, Portugal
Yazhuo Cao	King's College London, UK
David Clark	University College London, UK
Giordano D'Aloisio	Università degli Studi dell'Aquila, Italy
Santanu Dash	University of Surrey, UK
Arya Farahi	University of Texas at Austin, USA
Daniel Fortunato	University of Porto, Portugal
Sophie Fortz	King's College London, UK
Carlos Gavidia	Pontifica Universidad Católica del Perú, Peru
Jürgen Grossmann	Fraunhofer FOKUS, Germany
DongGyun Han	Royal Holloway, University of London, UK
Carol Hanna	University College London, UK
Nargiz Humbatova	Università della Svizzera italiana, Switzerland
Stefano Izzo	University of Naples Federico II, Italy
Gunel Jahangirova	King's College London, UK
Thierry Jéron	Inria, France
Fitsum Meshesha Kifetew	Fondazione Bruno Kessler, Italy
Gabriel Leach	University of Nottingham, UK
Yu Lei	University of Texas at Arlington, USA
Luis Llana	Universidad Complutense de Madrid, Spain
Yang Lu	York St John University, UK
Md Shadab Mashuk	University of Salford, UK
Radu Mateescu	Inria, France
Eñaut Mendiluze Usandizaga	Simula Research Laboratory, Norway
Héctor D. Menéndez	King's College London, UK
Mohammad Reza Mousavi	King's College London, UK
Mohammad Naiseh	Bournemouth University, UK
Grzegorz J. Nalepa	Jagiellonian University, Poland
Eneko Osaba	TECNALIA Research & Innovation, Spain
Angel Panizo Lledot	Universidad Politécnica de Madrid, Spain

Francesco Piccialli	University of Naples Federico II, Italy
Edoardo Prezioso	Università degli Studi di Napoli Federico II, Italy
Dominic Price	University of Nottingham, UK
Chaiyong Ragkhitwetsagul	Mahidol University, Thailand
Raj Kumar Rajaram Baskaran	University of Strathclyde, UK
Cristian Ramírez-Atencia	Universidad Politécnica de Madrid, Spain
Vincenzo Riccio	University of Udine, Italy
Victor Rodriguez-Fernandez	Universidad Politécnica de Madrid, Spain
Sébastien Salva	LIMOS, France
Hasan Sozer	Özyeğin University, Turkey
Valerio Terragni	University of Auckland, New Zealand
Andreas Ulrich	Siemens AG, Germany
Xinyi Wang	Simula Research Laboratory, Norway
Zhou Yang	Singapore Management University, Singapore
Xin Zhou	Singapore Management University, Singapore

Additional Reviewers

Wendelin Serwe
Abhishek Shrestha

Contents

Best Paper Award

Estimating Combinatorial t-Way Coverage Based on Matrix Complexity
Metrics 3
    Luiza Corpaci, Michael Wagner, Sebastian Raubitzek, Ludwig Kampel,
    Kevin Mallinger, and Dimitris E. Simos

Industry and Challenge Tracks

Enhancing RL Safety with Counterfactual LLM Reasoning 23
    Dennis Gross and Helge Spieker

GoNoGo: An Efficient LLM-Based Multi-agent System for Streamlining
Automotive Software Release Decision-Making 30
    Arsham Gholamzadeh Khoee, Yinan Yu, Robert Feldt,
    Andris Freimanis, Patrick Andersson Rhodin,
    and Dhasarathy Parthasarathy

Test Prioritization Based on the Coverage of Recently Modified Source
Code: An Industrial Case Study 46
    Hande Erol and Hasan Sözer

Mutation Testing and Code Generation

On the Variations of ChatGPT's Response Quality for Generating Source
Code Across Programming Languages 63
    Ángela González de Diego and Franz Wotawa

Reevaluating the Small-Scope Testing Hypothesis of Answer Set Programs 79
    Liliana Marie Prikler and Franz Wotawa

Advancing Code Vulnerability Detection

Enhancing Vulnerability Detection with Domain Knowledge:
A Comparison of Different Mechanisms 95
    Alessandro Marchetto and Rosmaël Zidane Lekeufack Foulefack

LLMs Can Check Their Own Results to Mitigate Hallucinations in Traffic
Understanding Tasks 114
  Malsha Ashani Mahawatta Dona, Beatriz Cabrero-Daniel, Yinan Yu,
  and Christian Berger

Enhanced Graph Neural Networks for Vulnerability Detection in Java
via Advanced Subgraph Construction 131
  Rosmaël Zidane Lekeufack Foulefack and Alessandro Marchetto

Short Papers

Mutating Clingo's AST with `clingabomino` 151
  Liliana Marie Prikler and Franz Wotawa

Towards a Knowledge Graph Based Approach for Vulnerable Code
Weaknesses Identification 159
  Martina Vecellio Reane, Daniele Dall'Anese, Rosmaël Z. L. Foulefack,
  and Alessandro Marchetto

Tutorial

Automatic Summarization Evaluation: Methods and Practices 169
  Héctor D. Menéndez and Aidan Dakhama

Journal First

Summary of ObfSec: Measuring the Security of Obfuscations
from a Testing Perspective 185
  Héctor D. Menéndez and Guillermo Suárez-Tangil

Health Track

A Trusted Friend in the Middle of the Night: End-User Perspectives
on Artificial Intelligence Informed Software Systems as a Decision-Making
Aid for Patients and Clinicians Navigating Uncertainty in Kidney
Transplant 193
  Laura R. Wingfield, Katie Wainwright, Simon Knight, and Helena Webb

Binary Classification Optimisation with AI-Generated Data 210
  Manuel Jesús Cerezo Mazón, Ricardo Moya García,
  Ekaitz Arriola García, Miguel Herencia García del Castillo,
  and Guillermo Iglesias

Responsible MLOps Design Methodology for an Auditing System
for AI-Based Clinical Decision Support Systems 217
*Pepita Barnard, John Robert Bautista, Aidan Dakhama, Arya Farahi,
Kazim Laos, Anqi Liu, and Héctor D. Menéndez*

Innovations in Software Testing and AI Compliance

Software System Testing Assisted by Large Language Models:
An Exploratory Study 239
*Cristian Augusto, Jesús Morán, Antonia Bertolino, Claudio de la Riva,
and Javier Tuya*

Continuous Auditing Based Conformity Assessment for AI Systems:
A Proof-of-Concept Evaluation 256
Dorian Knoblauch and Abhishek Shrestha

Improving Software Testing Reliability

Checking Test Suite Efficacy Through Dual-Channel Techniques 275
*Constantin Cezar Petrescu, Sam Smith, Alexis Butler,
and Santanu Kumar Dash*

Extending a Flakiness Score for System-Level Tests 292
Joanna Kisaakye, Mutlu Beyazıt, and Serge Demeyer

Advancements in Testing Methodologies

Autonomous Driving System Testing: Traffic Density Does Matter 315
Guannan Lou, Donghwan Shin, Neil Walkinshaw, and Robert M. Hierons

Annotation-Based Input Modeling for Combinatorial Testing 332
Markus Fugger, Manuel Leithner, and Dimitris E. Simos

Author Index 349

Best Paper Award

Estimating Combinatorial t-Way Coverage Based on Matrix Complexity Metrics

Luiza Corpaci[1] , Michael Wagner[2] , Sebastian Raubitzek[3] ,
Ludwig Kampel[2(✉)] , Kevin Mallinger[1,3] , and Dimitris E. Simos[2(✉)]

[1] Christian Doppler Laboratory for Assurance and Transparency in Software
Protection, University of Vienna, Vienna, Austria
{luiza.cristina.corpaci,kevin.mallinger}@univie.ac.at
[2] MATRIS Research Group, SBA Research, Vienna, Austria
{mwagner,lkampel,dsimos}@sba-research.org
[3] CORE Research Group, SBA Research, Vienna, Austria
sraubitzek2@sba-research.org

Abstract. Efficiently estimating combinatorial t-way coverage in software testing remains a significant challenge due to the high-dimensional complexity of modern software systems and the inherent complexity of the problem. This article explores a novel method that uses matrix complexity metrics as features in machine learning algorithms to estimate the t-way coverage of random test sets. Based on an input parameter model of the system under test (SUT) we derive complexity metrics from the singular value decomposition of the matrix representation of the test set. This makes our approach independent of the SUT's input space dimension and the size of the test set. Our approach provides a good estimation of the combinatorial t-way coverage while being faster and more scalable than a state of the art tool for the exact computation of combinatorial t-way coverage. Moreover, our experiments show a connection between the spectrum of singular values of a random test set and its t-way coverage. The use of complexity metrics as predictors in our machine learning pipeline adds a new dimension to the combinatorial testing domain, offering an additional tool for improving software testing processes.

Keywords: t-way Coverage · Machine Learning · Combinatorial
Testing · Random Testing · Complexity Metrics · Singular Value
Decomposition · Explainable Machine Learning

1 Introduction

Modern software and hardware systems have reached complexity levels that make it increasingly difficult to thoroughly test for a system's safety, reliability

---

L. Corpaci, M. Wagner, S. Raubitzek and L. Kampel—Equally contributing first authors.

© IFIP International Federation for Information Processing 2025
Published by Springer Nature Switzerland AG 2025
H. D. Menéndez et al. (Eds.): ICTSS 2024, LNCS 15383, pp. 3–20, 2025.
https://doi.org/10.1007/978-3-031-80889-0_1

and security. In recent years Combinatorial Testing (CT) has become a key technique in the software testing toolbox. CT is an input space coverage based testing strategy, i.e. the focus lies on systematically covering a prescribed set of combinations of input arguments of the System Under Test (SUT). In particular, for a given parameter t, called the *(interaction) strength*, the central notion of CT is *combinatorial t-way coverage*, or *t-way coverage* for short [14, Chapter 7]. It pertains to the appearance of parameter-value combinations of up to t input parameters, so-called *t-way interactions*, in vector representations of software tests. A thorough introduction to CT can be found in [14]. A prominent input space coverage criterion is *pairwise coverage* [8], where a tester wants to examine all pairs ($t = 2$) of parameter-value combinations through the tests of a test set. Empirical comparisons [34] with comparable software testing approaches favour CT in terms of fault detection ability. Further, empirical evidence, gathered through the analysis of software failure reports by Kuhn et al. [15] (and references therein), show that most of these failures are caused by combinations of at most four to six input parameters. They conclude that CT with test sets achieving full t-way coverage for appropriate strength t is pseudo-exhaustive, or at least "close" to exhaustive testing. This is the reason why CT is of particular interest when it comes to testing security-critical applications [28] or safety-critical systems [11]. In this article, we explore a novel method that uses matrix complexity metrics as features in machine learning algorithms to estimate combinatorial t-way coverage.

1.1   Preliminaries on Combinatorial t-Way Coverage Measurement

A necessary prerequisite for applying CT to an SUT is that the input, or configuration space of the system is modelled by means of an input parameter model (IPM) [7]. In its simplest form, an IPM enumerates parameters (also called factors or categories) and their respective domains, which contain the possible values each parameter can assume. Then, as also described in [7], each parameter value represents a non-empty partition of the input space. In practical testing problems, however, certain combinations of parameter-value assignments may be invalid for execution against the SUT. For practical applications, to avoid (attempted) execution of invalid test cases, one may formulate constraints between the input parameters and their values, to prevent considering (or generating) them in the first place. Such input space restrictions are generally considered part of the IPM and can be expressed, e.g. by explicitly listing invalid combinations of parameter-values, or by expressing the constraints in some first order logic. Provided an IPM, each test case for an SUT can be represented as a vector, say of length k. Then, each position of a vector corresponds to one input parameter, and the values in the vector represent the parameters' values. A test set containing N test cases for such an SUT can then be abstracted and represented as an $N \times k$ *matrix. For that reason, for the remainder of this work we use the terms matrices and test sets interchangeably.* Further, we assume that all input parameters of the SUT can take the same number of values v – an assumption that is certainly not met in the real-world, however, this does not stand in contrast with our approach or its evaluation, it rather facilitates the compact presentation of our experiments. Further, in this paper we only consider the case of unconstrained IPMs, also for the sake of keeping our experimental evaluation at a reasonable scale, as the treatment of constraints of different complexities (e.g. number and length of forbidden combinations) would add an additional layer of complexity to our experimental evaluation. The *combinatorial t-way coverage* that is central in combinatorial testing is defined as the percentage of all *t-way interactions* that appear in a test set, respectively in its matrix representation. A t-way interaction is defined as a combination of t different parameters of the IPM together with t values, one for each parameter. Analogue, it could be defined as a combination of t different columns of a matrix together with t values, one for each column. For an SUT with k parameters, where each parameter can take v different values, there are exactly $v^t \binom{k}{t}$ different t-way interactions, v^t different ones for each of the $\binom{k}{t}$ selections of t parameters. In the literature the concept of a t-way interaction is typically formalized as a set of pairs $\{(p_1, u_1), \ldots, (p_t, u_t)\}$, where $1 \leq p_1 < p_2 < \ldots < p_t \leq k$ represent the columns, and $u_1, \ldots, u_t \in \{0, \ldots, v-1\}$ represent the respective values. If all t-way interactions appear in a matrix, it is called *covering array* (CA) of strength t.

1 1 1 0
0 1 0 0
1 0 1 0
1 0 0 1
1 0 1 0

(a) Random matrix
H A_{rand}

1 0 1 1
1 1 0 1
0 1 1 1
1 1 1 0
0 0 0 0

(b) Covering array (CA)

Browser	IP	Processor	DBMS
Firefox	IPv6	Intel	MySQL
Firefox	IPv4	AMD	MySQL
Chrome	IPv4	Intel	MySQL
Firefox	IPv4	Intel	Oracle
Chrome	IPv6	AMD	Oracle

(c) Combinatorial test set from CA

Fig. 1. (a) Random matrix where entries are sampled uniformly at random, (b) covering array, and (c) combinatorial test set based on the CA in (b).

Figure 1 shows three matrices, a random matrix, a covering array and a 2-way combinatorial test set based on the latter. An example of a 2-way interaction for $k = 4$ columns is $\{(1,0), (3,1)\}$, which we may depict as $(0, \_, 1, \_)$. In the covering array given in Fig. 1b, this 2-way interaction appears in the third row, we also say it is *covered*. Since the matrix in Fig. 1b has full 2-way coverage, each 2-way interaction appears in at least one of its rows. On the other hand, the mentioned 2-way interaction is not covered by A_{rand} given in Fig. 1a, which does not achieve full 2-way coverage. When we iterate over all $2^2 \binom{4}{2} = 24$ 2-way interactions, we will find 5 of them not covered by any of the rows of A_{rand}, which therefore achieves only $19/24 = 79.1\dot{6}\%$ 2-way coverage. In Fig. 1c we give an *abstract* combinatorial test set for testing possible compositions of a PC where we test different browsers, internet protocol versions (IP), processors, and database management systems (DBMS). When we test all compositions described by the rows of this matrix, we will have examined every 2-way interaction of the components of the system. Although this is a very small example, it already points towards the complexity of combinatorial coverage measurement. A single vector of length k consists of $\binom{k}{t}$ different t-way interactions, each corresponding to the respective selections of t columns of the vector. To the best of the authors' knowledge, the only way to obtain certainty of the t-way coverage of a given test set for k parameters with v-ary domains, is to enumerate all $v^t \binom{k}{t}$ t-way interactions and iterate over the tests of the test set and check which t-way interactions are covered.

1.2   Motivation for t-Way Coverage Estimation

In practical applications, combinatorial testing can be applied as a complementary or supplementary method in combination with other software testing methods. In this case, it can be important to be able to *measure* the t-way coverage of existing, already performed software tests, which allows quantifying the number of untested t-way interactions, or in some cases extending the executed tests to achieve full t-way coverage. For example, a 2-way and 3-way combinatorial coverage measurement of existing tests of a validation framework of an Adobe product [30] (the reporting engine of Adobe Analytics) revealed, that despite millions of tests, significant fractions of input values and parameter-value combinations were not included in existing validation. In a separate study, CT was applied to different parts of the Adobe product, which features a high dimensional input space of over 2000 input parameters [29]. Such a high dimensional input space in addition to a large number of existing tests renders t-way coverage measurement by enumeration practically infeasible. The CT process in [29] is not based on extending existing tests, but on newly derived combinatorial test sets. Nevertheless, it revealed several undocumented constraints, and new failures in comparison to the previously applied random approach.

   These use case studies highlight the importance of being able to evaluate t-way coverage of a given test set in the application of CT. While for small and moderate sized problems, existing tools [13, 16] are sufficient to measure t-way coverage of existing test sets, the inherent combinatorial complexity of measuring t-way coverage makes them impractical when the tested system has a high dimensional input space. In addition to assessing combinatorial t-way coverage of existing test sets, a performant method to track and measure the t-way coverage is also critical for the generation of (optimized) combinatorial test sets and has been subject to previous research [1]. This is of particular interest for metaheuristic algorithms, as they rely on iteratively measuring the t-way coverage of candidate solutions. Notably, metaheuristics constitute the state of the art for generating combinatorial test sets for relatively *small* problem instances, see Torres-Jimenez et al. [32]. However, to make them applicable to larger problem instances a more scalable method for computing (or estimating) t-way coverage would be required. The present work aims to investigate a method that allows for a *fast* assessment of the t-way coverage of a given test set, by providing an estimation of its t-way coverage. To achieve this, we employ ideas from machine learning and complexity research. This intersection of disciplines allows the use of interpretable complexity metrics of data as a feature extraction method for machine learning approaches, as previously applied to time series and stock market data in particular, [19,23]. However, we extend these ideas to estimate the t-way coverage of random matrices, and thus to estimate the t-way coverage of randomly generated test sets.

Contribution. In this work, we utilize recent advances in matrix complexity metrics within machine learning models to estimate the combinatorial t-way coverage of test sets. In particular, the contributions of this article are:

1. The development of a novel approach to estimate the combinatorial t-way coverage of random test sets using matrix complexity metrics in a machine learning pipeline;
2. Our approach is agnostic to the size of the test sets. In more detail, our approach is applicable to test sets independent from the number of tests (N), the number of parameters (k) in the IPM, and therefore the length of the tests, and the size of their domains (v). Further, it works for different interaction strengths (t).
3. A comprehensive comparison against a baseline approach by means of an empirical validation on an extensive set of instances, i.e. for various sized randomly generated test sets for IPMs containing different numbers of parameters, for interaction strengths $t \in \{2, 3, 4\}$.
4. We are evaluating the link between the spectrum of singular values of randomly generated test sets and its t-way coverage.

At this point we want to stress that our approach is also applicable to estimate the t-way coverage of test sets that are not randomly generated.

Structure of the Paper. In the following, in Sect. 2 we present related work on t-way coverage estimation as well as complexity metrics used in combination with machine learning. Section 3 outlines our methodologies, discussing the integration of combinatorial testing techniques with complexity metrics derived from singular value decomposition. Section 5 describes the data generation, and how our machine learning approach is performed. Section 6 presents an experimental evaluation and a comparison of our models in terms of estimating t-way coverage of various random matrices, and thus for (synthetically generated abstract) random test sets. We conclude in Sect. 7 where we discuss the broader implications of our findings and suggest potential avenues for future research.

2   Related Work

Combinatorial Testing. Despite the various application domains of t-way coverage estimation outlined above, the topic has not been the focus of many research articles so far. Only recently, works investigating t-way coverage estimations seem to emerge. In 2022, Baranov et al. [3] introduced a Monte-Carlo approximation algorithm capable of estimating the coverage of partial test sets with certain approximation guarantees. Their proposed algorithm selects a specific number of t-way interactions uniformly at random such that the percentage of sampled t-way interactions that are covered is within a given approximation guarantee of the percentage of covered t-way interactions in the entire matrix with a given probability.

In 2019, Oh et al. [20] proposed a uniform sampling method of software tests (i.e. vectors) to enhance t-way coverage in software test generation. While their focus was on generating test sets, and not on measuring t-way coverage, their probabilistic analysis of experimental results is highly relevant to our work. In particular, they reason about the expected number of covered t-way interactions when uniformly sampling a certain number of test sets. For a single t-way interaction τ the probability of it being covered in a randomly selected test r specifying parameter values, each coming from a domain of size v is $\mathbb{P}(\tau \text{ covered by } r) = 1/v^t$, because r covers exactly one t-way interactions of the v^t many that can occur in the positions of τ. Thus, for a given (random) test set $\mathcal{S}$ with N such tests the probability of τ being covered is: $\mathbb{P}(\tau \text{ covered by } \mathcal{S}) = 1 - (1 - 1/v^t)^N$. Hence, we get further that for a given (random) test set with N such tests, the expected number of covered t-way interactions is:

$$\mathbb{E}(\text{Num. covered } t\text{-way interactions by } \mathcal{S}) = v^t \binom{k}{t}(1 - (1 - 1/v^t)^N). \quad (1)$$

We will compare our approach to this *baseline* in the experimental evaluation in Sect. 6.

Complexity Metrics and Machine Learning. The complexity of systems and their data remains an active area of research. Researchers have developed numerous theories and metrics to describe, explain, and indicate complexity at various levels. This article utilizes complexity metrics to analyze data, particularly matrices.

In a 2021 review, Raubitzek et al. [24] examined the integration of complexity metrics, such as the Hurst exponent and spectral entropy, into machine learning workflows. They found that these measures can enhance the accuracy and depth of analysis for time series predictions and offer new ideas on extracting features from data to be used for machine learning approaches. These ideas are further developed with specific applications for environmental and agricultural research in an article by Mallinger et al. [19]. Therein, the authors provide several examples along with corresponding code on utilizing complexity metrics in machine learning approaches within these fields. While these publications primarily focus on complexity metrics for time series data, many of these techniques also apply to any matrix-like data. Techniques such as the spectrum of Lyapunov exponents, and most notably for this paper, metrics based on *singular value decomposition* (SVD), require embedding the time series, with an appropriate embedding dimension [26]. This process involves constructing a correlation matrix, which is analyzed using the spectrum of singular values to determine the data's complexity. Thus, we can justify using SVD-based complexity metrics for analyzing any type of matrices. This means that our set of SVD-based complexity metrics applies to matrices in general, though our motivation and their initial use cases are rooted in time series analysis, [26]. This and similar approaches motivated us to develop our approach for estimating t-way coverage of matrices of any dimension, as described in the following section.

3   Methodologies for T-Way Coverage Estimation

For the exploration of the t-way coverage of test sets across different numbers of tests, numbers of input parameters in the underlying IPMs and domain sizes, the main challenges are posed by the different number of parameters in the IPM and the varying domain sizes. Addressing this problem requires an approach that can abstract the properties of the corresponding matrices in both a size-agnostic manner and a domain size-agnostic way. The characteristics of the spectrum of singular values are a useful tool to describe the properties of a matrix independent of its actual dimensions. Since matrices of different sizes yield different counts of singular values, we developed a scalable approach that computes a single scalar value by collapsing the spectrum of singular values into a metric. This method involves a series of transformations, as detailed below, which were chosen after considering similar approaches from the literature [19,24,27] in order to cover a diverse set of properties, serving as features for a regression-based approach to model the complexity of the t-way coverage measurement.

SVD-Based Matrix Complexity. Singular Value Decomposition (SVD) is a well-known tool used, e.g., for image compression, agnostic of the size and type of a given matrix [22]. The spectrum of singular values of a matrix A is obtained via a factorization of the form $A = U \Sigma U^{\dagger}$, where U and $U^{\dagger}$ are rotation matrices and Σ is a diagonal matrix, with real non-negative singular values $\sigma_1, \sigma_2, \ldots, \sigma_p$, where $p = \min(m,n)$ is the rank of matrix A. We further obtain normalized singular values as $\bar{\sigma}_i = \frac{\sigma_i}{\sum_{j=1}^{p} \sigma_j}$.

SVD suffers from the fact that the information of matrices with a low rank but a high number of rows and/or columns is compressed into a small number of singular values. Further, SVD does not provide an expressive spectrum of singular values for binary matrices. To cope with these insufficiencies, we perform three transformations to the regarded matrices, i.e., the test sets, before obtaining the spectrum of singular values. In the following we denote by A_{T} a matrix that is the original matrix A or any of its transforms defined below, i.e., $A_{\mathrm{T}} \in \{A, A_{\mathrm{S}}, A_{\mathrm{B}}, A_{\mathrm{B,S}}\}$. The transformations are defined as follows:

- $A_{\mathbf{S}}$, **we perform a square transformation:** This transformation serves to make matrices with significantly different numbers of rows and columns more expressive. We perform one of the following operations to get a matrix with maximal rank: $A \cdot A^{\mathrm{T}}$ or $A^{\mathrm{T}} \cdot A$
- $A_{\mathbf{B}}$, **we perform a row-wise Bloch transformation:** This transformation resolves the problem of varying domain sizes in the IPMs of the SUTs, which are leading to matrices over alphabets of different sizes v. In particular, it solves the problem of binary matrices which do not yield an SVD. This is done by the normalization appearing in the computation of the Bloch-transform A_{B}. $A_{\mathrm{B}(i,j)} = \frac{A_{(i,j)}}{\sqrt{\sum_j A_{(i,j)}^2}}$, [33].
- $A_{\mathbf{B,S}}$**:** Applied both the square and row-wise Bloch transformation.

Next, we apply complexity metrics based on the singular value decomposition of a matrix, focusing on extracting *relative* information from the spectrum of singular values, [25]. *Relative* in this context means that we disregard the absolute number of singular values and matrix sizes, making our approach agnostic to matrix dimensions.

In particular, we compute the following values based on the singular values of A, to which we collectively refer to as *SVD complexity metrics* in the following: their entropy (2), quantifying diversity within the distribution of the spectrum of singular values, [26]; their Fisher Information (3), measuring the amount of information that singular values convey relative to each other [18]; their spectral radius (4), useful for characterizing large random matrices, [2]; their condition number (5), highlighting matrices with significant disparities and thus addressing compressibility thereof, [5]; their relative decay (6), indicating the rate at which the singular values decrease; their energy (7), evaluating the dominance of the first k singular values in the total energy of the matrix; and their product (8).

- **Entropy of Singular Values**

$$SVentropy\,(A_\mathrm{T}) = -\sum_{i=1}^{p} \bar{\sigma}_i \log_2 \bar{\sigma}_i \tag{2}$$

- **Fisher Information**

$$Fisher\,(A_\mathrm{T}) = \sum_{i=1}^{p-1} \frac{[\bar{\sigma}_{i+1} - \bar{\sigma}_i]^2}{\bar{\sigma}_i} \tag{3}$$

- **Spectral Radius**

$$SpectralRad\,(A_\mathrm{T}) = \max_i |\sigma_i| \tag{4}$$

- **Condition Number**

$$CondNum\,(A_\mathrm{T}) = \frac{\max_i(\sigma_i)}{\min_i(\sigma_i)} \tag{5}$$

- **Relative Decay**

$$RelDecay\,(A_\mathrm{T}) = \frac{\sigma_i}{\sigma_{i+1}} \tag{6}$$

- **Singular Values Energy**

$$SVenergy\,(A_\mathrm{T}) = \frac{\sum_{i=1}^{k=3} \sigma_i^2}{\sum_{i=1}^{p} \sigma_i^2} \tag{7}$$

- **Singular Values Product**

$$SVproduct\,(A_\mathrm{T}) = \prod_{i=1}^{p} \sigma_i \tag{8}$$

Machine Learning. In this article, we draw inspiration from previous attempts to assess the complexity of systems and data using machine learning. In particular, one can construct time series data with particular complexities (their scaling exponents) and train a machine learning regressor using this data and the associated information/complexity and then use the trained model to assess the complexity of given data, as shown in [23]. In contrast, in this paper, we use our SVD complexity metrics (Eqs. (2)–(8)) as input for the machine learning model. However, similar to the scaling exponent approach [23], we predict a known ground truth of the regarded data: the t-way coverage of randomly generated test sets. To do so, we selected two widely used machine learning models, specifically a linear model - Lasso regression [31] - and a tree-based model - LightGBM [12] We chose these two regressors as a repesentation of sophisticated boost classifers and to determine whether the *t*-way coverage can be expressed as a linear combination of the regarded SVD metrics or if the non-linear, tree-based approach offers better performance, indicating that *t*-way coverage cannot be easily quantified solely through SVD-based complexity metrics and linear dependencies. Further, both of these algorithms are known to perform well on a variety of problems and can easily be implemented. To evaluate the performance of our models, we compute (1) the *root mean squared error* (RMSE) and (2) the *maximal residuals* between the model's output predicted *t*-way coverage and the exactly computed *t*-way coverage. Our approach employs model interpretability and explainability; for the linear model, we extract and normalize the feature coefficients. In contrast, the tree-based classifier allows for feature-importance analysis, which helps depict the features' relative importance.

Lasso [31] regression, a well-established linear regression method, uses a penalty term on the coefficients to achieve variable selection and regularization. This approach reduces the likelihood of overfitting by shrinking some coefficients to zero, which simplifies the model and improves interpretability, especially in high-dimensional settings.

LightGBM [12], is an advanced tree-based learning model based on gradient boosting. It was developed for rapid training speeds, reduced memory usage, and enhanced accuracy.

4   Performance Metrics

For the evaluation of our approach and the comparison with existing methods, we are using the following performance metrics.

RMSE (Root Mean Square Error). The Root Mean Square Error [21] provides a measure of the average error magnitude between the predicted $(\hat{y}_i)$ and the actual *t*-coverage values (y_i). Lower RMSE values indicate better predictive accuracy:

$$RMSE = \sqrt{\frac{1}{n}\sum_{i=1}^{n}(y_i - \hat{y}_i)^2} \tag{9}$$

Maximum Residual(s). Based on the RMSE, Eq. 9, we also used the maximal residual of each regression approach as a performance metric to assess the volatility of our estimates, this is related to the RMSE such that:

$$Max\,Residual = \max_i(y_i - \hat{y}_i) \tag{10}$$

5   Experimental Setup

Due to the absence of real-world test sets, we evaluate our models on random arrays, which can be understood as representing test sets for random testing of appropriate SUT. Figure 2 gives an overview of our experimental setup. Initially, we generated a dataset consisting of randomly generated test sets with various numbers of tests (N) for on various IPMs (without constraints) with varying numbers of parameters (k) and their domain sizes (v). These test sets are represented by random $N \times k$ matrices over different alphabets and of various dimensions N and k. The generation of these matrices together with the computation of their exact t-way coverage, is described in the following Subsect. 5.1. We then applied the selected transformations (square A_S, Bloch A_B and Bloch-square $A_{B,S}$) to these random matrices (test sets). Next, we computed the spectrum of singular values from each of these matrices and from these spectra the corresponding SVD complexity metrics (Eqs. (2)–(8)). We used this as the input for our machine learning models to predict the t-way coverage of the regarded test sets. We trained our models on 80% of the generated data using a 5-fold cross-validation with a Bayesian optimization approach to find the best model. We then tested these trained *best* models on the remaining 20% of the data to evaluate our approach. We compared these results to the previously introduced baseline, i.e., the probabilistic t-way coverage estimation given in Eq. (1). Furthermore, since we can always compute this baseline from the properties of a considered test set (its size N, number of parameters K, domain size v and strength t of interest), we also evaluated our models when adding this probabilistic t-way coverage estimation into our input features. This addition helps us understand how it affects both the linear and the nonlinear model. Adding this baseline estimation to our feature space might sound counterintuitive from the point of view of a machine learning practitioner but it makes sense in that this information can be computed from the underlying properties of the matrix and thus can be considered just another way of extracting features from our random test sets. These two ways to assemble our feature space are depicted on the left side of Fig. 2.

5.1   Data Generation

In order to evaluate the performance of our models, we consider t-way coverage measurement problems representing 64 *instances* of different classes of complexity (as also implied in [32, Sec. IX]), i.e. different selections of strength t, domain sizes v and number of parameters/columns k. We carefully selected the ranges for t, k and v based on appearing problems in real life, which range from tens to hundreds of input parameters up to thousand [29], as well as our computational limitations. In particular, we consider for each domain size $v \in \{2, 3, 4, 5\}$ and strength $t \in \{2, 3, 4\}$ the instances with $k \in \{20, 50, 100, 200, 500, 1000\}$ input parameters in the IPM, except for $t = 4$, where we had to skip the instances with $k = 500$ and $k = 1000$ input parameters in the IPM due to time- and memory-constraints of our computational infrastructure.

For each such instance, we computed a dataset consisting of 2000 randomly generated test sets, serving as the input data, as well as their t-way coverage, which serves as the target, resulting in a total of 128000 samples. Each test set, and the corresponding t-way coverage, was constructed using the following algorithm: First, a target t-way coverage is selected randomly between 50% and 99%. Afterwards, tests are added one by one to an initially empty test set, where

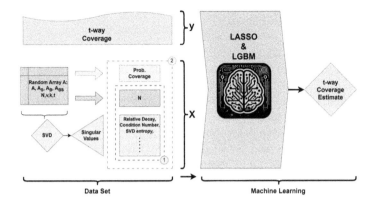

Fig. 2. Experimental setup and the compilation of the feature space. Left, underlined with *Dataset*: describes the structure of our dataset. The dataset consists of a feature space X and the target variable y: the t-way coverage. The feature space is constructed from the matrices A, A_S, A_B, A_{BS}, using SVD to obtain the complexity features. We then define two cases for our dataset, denoted as ① and ②, and marked by dashed lines, both including the number of rows N of the random matrix A. ① represents the dataset without our baseline probabilistic t-way coverage estimation (1), whereas ② includes it as a feature. Right: The *Machine Learning* part, trains the respective model to estimate the t-way coverage of an input matrix, respectively of a test set, based on the feature space.

each parameter-value of the new test is selected uniformly at random from the domain. After adding a test, we update the t-way coverage of the current test set. Once the target t-way coverage is exceeded, the algorithm terminates and the constructed random test set and its t-way coverage is added to the dataset. We selected a lower coverage bound of 50% because t-way coverage grows rapidly for initial tests. For example, for any instance with $t = v = 2$ any first test will already cover $\binom{k}{2}$, i.e. 25% of the $2^2\binom{k}{2}$ t-way interactions. Without a lower bound a quarter of the dataset would be test sets with a single (likely different) test with the same t-way coverage value.

Generating the entire dataset of 128000 random test sets together with their t-way coverage took over a month, despite generating between 15 and 30 random test sets in parallel on an AMD EPYC 7502P processor with 32 cores at 2.5 GHz base clock and 3.35 GHz boost clock and 128 GB of RAM. The main challenge in generating this data set is the exponential increase in the number of t-selections of parameters in the IPMs that need to be evaluated. For each test and each of the $\binom{k}{t}$ t-selections of parameters, the corresponding t-way interaction needs to be encoded to an integer and marked as covered. In addition, increasing the domain size v requires a significantly higher number of tests on average to achieve the same percentage of t-way coverage. For these reasons, we limit the strength used in our experiments to $t \leq 4$ and skip the instances with $k = 500$ and $k = 1000$ parameters in the IPM for $t = 4$.

6   Results and Discussion

In the following, we discuss the results of our conducted experiments presented in Fig. 3. We analyze where and to what extent the trained machine learning models perform well, i.e., where they are better than the baseline probabilistic estimator (1). We further discuss which features (complexity metrics) are important in this process, and how this provides insights into the connection between t-way coverage and singular value decomposition. Supplementary information, such as additional visualizations and detailed numerical results (containing the RMSE and maximal residuals for all experiments) are available online[1].

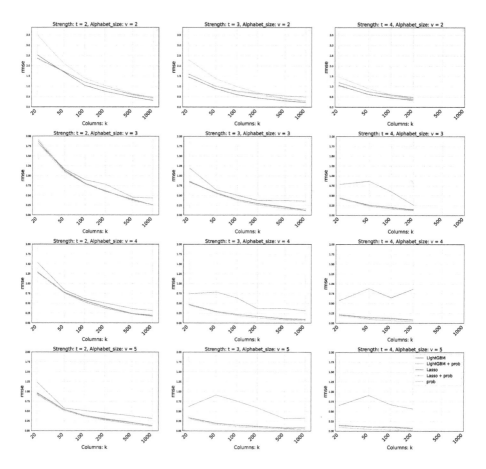

Fig. 3. RMSE comparison between the probabilistic estimator ("prob") and "Lasso"/"LightGBM" both with and without the probabilistic estimator ("+ prob") used as an input feature, for all combinations of strength t, number of parameters in the IPM k, and domain size v.

---

[1] Available at: https://srd.sba-research.org/data/ml4ct/mcm4cce/.

Figure 3 shows that our machine learning approach can outperform the probabilistic baseline estimate (1), particularly for binary test sets, i.e. domain size $v = 2$. Here, the LightGBM estimates always outperform the probabilistic estimate, both with and without the baseline included. The Lasso regressor, however, performs worse than the baseline for increasing numbers of parameters k. For other domain sizes, we see that LightGBM is always very close to the baseline, sometimes outperforming it and sometimes being just very close. The Lasso regressor without the probabilistic estimation as feature input performs worse, while when including it, "Lasso+prob" performs similarly to the baseline. This indicates that t-way coverage and the spectrum of singular values are better predicted by models that accommodate non-linear behavior, such as LightGBM. It also suggests that the information in the baseline estimate, cannot be linearly derived from our SVD metrics. We note that the Lasso regressor without the probabilistic estimate exhibits alternating performance for an increasing number k of parameters, as can be seen in several graphs of Fig. 3. However, for the three other models, the RMSE values get smaller for increasing domain sizes and increasing numbers of parameters k of the randomly generated test sets.

Overall, there are cases and instances, particularly for domain size $v = 2$, where our machine learning approaches perform well. Moreover, the trained LightGBM models allow for improvement over the regarded baseline throughout all binary instances, see the first line of graphs in Fig. 3 where $v = 2$, but particularly perform well with respect to the baseline for low numbers of columns k. Additionally, we would like to note that the uniform sampling used in generating the random test sets likely enhanced the performance of the probabilistic baseline estimation. In practice, however, test sets manually created or partial combinatorial test sets often contain dependencies or other inner structure that deviates from uniform sampling. Our metrics based on SVD *might be able* to model these dependencies and, therefore, perform significantly better than the baseline approach in these cases. Since this paper is dedicated to randomly generated test sets, we leave the investigation of this hypothesis for future work.

Moreover, when comparing to the runtimes of CAmetrics [16], to the computation of the SVD-based features added to the prediction time of our ML models, we identified a speed-up of a factor of 2.7 to 25 across all considered instance complexities, demonstrating that ML based estimation of t-way coverage bears improved time efficiency over precise computation of t-way coverage.

Table 1. This table displays the top ten features on average for each model across all instances, i.e., different domain sizes, strengths, and input parameters, in the two distinct datasets: one including the baseline estimate and the other not including the baseline estimate.

	Lasso	Lasso + prob	LightGBM	LightGBM + prob
1	SVentropy(A)	prob(A)	N(A)	N(A)
2	SpectralRad(A)	SpectralRad(A)	Fisher(A_B)	RelDecay(A_S)
3	RelDecay(A_{BS})	SVenergy(A)	Fisher(A_{BS})	Fisher(A_B)
4	N(A)	N(A)	Fisher(A)	Fisher(A_{BS})
5	RelDecay(A_S)	SVentropy(A_{BS})	RelDecay(A_S)	Fisher(A)
6	RelDecay(A)	SVentropy(A)	SVenergy(A_B)	Fisher(A_S)
7	SVentropy(A_S)	RelDecay(A_S)	Fisher(A_S)	SVenergy(A_B)
8	RelDecay(A_B)	SVentropy(A_S)	SVenergy(A)	SVenergy(A)
9	SVProduct(A_B)	SVenergy(A_B)	SVenergy(A_S)	SVenergy(A_S)
10	SVenergy(A_S)	RelDecay(A_{BS})	SpectralRad(A)	SpectralRad(A)

Further, to analyze how important the individual features are in our trained models, we performed a feature importance analysis [17] for the LightGBM models. We took the absolute value of the coefficients associated with each feature for the Lasso regressor. Additionally, both of these feature importance *metrics* were normalized to yield comparable results, which are averaged and collected over all instances in Table 1, showing which features are the most important ones for each regressor.

Our feature importance analysis shows that for both LightGBM approaches, the number of rows of the matrix is the most important feature. This makes sense because the t-way coverage depends largely on the number of tests in a random test set, as an increased number of tests allows for more possible combinations to be covered. Furthermore, as one would expect for the Lasso regressor with the baseline included, the best regressors use this baseline to get a good estimate of the t-way coverage. Another important feature of the Lasso regressor is the entropy of the singular values of the non-transformed matrix A. In contrast to the results for the Lasso regressor, we do not see the probabilistic baseline estimate - *prob* - among the top ten results of the LightGBM regressor that can also use the baseline to estimate the t-way coverage, meaning that the combination of other metrics is more expressive when trained on the actual/ground-truth t-way coverage. Observing the other important metrics, we see that the relative decay and Fisher's information of various transformed matrices are among the top ten features for both Lasso and LightGBM. Additionally, the spectral radius of a non-transformed matrix, i.e., the largest singular value, is particularly important. Summarizing, the manner in which the singular values descend, as described by relative decay (6) and Fisher's information (3), provides the most significant insights among the SVD metrics. This implies that, considering SVD can be used to compress the information of matrices; the granularity and information density described by the spectrum of singular values descends are important. Hypothesizing – There is a link between a random test set's t-way coverage and the information density described by the spectrum of singular values of the corresponding matrix. Thus, the SVD information density of the parameters in the IPM and the tests govern the behavior of our machine learning models.

7 Conclusion and Future Work

We introduced and explored a novel approach for estimating combinatorial t-way coverage of uniform test sets using matrix complexity metrics and explainable machine learning techniques. Our method shows improved performance compared to the baseline probabilistic estimator for binary random test sets and similar performance for larger domain sizes ($v > 2$). Moreover, when comparing to the runtimes of CAmetrics [16], the computation of the SVD-based features added to the prediction time shows better time efficiency. This speed advantage indicates that our method can quickly estimate combinatorial t-way coverage, not necessarily as a replacement for exact combinatorial t-way coverage measurement, but rather as a complementary tool.

Our use of singular value decomposition (SVD) based complexity metrics provides a framework that is agnostic to the size of the regarded test sets and the underlying IPMs and further allows us to reason about feature interpretability in this context. This is linked to our choices of machine learning models. Regarding the comparison between a tree-based and a linear model, if our Lasso regressor had shown comparable performance, this would have meant that we could describe the t-way coverage as a linear combination of different aspects of our spectrum of singular values. However, since this is not the case, we can infer that this relationship is rather non-linear and that one cannot simply express the t-way coverage of a test set with information from the spectrum of singular values. This is supported by the tree-based model LightGBM outperforming Lasso in our experiments. In short, the relationship between the singular values of a test set and its t-way coverage is more intricate than a linear relationship.

Finally, while our ML models show good performance for t-way coverage estimation, the results confirm that they cannot replace exact combinatorial t-way coverage measurement. They can, however, offer a complementary method that efficiently provides a close approximation, this can be helpful in practice to quickly assess t-way coverage of existing test sets, or in heuristic algorithms for the construction of combinatorial test sets to evaluate intermediate solutions.

For future work, first and foremost, we want to reproduce the results of our presented approach when applied to IPMs with heterogeneous parameter domains as well as IPMs with constraints. Another avenue of future work is to further enhance our approach in terms of speed. One way for doing so would be to explore the applicability of randomized SVD and/or randomized linear algebra in this context [4,6,9]. Employing randomized SVD could potentially speed up the SVD process, which is one of the bottlenecks of our approach. Moreover, introducing randomness might also enrich our training dataset. Although this might seem counterintuitive for a relatively static property such as t-way coverage, slightly randomized or augmented datasets can lead to improved learning by the machine learning models used, [10].

Acknowledgments. SBA Research (SBA-K1) is a COMET Centre within the COMET – Competence Centers for Excellent Technologies Programme and funded by BMK, BMAW, and the federal state of Vienna. COMET is managed by FFG. Additionally, the financial support by the Austrian Federal Ministry of Labour and Economy, the National Foundation for Research, Technology and Development and the Christian Doppler Research Association is gratefully acknowledged.

Disclosure of Interests. The authors have no competing interests to declare that are relevant to the content of this article.

References

1. Ahmed, B.S., Gambardella, L.M., Zamli, K.Z.: A new approach to speed up combinatorial search strategies using stack and hash table. In: 2016 SAI Computing Conference (SAI), pp. 1217–1222 (2016)
2. Alt, J., Erdős, L., Krüger, T.: Spectral radius of random matrices with independent entries. Probab. Math. Phys. **2**(2), 221–280 (2021)
3. Baranov, E., Chakraborty, S., Legay, A., Meel, K.S., Variyam, V.N.: A scalable t-wise coverage estimator. In: Proceedings of the 44th International Conference on Software Engineering, pp. 36–47 (2022)
4. Benjamin Erichson, N., Brunton, S.L., Nathan Kutz, J.: Compressed singular value decomposition for image and video processing. In: Proceedings of the IEEE International Conference on Computer Vision (ICCV) Workshops (2017)
5. Edelman, A.: Eigenvalues and condition numbers of random matrices. SIAM J. Matrix Anal. Appl. **9**(4), 543–560 (1988)
6. Erichson, N.B., Voronin, S., Brunton, S.L., Kutz, J.N.: Randomized matrix decompositions using R. J. Stat. Softw. **89**(11) (2019)
7. Grindal, M., Offutt, J.: Input parameter modeling for combination strategies. In: Proceedings of the 25th Conference on IASTED International Multi-Conference: Software Engineering, SE 2007, pp. 255–260. ACTA Press, Anaheim (2007)
8. Grindal, M., Offutt, J., Andler, S.F.: Combination testing strategies: a survey. Softw. Test. Verif. Reliabil. **15**(3), 167–199 (2005)
9. Halko, N., Martinsson, P.G., Tropp, J.A.: Finding structure with randomness: probabilistic algorithms for constructing approximate matrix decompositions. SIAM Rev. **53**(2), 217–288 (2011)
10. Jackson, P.T., Abarghouei, A.A., Bonner, S., Breckon, T.P., Obara, B.: Style augmentation: data augmentation via style randomization. In: Conference on Computer Vision and Pattern Recognition (CVPR) Workshops, vol. 6, pp. 10–11 (2019)
11. Jayakumar, A.V., et al.: Systematic software testing of critical embedded digital devices in nuclear power applications. In: IEEE International Symposium on Software Reliability Engineering Workshops (ISSREW), pp. 85–90. IEEE (2020)
12. Ke, G., et al.: LightGBM: a highly efficient gradient boosting decision tree. In: Proceedings of the 31st International Conference on Neural Information Processing Systems, NIPS 2017, pp. 3149–3157. Curran Associates Inc., Red Hook (2017)

13. Kuhn, D.R., Mendoza, I.D., Kacker, R.N., Lei, Y.: Combinatorial coverage measurement concepts and applications. In: 2013 IEEE Sixth International Conference on Software Testing, Verification and Validation Workshops, pp. 352–361 (2013)
14. Kuhn, D., Kacker, R., Lei, Y.: Introduction to Combinatorial Testing. Chapman & Hall/CRC Innovations in Software Engineering and Software Development Series, 1st edn. Taylor & Francis (2013)
15. Kuhn, R., Kacker, R.N., Lei, Y., Simos, D.: Input space coverage matters. Computer **53**(1), 37–44 (2020)
16. Leithner, M., Kleine, K., Simos, D.E.: CAMETRICS: a tool for advanced combinatorial analysis and measurement of test sets. In: 2018 IEEE International Conference on Software Testing, Verification and Validation Workshop (ICSTW), pp. 318–327 (2018)
17. Louppe, G., Wehenkel, L., Sutera, A., Geurts, P.: Understanding variable importances in forests of randomized trees. In: Advances in Neural Information Processing Systems, vol. 26. Curran Associates, Inc. (2013)
18. Makowski, D., et al.: NeuroKit2: a python toolbox for neurophysiological signal processing. Behav. Res. Methods **53**(4), 1689–1696 (2021)
19. Mallinger, K., Raubitzek, S., Neubauer, T., Lade, S.: Potentials and limitations of complexity research for environmental sciences and modern farming applications. Curr. Opin. Environ. Sustain. **67**, 101429 (2024)
20. Oh, J., Gazzillo, P., Batory, D.: t-wise coverage by uniform sampling. In: Proceedings of the 23rd International Systems and Software Product Line Conference-Volume A, pp. 84–87 (2019)
21. Pedregosa, F., et al.: Scikit-learn: machine learning in Python. J. Mach. Learn. Res. **12**, 2825–2830 (2011)
22. Prasantha, H., Shashidhara, H., Balasubramanya Murthy, K.: Image compression using SVD. In: International Conference on Computational Intelligence and Multimedia Applications (ICCIMA 2007), vol. 3, pp. 143–145 (2007)
23. Raubitzek, S., Corpaci, L., Hofer, R., Mallinger, K.: Scaling exponents of time series data: a machine learning approach. Entropy **25**(12), 1671 (2023)
24. Raubitzek, S., Neubauer, T.: Combining measures of signal complexity and machine learning for time series analysis: a review. Entropy **23**(12) (2021)
25. Raubitzek, S., Schrittwieser, S., Lawitschka, C., Mallinger, K., Ekelhart, A., Weippl, E.: Code obfuscation classification using singular value decomposition on grayscale image representations. In: SECRYPT (2024)
26. Roberts, S.J., Penny, W., Rezek, I.: Temporal and spatial complexity measures for electroencephalogram based brain-computer interfacing. Med. Biol. Eng. Comput. **37**(1), 93–98 (1999)
27. Schrittwieser, S., et al.: Modeling obfuscation stealth through code complexity. In: Computer Security. ESORICS 2023 International Workshops, pp. 392–408. Springer, Cham (2024)
28. Simos, D.E., Kuhn, R., Voyiatzis, A.G., Kacker, R.: Combinatorial methods in security testing. Computer **49**(10), 80–83 (2016)
29. Smith, R., et al.: Applying combinatorial testing to large-scale data processing at Adobe. In: 2019 IEEE International Conference on Software Testing, Verification and Validation Workshops (ICSTW), pp. 190–193 (2019)
30. Smith, R., Jarman, D., Bellows, J., Kuhn, R., Kacker, R., Simos, D.: Measuring combinatorial coverage at adobe. In: IEEE International Conference on Software Testing, Verification and Validation Workshops (ICSTW), pp. 194–197 (2019)
31. Tibshirani, R.: Regression shrinkage and selection via the lasso. J. Roy. Stat. Soc.: Ser. B (Methodol.) **58**(1), 267–288 (2018)

32. Torres-Jimenez, J., Izquierdo-Marquez, I., Avila-George, H.: Methods to construct uniform covering arrays. IEEE Access **7**, 42774–42797 (2019)
33. Wagner, M., Kampel, L., Simos, D.E.: Quantum-inspired evolutionary algorithms for covering arrays of arbitrary strength. In: Analysis of Experimental Algorithms, pp. 300–316. Springer, Cham (2019)
34. Wu, H., Nie, C., Petke, J., Jia, Y., Harman, M.: An empirical comparison of combinatorial testing, random testing and adaptive random testing. IEEE Trans. Softw. Eng. **46**(3), 302–320 (2020)

Industry and Challenge Tracks

Enhancing RL Safety with Counterfactual LLM Reasoning

Dennis Gross[(✉)] and Helge Spieker

Simula Research Laboratory, Oslo, Norway
dennis@simula.no

Abstract. *Reinforcement learning (RL)* policies may exhibit unsafe behavior and are hard to explain. We use counterfactual large language model reasoning to enhance RL policy safety post-training. We show that our approach improves and helps to explain the RL policy safety.

Keywords: Model Checking · Explainable Reinforcement Learning · Large Language Models

1 Introduction

Reinforcement learning (RL) has transformed technology [19].

An RL agent learns a *policy* to achieve an objective by acting and receiving rewards from the environment. A *neural network (NN)* represents the policy, mapping state observations to actions, with each observation consisting of features characterizing the environment [8].

Unfortunately, learned policies are not guaranteed to avoid *unsafe behavior* [7], as rewards often do not fully capture complex safety requirements [21].

To resolve the issue mentioned above, formal verification methods like *model checking* have been proposed to reason about the safety of RL [10,12]. Model checking is not limited by properties that can be expressed by rewards but support a broader range of properties that can be expressed by *probabilistic computation tree logic (PCTL)* [11].

However, trained NN policies obscure their inner workings, and it is essential in the context of explainable RL [3] to understand them. Explaining RL policies through counterfactual action outcomes can help non-experts understand policy preferences by depicting the trade-offs between alternative actions [2]. A counterfactual explanation answers the question "Why *action 1* rather than *action 2?*", where *action 1* is the fact that occurred and *action 2* is a hypothetical alternative that the user might have expected [17].

Unfortunately, it may be difficult to decide which state to look at for a non-expert and which alternative action to choose [1].

Here, *large language models (LLMs)* may help explain RL policy outcomes [16,18]. LLMs are designed to understand and generate human-like text by learning from vast text data.

© IFIP International Federation for Information Processing 2025
Published by Springer Nature Switzerland AG 2025
H. D. Menéndez et al. (Eds.): ICTSS 2024, LNCS 15383, pp. 23–29, 2025.
https://doi.org/10.1007/978-3-031-80889-0_2

In this work, we apply model checking to identify states that may lead to safety violations because of the policy action selection and use an LLM to explain and determine which alternative action may be a better choice.

Our approach takes three inputs: a *Markov Decision Process (MDP)* representing the RL environment, a trained policy, and a PCTL formula for safety measurements. We *incrementally build* only the reachable parts of the MDP, guided by the trained policy [8]. We verify the policy's safety using the *Storm* model checker [13] and the PCTL formula. From the verified model, we extract states that directly lead to a safety violation through a policy action.

For each extracted state, we provide the RL environment information and the state with its action leading to a safety violation to the LLM, asking it to explain the mistake and suggest a safer alternative.

Then, we reverify the policy with the action alternatives concerning safety properties in the RL environment.

In experiments, we show that an LLM can indeed explain failures, propose valid alternative actions, and improve the safety performance of trained RL policies by forcing the policy to select the LLM alternative action. We compare our approach to a baseline approach [2] that always chooses naively the second most favored action at the current state.

To summarize our **main contribution**, we combine model checking with explainable RL and LLMs to explain safe policy decision-making and propose explainable alternative action selections at safety-critical states that improve the safety performance of the trained RL policies post-training.

Related Work. Although there is work combining LLMs with RL [5], work that focuses on counterfactual reasoning [1,2], as well as using LLMs to explain trajectories concerning reward performance [18], these studies do not address safety. There exists a variety of related work focusing on the trained RL policy verification [6,14,15,23]. Safe RL, such as RL policy shielding [4], steers the policy during training to satisfy safety properties. In comparison, we combine model checking with LLMs to propose explainable alternative actions post-training. There exists work that combines explainability with safety in explaining NN policy interconnections [9]. However, we additionally use the results to improve the safety of the trained policies.

2   Background

Probabilistic Model Checking. A *probability distribution* over a set X is a function $\mu\colon X \to [0,1]$ with $\sum_{x\in X} \mu(x) = 1$. The set of all distributions on X is $Distr(X)$.

Definition 1 (MDP). *A MDP is a tuple $M = (S, s_0, Act, Tr, rew, AP, L)$ where S is a finite, nonempty set of states; $s_0 \in S$ is an initial state; Act is a finite set of actions; $Tr\colon S \times Act \to Distr(S)$ is a partial probability transition function; $rew\colon S \times Act \to \mathbb{R}$ is a reward function; AP is a set of atomic propositions; $L\colon S \to 2^{AP}$ is a labeling function.*

We employ a factored state representation where each state s is a vector of features $(f_1, f_2, ..., f_d)$ where each feature $f_i \in \mathbb{Z}$ for $1 \leq i \leq d$ (state dimension). MDPS can be modeled with the formal language called PRISM[1].

A *memoryless deterministic policy* π for an MDP M is a function $\pi \colon S \to Act$ that maps a state $s \in S$ to action $a \in Act$. Applying a policy π to an MDP M yields an *induced discrete-time-Markov chain (DTMC) D*, where all non-determinism is resolved. Storm [13] allows the verification of PCTL properties of induced DTMCs to make, for instance, safety measurements. In a slight abuse of notation, we use PCTL state formulas to denote probability values. For instance, in this paper, $P(\Diamond \text{event})$ denotes the probability of eventually reaching the event.

The standard learning goal for RL is to learn a policy π in an MDP such that π maximizes the accumulated discounted reward [3], that is, $\mathbb{E}[\sum_{t=0}^{N} \gamma^t R_t]$, where γ with $0 \leq \gamma \leq 1$ is the discount factor, R_t is the reward at time t, and N is the total number of steps.

Large Language Models. In our setting, an LLM is a black-box function that takes input text and outputs text. For details on training LLMs, we refer the reader to [22].

3   Methodolodgy

We first incrementally build the induced DTMC of the policy π and the MDP M as follows. For every reachable state s via the trained policy π, we query for an action $a = \pi(s)$. In the underlying MDP M, only states s' reachable via that action $a \in A(s)$ are expanded [8]. The resulting DTMC D induced by M and π is fully deterministic, with no open action choices, and is passed to the model checker Storm for verification, yielding the *exact* safety measurement result m.

Then, we extract all the state-action pairs that led via their transitions to safety violations (based on the PCTL formula). Afterwards, for each state-action-pair, we input a description of the RL environment, state-action pair, and the question "What went wrong during execution?" into an LLM that outputs a human-readable explanation and proposes an alternative action at each stage of the extracted state-action pairs to improve the RL policy performance concerning the safety property (see Example 1 for LLM input and Example 2 for the corresponding LLM output).

Example 1 (LLM input).   In the Cleaning Agent environment, a robotic agent is tasked with cleaning rooms... Negative state feature values indicates terminal states. The action space is: NEXT for changing rooms if room is clean or blocked... CLEAN for cleaning a room... What went wrong with likelihood prob in the state [dirt level = 3, blocked = false] with action NEXT ending up in [dirt level = −1, blocked = false]. Explain it to me.

Example 2 (LLM Ouput).   The agent left the dirty room that nobody was taking care of. An alternative action would be to use the clean action.

---

[1] PRISM manual, http://www.prismmodelchecker.org/manual/.

Finally, we rebuild the induced DTMC D' via the alternative actions and verify it again to get a new safety measurement result m'.

Limitations. This approach focuses on explainable safety repairs fixable one state before a violation and supports memoryless policies in MDP environments, limited by state space and transitions [8].

4   Experiments

We present a private environment (to ensure it was not part of LLM training), trained RL policy, safety repair methods, and technical setup before evaluating explainable safety repairs in various scenarios[2].

Environment. A robotic agent cleans rooms while avoiding collisions and conserving energy. The state includes room cleanliness, slipperiness, and the agent's battery level. The agent is rewarded for correct actions, and the environment terminates upon collisions, energy depletion, or cleaning an already clean room.

$$S = \{(\text{dirt1, dirt2, energy, slippery level, room blocked}), \dots \}$$
$$Act = \{\text{next room, charge option1, charge option2,}$$
$$\text{clean1 option1, clean1 option2, clean2 option1,}$$
$$\text{clean2 option2, all purpose clean, idle}\}$$

$$rew = \begin{cases} 20 \cdot dirt*, & \text{if clean* operation for dirt* successful.} \\ 20 \cdot dirt1 \cdot dirt2, & \text{if all purpose clean operation successful.} \\ 20, & \text{if changing room correctly.} \\ 10, & \text{if idle when slippery level} > 0 \text{ an room not blocked.} \\ 10, & \text{if charging starts between energy} > 0 \text{ and energy} \leq 2. \\ 0, & \text{otherwise.} \end{cases}$$

RL Policy Training. We trained an RL policy using deep Q-learning [19] with 4 hidden layers of 512 neurons each. Training parameters were a batch size of 64, epsilon decay of 0.99999, minimum epsilon 0.1, initial epsilon 1, γ 0.99, and target network updates every 1024 steps. The policy achieved an average reward of 67.8 over 100 episodes in 27,709 epochs.

Counterfactual Safety Reasoning Methods. We compare three counterfactual safety reasoning methods: LLM with a MDP encoded in PRISM, LLM with natural language RL environment description, and a baseline method selecting the second-best policy choice [2]. We use the state-of-the-art GPT4-turbo API [20]. We only append the most likely token during text generation to ensure deterministic output and avoid excessive sampling.

---

[2] The code is available at https://github.com/LAVA-LAB/COOL-MC/tree/xrl_llm_safety.

Technical Setup. We executed our benchmarks in a docker container with 16 GB RAM, and an 12th Gen Intel Core i7-12700H × 20 processors with the operating system Ubuntu 20.04.5 LTS. For model checking, we use Storm 1.7.0.

Do LLM Alternatives Enhance Safety? The results via the different methods are illustrated in Table 1. The LLM, with a natural language explanation of the underlying environment, improved safety performance to avoid running out of energy. In other cases, our approach matches the baseline's performance but additionally explains why we choose the alternative actions. Inputting the MDP's PRISM encoding into the LLM yields poor results. One reason could be that LLMs are more trained on natural language than PRISM code.

Table 1. Different safety policy repair methods and the reachability probability of the unsafe behavior. Lower values are better.

PCTL Query	Original	LLM Desc.	LLM PRISM	Baseline
$P(\Diamond$ no energy)	0.603	0.406	0.422	0.660
$P(\Diamond$ wrong charge)	0.018	0.013	0.013	0.013
$P(\Diamond$ wrong room switch)	0.023	0.000	0.000	0.000
$P(\Diamond$ wrong idle)	0.023	0.000	0.050	0.000

Are LLM Explanations of Failures Acceptable? We analyze the correctness of the action alternatives that were explained. For the safety measure of running out of energy, we reviewed the first 44 explanations. An explanation is deemed correct if both the explanation and proposed action are sensible (we recognize that it may be subjective). For example, the ratio of correct explanations $P(\Diamond$no energy) was about 3/4, indicating its potential for explainable policy improvements.

Additional Observations. Action parsing was successful, with only 1 out of 99 LLM outputs having a format issue. The LLM approach is highly sensitive to the environment description. For example, with a specific description for $P(\Diamond$ no energy), we achieved a probability of 0.265. However, using a more generic description for all PCTL queries (which is used in the Table 1), the probability increased to 0.406.

5   Conclusion

We used model checking with LLMs for counterfactual safety reasoning, showing LLMs can explain and improve RL policy safety. Future work includes integrating this into safe RL and exploring visual and multi-modal LLMs[3].

[3] Funded by the EU under grant agreement number 101091783 (MARS Project) and as part of the Horizon Europe HORIZON-CL4-2022-TWIN-TRANSITION-01-03.

References

1. Amitai, Y., Amir, O.: "I don't think so": summarizing policy disagreements for agent comparison. In: AAAI, pp. 5269–5276. AAAI Press (2022)
2. Amitai, Y., Septon, Y., Amir, O.: Explaining reinforcement learning agents through counterfactual action outcomes. In: AAAI, pp. 10003–10011. AAAI Press (2024)
3. Bekkemoen, Y.: Explainable reinforcement learning (XRL): a systematic literature review and taxonomy. Mach. Learn. **113**(1), 355–441 (2024)
4. Carr, S., Jansen, N., Junges, S., Topcu, U.: Safe reinforcement learning via shielding under partial observability. In: AAAI, pp. 14748–14756. AAAI Press (2023)
5. Du, Y., et al.: Guiding pretraining in reinforcement learning with large language models. In: ICML (2023)
6. Eliyahu, T., Kazak, Y., Katz, G., Schapira, M.: Verifying learning-augmented systems. In: SIGCOMM, pp. 305–318. ACM (2021)
7. García, J., Fernández, F.: A comprehensive survey on safe reinforcement learning. J. Mach. Learn. Res. **16**, 1437–1480 (2015)
8. Gross, D., Jansen, N., Junges, S., Pérez, G.A.: COOL-MC: a comprehensive tool for reinforcement learning and model checking. In: Dong, W., Talpin, J.P. (eds.) SETTA 2022. LNCS, vol. 13649, pp. 41–49. Springer, Cham (2022). https://doi.org/10.1007/978-3-031-21213-0_3
9. Groß, D., Spieker, H.: Safety-oriented pruning and interpretation of reinforcement learning policies. In: Proceedings of the 32nd European Symposium on Artificial Neural Networks, Computational Intelligence and Machine Learning (ESANN) (2024)
10. Hahn, E.M., Perez, M., Schewe, S., Somenzi, F., Trivedi, A., Wojtczak, D.: Omega-regular objectives in model-free reinforcement learning. In: Vojnar, T., Zhang, L. (eds.) TACAS 2019. LNCS, vol. 11427, pp. 395–412. Springer, Cham (2019). https://doi.org/10.1007/978-3-030-17462-0_27
11. Hansson, H., Jonsson, B.: A logic for reasoning about time and reliability. Formal Aspects Comput. **6**(5), 512–535 (1994)
12. Hasanbeig, M., Kroening, D., Abate, A.: Deep reinforcement learning with temporal logics. In: Bertrand, N., Jansen, N. (eds.) FORMATS 2020. LNCS, vol. 12288, pp. 1–22. Springer, Cham (2020). https://doi.org/10.1007/978-3-030-57628-8_1
13. Hensel, C., Junges, S., Katoen, J., Quatmann, T., Volk, M.: The probabilistic model checker Storm. Int. J. Softw. Tools Technol. Transf. **24**(4), 589–610 (2022)
14. Jin, P., Wang, Y., Zhang, M.: Efficient LTL model checking of deep reinforcement learning systems using policy extraction. In: SEKE (2022)
15. Kazak, Y., Barrett, C.W., Katz, G., Schapira, M.: Verifying deep-RL-driven systems. In: NetAI@SIGCOMM, pp. 83–89. ACM (2019)
16. Kroeger, N., Ley, D., Krishna, S., Agarwal, C., Lakkaraju, H.: Are large language models post hoc explainers? CoRR abs/2310.05797 (2023)
17. Lipton, P.: Contrastive explanation. Roy. Inst. Philos. Suppl. **27**, 247–266 (1990)
18. Lu, W., Zhao, X., Spisak, J., Lee, J.H., Wermter, S.: Mental modeling of reinforcement learning agents by language models. arXiv preprint arXiv:2406.18505 (2024)
19. Mnih, V., et al.: Playing Atari with deep reinforcement learning. CoRR abs/1312.5602 (2013)

20. OpenAI: GPT-4 technical report. CoRR abs/2303.08774 (2023)
21. Vamplew, P., et al.: Scalar reward is not enough: a response to silver, Singh, Precup and Sutton (2021). AAMAS **36**(2), 41 (2022)
22. Vaswani, A., et al.: Attention is all you need. In: NIPS, pp. 5998–6008 (2017)
23. Zhu, H., Xiong, Z., Magill, S., Jagannathan, S.: An inductive synthesis framework for verifiable reinforcement learning. In: PLDI, pp. 686–701. ACM (2019)

GoNoGo: An Efficient LLM-Based Multi-agent System for Streamlining Automotive Software Release Decision-Making

Arsham Gholamzadeh Khoee[1,2](✉) [ID], Yinan Yu[1] [ID], Robert Feldt[1] [ID],
Andris Freimanis[2], Patrick Andersson Rhodin[2],
and Dhasarathy Parthasarathy[2] [ID]

[1] Department of Computer Science and Engineering,
Chalmers University of Technology, Gothenburg, Sweden
{khoee,yinan,robert.feldt}@chalmers.se
[2] Volvo Group, Gothenburg, Sweden
{andris.freimanis,patrick.andersson,dhasarathy.parthasarathy}@volvo.com

Abstract. Traditional methods for making software deployment decisions in the automotive industry typically rely on manual analysis of tabular software test data. These methods often lead to higher costs and delays in the software release cycle due to their labor-intensive nature. Large Language Models (LLMs) present a promising solution to these challenges. However, their application generally demands multiple rounds of human-driven prompt engineering, which limits their practical deployment, particularly for industrial end-users who need reliable and efficient results. In this paper, we propose GoNoGo, an LLM agent system designed to streamline automotive software deployment while meeting both functional requirements and practical industrial constraints. Unlike previous systems, GoNoGo is specifically tailored to address domain-specific and risk-sensitive systems. We evaluate GoNoGo's performance across different task difficulties using zero-shot and few-shot examples taken from industrial practice. Our results show that GoNoGo achieves a 100% success rate for tasks up to Level 2 difficulty with 3-shot examples, and maintains high performance even for more complex tasks. We find that GoNoGo effectively automates decision-making for simpler tasks, significantly reducing the need for manual intervention. In summary, GoNoGo represents an efficient and user-friendly LLM-based solution currently employed in our industrial partner's company to assist with software release decision-making, supporting more informed and timely decisions in the release process for risk-sensitive vehicle systems.

Keywords: LLMs · LLM-based Multi-agent · Software Release Assistant · Table Analysis Automation · Risk-sensitive Systems

© IFIP International Federation for Information Processing 2025
Published by Springer Nature Switzerland AG 2025
H. D. Menéndez et al. (Eds.): ICTSS 2024, LNCS 15383, pp. 30–45, 2025.
https://doi.org/10.1007/978-3-031-80889-0_3

1 Introduction

In the automotive industry, decisions about when to release software, particularly embedded software in risk-sensitive systems, carry immense weight. The complexity of modern vehicles, with their multiple levels of integration, further complicates this process. Each integration level involves one or more gating steps, with tests conducted to verify whether gate criteria are fulfilled. Gate failures can delay the integration of all dependent subsystems, regardless of their individual quality. In this intricate process, release managers, bearing the responsibility of gatekeeping could greatly benefit from assistance to make faster and better decisions.

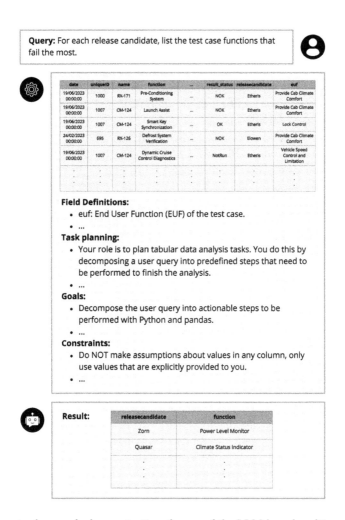

Fig. 1. An actual example demonstrating the use of the LLM-based multi-agent system for automating ad-hoc tabular data analysis.

Large language models (LLMs) present an interesting avenue for providing such assistance. In particular, LLMs have demonstrated strong capabilities in zero- and few-shot settings with in-context learning [5]. Recent advancements have improved reasoning [32], exemplar selection, and prompt design [7]. Companies now use LLMs for software engineering tasks like API testing, code generation, and documentation and research studies have already shown test automation improvements over the state-of-the-art [28].

However, when applying LLMs to *risk-sensitive domain-specific* tasks, several unique challenges must be addressed. In our research with industrial partners, the most prominent challenges include 1) Incorporating specific logic and terminology relevant to the domain; 2) Understanding and parsing high-level queries or vague language used by non-expert stakeholders and translating them into actionable plans, 3) Enabling interpretability so that domain experts can explain system functionality to stakeholders without excessive complexity, 4) Operating efficiently to meet the time-critical demands of organizational applications, mitigating potential bottlenecks related to limited LLM licensing or infrastructure, and 5) Designing the system to enable ease of troubleshooting and maintenance, ensuring that any issues can be quickly identified and resolved.

To address these challenges, we propose a multi-agent system that encodes domain-specific requirements using in-context learning. This system comprises two primary LLM agents: a Planner and an Actor (refer to Fig. 2). The Planner, which forms the core of the system, comprehends and decomposes user queries into step-by-step instructions for data analysis [14]. The Actor then synthesizes and generates executable scripts from these higher-level instructions. Within the Actor, a coder LLM utilizes the self-reflection mechanism besides a memory to produce the most effective Python script optimized for querying the given data for each instruction generated by the Planner [1,28].

This system provides an interface for end-users at our industrial partner, illustrated by Fig. 1, which shows a real-world example of its use. It allows end-users, like release managers, to interpret results from a business and safety perspective without needing detailed technical knowledge. For example, they can simply receive a short table that reports the test case functions that have failed the most for each release candidate as shown in Fig. 1. By reviewing this information, release managers can make well-informed decisions on whether to release the software or not, ensuring that it meets both business objectives and safety standards in the automotive industry. This approach can significantly reduce time and resources by eliminating the need for various database and programming experts to achieve the desired results for end-users. Our agent automates test data analysis across multiple vehicle development integration levels, providing detailed reports on component functionality and system interactions. This assists release managers in making informed decisions about software readiness for release, accelerating development while enhancing gatekeeping reliability. Our contributions can be summarized as follows:

- We highlight the practicality of the proposed LLM-based intelligent assistant in making software release decisions within the automotive industry. This is achieved by enhancing two key capabilities:
  - **Domain-specificity:** We design a framework to handle unstructured queries from non-expert stakeholders in the automotive industry by mapping generic language to domain-specific logic using in-context learning.
  - **Risk-sensitivity:** We incorporate two predefined atomic operations to restrict the action space and improve the risk-sensitive aspect of the planner.
- Experiments on a total of 50 crafted test queries show that our proposed system is effective at analyzing data and deriving the required insights for software release decision-making.
- Our system, now deployed and actively used within our industrial partner's company, has demonstrated significant improvements in the software release decision-making process besides saving time, improving accessibility, reducing reliance on specialized analysts, and accelerating overall workflow.

The remainder of this paper is structured as follows: Sect. 2 provides an overview of the manual process behind automotive software release decisions and the need for streamlining operations. Section 3 details our approach, including a description of the architecture of our LLM-based multi-agent system and an explanation of the Planner and Actor agents. Furthermore, in Sect. 4, we present our experimental setup and results. Section 6 provides an overview of similar research in LLMs for data analysis. Finally, Sect. 7 concludes the paper by summarizing key findings and discussing the broader implications of our work in the context of industrial software release management and risk-sensitive systems.

2   Manual Process of Release Decisions: Insights From the Industry

Deciding to go ahead, or not, with a software release in the automotive industry is a complex task involving multiple stakeholders and extensive data analysis. This section reviews the current, and typical of the industry at large, manual workflow and the need for streamlining.

Vehicle development progresses through multiple phases, each becoming more complex as more components are integrated. Numerous tests are conducted at each stage to ensure functionality and identify revisions, generating vast amounts of data. Software components require repeated testing and validation, adding to this data.

Project managers, verification engineers, and quality engineers need clear analytics and insights from these tests in order to make software release decisions. Extracting essential information is time-consuming. Quality engineers analyze data for continuous improvement, while release engineers need specific information to make informed release decisions.

Within this process, statisticians provide an overall view of the data to project managers and quality engineers for future business decisions. Manual data processing is necessary due to the critical nature of these decisions and their impact on consumer safety. However, this approach is time-consuming and prone to errors, partly due to the differing perspectives of technical data analyzers and statisticians, who may not fully understand the project managers' goals.

A critical and typical stage in this process is "Testing on Closed Track", where vehicles equipped with the necessary software release undergo systematic and rigorous testing of their systems in a controlled environment. After these tests, release managers analyze large amounts of data to decide whether to move to the next test stage. This involves manually querying data to generate reports that support informed decisions. Errors or delays in this analysis can hinder timely software release, affect business goals, and delay subsystem integration.

The deployment of an intelligent assistant has the potential to facilitate software release decisions in the automotive industry [20], particularly during the critical testing on a closed track phase. In this work, we have focused on designing such an LLM-based multi-agent system to address the challenges of this specific stage. By rapidly processing test data from closed track testing, the system can generate comprehensive reports tailored to different stakeholders' needs. For example, it can quickly compile summaries of failed tests, highlight software performance trends across vehicle models, or analyze a specific component's behavior under various conditions. Consequently, this reduces the time spent on initial analysis, allowing release managers to focus on interpreting results and making informed decisions. This not only accelerates the development process but also enhances the accuracy and reliability of the information used in release decisions, ultimately contributing to maintaining high safety and quality standards in automotive software development.

3   GoNoGo: Intelligent Software Release Assistant

3.1   System Requirements

After discussing current needs and opinions about the software release analysis and decision-making processes with our industrial partner, we identified the following main challenges in automating data analysis:

Understanding User Queries The system must interpret queries, typically presented in natural language [17], within the specific domain context, using any provided domain-specific knowledge.

Translating User Queries to Actionable Steps The system needs to convert the user's query into concrete steps, breaking down complex queries into simpler tasks, determining the order of operations, and selecting appropriate data manipulation or analysis techniques. Additionally, the action space must be carefully managed to adhere to risk-sensitive requirements.

Execution and Result Preparation The system must execute the planned actions, interact with data using scripts (e.g., querying databases, performing calculations, applying filters), and compile the results into the desired format for the user.

These steps rely heavily on the LLM's domain-specific knowledge and reasoning ability, crucial for effective query instruction planning [18]. Consequently, this work explores techniques for enhancing the reasoning capabilities of LLM agent systems, particularly for the analysis of tabular data in industrial contexts.

3.2   System Architecture

Our approach to automating tabular data analysis leverages LLMs to create an intelligent system capable of interpreting natural language queries, executing complex analyses, and delivering desired results. The system architecture consists of two main components: the Planner supported by a Knowledge Base and Examples for few-shot learning and the Actor including coder LLM, memory module, and some Plugin components. Figure 2 illustrates the overall architecture of the developed system.

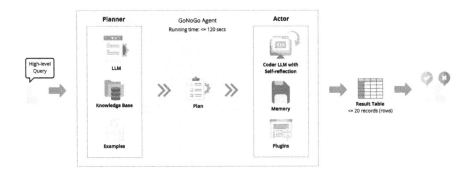

Fig. 2. Architecture of the LLM-based multi-agent system GoNoGo along with the illustration of the interaction procedure of the system. GoNoGo receives high-level queries from the end user, performs the required data manipulations, and outputs the result table as a decision support resource. GoNoGo comprises a Planner agent, which interprets queries and devises analysis strategies using Chain-of-Thought prompting and self-consistency, supported by a *Knowledge Base* and *Examples* for few-shot learning. The Actor includes a Coder LLM with a *Self-reflection* mechanism, utilizing *Memory* and *Plugins* for code generation and error resolution. The total running time of GoNoGo for one user query is approximately 120 s, which satisfies typical user requirements.

Planner. The Planner is the core of our system, responsible for interpreting user queries and devising appropriate analysis strategies. One of the core challenges of designing an LLM-based multi-agent system is the inherent inaccuracy of prompting. As decision-making becomes more distributed over multiple LLM agents, the uncertainty within the multi-agent system increases. To mitigate this, we centralize the complexity within the Planner, which is responsible for the majority of design choices. By focusing on the Planner as the main agent for refinement, we aim to create a system that is both interpretable and easily maintainable.

Our problem consists of two main aspects: domain-specificity and risk-sensitivity. These two characteristics frequently manifest together in real-world applications, particularly in fields such as healthcare and automotive, where unreliability and inaccuracies can have significant consequences. However, there is a noticeable gap in addressing both aspects simultaneously, let alone demonstrating such systems in practice. As part of our system, we want to explicitly address both of these aspects. As the Planner is the component with the most decision-making responsibility, these two requirements are encoded into the Planner prompts as depicted in Fig. 3.

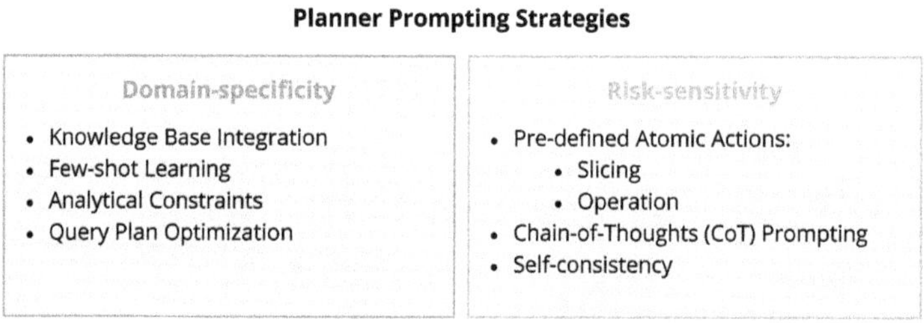

Planner Prompting Strategies

Domain-specificity	Risk-sensitivity

• Knowledge Base Integration
• Few-shot Learning
• Analytical Constraints
• Query Plan Optimization
	• Pre-defined Atomic Actions:
	   • Slicing
	   • Operation
	• Chain-of-Thoughts (CoT) Prompting
	• Self-consistency

Fig. 3. Planner prompting strategies addressing domain-specificity and risk-sensitivity in the LLM-based agent system for tabular data analysis.

Domain-Specificity. The Planner utilizes a Knowledge Base containing a structured description of the data and its attributes to provide the necessary context and domain-specific information in the prompts given to the LLM, enhancing the system's performance and applicability [15]. The Knowledge Base serves as a comprehensive repository of metadata, including detailed descriptions of data tables, possible states and values for essential fields, and domain-specific terminologies, as well as the semantic meanings of various data elements. This enables the system to understand and interpret high-level queries and devise appropriate analysis plans by using this information as input prompts for the Planner, taking advantage of in-context learning. This integration ensures that the entire pipeline, from query interpretation to result generation, is informed by relevant domain knowledge, enabling the LLM agent to provide more accurate, relevant, and specialized responses to user queries.

In our system architecture, we also feed some input-output pairs as examples into the Planner, allowing few-shot learning alongside the Knowledge Base. This combination enables the Planner to interpret user queries more effectively, drawing on both general knowledge and specific task examples to formulate appropriate analysis plans. This approach makes the system a powerful tool for automated tabular data analysis across various industries and use cases.

Helpful prompts serve as constraints, enhancing the LLM's reasoning capabilities [13]. For example, constraints help the model understand that queries should account for more than just binary states for some fields. Retrieving records with 'A' and its opposite doesn't always mean retrieving all records, as other non-binary states might exist. For instance, 'successful' and 'failed' tests don't encompass all possible test statuses; there may be additional statuses to consider, such as 'N/A', that the model should take into account.

The focus is on pushing the model to generate an optimized query plan. This involves narrowing down data through filtering and selection before performing sorting and other operations on the reduced dataset to minimize processing. Accordingly, designed constraints help the agent explore the characteristics of each field and the data, providing more accurate planning.

Risk-Sensitivity. We guide the Planner with two pre-defined atomic actions to limit the action space of the planner: slicing and operation. Slicing involves specifying the columns to select and the conditions for filtering rows from the data to be analyzed. Operation involves describing the operations (such as max, mean, count, etc.) to be performed on the values of one or more columns of the data obtained from the slicing step. The steps should be returned as a Python list, with each step described in natural language, including all relevant values and column names.

Also, we leverage Chain-of-Thought (CoT) prompting to further enhance the reasoning capabilities of our LLM-based agent [23]. This technique incorporates intermediate reasoning steps into the prompt, guiding the model to break down complex problems into smaller, more manageable steps [33]. This approach mimics human-like reasoning and problem-solving processes. Additionally, CoT prompting makes the agent's decision-making process more transparent by explicitly showing the reasoning steps, allowing users to understand how the agent arrived at a particular conclusion or analysis result.

We combine CoT prompting with few-shot learning by providing examples that not only show input-output pairs but also include the intermediate reasoning steps. This synergy further enhances the agent's ability to handle diverse and complex data analysis tasks [10].

To further improve reasoning, we employ self-consistency in conjunction with CoT prompting. This involves generating multiple independent reasoning paths for the same query, comparing them for consistency, and using majority voting to determine the most reliable outcome [22]. By considering multiple reasoning paths, the system becomes less likely to be misled by a single flawed chain of thought. As a result, for queries with potential ambiguity, self-consistency can help identify different valid interpretations and provide a more comprehensive answer.

Actor. The Actor is responsible for carrying out the analysis plans devised by the Planner. It consists of several interacting components: Coder LLM with Self-reflection, Memory, and Plugins, as depicted in Fig. 2.

The Coder LLM is responsible for generating executable scripts based on the Planner's instructions. This component is crucial as it translates abstract plans into concrete, executable code that can interact with the data using the required Plugins and perform the necessary analysis. It includes a Self-reflection mechanism, which works in tandem with a Memory module. This Memory stores generated code, error messages, execution results, and contextual information about the current task [8].

The Self-reflection mechanism is a sophisticated process that allows the Coder LLM to critically analyze its own output and decision-making process. When an error occurs during script execution, the Self-reflection mechanism activates, providing feedback to the Coder LLM. This feedback loop enables the LLM to analyze error messages within the task context [11,28], facilitating iterative improvement of the generated code.

The Self-reflection mechanism offers several advantages: It enables the Coder LLM to autonomously identify and correct errors by continuously analyzing and reflecting on its own output, thereby reducing the need for external debugging and intervention. This mechanism promotes a cycle of continuous improvement, allowing each iteration to refine the scripts for progressively better performance and reliability [25]. By utilizing the Memory module, the Coder LLM can make context-aware adjustments, considering previous errors, execution results, and specific task requirements, which leads to more precise and contextually appropriate code generation. Automated error correction and iterative refinement result in a more efficient coding process, speeding up the development cycle and enhancing the robustness and reliability of the final scripts. Additionally, the self-reflective capabilities minimize the need for human intervention in the debugging process, enabling engineers to focus on more complex and high-level tasks.

This architecture enables the Actor to not only generate code for data analysis tasks but also to troubleshoot and improve its own output, resulting in a more robust and reliable automated data analysis system.

3.3   System Implementation

The system uses Azure OpenAI's GPT-3.5 Turbo for both the Planner and Actor agents. The Planner utilizes specially designed prompts for task planning, defining the entire data analysis task by specifying the details of each step in the plan. Moreover, the Actor uses predefined prompts to generate the required Python code for executing each step of the provided plan with the pandas library, performing tasks on the given data.

4   Experiments

4.1   Data

The data used for analysis at our industrial partner is called "GoNoGo" data and is updated after testing each function of every software component in each vehicle. This internal company data contains about 40 different fields and is critical for release decisions, as it includes detailed information regarding the performance and functionality of software components. It provides the necessary information for determining whether to advance a vehicle to the next phase of development and allow it to be driven on open roads. Although the data is updated after each test, we used a dataset of 55,000 records to report our experiments.

Stakeholders often ask questions like "What are the test case functions that fail the most for release candidate X?" or "What is the Y-status of X?" where X is the release candidate's name and Y is a specific functionality. Answering these questions requires domain knowledge and an understanding of the data to extract and communicate the answers accurately. By analyzing this data, release managers can determine if a vehicle meets the necessary criteria to progress to the next development phase or be driven on public roads. This ensures that only vehicles that meet stringent safety and quality standards are advanced, maintaining high standards in automotive software development.

4.2   Benchmark Overview

To evaluate the GoNoGo system's performance, we developed a benchmark based on 15 initial analysis tasks. These tasks were defined with the help of release engineers, quality engineers, and verification engineers. We identified the most common high-level queries and criteria frequently used by these end users in their workflows. Our goal was to design tasks that capture the nuances and complexity of the demanding queries necessary for their decision-making processes. These tasks were then translated into explicit table analysis queries that GoNoGo could process, ensuring that the benchmark reflects real-world scenarios and challenges typically encountered by these professionals. We created definitive ground-truth solutions for these queries using Python, breaking down the solutions into smaller code chunks representing operations such as filtering, grouping, and sorting. For each query, we generated a series of query ablations by incrementally adding code chunks and formulating corresponding queries that these chunks would solve. This method expanded our original 15 queries into 50 query ablations, each with a corresponding ground-truth solution and Python code.

In this way, we established queries with four levels of difficulty:

Level 1 These are the simplest queries, typically involving a single operation such as filtering or sorting.
Level 2 These queries combine two or three basic operations, such as multiple filtering followed by sorting.

Level 3 These queries involve more than three operations, potentially including grouping and aggregating.

Level 4 These are the most complex queries, requiring multiple advanced operations such as grouping and aggregating, for calculating statistics, beyond basic filtering and sorting.

This incremental approach to query complexity allows us to assess GoNoGO's performance at various levels of difficulty. It helps identify at which point, if any, the system's performance begins to degrade, and provides insights into its capabilities in handling increasingly complex table analysis tasks.

This benchmark allows for objective evaluation of the GoNoGo's ability to handle increasingly complex table analysis tasks, ensuring a comprehensive assessment of its performance across a spectrum of difficulty levels.

4.3   Evaluation

The evaluation process involves comparing the GoNoGo system's results against manually generated ground-truth results. The comparison is based on a strict matching criterion [9]. For a match to be considered successful, the system's output must contain the same columns as the ground truth. Additionally, each record in the system's output must exactly match a corresponding record in the ground truth, including all values across different fields. The system's output must also contain the same number of records as the ground truth, with no missing or extra entries. This strict matching ensures that the output is not just similar, but identical in structure and content to the expected result. If the agent's output satisfies all these criteria when compared to the ground truth, the task is marked as successful; otherwise, it is considered a failure. The model's performance is then quantified by calculating the success rate, defined as the ratio of successful tasks to the total number of tasks.

4.4   Results

We present our experiment results on the GoNoGo system in Table 1. We evaluated its performance across different levels of task difficulty using 0-shot, 1-shot, 2-shot, and 3-shot examples. GoNoGo achieved high performance with 3-shot examples.

Initially, we assessed GoNoGo's ability to handle the simplest queries involving basic operations like filtering or sorting (Level 1). We then incrementally increased the complexity by including queries that combined Level 1 and Level 2 difficulties, followed by those incorporating Level 1 to Level 3 difficulties. Finally, we evaluated GoNoGo's performance on the full spectrum of tasks, including the most complex queries (Level 4), which require multiple operations such as filtering, sorting, grouping, and calculating statistics.

Our observations indicate that GoNoGo with 3-shot examples is particularly effective for solving queries with task difficulty up to Level 2 and can handle these tasks without error. For more complex tasks involving Level 3 or Level 4

Table 1. Performance evaluation of the GoNoGo system with varying numbers of example queries across different levels of task difficulty.

# Examples	Task Difficulty	# Total Tasks	# Success	# Failed	Performance
0-shot	1	16	3	13	18.75%
	1-2	32	6	26	18.75%
	1-3	44	9	35	20.45%
	1-4	50	11	39	22%
1-shot	1	16	15	1	93.75%
	1-2	32	27	5	84.37%
	1-3	44	32	12	72.72%
	1-4	50	34	16	68%
2-shot	1	16	16	0	100%
	1-2	32	31	1	96.87%
	1-3	44	38	6	86.36%
	1-4	50	41	9	82%
3-shot	1	16	16	0	100%
	1-2	**32**	**32**	**0**	**100%**
	1-3	**44**	**41**	**3**	**93%**
	1-4	**50**	**45**	**5**	**90%**

difficulties, human intervention is recommended to perform the necessary manipulations and computations, rather than relying solely on the automated system.

5   Threats to Validity

We identify the following threats to the validity of our study:

Limitation of the Created Benchmark Our study relies on a benchmark specifically created for evaluating the system. While this benchmark is designed to be comprehensive, it may not cover all potential scenarios and edge cases encountered in real-world applications. Efforts have been made to design queries and tasks to be as comprehensive as possible by involving verification engineers to mitigate subjectiveness. However, despite these efforts, the limitation remains that it may not capture every potential scenario and edge case. This limitation could affect the generalizability and robustness of our findings.

Selection of the Foundation Model The choice of the foundation model, in this case GPT-3.5 Turbo, which is considered a widely used LLM in recent studies, might influence the results. Different foundation models, such as GPT-4, GPT-4o, Claude 3, or LLaMA 3, may yield better performance levels and interpretations of the same tasks. However, we limited the project to using GPT-3.5 Turbo and focused on improving its reasoning and planning capabilities. Besides, our framework is flexible and can be easily applied to different pre-trained models. The dependency on a single model means that our conclusions may not hold if another model were used.

6   Related Work

The application of tabular data in machine learning holds significant potential, ranging from few-shot learning for data analysis to end-to-end data pipeline automation.

Integrating LLM with tabular data presents several substantial challenges [4]. Most foundation models are not trained on tabular data, making it difficult for them to process and interpret this type of data effectively. To mitigate this issue, pre-training LLMs using tabular data or fine-tuning on specific tasks are two commonly adopted options. [16] described different phases and strategies for LLM training, and [19] provided guidelines for enterprises who are interested in fine-tuning LLMs.

In particular, recent literature has seen a growing interest in pre-training and self-supervised learning (SSL) approaches using tabular data. [21] emphasizes SSL for non-sequential tabular data (SSL4NS-TD), categorizing methods into predictive, contrastive, and hybrid learning, and discussing application issues such as automatic data engineering and cross-table transferability. In contrast, [30] introduces TapTap, a novel table pre-training method that enhances tabular prediction and generates synthetic tables for various applications. Finally, [26] introduces Tabular data Pre-Training via Meta-representation (TabPTM), which enables training-free generalization across heterogeneous datasets by standardizing data representations through distance to prototypes. The common theme across these works is the enhancement of tabular data handling through innovative pre-training and SSL techniques, though they differ in their specific methodologies and application focuses, ranging from generating synthetic data to improving model generalization and manipulation capabilities. [29] proposes Tabular Foundation Models (TabFMs), leveraging a pre-trained LLM fine-tuned on diverse tabular datasets to excel in instruction-following tasks and efficient learning with scarce data.

Pre-training aims to enhance LLMs' capability of handling tabular data in general. However, it does not necessarily improve their performance on specific tasks. On the other hand, fine-tuning pre-trained LLMs have demonstrated potential for enhancing tabular data manipulation on specific tasks. [31] introduced TableLLM, a robust 13-billion-parameter model designed for handling tabular data in real-world office scenarios. In particular, TableLLM incorporates reasoning process extensions and cross-way validation strategies, outperforming existing general-purpose and tabular-focused LLMs. [12] explored zero-shot and few-shot tabular data classification by prompting LLMs with serialized data and problem descriptions, achieving superior performance over traditional deep-learning methods and even strong baselines like gradient-boosted trees. [34] addressed question answering over hybrid tabular and textual data, fine-tuning

LLaMA 2 using a step-wise pipeline, resulting in TAT-LLM, which outperforms both prior fine-tuned models and large-scale LLMs such as GPT-4 on specific benchmarks. [24] focused on applying LLMs to predictive tasks in tabular data, enhancing LLM capabilities through extensive training on annotated tables.

Industrial Considerations. One known issue is that LLMs often memorize tabular data verbatim, leading to overfitting. [2] highlights that despite their non-trivial generalization capability, LLMs perform better on datasets they were exposed to during training compared to new, unseen datasets. This indicates a tendency towards memorization, necessitating robust testing and validation protocols. This issue is particularly critical for companies' internal data and tasks that a foundation model has not encountered before, as public benchmarks do not necessarily predict performance on these internal tasks. In addition, it is worth noting that some applications have stringent data privacy policies, a concern increasingly being addressed in the literature [3,6,27]. In our work, we assume that the data resides within a secure local network, and we do not address data privacy issues in this paper. In industrial settings, practical constraints such as interpretability, user-centric adaptation, ease of development and maintenance, latency requirements, and IT infrastructure limitations are crucial. Our objective is to design a system that addresses these industrial needs without unnecessary complexity and excessive resources typically required by pre-training and fine-tuning LLMs.

7 Conclusion

We present the GoNoGo, an LLM-based multi-agent system designed to streamline software release decisions in the automotive industry by analyzing and deriving insights from real-world data using Python code. We have employed this system within our industrial partner's company, which is significantly assisting release managers and reducing the number of engineers engaged in this process, allowing them to focus on their high-level tasks.

The impact of our system extends beyond automation, transforming how automotive companies manage their software release cycles. It reduces the time and effort required for data analysis while increasing decision accuracy and reliability. This shift allows engineers and managers to focus on higher-level tasks, accelerating the overall development and deployment process by bridging the gap between raw data and actionable insights, driving the industry towards more efficient, data-driven software release practices. Without GoNoGo in place, our industrial partner would experience more wasted time and effort across various teams and employees, with the decision-making process becoming significantly prolonged. Pilot users have reported saving approximately 2 h per person each time they make a decision, highlighting the system's positive impact on efficiency and the industrial partner's overall business goals.

Acknowledgement. This work was partially supported by the Wallenberg AI, Autonomous Systems and Software Program (WASP) funded by the Knut and Alice Wallenberg Foundation.

References

1. Austin, J., et al.: Program synthesis with large language models. arXiv preprint arXiv:2108.07732 (2021)
2. Bordt, S., Nori, H., Rodrigues, V., Nushi, B., Caruana, R.: Elephants never forget: memorization and learning of tabular data in large language models. arXiv preprint arXiv:2404.06209 (2024)
3. Boudewijn, A.T.P., et al.: Privacy measurements in tabular synthetic data: state of the art and future research directions. In: NeurIPS 2023 Workshop on Synthetic Data Generation with Generative AI (2023)
4. van Breugel, B., van der Schaar, M.: Why tabular foundation models should be a research priority (2024)
5. Brown, T., et al.: Language models are few-shot learners. Adv. Neural. Inf. Process. Syst. **33**, 1877–1901 (2020)
6. Carey, A.N., Bhaila, K., Edemacu, K., Wu, X.: DP-TabICL: in-context learning with differentially private tabular data. arXiv preprint arXiv:2403.05681 (2024)
7. Chang, Y., et al.: A survey on evaluation of large language models. ACM Trans. Intel. Syst. Technol. **15**(3), 1–45 (2024)
8. Chen, X., Lin, M., Schärli, N., Zhou, D.: Teaching large language models to self-debug. arXiv preprint arXiv:2304.05128 (2023)
9. Chiang, W.L., et al.: Chatbot arena: an open platform for evaluating LLMs by human preference. arXiv preprint arXiv:2403.04132 (2024)
10. Dagdelen, J., et al.: Structured information extraction from scientific text with large language models. Nat. Commun. **15**(1), 1418 (2024)
11. Dyachenko, Y., Nenkov, N., Petrova, M., Skarga-Bandurova, I., Soloviov, O.: Approaches to cognitive architecture of autonomous intelligent agent. Biol. Inspir. Cogn. Archit. **26**, 130–135 (2018)
12. Hegselmann, S., Buendia, A., Lang, H., Agrawal, M., Jiang, X., Sontag, D.: TabLLM: few-shot classification of tabular data with large language models (2023)
13. Huang, J., Chang, K.C.C.: Towards reasoning in large language models: a survey. arXiv preprint arXiv:2212.10403 (2022)
14. Khot, T., et al.: Decomposed prompting: a modular approach for solving complex tasks. arXiv preprint arXiv:2210.02406 (2022)
15. Liu, P., Yuan, W., Fu, J., Jiang, Z., Hayashi, H., Neubig, G.: Pre-train, prompt, and predict: a systematic survey of prompting methods in natural language processing. ACM Comput. Surv. **55**(9), 1–35 (2023)
16. Patil, R., Gudivada, V.: A review of current trends, techniques, and challenges in large language models (LLMs). Appl. Sci. **14**(5), 2074 (2024)
17. Rahimi, A., Veisi, H.: Integrating model-agnostic meta-learning with advanced language embeddings for few-shot intent classification. In: 2024 32nd International Conference on Electrical Engineering (ICEE), pp. 1–5. IEEE (2024)
18. Valmeekam, K., Marquez, M., Sreedharan, S., Kambhampati, S.: On the planning abilities of large language models-a critical investigation. Adv. Neural. Inf. Process. Syst. **36**, 75993–76005 (2023)
19. VM, K., Warrier, H., Gupta, Y., et al.: Fine tuning LLM for enterprise: practical guidelines and recommendations. arXiv preprint arXiv:2404.10779 (2024)

20. Wang, L., et al.: A survey on large language model based autonomous agents. Front. Comp. Sci. **18**(6), 186345 (2024)
21. Wang, W.Y., Du, W.W., Xu, D., Wang, W., Peng, W.C.: A survey on self-supervised learning for non-sequential tabular data. arXiv preprint arXiv:2402.01204 (2024)
22. Wang, X., et al.: Self-consistency improves chain of thought reasoning in language models. arXiv preprint arXiv:2203.11171 (2022)
23. Wei, J., et al.: Chain-of-thought prompting elicits reasoning in large language models. Adv. Neural. Inf. Process. Syst. **35**, 24824–24837 (2022)
24. Yang, Y., Wang, Y., Sen, S., Li, L., Liu, Q.: Unleashing the potential of large language models for predictive tabular tasks in data science (2024)
25. Yao, S., Zhao, J., Yu, D., Du, N., Shafran, I., Narasimhan, K., Cao, Y.: ReAct: synergizing reasoning and acting in language models. arXiv preprint arXiv:2210.03629 (2022)
26. Ye, H.J., Zhou, Q., Zhan, D.C.: Training-free generalization on heterogeneous tabular data via meta-representation (2023)
27. Ye, J., Du, M., Wang, G.: DataFrame QA: a universal LLM framework on DataFrame question answering without data exposure (2024)
28. Yoon, J., Feldt, R., Yoo, S.: Intent-driven mobile GUI testing with autonomous large language model agents. In: 2024 IEEE Conference on Software Testing, Verification and Validation (ICST). IEEE (2024)
29. Zhang, H., Wen, X., Zheng, S., Xu, W., Bian, J.: Towards foundation models for learning on tabular data. arXiv preprint arXiv:2310.07338 (2023)
30. Zhang, T., Wang, S., Yan, S., Li, J., Liu, Q.: Generative table pre-training empowers models for tabular prediction. arXiv preprint arXiv:2305.09696 (2023)
31. Zhang, X., et al.: TableLLM: enabling tabular data manipulation by LLMs in real office usage scenarios (2024)
32. Zhang, Z., et al.: Igniting language intelligence: the Hitchhiker's guide from chain-of-thought reasoning to language agents. arXiv preprint arXiv:2311.11797 (2023)
33. Zhou, D., et al.: Least-to-most prompting enables complex reasoning in large language models. arXiv preprint arXiv:2205.10625 (2022)
34. Zhu, F., Liu, Z., Feng, F., Wang, C., Li, M., Chua, T.S.: TAT-LLM: a specialized language model for discrete reasoning over tabular and textual data (2024)

Test Prioritization Based on the Coverage of Recently Modified Source Code: An Industrial Case Study

Hande Erol[1,2] and Hasan Sözer[2(✉)]

[1] Vestel Electronics, Manisa, Turkey
hande.erol@vestel.com.tr
[2] Ozyegin University, İstanbul, Turkey
hasan.sozer@ozyegin.edu.tr

Abstract. Regression tests are re-executed to ensure quality and lack of side-effects after software changes to incorporate new/improved functionalities and/or bug fixes. Prioritizing these tests for detecting faults earlier can increase productivity especially when the testing duration increases. We conduct an industrial case study in the consumer electronics domain, where regression tests take several weeks to complete. We evaluate the effectiveness of a test prioritization approach in terms of the rate of early fault detection. We analyze test cases individually but apply prioritization at a higher granularity level, where we prioritize weekly test plans rather than individual test cases. Our approach gives higher priority to those test cases that cover the recently modified parts of the source code. We use 3 Digital TV projects as subject systems. We compare the effectiveness of the original execution order of test cases with the alternative ordering as suggested by our approach. Results show that the alternative ordering is more effective in finding faults earlier for all the 3 subject systems, where the rate of early fault detection can be increased by up to 38%.

Keywords: Test case prioritization · regression testing · rate of early fault detection · repository mining · industrial case study

1 Introduction

Software systems have to be maintained and they are usually extended with new features. Regression testing is performed to ensure quality and lack of bugs or side effects that might be caused by maintenance activities and extensions [37]. However, the size of test suites used for regression testing tends to increase over time. The increasing size of the test suite inevitably increases the test execution time. A regression test suite might include millions of test cases [15], which take multiple weeks to execute. For example, test execution time was reported as 7 weeks for an actual product that has around 20,000 lines of code only [30].

It might turn out to be infeasible to execute all the test cases in the regression test suite due to resource constraints. In this respect, test case selection [5,17], test suite reduction [29,32] or test suite minimization [26] approaches can be

H. D. Menéndez et al. (Eds.): ICTSS 2024, LNCS 15383, pp. 46–59, 2025.
https://doi.org/10.1007/978-3-031-80889-0_4

applied [37]. It might be possible or necessary [8] to execute all the test cases. However, increasing test duration would still be a problem since the detection of some faults are delayed. In this respect, test case prioritization (TCP) [30,39] can be applied to change the execution order of test cases such that faults can be detected as early as possible [10,19,31]. Early fault detection and as such early feedback for developers can increase productivity especially when the testing duration is long. TCP can be also employed as a means of test case selection, where test execution can continue in the suggested ordering of test cases until the resources are consumed [12].

TCP can be performed based on various properties of test cases such as their cost [7], code coverage [35,38], the priority of the verified requirements [34], and historical data regarding their fault detection effectiveness [18]. Hereby, code coverage is measured as the percentage of the source code (e.g., statements) executed by a test case. The expectation is that higher code coverage leads to a greater chance of detecting faults [16]. Therefore, a test case with a high code coverage is prioritized over those that have lower code coverage.

In this paper, we present an industrial case study from the consumer electronics domain. The goal of the study is to evaluate the effectiveness of a TCP approach that is based on code coverage. We apply TCP at a higher granularity level compared to previous studies. Although we analyze test cases individually, we prioritize weekly test plans rather than individual test cases. We select the set of tests to be applied each week. In particular, we prioritize those tests that cover the recently modified source code elements. Our rationale is that faults are more likely to be introduced in recently changed sources files. This assumption was validated in empirical studies on fault prediction where, source code changes have been measured to be used as input for prediction models to achieve high accuracy [2,23].

We use 3 Digital TV projects as subject systems for our case study. We apply prioritization of tests spanning 7 weeks for each of these systems. We compare the effectiveness of the ordering obtained with our prioritization approach to that of the existing ordering as the baseline. We measure effectiveness in terms of the rate of early fault detection by using the $APFD_c$ metric [9]. Results show that the alternative ordering is more effective in finding faults earlier for all the 3 subject systems, where the rate of early fault detection can be increased by up to 38%.

The rest of this paper is organized as follows. We provide a summary of the related studies in the following section. We explain the implemented TCP approach and the case study design in Sect. 3. We present and discuss the results in Sect. 4. Finally, we conclude the paper in Sect. 5.

2 Related Work

TCP has been studied for more than two decades and the number of studies published in this area has increased over time [20]. An analysis of these studies suggests that most of these have mainly investigated effective criteria for TCP.

The focus of researchers has shifted to prioritization algorithms and empirical studies in the last decade as the research area became more mature [20]. Yet, the number of empirical studies is still not high, especially for those that are conducted in an industrial context. This study contributes to filling this gap.

One can not predict the fault-detection capability of a test case directly. Hence, various criteria are proposed for prioritizing test cases, assuming that these criteria provide indirect measures to approximate fault-detection capability. These measures include mutation score [21,33], code coverage [24,30], code complexity [3], and the number of faults that are detected in the history [3,4]. The most used criterion is structural coverage, where a test case gets a priority based on the percentage of structural units it covers [20]. These units can be system states [14] or units in the source code [24,30] at various levels of granularity like statements, branches, and functions [24]. Most studies aim at improving the overall code coverage [36]. Change impact-based criteria have also shown to be effective [5,13,25,27]. There are several studies, which focus on changed code units to calculate risk [6] or to detect refactoring faults [1]. In this study, our prioritization criterion is the number of changes made on the source code elements that are covered by test cases. This criterion is based on the assumption that faults are more likely to be introduced in recently and mostly changed sources files. Empirical studies show that this measure can be used as input for achieving high accuracy in fault prediction [2,23]. Hence, we believe that it can be a good candidate for an indirect measure regarding fault-detection capability.

There have been a number of industrial case studies to evaluate the effectiveness of TCP techniques in the last decade. One of the earlier ones shows the effectiveness of TCP based on failure prediction and change risk analysis applied on the Microsoft Windows Vista operating system [6]. Another one [3] utilizes code coverage, code complexity, and historical data on previously detected faults for TCP. Hereby, the subject of the study is another Microsoft product and the employed TCP approach clusters test cases based on the utilized criteria. Test cases in the same cluster are assumed to have similar fault detection ability. ROCKET [22] priorities test cases that detected more faults in recent testing activities. It was applied on a video conferencing software and results showed that 30% of the known faults can be revealed by executing 20% of the test cases. Finally, a coverage-based TCP was evaluated with an industrial case study, where a simulation software system was selected as the subject [24]. Results of the study showed that coverage criteria at a finer granularity lead to better early fault detection rates and the use of modification information does not significantly impact the results. However, the study ignored the difference in execution duration for test cases, which can significantly vary in the consumer electronics domain. We exploit modification information in our study and we observe improvement in early fault detection rates when we prioritize tests that cover the recently modified source code elements.

Our study is one of the few industrial case studies on TCP from the consumer electronics domain. TCP is very important for this domain in particular since regression tests take several weeks to complete. There are also certification tests for which test case minimization or selection approaches are not applicable [8]. All the test cases have to be executed and none of them can be omitted. However, TCP can help for detecting faults earlier. Our case study investigates to what extent TCP can improve the early fault detection rate. We apply TCP at a higher granularity level as a major difference with respect to the previous studies. In fact, we do not prioritize test cases individually. We prioritize weekly test plans instead. However, we analyze source code changes and their coverage by each test case at the statement level. We present our approach and the case study design in the following section.

3   Case Study Design

We explain our case study design in this section. Our goal is to investigate the amount of improvement, if any, that can be achieved in early fault detection rate by TCP. We evaluate a TCP approach that gives higher priority to those test cases that cover the recently modified source code elements mostly. Hence, our research question is formulated as follows.

> *To what extent the rate of early fault detection can be increased by prioritizing test cases based on their coverage of the recently modified source code elements?*

We explain the implemented TCP approach in the following subsection. Then, we explain the evaluation metric we employed. We conclude the section with the explanation of subject systems and data collection procedures.

3.1   Implemented Prioritization Approach

We conducted our case study on Digital TV systems being developed and maintained at Vestel[1], which is one the largest consumer electronics companies in Europe. Digital TV systems are commissioned on a weekly basis by this company. Test cases are grouped into a set of test suites based on the tested features of these systems. These test suites are grouped to be applied as part of a set of test plans, each of which are executed within a week. In our approach, we prioritize these weekly test plans rather than individual test cases.

We developed a tool that keeps mappings among test plans, test suites, test cases, and the set of source files covered during the execution of these test cases. We also developed scripts to analyze SVN[2] commit logs and identify source code changes. We followed the steps listed below for prioritizing the execution of test plans:

1. We create an association between each test plan and a set of test suites;
2. We create an association between each test suite and a set of test cases;

---

[1] http://www.vestel.com.tr.
[2] https://subversion.apache.org/.

3. We create an association between each test case and a set of source files it covers during execution;
4. We collect the number of changes for each source file;
5. We calculate the *associated change count* for each test case by summing up the number of changes for all the files that are associated with the test case;
6. We calculate the associated change count for each test plan by summing up this count for all the test cases that are included in all the test suites associated with the plan;
7. We sort test plans in descending order based on the associated change count to determine the prioritization order.
8. We prioritize a test plan with the shorter execution time over others with the same associated change count.

The rate of early fault detection achieved by original test plan ordering, which has been used by the company, is compared to that of ordering based on this TCP approach. We explain the evaluation metric used for this comparison in the following.

3.2   Evaluation Metric

We measure effectiveness in terms of the rate of early fault detection by using the $APFD_c$ metric [9], which is introduced as a variant of the APFD (Average Percentage Faults Detected) metric [31] for rewarding units of fault severity detected per unit test cost. We measure test cost in terms of the time it takes to execute a test suite. However, fault severity is measured in ordinal scale for the experimental objects we utilize in our case study. Hence, calculating the cumulative severity of detected faults is not a proper way of quantifying a kind of weighted contribution. Arithmetic operations have no meaning in ordinal scale [11], when severity levels do not reflect the absolute value/criticality of faults [8]. For instance, a fault with severity scale 1 is not four times severe than a fault with a severity scale 4. On the other hand, test suites have a high variance in terms of their cost. One test suite can be completed within a day, whereas another one can take multiple days to complete. Therefore, we used the $APFD_c$ metric to take this variance into account.

3.3   Data Collection

We used 3 Digital TV projects as experimental objects, and used their test plans for evaluating our TCP approach. We refer to these projects as *P1*, *P2*, and *P3* in the rest of the paper. Each of these projects have 7 test plans. A week is allocated for each of these test plans. Table 1 shows the original plan executed for 7 weeks for *P1*, for instance. The second column lists the sequence of test suites included in the plan, enumerated from 1 to 42.

The third column lists the number of changes associated with the test suites that are included in the plan for the corresponding week. For instance, there are 64 changes applied on source code statements that are covered by the execution

Table 1. The original ordering of weekly test plans for *P1*.

Week #	Test Suites	# of Changes	# of Faults
1	[1–6]	64	46
2	[7–13]	133	89
3	[14–23]	280	296
4	[24–27]	14	22
5	[28–33]	65	23
6	[34–37]	181	155
7	[38–42]	312	301

Table 2. The suggested ordering of weekly test plans for *P1*.

Week #	Test Suites	# of Changes	# of Faults
1	[38–42]	312	301
2	[14–23]	280	296
3	[34–37]	181	155
4	[7–13]	133	89
5	[28–33]	65	23
6	[1–6]	64	46
7	[24–27]	14	22

of test cases included in test suites 1, 2, 3, 4, 5, and 6 within the first week. The last column of Table 1 shows the number of faults detected. We analyzed a total of 13,316 source code changes (commits) from SVN repositories of projects registered between late 2017 and mid-2018. All the data regarding the detected faults at the end of each test cycle are collected from JIRA[3], which is the bug tracking system used by the company. After each test session, any detected bugs are reported as issues, with each issue linked to the unique number of the test case in which the bug was found. This allows for easy collection of detected bugs and their associated test cases through a simple query[4].

Our TCP approach suggests an ordering that is based on the number of associated changes (i.e., the third column of Table 1). For instance, the suggested ordering for the execution of test plans for *P1* would be as shown in Table 2. We can see in this table that the majority of the faults can be detected much earlier when the suggested ordering is applied. Overall results that are obtained in our case study are presented in the following section.

4   Results and Discussion

We compiled the results for *P1*, *P2*, *P3*, over a period of 7 weeks. Results for *P1* with the original test plan ordering are depicted in Fig. 1. It shows the number of changes and the number of faults associated with the set of test cases that are scheduled for each of the 7 weeks. Figure 2 depicts the same results that are obtained when the suggested test plan ordering is used. We can observe a high correlation between the number of changes and the number of detected faults. Pearson Correlation Coefficient (PCC) [28] was calculated as 0.98. The majority of faults are detected in weeks 3 and 7 when the original test plan ordering is used (See Fig. 1). The corresponding test plans are prioritized in the suggested ordering and as such, the majority of faults are detected in the first two weeks (See Fig. 2).

---

[3] https://www.atlassian.com/software/jira.
[4] We cannot share the raw data due to confidentiality.

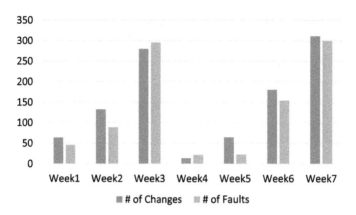

Fig. 1. Results for *P1* with the original test plan ordering.

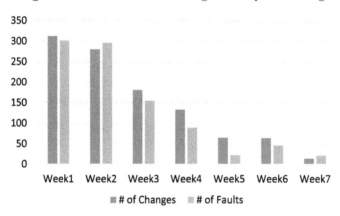

Fig. 2. Results for *P1* with the suggested test plan ordering.

Figure 3 depicts the percentage of faults detected with the original and the suggested ordering of test plans executed throughout the period of 7 weeks for *P1*. The percentage of faults are aligned on the x-axis between 0 and 100. The coloring scheme shows when, i.e., in each week, these faults are detected. We can observe a significant improvement in the rate of early fault detection. Only 4% of the faults can be detected in the first week when the original test plan ordering is used. This rate goes up to 32% with the suggested ordering. Likewise, at the end of week 2, approximately 14% of the faults can be detected with the original test plan order. On the other hand, about 64% of the faults can be detected by the end of week 2 when the suggested order is used.

Results for *P2* are depicted in Fig. 4 and Fig. 5, when the original test plan ordering and the suggested test plan ordering are used, respectively. Although the level of correlation between the number of changes and the number of detected

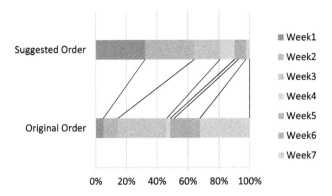

Fig. 3. Percentage of faults detected with the original and the suggested ordering of test plans executed throughout the period of 7 weeks for *P1*.

faults is lower when compared to *P1*, it is still significantly high. PCC was calculated as 0.87. Week 3 stands out as the week where both the number of changes and the number of detected faults are the highest (See Fig. 4). The corresponding test plan is scheduled for the first week when the suggested ordering is used (See Fig. 5) and the rate of early fault detection is significantly increased.

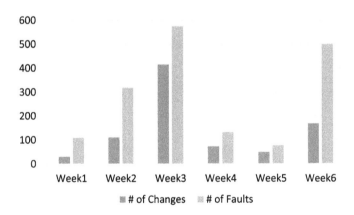

Fig. 4. Results for *P2* with the original test plan ordering.

Figure 6 depicts the percentage of faults detected with the original and the suggested ordering of test plans executed throughout the period of 7 weeks for *P2*. We can observe a significant improvement in the rate of early fault detection for this project as well. Only 6% of the faults can be detected in the first week when the original test plan ordering is used. This rate goes up to 33% with the suggested ordering. Likewise, at the end of week 2, approximately 25% of the faults can be detected with the original test plan order. On the other hand,

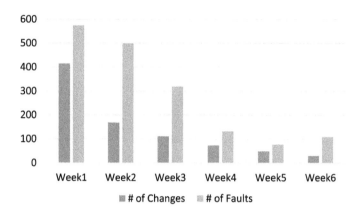

Fig. 5. Results for *P2* with the suggested test plan ordering.

about 62% of the faults can be detected by the end of week 2 when the suggested order is used.

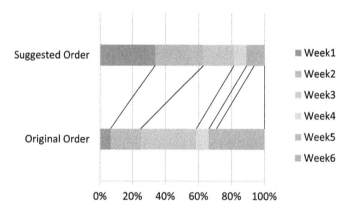

Fig. 6. Percentage of faults detected with the original and the suggested ordering of test plans executed throughout the period of 7 weeks for *P2*.

Results for *P3* are depicted in Fig. 7 and Fig. 8, when the original test plan ordering and the suggested test plan ordering are used, respectively. The level of correlation between the number of changes and the number of detected faults is almost the same as what was observed for *P2*. PCC was calculated as 0.87. Weeks 3 and 6 stand out as the weeks where both the number of changes and the number of detected faults are relatively higher (See Fig. 7). The corresponding test plans are scheduled for the first two weeks when the suggested ordering is used (See Fig. 8).

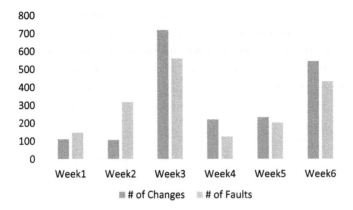

Fig. 7. Results for *P3* with the original test plan ordering.

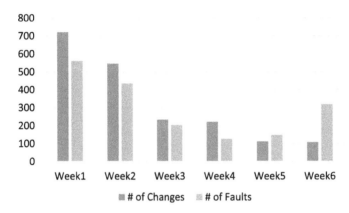

Fig. 8. Results for *P3* with the suggested test plan ordering.

The rate of early fault detection is significantly increased for *P3* as well. Figure 9 depicts the percentage of faults detected with the original and the suggested ordering of test plans executed throughout the period of 7 weeks for *P3*. Only 8% of the faults can be detected in the first week when the original test plan ordering is used. This rate goes up to 31% with the suggested ordering. Likewise, at the end of week 2, approximately 26% of the faults can be detected with the original test plan order. On the other hand, about 55% of the faults can be detected by the end of week 2 when the suggested order is used.

Table 3 lists the previously reported PCC values as well as the $APFD_c$ values calculated for both the original and suggested ordering of test plans for all the projects. The last column shows the amount of improvement obtained when the suggested ordering is used instead of the original ordering. The ratio of improvement is calculated as approximately 33%, 38%, and 33%, for *P1*, *P2*, and *P3*, respectively. We discuss validity threats for our evaluation in he following.

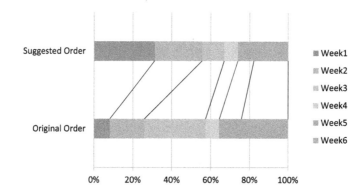

Fig. 9. Percentage of faults detected with the original and the suggested ordering of test plans executed throughout the period of 7 weeks for *P3*.

Table 3. Correlation between the number of faults detected by test plans and the number of changes associated with them, $APFD_c$ values for alternative test plan orderings, and the ratio of improvement for all the projects.

Project	PCC	Original Order	Suggested Order	Improvement Ratio (%)
P1	0.983	28.75	38.12	32.59
P2	0.872	48.13	66.16	37.46
P3	0.866	48.48	64.54	33.12

4.1   Threats to Validity

Our empirical study is subject to external validity threats since all the 3 experimental objects are Digital TV projects that are developed and maintained by the same company. Our results might not be generalized in other application domains. The approach might not be even applicable if test cases are not organized into a set of test suites and the testing process is not organized with a series of test plans each of which executes a set of test suites. We present our conclusions in the following section.

5   Conclusion

We evaluate the effectiveness of a coarse-grained test case prioritization approach, where we prioritize test plans rather than prioritizing individual test cases. Each test plan executes a set of test suites, and each test suite includes a set of test cases. We analyze test cases individually to measure their coverage of the recently modified source code elements. Then we calculate the coverage of the overall test plan based on these measurements. We prioritize test plans based on their coverage.

We conduct an industrial case study in the consumer electronics domain, where regression tests take several weeks to complete. We use 3 Digital TV projects as subject systems. We compare the effectiveness of the original execution order of test plans with the alternative ordering as suggested by our approach. Results show that the suggested ordering is more effective in finding faults earlier for all the 3 subject systems, where the rate of early fault detection ranges between 33% and 38%. The correlation between the number of faults detected by a test plan and its coverage of modified source code elements ranges between 0.87 and 0.98.

Acknowledgment. We would like to thank software developers and test engineers at Vestel for supporting our case study.

References

1. Alves, E., Machado, P., Massoni, T., Kim, M.: Prioritizing test cases for early detection of refactoring faults. Softw. Test. Verif. Reliabil. **26**(5), 402–426 (2016)
2. Bell, R., Ostrand, T., Weyuker, E.: Does measuring code change improve fault prediction? In: Proceedings of the 7th International Conference on Predictive Models in Software Engineering, pp. 1–8 (2011)
3. Carlson, R., Do, H., Denton, A.: A clustering approach to improving test case prioritization: an industrial case study. In: Proceedings of the 27th IEEE International Conference on Software Maintenance, pp. 382–391 (2011)
4. Cho, Y., Kim, J., Lee, E.: History-based test case prioritization for failure information. In: Proceedings of the 23rd Asia-Pacific Software Engineering Conference, pp. 385–388 (2016)
5. Cingil, T., Sozer, H.: Black-box test case selection by relating code changes with previously fixed defects. In: Proceedings of the International Conference on Evaluation and Assessment in Software Engineering, pp. 30–39 (2022)
6. Czerwonka, J., Das, R., Nagappan, N., Tarvo, A., Teterev, A.: CRANE: failure prediction, change analysis and test prioritization in practice – experiences from windows. In: 2011 Fourth IEEE International Conference on Software Testing, Verification and Validation, pp. 357–366 (2011)
7. Dirim, S., Ozener, O., Sozer, H.: Prioritization and parallel execution of test cases for certification testing of embedded systems. Softw. Qual. J. 1–26 (2022)
8. Dirim, S., Sozer, H.: Prioritization of test cases with varying test costs and fault severities for certification testing. In: Proceedings of the IEEE International Conference on Software Testing, Verification and Validation Workshops, pp. 386–391 (2020)
9. Elbaum, S., Malishevsky, A., Rothermel, G.: Incorporating varying test costs and fault severities into test case prioritization. In: Proceedings of the 23rd International Conference on Software Engineering, pp. 329–338 (2001)
10. Elbaum, S., Malishevsky, A., Rothermel, G.: Test case prioritization: a family of empirical studies. IEEE Trans. Softw. Eng. **28**(2), 159–182 (2002)
11. Fenton, N., Pfleeger, S.: Software Metrics: A Rigorous and Practical Approach, 3rd edn. CRC Press, Boca Raton (2014)
12. Hao, D., Zhang, L., Zang, L., Wang, Y., Wu, X., Xie, T.: To be optimal or not in test-case prioritization. IEEE Trans. Softw. Eng. **42**(5), 490–505 (2016)
13. Haraty, R., Mansour, N., Moukahal, L., Khalil, I.: Regression test cases prioritization using clustering and code change relevance. Int. J. Softw. Eng. Knowl. Eng. **26**(05), 733–768 (2016)

14. He, Z., Bai, C.: GUI test case prioritization by state-coverage criterion. In: Proceedings of the IEEE/ACM 10th International Workshop on Automation of Software Test, pp. 18–22 (2015)
15. Herzig, K., Greiler, M., Czerwonka, J., Murphy, B.: The art of testing less without sacrificing quality. In: Proceedings of the 37th International Conference on Software Engineering, pp. 483–493 (2015)
16. Huang, R., Zhang, Q., Towey, D., Sun, W., Chen, J.: Regression test case prioritization by code combinations coverage. J. Syst. Softw. **169**, 110712 (2020)
17. Kazmi, R., Jawawi, D., Mohamad, R., Ghani, I.: Effective regression test case selection: a systematic literature review. ACM Comput. Surv. **50**(2), 1–32 (2017)
18. Khalilian, A., Azgomi, M., Fazlalizadeh, Y.: An improved method for test case prioritization by incorporating historical test case data. Sci. Comput. Program. **78**(1), 93–116 (2012)
19. Khatibsyarbini, M., Isa, M., Jawawi, D., Tumeng, R.: Test case prioritization approaches in regression testing: a systematic literature review. Inf. Softw. Technol. **93**, 74–93 (2018)
20. Lou, Y., Chen, J., Zhang, L., Hao, D.: A survey on regression test-case prioritization. In: Advances in Computers, vol. 113, pp. 1–46. Elsevier (2019)
21. Luo, Q., Moran, K., Poshyvanyk, D., Penta, M.D.: Assessing test case prioritization on real faults and mutants. In: Proceedings of the IEEE International Conference on Software Maintenance and Evolution, pp. 240–251 (2018)
22. Marijan, D., Gotlieb, A., Sen, A.: Test case prioritization for continuous regression testing: an industrial case study. In: Proceedings of the IEEE International Conference on Software Maintenance, pp. 540–543 (2013)
23. Moser, R., Pedrycz, W., Succi, G.: Analysis of the reliability of a subset of change metrics for defect prediction. In: Proceedings of the Second ACM-IEEE International Symposium on Empirical Software Engineering and Measurement, pp. 309–311 (2008)
24. Nardo, D.D., Alshahwan, N., Briand, L., Labiche, Y.: Coverage-based test case prioritisation: an industrial case study. In: Proceedings of the IEEE Sixth International Conference on Software Testing, Verification and Validation, pp. 302–311 (2013)
25. Nguyen, C., Marchetto, A., Tonella, P.: Change sensitivity based prioritization for audit testing of webservice compositions. In: Proceedings of the 4th IEEE International Conference on Software Testing, Verification and Validation Workshops, pp. 357–365 (2011)
26. Ozener, O., Sozer, H.: An effective formulation of the multi-criteria test suite minimization problem. J. Syst. Softw. **168**, 110632 (2020)
27. Panda, S., Munjal, D., Mohapatra, D.: A slice-based change impact analysis for regression test case prioritization of object-oriented programs. Adv. Softw. Eng. **2016**(1), 7132404 (2016)
28. Pearson, K.: Note on regression and inheritance in the case of two parents. Proc. Roy. Soc. London Ser. **I**(58), 240–242 (1895)
29. Rothermel, G., Harrold, M.J, Von Ronn, J., Hong, C.: Empirical studies of test suite reduction. Softw. Test. Verif. Reliabil. **4**(2), 219–249 (2002)
30. Rothermel, G., Untch, R.H., Chu, C., Harrold, M.J.: Prioritizing test cases for regression testing. IEEE Trans. Softw. Eng. **27**(10), 929–948 (2001)
31. Rothermel, G., Untch, R., Chu, C., Harrold, M.: Test case prioritization: an empirical study. In: Proceedings of the IEEE International Conference on Software Maintenance, pp. 179–188 (1999)

32. Shi, A., Gyori, A., Mahmood, S., Zhao, P., Marinov, D.: Evaluating test-suite reduction in real-world software evolution. In: Proceedings of the International Symposium on Software Testing and Analysis, pp. 84–94 (2018)
33. Shin, D., Yoo, S., Papadakis, M., Bae, D.: Empirical evaluation of mutation-based test case prioritization techniques. Softw. Test. Verif. Reliab. **29**(1–2), e1695 (2019)
34. Srikanth, H., Hettiarachchi, C., Do, H.: Requirements based test prioritization using risk factors: an industrial study. Inf. Softw. Technol. **69**, 71–83 (2016)
35. Wang, S., Nam, J., Tan, L.: QTEP: quality-aware test case prioritization. In: Proceedings of the 2017 11th Joint Meeting on Foundations of Software Engineering, ESEC/FSE 2017, pp. 523–534. Association for Computing Machinery, New York (2017)
36. Yadav, D.K., Dutta, S., Azad, C.: Study and analysis of test case prioritization technique. In: Nath, V., Mandal, J. (eds.) Nanoelectronics, Circuits and Communication Systems, pp. 469–481. Springer, Singapore (2021)
37. Yoo, S., Harman, M.: Regression testing minimization, selection and prioritization: a survey. Softw. Test. Verif. Reliab. **22**(2), 67–120 (2012)
38. You, D., Chen, Z., Xu, B., Luo, B., Zhang, C.: An empirical study on the effectiveness of time-aware test case prioritization techniques. In: Proceedings of the 2011 ACM Symposium on Applied Computing, pp. 1451–1456 (2011)
39. Zhang, L., Hao, D., Zhang, L., Rothermel, G., Mei, H.: Bridging the gap between the total and additional test-case prioritization strategies. In: Proceedings of the 35th International Conference on Software Engineering, pp. 192–201 (2013)

Mutation Testing and Code Generation

On the Variations of ChatGPT's Response Quality for Generating Source Code Across Programming Languages

Ángela González de Diego[1] and Franz Wotawa[2(✉)] (iD)

[1] Graz University of Technology, Graz, Austria
`a.gonzalezdediego@student.tugraz.at`
[2] CD Lab for Quality Assurance Methodologies for Automated Cyber-Physical Systems, Institute of Software Technology, Graz University of Technology, Graz, Austria
`wotawa@ist.tugraz.at`
`https://www.tugraz.at/institute/ist`

Abstract. The rise of Large Language Models, particularly the Chat-GPT model, has transformed the field of natural language information processing and has led to widespread adoption in a diverse range of applications and across a multitude of industries. In this paper, we focus on assessing the quality of the responses generated by Chat-GPT for the code generation tasks using seven different programming languages. We selected the languages considering diversity in terms of the fields of application, philosophies, and popularity. We carried out an experimental evaluation utilizing different introductory coding examples for each of the programming languages using the pass@k metric for evaluation. The results indicate a correlation between the effectiveness of the model and the popularity of programming languages.

Keywords: Large language models for programming · Experimentally evaluating code generation using LLMs · ChatGPT for programming

1 Introduction

Artificial Intelligence has undergone a profound evolution in recent years with the success of improved machine learning approaches and their use in computer vision and natural language processing applications. For the latter application domain, the development of Large Language Models (LLMs) represents a significant advance since these systems have the ability to understand and generate coherent responses using human-like language. Their operation is based on the ability to predict the likelihood of a token, considering the preceding context or the surrounding context as inputs. These unsupervised systems receive as input a token, which can be a character, a word, or a string, and generate as output a prediction in the form of punctuation or string [5,6].

To achieve this, the models employ large-scale architectures and are trained on large volumes of data, allowing them to be applied in various fields such as

© IFIP International Federation for Information Processing 2025
Published by Springer Nature Switzerland AG 2025
H. D. Menéndez et al. (Eds.): ICTSS 2024, LNCS 15383, pp. 63–78, 2025.
https://doi.org/10.1007/978-3-031-80889-0_5

natural language processing (NLP), language translation, and text generation. Although LLMs achieve satisfactory performance, it is common to find unusual and undesired behaviors in these models, as they generate responses without precise correspondence with the user's goals. This is due to a discrepancy between the language modeling and user objectives, which are to follow instructions accurately and safely [28,35].

Alongside the evolution of Artificial Intelligence algorithms and the massive quantities of available data, there has been a growing interest in conversational agents. Initially, chatbots were designed to perform specific tasks. Due to their potential for a broad range of applications, many were developed using NLP to attempt to respond to user queries by retrieving information. Some examples include social bots that flooded Twitter (2010) or intelligent agents that retrieve information and send notifications, such as Siri (2011), Alexa (2014), Cortana (2014), and Google Assistant (2016) [10]. With the development of large language models and the need to provide real-time feedback on unstructured data, new models, like the Generative Pre-trained Transformer (GPT), have been developed. These models use transformer architectures of neural networks to apply generative and discriminative algorithms that are capable of forecasting the probability of word sequences [36].

The rapid development and popularization of LLMs have, in turn, triggered changes in the programming field. This development has led to the idea that machines, guided by concrete specifications, can write code [24]. Furthermore, the release of ChatGPT-3 by OpenAI was a milestone. OpenAI observed that GPT-3 possessed the ability to generate simple Python programs from docstrings, although its abilities in code generation were initially limited because it was not explicitly trained for this function [9]. Nevertheless, the models have evolved substantially. Examples of the most recent models are OpenAI's GPT-3.5 and GPT-4, Google's Gemini [16], Claude [11] and Microsoft's Copilot [25] leading to efficient code generation tools like ChatGPT [9], GitHub Copilot [15], Amazon CodeWhisperer [3], and Tabnine [34].

In this paper, we do not consider evaluating code generation tools on performing their task again. Instead, we focus on whether there is a difference in the code generation capabilities of LLMs over various programming languages used as target languages for code generation. In particular, we focus on ChatGPT (in Version 3.5 [28]) and its capabilities to generate programs for the programming languages Python, Java, C, JavaScript, Lisp, Smalltalk, and SML, considering smaller and simpler programming tasks. Note that we selected ChatGPT 3.5 because it is one of the most advanced and accessible versions of OpenAI. Unlike the OpenAI API and later versions like ChatGPT 4, it does not require a paid subscription.

It is worth noting that there are many data sets available for evaluating LLMs when performing coding tasks, including HumanEval, APPS, and MBPP [7,9]. However, as pointed out by an AlphaCode study [22] the APPS dataset generated false positives during the evaluation. In a recent paper [39], the authors pointed out that HumanEval and MBPP have significant biases, as they represent a very limited subset of programming concepts. Moreover, there is a lack of transparency regarding the selection process and problem categories included in these datasets [39]. We created our own dataset because of these reasons and our focus on different programming languages.

In summary, we wanted to tackle the research question of whether the programming language influences the solution given back by an LLM, particularly ChatGPT, for a given basic programming task. More specifically, we wanted to know whether the popularity of a programming language impacts the outcome of ChatGPT. We might expect such an impact to exist because fewer example programs are available for training. However, to our knowledge, no result has been published justifying this impact.

We structure this paper as follows: First, we discuss background information, including available work and the evaluation method. Afterward, we discuss the methodologies behind our experimental analysis, followed by an in-depth discussion of the obtained results. Finally, we summarize the content of the paper.

2   Background

Evaluating LLMs and other machine learning-based tools for any software engineering task requires a standardized task description and an evaluation procedure for its output. In this section, we mainly report on the evaluation metrics already used in the scientific literature for this purpose.

BLEU Metrics: The Bilingual Evaluation Understudy (BLEU) metric has been widely employed in the literature [2,14,30] for the evaluation of code generation models. BLEU [29] was initially developed as a metric for evaluating machine translation tasks. The basis of its operation is based on the search and counting of n-word sequence matches (called n-grams) between the target translation and the output generated by the model. Consequently, the quality of the translation is directly proportional to the number of matches found.

In code generation, the BLEU metric is employed to assess the degree of similarity between the generated code and a set of correct solutions. The metric allows for the evaluation of the generated syntax and programming structures. However, recent studies have demonstrated that this metric has significant limitations. It only evaluates the syntactic similarity of the target code, which does not imply that the code is executable or correct. BLEU does not consider specific characteristics of programming languages, such as language-specific keywords, syntactic accuracy, and semantic correctness [31]. Consequently, evaluating code generation models based on matching generated code with a correct solution is not an optimal approach [9].

This also holds for extensions like CodeBLEU, which was introduced in 2020 as an adaptation of the BLEU metric, which was developed to evaluate the quality of generated code [26,41]. Despite improvements in metrics, recent studies continue to indicate that metrics based on the textual match between the generated code and the reference code fail to capture the practical utility of it. In software development, it is possible to implement the same operations in different ways. However, what truly determines their effectiveness is whether their performance is equivalent. Therefore, it has been shown that in the evaluation of code generation, the main focus should be on the analysis of functional equivalence rather than looking for superficial similarities [13, 40].

Pass@k: Given the potential for performing similar tasks and operations in diverse ways, the effectiveness of evaluating code generation lies in determining whether the compiled and executed code is correct and whether the intended task has been fulfilled rather than focusing on the software implementation. To this end, execution-based metrics are employed, which analyze functional correctness by executing a series of unit tests. These metrics emulate the typical behavior of human developers, who carry out a series of tests to identify potential error cases and debug the code [40].

Pass@k is an execution-based metric initially proposed by Kulal in 2019 [19] and further refined by OpenAI in 2021 [9]. This metric assesses the accuracy of generated code in terms of precision and semantic similarity. It determines whether the code is functionally correct and executable and whether it fulfills the desired functionality, taking into account that it is possible to implement different but functionally correct solutions.

For each problem, the model generates n different solutions. In addition, a series of unit tests are generated that the solution must pass to be considered correct. If a single test fails, the solution is considered to not meet the necessary requirements to be valid and is marked as failed. Then, it is evaluated if at least one of the first k solutions is correct, with $n \geq k$. If at least one of the first k solutions generated passes all the defined unit tests, the model is considered to have produced a valid answer for that problem. Mathematically, this represents the probability that at least one of the top k solutions generated is correct. The following formula defines this probability:

$$pass@k = \mathbf{E}_{problems} \left[1 - \frac{\binom{n-c}{k}}{\binom{n}{k}} \right]$$

where n is the number of solutions generated by the model $(n \geq k)$, c is the number of correct solutions for that problem $(c \geq n)$ and k is the number of the first solutions taken into account for the evaluation.

For evaluating ChatGPT 3.5, we rely on *pass@k* as the evaluation metrics.

3   Methodology

In the following subsections, we discuss the methodology behind our experimental evaluation in detail. A replication package comprising programs, the test cases, the datasets, and the results are available on Zendo (https://zenodo.org/records/13837722?token=eyJhbGciOiJIUzUxMiJ9.eyJpZCI6IjRhNDY0YTAzLTU1YzctNDE2MS1hZWQ1LTQ0NTEyOGZhNDhhNCIsImRhdGEiOnt9LCJyYW5kb20iOiI4ZmIzMzgyNjY0M2QyZjQwOTk2YjljYTIyNGE5ODFhOCJ9.4qdAFHI-PrtCB-awqeX-cIYU6GcH9_k95ljXvwvmA8U1fvlje8WcpcE5aNmKhZqdSpZWbbBQZ_KGeAR_sAwHng).

Table 1. Programming languages and their development environments

Programming language	Paradigm	Compiler/Interpreter	IDE
C	Imperative	MinGW Compiler Suite	Code::Blocks
Java	Object-Oriented	Compiler for Java (ECJ)	Eclipse IDE
Python	Multi-paradigm	CPython	Google Colab
Javascript	Multi-paradigm	Node.js	Visual Studio Code
SmallTalk	Object-Oriented	Clang (incorporated in the VM)	Squeak
Standard ML (SML)	Functional	Standard ML of New Jersey (SML/NJ)	Visual Studio Code
Common Lisp	Multi-paradigm	SBCL (Steel Bank Common Lisp)	Visual Studio Code

3.1 Selected Programming Languages

This study aims to analyze the influence of the programming language used in the response generation of ChatGPT. There is a wide range of programming languages, which vary in terms of both complexity and simplicity and are characterized by different paradigms. The specific characteristics of each language can significantly influence the problem-solving logic and, thus, the quality and efficiency of the generated responses.

For the study, we selected seven programming languages, which we show in Table 1. When selecting these languages, we considered covering a broad and diverse set of paradigms, purposes, application domains, and popularity. The language paradigms include object-oriented, functional, imperative, and multi-paradigm languages. Some languages like LISP or Smalltalk have been used more widely in the past but are not that present anymore.

3.2 Setup

The setup comprises ChatGPT 3.5, the code generation prompt, the used programming tasks, and their evaluation using software testing.

Code Generation Prompt: Interaction with LLM models occurs through prompts. These are instructions or questions articulated in natural language that provide a defined context, indicate what information is relevant, and direct both the form and specific content of the answers generated by the model. In applications like ChatGPT, prompts are presented in an interactive dialog format. This allows the user to pose queries to which the model responds sequentially [37,38]. It is essential to remember that the quality of the responses from a model is directly proportional to the clarity and precision of the prompt provided by the user. Therefore, to take full advantage of ChatGPT's capabilities, it is essential to develop well-structured and detailed prompts [37].

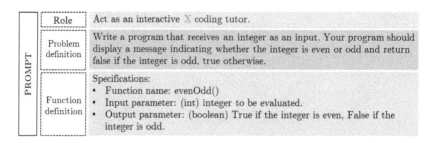

Fig. 1. Prompt definition for code generation tasks.

For our experimental analysis, we structured the generated prompts in three parts, as shown in Fig. 1. First, we establish the role of ChatGPT as a coding tutor for each of the languages to be analyzed. The letter "X" represents the name of the language under evaluation, and the corresponding name is substituted for it. Then, we provide the statement of the exercise to be solved. The statements have been adapted from their original version to be able to implement the tests in a more automated way. Finally, we give a description comprising information regarding the name that the function should take and the type and number of input and output parameters.

Programming Exercises: The dataset designed for our evaluation comprises 10 basic programming exercises where the objective was to choose tasks that belong to introductory programming courses. For this purpose, we review introductory programming literature [20,21,32,33] focusing on Python because it is most commonly used. For selecting the task, we wanted to cover fundamental concepts of programming, such as:

- **Data input/output:** Handling of data reading and writing in files and data output by console and input passed to the function as a string. The data reading by console has been excluded to facilitate the automation of the associated tests.
- **Mathematical algorithms:** Resolution of mathematical exercises that require the implementation of algorithms.
- **String operations:** Basic operations with strings such as concatenation, transformation, or substring search.
- **Flow control - if-else statements:** Use of conditional statements to control program flow.
- **Flow control - loops:** Use of loops to control program flow.
- **Functions:** Design of simple functions, parameter passing, and function calls.
- **Boolean logic:** Use of boolean operations for decision-making.

Table 2 summarizes the final 10 selected exercises and their main features. In addition, to the programs, we required test suites for checking the correctness. We generated the test cases manually, focusing on checking the functionality of the respective programs. Each test case is a unit test for a program comprising inputs and the expected output value. On average, 5.3 tests have been carried out, ranging between 4 and 9 tests per exercise.

Table 2. Programming exercises categorized.

Exercise ID	Exercise	Categories	#Tests
1	*Even or Odd?*	Mathematical algorithms, Data input/output, Flow control: if-else statements, Boolean logic	6
2	*Sort 3 Integers*	Mathematical algorithms, Functions, Data input/output	4
3	*Check a password*	Functions, Data input/output, String operations, Boolean logic	9
4	*Is a String a Palindrome?*	Data input/output, Flow control: if-else statements, Flow control: loops, String operations, Boolean logic	6
5	*Read, write file*	Functions, Data input/output	5
6	*Find and replace*	Flow control: if-else statements, Flow control: loops, String operations, Boolean logic	6
7	*Pig Latin*	Flow control: if-else statements, String operations, Data input/output, Boolean logic	5
8	*Title case*	Flow control: if-else statements, Flow control: loops, String operations, Functions, Data input/output, Boolean logic	4
9	*Random Shuffle*	Flow control: loops, String operations, Mathematical algorithms, Data input/output, Boolean logic	4
10	*Factorial calculation*	Flow control: if-else statements, Mathematical algorithms, Functions, Data input/output, Boolean logic	4

Figure 2 illustrates the distribution of exercises across the categories defined in the dataset. The most relevant category is data input/output, which is the only one present in all exercises. It is the first concept taught in any programming literature. It is common for most programs to receive data input from an external source, perform some form of data processing or conversion, and return the data as an output. Data input/output is followed by Boolean logic and the flow control category, and both of them are important in developing structured programs.

For more information regarding the programming tasks and their parameters, we refer to [12].

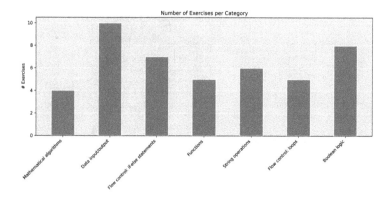

Fig. 2. Category distribution across the exercises.

Running the Experiments: For each programming task and programming language, we asked ChatGPT 3.5 for a solution, i.e., a running program, 5 times. We used the manually generated test cases for each solution to justify whether a program passed or failed. It is worth noting that we consider a solution to be passing if it passes all given test cases. Otherwise, it was classified as failing. To automate the classification process of solutions, we implemented a testing procedure for all different programming languages. The testing procedure executes the manually generated test cases and checks the outcome for correctness using the expected values. Furthermore, we used the classifications to obtain a *pass@k* metrics value for all programming languages as the final outcome of the experimental evaluation.

4   Experimental Results

We ran the experiments as described in the previous section to obtain the *pass@k* values. In Table 3 we depict the resulting metric values for each considered programming language.

The results of the metric can be divided into two distinct groups. The first group comprises Python, Java, C, and JavaScript programming languages, which achieve a high score. The probability that the first answer generated by the model is valid is approximately 90% for these languages, and it reaches 100% for higher values of k. Therefore, for these languages, it is highly probable that the first answer generated by the model is valid. It can be reasonably assumed that, when querying the model to solve a basic programming exercise, the model will provide the solution in the first five queries for these languages. Furthermore, it is also highly likely that the first solution provided by the model is valid. The

Table 3. Comparison of average *pass@k* metrics across various programming languages.

	Pass@1	*Pass@2*	*Pass@3*	*Pass@4*	*Pass@5*
Python	0.98	1.00	1.00	1.00	1.00
Java	0.92	0.97	0.99	1.00	1.00
C	0.92	1.00	1.00	1.00	1.00
JavaScript	0.86	0.95	0.99	1.00	1.00
Lisp	0.60	0.73	0.81	0.86	0.90
Squeak	0.56	0.60	0.60	0.60	0.60
SML	0.32	0.37	0.39	0.40	0.40

second group comprises the languages with the lowest scores: Lisp, Squeak, and SML. The probability of the first answer being correct is approximately 60% for Lisp and Squeak and 30% for SML. Consequently, the first answer generated by the model is generally not correct. For higher values of k, the only language that significantly increases the probability of generating good answers is Lisp, reaching 90% in the top five answers. On the other hand, Squeak does not show any improvement, remaining at a probability of 60%. This behavior indicates that if the model is not able to produce a correct solution among the initial solutions, it is not able to adapt and generate solutions with greater diversity. SML does exhibit an improvement as k increases, although this is not statistically significant. The probability that the first answer generated is valid increases from 32% to 40% for the top 5 answers. This indicates that the space of generated solutions is not particularly diverse for this language.

The comparison between these two groups, as well as the evolution of the *pass@k* value for different values of k within the same language, can be observed in the radar diagram in Fig. 3. In this graph, each programming language is represented on an axis, with the distance from the center representing the *pass@k* score. A different color represents each value of k.

The pass rate is defined as the percentage of solutions generated by the model that passes all unit tests. Figure 4 represents the heatmap with the pass rate of each exercise for each of the seven programming languages.

It can be observed that the most successfully solved exercises for each of the seven languages are Exercise 1, *Even or Odd?*, which only failed for SML, and Exercise 9, *Random Shuffle*, which experienced failures in two languages, SML and Squeak. The *Even or Odd?* exercise is a relatively simple exercise, and the modulus operator is universal in most languages, which contributes to its implementation varying slightly between languages. The success of the *Random Shuffle* exercise may be due to the fact that it relies primarily on randomization functions defined in standard libraries of most languages. Most exercises experience some errors in three languages. The exercises with the highest number of errors are exercises 7, *Pig Latin* and exercise 10, *Factorial*. Both of these exercises

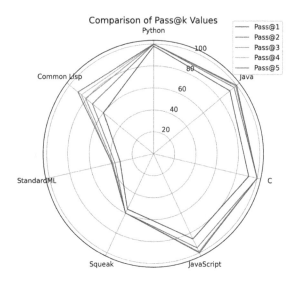

Fig. 3. *Pass@k* metric (%) by programming language.

contain errors in four programming languages. The difficulty of *Pig Latin* maybe because this exercise requires complex string manipulation for which an understanding of specific linguistic rules is necessary. Not all languages incorporate advanced string-handling functions, which can make it challenging to handle. The utilization of recursive iterations in the *Factorial* exercise can lead to inefficiencies in loop handling and stack management, as a seemingly uncomplicated operation can result in the calculation of very large numbers very quickly.

GitHub provides insight reports on the data uploaded to the platform by developers each year. Among the statistics provided, we find a ranking of the most used programming languages, with its last update in 2023 [17]. This ranking is created by counting the programming language used in a repository to which code has been pushed. This ranking shows the 50 most used programming languages globally, allowing them to be filtered by economy. Furthermore, GitHub provides a ranking with statistics on pull requests and pushes executed for each programming language annually, with the last update in 2024 [23]. In contrast, the TIOBE Programming Community index [1], also referenced on GitHub, provides a ranking of the popularity of programming languages based on the opinion of expert programmers rather than on the amount of code written for the languages. The analysis of pull requests on GitHub is of particular relevance, as it demonstrates the quantity of code added for different languages and reflects their utility and quality, as assessed by other developers.

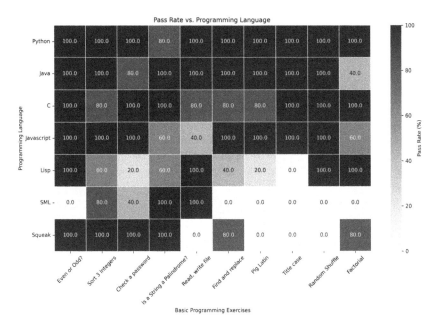

Fig. 4. Heatmap of pass rate distribution by programming language.

Table 4 presents the position of the programming languages under study in the GitHub pull request ranking, with a comparison to the TIOBE ranking. It can be observed that the four languages previously classified in the first group with the best $pass@k$ results are within the top ten positions of the rankings. This indicates that these languages are highly used in software development. Many LLMs are trained using data extracted from internet platforms, including GitHub. Consequently, the models are well suited to processing and generating code in these languages. In the case of $pass@1$, the results obtained for C are superior to those of Javascript and equal to those of Java, with C even obtaining a superior result than Java in $pass@2$ and $pass@3$. This may be attributed to the fact that C allows for greater control than Java over the logic applied to the exercise, as it is a low-level language. With regard to $pass@5$, all languages exhibit uniform performance. This suggests that the model has achieved optimal tuning with these languages, reflecting their widespread prevalence and use in software development.

The results of the second group of languages that have been analysed, show that they are notably inferior, occupying the lowest positions in the ranking. Lisp appears in the top 40, although it should be noted that Common Lisp does not appear, but rather Emacs Lisp, a different dialect that uses dynamic scoping rules instead of lexical scoping rules. Smalltalk(Squeak) is situated at the lower positions of the ranking, while SML is not included in either of the two. The low popularity of these programming languages is reflected in the $pass@k$ metrics obtained for them and, in turn, in the less effective training of the model for these languages. Lisp's *pass@k* value does improve for higher values of k, which may be a consequence of the structural similarities with the Emacs Lisp dialect. The significant disparity in popularity between Lisp and Smalltalk(Squeak) is also reflected in the divergence of their *pass@k* metrics. Smalltalk(Squeak) exhibits the second worst metric, which remains unchanged as k increases, indicating its limited usage. In contrast, SML has the worst metric, which is consistent with its absence in the popularity ranking.

The strong correlation between programming languages' popularity and functional correctness demonstrates a significant imbalance in ChatGPT's training data. Data from popular programming languages are substantially more prevalent, highlighting the importance of both the volume and diversity of training data in the development of large language models.

Table 4. Comparison of GitHub [23] and TIOBE [1] rankings for the selected programming languages.

GitHub Ranking	TIOBE Index Ranking	Programming Language
1	1	Python
2	4	Java
4	7	JavaScript
9	3	C
30	36	Emacs Lisp
47	Between 51–100	Smalltalk
Not inside the ranking	Not inside the ranking	SML

Figure 5 shows a comparison of the *pass@1* metric obtained in our dataset and in other code generation benchmark datasets. In all cases, the value of *pass@1* is obtained when making inferences to the GPT-3.5 model using Python as a programming language, as this is the dominant language in the literature.

The HumanEval [9] benchmark dataset is the most widely used in the literature and was proposed by OpenAI for the evaluation of LLMs in code-generation tasks. The tests conducted on this dataset indicate that the probability of the first generated answer being correct is 77% [27], the highest among the three benchmark datasets. MBPP [4] dataset scores slightly lower with 72% [8]. The xCodeEval [18] dataset scores significantly worse than the previous two datasets, with a value of 44% [8]. The Basic Programming Exercises dataset exhibits the highest performance for this programming language, with a 98% probability that the first solution generated by the model is valid.

HumanEval contains 164 programming challenges crafted by hand. These challenges range from mathematical exercises to algorithms and tests of the model's understanding of the language. This dataset exhibits a degree of variability in complexity, aiming to evaluate the model's understanding of the language. The MBPP dataset is composed of almost 1,000 short Python problems. These can be categorized as either simple problems that can be solved with basic knowledge or as more complex problems that require a certain degree of knowledge of the language. These exercises have been created with a balance of complexity in order to create a solid dataset for evaluating language models. xCodeEval is a multilingual dataset containing 7,500 problems classified into seven distinct tasks. Due to the large number of programming languages and tasks it defines, this dataset presents a greater challenge in defining its problems. Consequently, it is a challenging dataset for models, with performance below that of other datasets.

The exercises selected for the creation and evaluation of the dataset have been selected from introductory Python programming literature. Therefore, the code fragments generated by the model are relatively simple in comparison to the ones in the remaining datasets. The problems to be solved have less ambiguity in the code to be generated and are more straightforward tasks, having optimized the prompt introduced for this purpose. Consequently, the simplicity of the exercises and the clarity of the prompt used to generate the data to be evaluated have led to significantly superior results being obtained than those obtained from other datasets used in the evaluation of LLM code-generation tasks.

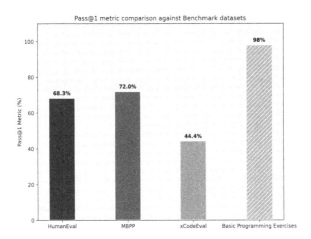

Fig. 5. Comparison of *pass@1* between Basic Programming Exercises dataset and benchmark datasets.

Threats to Validity. Like all empirical and experimental evaluations, there are a lot of threats to validity worth mentioning. These include the choice of programming tasks, the selection of only ChatGPT as LLM, the selection of used test cases, and the used prompt (which we drafted carefully). All these choices impact the outcome. However, we used ChatGPT because of its popularity. We selected the programming tasks because they can be considered basic exercises, and we developed the test cases manually, intending to check the implemented functionality. The test cases might not cover all possible faults. Hence, the outcome of the experiments might be too optimistic. In addition, we might have introduced faults when carrying out the experiments, e.g., having bugs in the testing procedure. To mitigate this influence, we carefully checked all the steps of the experiments.

5   Conclusions

In this paper, we investigated the use of ChatGPT 3.5 for programming, considering different programming languages and several programming tasks from introductory courses on programming. We selected ChatGPT 3.5 due to its free availability for experiments. As a result, we observed a strong bias in the model performance of popular and less popular programming languages. This differentiation seems to be a consequence of the abundance of publicly available content in repositories such as GitHub for each programming language. Future research might consider other versions of ChatGPT or other large language models, different and maybe more difficult programming tasks, and different programming languages.

Acknowledgments. The financial support by the Austrian Federal Ministry for Digital and Economic Affairs, the National Foundation for Research, Technology and Development, Austria, and the Christian Doppler Research Association is gratefully acknowledged.

Disclosure of Interests. The authors have no competing interests to declare relevant to this article's content.

References

1. TIOBE Index (2024). https://www.tiobe.com/tiobe-index/. Accessed 10 June 2024
2. Ahmad, W., Chakraborty, S., Ray, B., Chang, K.W.: A transformer-based approach for source code summarization. In: Jurafsky, D., Chai, J., Schluter, N., Tetreault, J. (eds.) Proceedings of the 58th Annual Meeting of the Association for Computational Linguistics, pp. 4998–5007. Association for Computational Linguistics (2020). https://doi.org/10.18653/v1/2020.acl-main.449, https://aclanthology.org/2020.acl-main.449
3. Amazon Web Services: AWS CodeWhisperer. https://aws.amazon.com/es/codewhisperer/. Accessed 04 Apr 2023
4. Austin, J., et al.: Program synthesis with large language models. arXiv:2108.07732 [cs] (2021)
5. Belgacem, A., Bradai, A., Beghdad Bey, K.: ChatGPT backend: a comprehensive analysis. In: ChatGPT Backend: A Comprehensive Analysis, pp. 1–6 (2023). https://doi.org/10.1109/ISNCC58260.2023.10323792
6. Bender, E.M., Gebru, T., McMillan-Major, A., Shmitchell, S.: On the dangers of stochastic parrots: can language models be too big? In: Proceedings of the 2021 ACM Conference on Fairness, Accountability, and Transparency, FAccT 2021, pp. 610–623. Association for Computing Machinery, New York (2021). https://doi.org/10.1145/3442188.3445922

7. Cassano, F., et al.: MultiPL-E: a scalable and extensible approach to benchmarking neural code generation (2022). https://doi.org/10.48550/ARXIV.2208.08227, https://arxiv.org/abs/2208.08227
8. Chen, J., et al.: Divide-and-conquer meets consensus: unleashing the power of functions in code generation (2024). https://doi.org/10.48550/ARXIV.2405.20092, https://arxiv.org/abs/2405.20092. Version Number: 1
9. Chen, M., et al.: Evaluating large language models trained on code (2021). https://doi.org/10.48550/ARXIV.2107.03374, https://arxiv.org/abs/2107.03374
10. Clark, L., et al.: What makes a good conversation?: challenges in designing truly conversational agents. In: Proceedings of the 2019 CHI Conference on Human Factors in Computing Systems, pp. 1–12. ACM, Glasgow (2019). https://doi.org/10.1145/3290605.3300705, https://dl.acm.org/doi/10.1145/3290605.3300705
11. Claude AI: Claude AI. https://claude.ai/login. Accessed 04 Apr 2023
12. de Diego, Á.G.: Design and analysis of ChatGPT's response quality across programming languages. Master's thesis, Graz University of Technology, Universidad Politecnica de Madrid Escuela Tecnica Superior de Ingenieros de Telecomunicacion (2024)
13. Dong, Y., Ding, J., Jiang, X., Li, G., Li, Z., Jin, Z.: CodeScore: evaluating code generation by learning code execution (2023). https://doi.org/10.48550/ARXIV.2301.09043, https://arxiv.org/abs/2301.09043
14. Feng, Z., et al.: CodeBERT: a pre-trained model for programming and natural languages. In: Cohn, T., He, Y., Liu, Y. (eds.) Findings of the Association for Computational Linguistics: EMNLP 2020, pp. 1536–1547. Association for Computational Linguistics (2020). https://doi.org/10.18653/v1/2020.findings-emnlp.139, https://aclanthology.org/2020.findings-emnlp.139
15. GitHub: GitHub Copilot: Your AI Pair Programmer (2024). https://github.com/features/copilot. Accessed 04 Apr 2024
16. Google: Gemini. https://gemini.google.com/. Accessed 04 Apr 2024
17. Innovation Graph: Global metrics on programming languages (2023). https://innovationgraph.github.com/global-metrics/programming-languages
18. Khan, M.A.M., Bari, M.S., Do, X.L., Wang, W., Parvez, M.R., Joty, S.: xCodeEval: a large scale multilingual multitask benchmark for code understanding, generation, translation and retrieval (2023). https://doi.org/10.48550/ARXIV.2303.03004, https://arxiv.org/abs/2303.03004. Version Number: 4
19. Kulal, S., et al.: SPoC: search-based pseudocode to code (2019). https://doi.org/10.48550/ARXIV.1906.04908, https://arxiv.org/abs/1906.04908. Version Number: 1
20. Lambert, K.A., Osborne, M.: Fundamentals of Python: From First Programs Through Data Structures, International edn. Course Technology, Cengage Learning, Boston (2010)
21. Lerner, R.: Python Workout: 50 Ten-Minute Exercises. Manning Publications Co., Shelter Island (2020). oCLC: on1121083840
22. Li, Y., et al.: Competition-level code generation with AlphaCode. Science **378**(6624), 1092–1097 (2022). https://doi.org/10.1126/science.abq1158, arXiv:2203.07814 [cs]
23. Madnight: GitHub Pull Requests Statistics 2024 (2024). https://madnight.github.io/githut/#/pull_requests/2024/1. Accessed 10 June 2024
24. Manna, Z., Waldinger, R.J.: Toward automatic program synthesis. Commun. ACM **14**(3), 151–165 (1971). https://doi.org/10.1145/362566.362568
25. Microsoft: Microsoft Copilot. https://copilot.microsoft.com/. Accessed 04 Apr 2023

26. Microsoft: CodeXGLUE: A Machine Learning Benchmark Dataset for Code Under-standing and Generation (2023). https://github.com/microsoft/CodeXGLUE/tree/main. Accessed 04 Apr 2023

27. Murdza, J.: Humaneval results (2023). https://github.com/jamesmurdza/humaneval-results/tree/main

28. Ouyang, L., et al.: Training language models to follow instructions with human feedback (2022). https://doi.org/10.48550/ARXIV.2203.02155, https://arxiv.org/abs/2203.02155. arXiv Version Number: 1

29. Papineni, K., Roukos, S., Ward, T., Zhu, W.J.: BLEU: a method for automatic evaluation of machine translation. In: Proceedings of the 40th Annual Meeting on Association for Computational Linguistics - ACL 2002, p. 311. Association for Computational Linguistics, Philadelphia (2001). https://doi.org/10.3115/1073083.1073135, http://portal.acm.org/citation.cfm?doid=1073083.1073135

30. Parvez, M.R., Ahmad, W.U., Chakraborty, S., Ray, B., Chang, K.W.: Retrieval augmented code generation and summarization (2021). https://doi.org/10.48550/ARXIV.2108.11601, https://arxiv.org/abs/2108.11601

31. Ren, S., et al.: CodeBLEU: a method for automatic evaluation of code synthesis (2020). https://doi.org/10.48550/ARXIV.2009.10297, https://arxiv.org/abs/2009.10297

32. Stephenson, B.: The Python Workbook: A Brief Introduction with Exercises and Solutions, 1st edn., 2014 edn. Springer, Cham (2014). https://doi.org/10.1007/978-3-319-14240-1

33. Sweigart, A.: python programming exercises, gently explained, 2nd print-ing edn. (2022). https://www.amazon.com/Python-Programming-Exercises-Gently-Explained-ebook/dp/B0BGYJ7G6T. Licensed under Creative Commons Attribution-NonCommercial-ShareAlike 4.0 International (CC BY-NC-SA 4.0)

34. Tabnine: Tabnine: Your AI Coding Assistant. https://www.tabnine.com/ai-coding-assistant. Accessed 04 Apr 2023

35. Teubner, T., Flath, C.M., Weinhardt, C., Van Der Aalst, W., Hinz, O.: Welcome to the era of ChatGPT et al.: the prospects of large language models. Bus. Inf. Syst. Eng. **65**(2), 95–101 (2023). https://doi.org/10.1007/s12599-023-00795-x

36. Vaswani, A., et al.: Attention is all you need (2017). https://doi.org/10.48550/ARXIV.1706.03762, https://arxiv.org/abs/1706.03762. arXiv Version Number: 7

37. White, J., et al.: A prompt pattern catalog to enhance prompt engineer-ing with ChatGPT (2023). https://doi.org/10.48550/ARXIV.2302.11382, https://arxiv.org/abs/2302.11382

38. White, J., Hays, S., Fu, Q., Spencer-Smith, J., Schmidt, D.C.: ChatGPT prompt patterns for improving code quality, refactoring, requirements elicitation, and soft-ware design (2023). https://doi.org/10.48550/ARXIV.2303.07839, https://arxiv.org/abs/2303.07839

39. Yadav, A., Singh, M.: PythonSaga: redefining the benchmark to evaluate code generating LLM. arXiv:2401.03855 [cs] (2024)

40. Yan, W., Tian, Y., Li, Y., Chen, Q., Wang, W.: CodeTransOcean: a comprehen-sive multilingual benchmark for code translation (2023). https://doi.org/10.48550/ARXIV.2310.04951, https://arxiv.org/abs/2310.04951

41. Zhu, M., Jain, A., Suresh, K., Ravindran, R., Tipirneni, S., Reddy, C.K.: XLCoST: a benchmark dataset for cross-lingual code intelligence (2022). https://doi.org/10.48550/ARXIV.2206.08474, https://arxiv.org/abs/2206.08474

Reevaluating the Small-Scope Testing Hypothesis of Answer Set Programs

Liliana Marie Prikler[(✉)] and Franz Wotawa

Institute of Software Technology, Graz University of Technology, 8010 Graz, Austria
`liliana.prikler@ist.tugraz.at`

Abstract. As we increasingly rely on artificial intelligence systems, we must ensure that those systems are reliable and need to know how much we can rely on them. In software quality assurance, testing is a useful method to highlight and fix issues during development to avoid unexpected behavior after the system has been deployed. Artificial intelligence engineers are increasingly becoming aware of quality assurance as a requirement. Previous results in the area of answer set programming suggest that a high proportion of errors can be found when testing a program against a small scope, i.e. by inputs from a small domain. However, these results are based on assumptions that may be impractical for testing. To find out whether small scopes remain sufficient in practice, we evaluate several benchmarks against actual test oracles. Our findings suggest that small scopes can indeed find a high proportion of errors, but results depend on the observed benchmark and appropriate test oracles are required to achieve reliable scores.

Keywords: Answer set programming · Mutation testing · Small-scope hypothesis

1 Introduction

Although software testing has a long history, the literature on testing knowledge-based systems, in general, and answer set programs, in particular, is quite shallow. Coverage criteria were first introduced in [11], the success of random and structure-based testing strategies, when measured against mutation scores investigated a year later [12].

The main body of our research deals with the small-scope testing hypothesis [13], which roughly states that an answer set program can be sufficiently tested by only considering a small subset of "all possible inputs" (cf. [10]). While this hypothesis does not hold in general, empirical evidence suggests that it does hold for a large class of practical problems, see [13]. However, these previous results rely on invisible choices and a test oracle that is trivially true for the program under test. To overcome these issues and investigate the small-scope hypothesis further, we partially replicate the study and add new examples.

© IFIP International Federation for Information Processing 2025
Published by Springer Nature Switzerland AG 2025
H. D. Menéndez et al. (Eds.): ICTSS 2024, LNCS 15383, pp. 79–92, 2025.
https://doi.org/10.1007/978-3-031-80889-0_6

Other works consider unit tests for answer set programming [2,5], or random testing [8], while some choose to focus on particular applications of answer set programming, such as diagnosis [19]. However, it appears that the small-scope testing hypothesis is not really invoked in any of them.

In mutation testing [4], a test suite for a given program is scored on how well it distinguishes the "correct" program from slightly altered ones that have particular flaws introduced (the mutants). We say that a mutant is killed (or detected) if there is a test such that the original program passes that test while the mutant fails.

The rest of this paper is laid out as follows. In Sect. 2, we discuss the setup of our experiments, in particular guidelines for input generation, mutant generation, test suite layout and mutation analysis workflow. Our results are shown in Sect. 3 with a paragraph per benchmark detailing choices made for that benchmark and interpreting their outcome, followed by a slightly longer discussion of the overall results in Sect. 4. We address potential threats to their validity in Sect. 5, and finally conclude the paper in Sect. 6.

2   Experimental Setup

We use benchmarks from the Fifth ASP competition [3] and process them as follows:

1. We modify the included test scripts to make use of the Clingo [7] solver, and translate the problem encodings to Abstract Gringo [6] as needed.
2. We label the set of 20 selected instances, included already with the benchmark, as "selected".
3. We generate mutants of the problem encoding.
4. We write an input generator for the problem following the setup of [13].
5. We run the input generator to produce some test inputs. We label this set of instances as "generated".
6. We evaluate the original encoding and all our mutants on the "selected" and "generated" instances.
7. We compare the runs of the mutants against the original encoding.
8. We aggregate the results from the above and compare them with each other, as well as some target scores.

We use `clingabomino`[1] to generate mutants of the problem encodings. Table 1 shows the mutation operators implemented in `clingabomino`. Most of them result in super-sets of the mutation operators from [13], but some do not: particularly, the `delete-literals` operation does not delete the head of a rule if it is a single literal.[2] In addition, `clingabomino` allows us to study programs (and mutants) that use language features specific to Abstract Gringo, such as double negations (cf. [6]).

---

[1] https://git.ist.tugraz.at/clingabomino/clingabomino.
[2] Clingo represents the empty head using an invisible NOGOOD literal.

For our test suite, we include some benchmarks that were already used in [13], and others that were not. For space reasons, we restrict ourselves to a particular set of benchmarks, that highlight our main findings.

We use answer set programming to generate instances, but unlike [13], we consider both satisfiable and unsatisfiable instances—thus, out of necessity, our instance generators are encoding-agnostic. We run each instance generator with parameters that have been chosen to yield between 100 and 1000 instances per benchmark. Intuitively, more tests provide more chances at detecting a mutant, but also increase the amount of computation needed. We thus understand "small scope" to also mean "low in number".

For a given list of instances, we evaluate all mutants on all instances, using parallel execution [17] and timeouts to limit our computing to a "reasonable" duration. On a MacPro6.1 running a 12-Core Intel Xeon E5 processor at 2.7 GHz, with 64 GB of RAM, a 30 MB shared L3 cache and a 256 KB L2 cache per processor, it takes a few hours to a day to complete one benchmark.[3]

Each check gives a single line as response—shown in Table 2—which we match up according to the rules in Table 3 to reveal the liveliness of a mutant. In short, the result is FAIL if the script is invoked wrongly or there is a reason to believe that the input program (or the test script) is broken, KILLED if the mutant can reasonably be shown to be wrong, DONTKNOW if there are unclear results that could possibly be determined either way with some stricter rules, and ALIVE otherwise.

After performing this comparison between the encoding and every mutant, we compute the mutation score s as

$$s = \frac{\text{KILLED}}{\text{ALL}} \tag{1}$$

and the failure rate f as

$$f = \frac{\text{FAIL}}{\text{ALL}}. \tag{2}$$

While the mutation score is a well-established metric in literature, we use the failure rate to indicate how broken our process (read: more often than not the underlying test script) is. The sum $s + f$ gives an upper limit for the mutation score, assuming that all FAILing results can be killed by handling whichever error they trigger more carefully.

To see whether the results from [13] can be backed up, we use two strategies:

- If [13] ran the same benchmark, we check to see whether our results are within or near expectations, where our expectations are given by a scope that provides a similar number of inputs.

---

[3] These execution times need to be taken with a spoonful of salt and can not be compared to [13], as we generate more mutants and run the tests on all instances while only limiting the time allowed to generate the answer sets, but not the time for validating them in a test script.

Table 1. Mutation operators for ASP supported by `clingabomino`. Most operators have similar semantics to the ones in [13]; note, however, the compression into fewer operators, and the change in semantics for delete-literals.

Operation	Original Rules	Examples Mutant
delete-rules	`p(X) :- q(X). q(X) :- r(X).`	`p(X) :- q(X).`
	`good(x-men). :- good(X),evil(X).`	`good(x-men).`
	`good(x-men). :- good(X),evil(X).`	`:- good(X), evil(X).`
delete-literals	`norm(X) :- p(X), not ab(X).`	`norm(X) :- p(X).`
	`{ left(C); right(C) } :- choice(C).`	`{ left(C) } :- choice(C).`
twiddle-default-negations	`p :- q(X,Y), t(Y).`	`p :- q(X,Y), not t(Y).`
	`p :- q(X,Y), not r(X).`	`p :- q(X,Y), r(X).`
twiddle-double-negations	`p :- q(X,Y), not t(Y).`	`p :- q(X,Y), not not t(Y).`
	`p :- q(X,Y), not not r(X).`	`p :- q(X,Y), not r(X).`
positive-double-negations	`p :- q(X,Y), t(Y).`	`p :- q(X,Y), not not t(Y).`
	`p :- q(X,Y), not not t(Y).`	`p :- q(X,Y), t(Y).`
twiddle-strong-negations	`person(X) :- mutant(X).`	`person(X) :- -mutant(X).`
	`norm(X) :- -mutant(X).`	`norm(X) :- mutant(X).`
rename-predicates	`r(X,Y):- e(X,Y). :- e(a,b).`	`r(X,Y):- e(X,Y). :- r(a,b).`
wronguarde	`:- succ(X,Y), Y > X.`	`:- succ(X,Y), Y >= X.`
advanced-arithmetics	`next(X,Y) :- r(X;Y),Y=X+1.`	`next(X,Y) :- r(X;Y),Y=X*1.`
twiddle-bounds	`1 {guess(X)} N :- max(N).`	`1 {guess(X)} (N-1) :- max(N).`
twiddle-weights	`ok :- 2 #sum {V: val(P,V)} 8.`	`ok :- 2 #sum {V+1: val(P,V)} 8.`
off-by-one	`next(N, N+1) :- number(N).`	`next(N, N+2) :- number(N).`
transpose-arguments	`less(X,Y) :- n(X,Y),X < Y.`	`less(Y,X) :- n(X,Y),X < Y.`
constant-variables	`p(a;b). fail :- p(X).`	`p(a;b). fail :- p(a).`
replace-variables	`first(X) :- rel(X,Y).`	`first(Y) :- rel(X,Y).`
variable-constants	`ok :- exit(1,Y),grid(X,Y).`	`ok :- exit(X,Y), grid(X,Y).`
replace-constants	`first(alpha). last(omega).`	`first(omega). last(omega).`

Table 2. Checker outputs and their meaning. A TIMEOUT occurs before the checker is called if a given program-instance pair exceeded the arbitrarily chosen time limit of 10 s.

Output	Meaning
OK	The program passed the check
FAIL	The program failed the check
DONTKNOW	The check is inconclusive (mostly UNSATISFIABLE results)
ERROR	The check itself failed
TIMEOUT	We did not run the check, because no answer set was computed in time

– If they did not, we consider an arbitrarily chosen **high** score of >75% as an indicator of successful testing and a *baseline* score of >60% as an indicator of moderate success. In our tables, we highlight where the high and baseline scores are met using a bold and italic fonts respectively. In both cases, we consider only the mutation score s, rather than the upper limit $s + f$.

Table 3. Comparison outputs and their meaning, in order of precedence. Note the many ways a comparison may FAIL.

Output	Meaning
FAIL	mismatching number of tests, or the reference program FAILed a test, or reference DONTKNOW vs mutant OK, or any reported ERROR
KILLED	the mutant FAILed a test, or reference OK vs mutant DONTKNOW
DONTKNOW	No OK-pair between the programs, or at least one OK with different optimum
ALIVE	At least one OK-pair between the programs

As a separate indicator, we also compare the results of the generated small scopes against the selected instances of the competition, which were used to evaluate both solvers and encodings in the competition.

In order to study the relationship between mutant operators and survivability, we compute the mutation score for each operator separately, as well as a total score for all of them together. This technically gives us (at least) two mutation scores for all mutants: one, in which each operator is given weight proportional to the number of mutants it produced, and one, in which each operator is given uniform weight. In this paper, we compute s and f for "all" mutants according to Eqs. (1) and (2), which is equivalent to giving each operator a proportional weight.

3   Results

In this section, we present our results with respect to the various benchmarks analyzed. We will discuss each benchmark before attempting to generalize our findings.

Connected Maximum-Density Still Life. We start out with a somewhat peculiar benchmark, which has only input fact to generate. In this benchmark, the task for the problem encoding is to find a configuration of Conway's Game of Life, which, when placed in a square board of size d, remains unchanged as the game continues (i.e., a fixed-point). We evaluate the test suite on "small" board sizes ranging from 2 to 15, resulting in Table 4. As we can see, the number of caught mutants gradually increases but eventually fluctuates and plateaus.

If instead of calculating the mutation score per board size we mark a mutant as killed if it is killed at any board size, we arrive at a mutation score of 42.97% (rounded up). This is still too small for hitting baseline performance. We further discover that some board sizes are redundant: aggregating only the sizes 2, 3, 4, 5, 6, 11, and 14 yields the same overall mutation score.

Table 4. Mutation scores for the Connected Maximum-Density Still Life benchmark. Each benchmark only consists of a single fact `size(%d)`. with `%d` being the column headers. Sizes 7–10 have been omitted for the sake of space. The failure rate f is 0 for all sizes.

mutants	2	3	4	5	6	...	11	12	13	14	15
all	0.188	0.248	0.276	0.399	0.399	...	0.389	0.384	0.393	0.392	0.390
delete-rules	0.080	0.200	0.280	0.360	0.360	...	0.320	0.360	0.360	0.360	0.360
delete-literals	0.341	0.366	0.366	0.512	0.512	...	0.463	0.512	0.488	0.488	0.488
twiddle-default-negations	0.365	0.413	0.460	0.571	0.556	...	0.556	0.540	0.556	0.556	0.556
twiddle-double-negations	0.250	0.375	0.375	0.500	0.375	...	0.500	0.500	0.500	0.500	0.500
positive-double-negations	0.418	0.436	0.436	0.455	0.455	...	0.455	0.455	0.455	0.455	0.455
twiddle-strong-negations	0.087	0.188	0.232	0.290	0.290	...	0.275	0.275	0.290	0.290	0.290
rename-predicates	0.131	0.211	0.242	0.376	0.369	...	0.346	0.346	0.342	0.356	0.349
wronguarde	0.429	0.429	0.543	0.571	*0.600*	...	*0.600*	*0.600*	*0.600*	*0.600*	*0.600*
advanced-arithmetics	0.000	0.015	0.076	0.091	0.106	...	0.091	0.121	0.091	0.121	0.091
twiddle-bounds	0.214	0.143	0.214	0.357	0.429	...	0.429	0.429	0.429	0.429	0.429
twiddle-weights	0.000	0.000	0.000	0.000	0.000	...	0.000	0.000	0.000	0.000	0.000
off-by-one	0.065	0.152	0.161	0.298	0.280	...	0.276	0.280	0.292	0.264	0.267
transpose-arguments	0.000	0.027	0.095	0.324	0.338	...	0.378	0.270	0.351	0.351	0.351
constant-variables	0.159	0.212	0.246	0.373	0.373	...	0.361	0.347	0.367	0.365	0.365
replace-variables	0.305	0.368	0.373	0.524	0.537	...	0.521	0.521	0.524	0.526	0.524
variable-constants	0.568	*0.614*	*0.659*	*0.659*	*0.659*	...	*0.659*	*0.659*	*0.659*	*0.659*	*0.659*
replace-constants	0.278	0.333	0.389	0.481	0.500	...	0.500	0.500	0.500	0.500	0.500

Graph Coloring. Onto our first benchmark with more than a single input fact, we encounter a typical problem of graphs, which is coloring them with a number of colors. Our input generator generates any graph with ≤ 4 vertices and ≤ 3 colors. We don't exclude graphs that cannot be colored with that many colors but use some isomorphism-breaking heuristics in the input generator. A limited number of self-links (1) are also permitted in the input. In total, there are 308 generated instances.

We evaluate the test suite on the instances thus generated, as well as the selected instances of the ASP competition, with results appearing in the "selected" and "generated" columns of Table 5 respectively. Upon inspecting these results, we noticed that there was some overlap in the killed mutants, but also that both approaches caught different mutants. We were able to attribute this difference to the use of numbers (generated instances) or symbols (selected instances) for the colors. We thus instructed the generator to produce numbered *shades* of an otherwise unspecified color instead, resulting in the "generated'" column.

Comparison to prior findings [13] would leave us to expect some value between 0.43% and 0.95% of killed mutants. Indeed, all our mutant scores fall into this

Table 5. Results for the Graph Coloring benchmark. The "generated'" instances are nearly identical to the "generated" ones. Only facts relating to color names have been changed.

mutants	generated		generated'		selected		target [13]
	s	*f*	*s*	*f*	*s*	*f*	
all	0.552	0.126	0.577	0.119	0.549	0.000	**0.95**
delete-rules	0.455	0.182	0.455	0.182	0.455	0.000	
delete-literals	*0.667*	0.067	*0.667*	0.067	*0.600*	0.000	
twiddle-default-negations	*0.692*	0.077	*0.692*	0.077	*0.654*	0.000	
twiddle-double-negations	**0.750**	0.000	**0.750**	0.000	**0.750**	0.000	
positive-double-negations	*0.682*	0.000	*0.682*	0.000	*0.682*	0.000	
twiddle-strong-negations	0.452	0.161	0.452	0.161	0.452	0.000	
rename-predicates	0.509	0.182	0.509	0.170	0.509	0.000	
wronguarde	*0.720*	0.040	*0.720*	0.040	0.520	0.000	
advanced-arithmetics	0.000	0.000	0.000	0.000	0.000	0.000	
twiddle-bounds	*0.600*	0.100	*0.600*	0.100	0.300	0.000	
off-by-one	0.526	0.164	0.509	0.103	0.457	0.000	
transpose-arguments	0.273	0.136	0.500	0.136	0.500	0.000	
constant-variables	0.480	0.120	0.540	0.180	0.560	0.000	
replace-variables	*0.643*	0.086	*0.707*	0.100	*0.693*	0.000	
variable-constants	**0.833**	0.000	**1.000**	0.000	**0.833**	0.000	

range, but at the same time, they fall short of the baseline score unless counting failed mutants as killed. Still, the mutation score is slightly higher for the generated instances. In both cases, weak support for the small-scope hypothesis was shown.

Graceful Graphs. Since we are already dealing with graph problems, we included another benchmark from the competition, which does not appear in [13]. First described as β-valuations [16], a graph is considered *graceful*, if there exists a vertex labelling consisting of the numbers 1 to n, where n is the number of vertices, such that edge labels—computed by the difference between the vertex labels—are distinct. For this benchmark, we generate 768 instances of graphs with up to 5 vertices. The results can be seen in Table 6. Again, the mutation score is slightly higher for the generated instances, but this time both selected and generated instances meet the high score on most mutation operators.

Crossing Minimization. A classical graph problem in hierarchical drawings is the minimization of crossings in a layered graph. We generate instances by sorting 5 vertices into 3 layers, producing 240 instances. This benchmark shows an interesting pattern in its results (see Table 7), as the sum of killed and failing mutants stays the same across instance sets, but the generated instances skew more towards failure.

Table 6. Results for the Graceful Graphs benchmark.

mutants	generated		selected	
	s	*f*	*s*	*f*
all	**0.935**	0.000	**0.895**	0.000
delete-rules	**1.000**	0.000	**1.000**	0.000
delete-literals	**0.944**	0.000	**0.833**	0.000
twiddle-default-negations	**1.000**	0.000	**0.946**	0.000
positive-double-negations	*0.676*	0.000	*0.649*	0.000
twiddle-strong-negations	**1.000**	0.000	**1.000**	0.000
rename-predicates	**0.939**	0.000	**0.909**	0.000
wronguarde	**0.867**	0.000	**0.800**	0.000
advanced-arithmetics	**0.813**	0.000	*0.656*	0.000
twiddle-bounds	**0.917**	0.000	**0.750**	0.000
twiddle-weights	0.333	0.000	0.333	0.000
transpose-arguments	**0.925**	0.000	**0.925**	0.000
constant-variables	**0.973**	0.000	**0.953**	0.000
replace-variables	**0.974**	0.000	**0.922**	0.000
variable-constants	**0.917**	0.000	**0.917**	0.000
replace-constants	**0.750**	0.000	0.500	0.000

Hanoi Towers. Returning to a benchmark with a target value, we consider the task of moving disks on a Hanoi tower arrangement. With three disks and a one-time unit, we get 380 instances—slightly fewer than reported for the scope "7". We could thus be led into assuming a score close to 77% being met, but as can be seen in Table 8, this is not the case. In fact, the generated instances fail to meet baseline performance by a small margin and are outperformed by the selected instances.

Knight Tour (with Holes). Given an $n \times n$ chess board, a knight tour is a sequence of moves that can be performed by a knight, which starts in any square, travels exactly once to each square on the board, and finally returns to the origin. It is thus an interesting instance of the Hamiltonian Cycle problem. By adding holes that the knight must not touch[4], we avoid situations akin to the Connected Maximum-Density Still Life benchmark, where only one input fact is given.

This benchmark has a few surprises for us. With a board of $n = 4$ and $1 \leq \#holes \leq 3$, we generate 696 inputs—far fewer than report for any scope in [13]. However, not only does it beat the selected instances by a landslide, it also meets our high mutation score requirement. The key to the parameterization of our instance generator appears to be that both satisfiable and unsatisfiable

---

[4] You may imagine the floor to be lava.

Table 7. Results for the Maximum Clique benchmark. Note how $s + f$ is the same across the two instance sets, but the generated instances are likelier to trigger a failure.

mutants	generated		selected	
	s	f	s	f
all	0.324	0.414	0.510	0.228
delete-rules	0.333	0.667	*0.667*	0.333
delete-literals	0.429	0.286	0.429	0.286
twiddle-default-negations	0.500	0.500	**0.800**	0.200
twiddle-double-negations	0.500	0.500	**1.000**	0.000
positive-double-negations	0.500	0.167	0.500	0.167
twiddle-strong-negations	0.300	0.500	0.500	0.300
rename-predicates	0.389	0.444	0.500	0.333
wronguarde	0.000	0.600	0.000	0.600
twiddle-bounds	0.000	1.000	0.500	0.500
off-by-one	0.206	0.412	0.412	0.206
transpose-arguments	0.000	0.000	0.000	0.000
constant-variables	0.292	0.375	0.458	0.208
replace-variables	0.450	0.350	*0.700*	0.100

instances need to be generated, whereas the selected instances struggle to deal with the restrictive timeouts.

Permutation Pattern Matching. The permutation pattern matching benchmark searches for match between permutations of the sequences $1, \ldots, T$ and $1, \ldots, P$, with $T > P$. For $T \leq 4$ and $P \in \{2, 3\}$, we find 204 generated instances. As shown in Table 10, both instance sets catch a very high number of mutants, with the generated instances yielding a slightly higher score.

4   Discussion

As we can see from various benchmarks, small scopes do appear to be able to highlight some or even many potential mistakes—in line with the small-scope testing hypothesis [13]. However, the extent to which they do so varies greatly between benchmarks:

- *Graph colouring*, *Graceful graphs* and *Permutation pattern matching* show quite similar results between generated and selected inputs. While *Graph colouring* misses baseline performance due to failures (and falls way short of the target), the other two meet the high mutation score.
- *Maximum clique* and *Hanoi towers* see worse mutation scores in the generated inputs w.r.t. the selected inputs. A baseline or even a high score could be met if failures were addressed. Still, the *Hanoi towers* benchmark in particular would not meet the target score even then.

Table 8. Results for the Hanoi Towers benchmark. Note how the generated instances fall short the 60% baseline, whereas the selected instances from the competition meet it. Also note the higher $f$ailure rate among the selected instances.

mutants	generated		selected		target [13]
	s	f	s	f	
all	0.599	0.086	*0.668*	0.132	**0.77**
delete-rules	0.400	0.100	0.350	0.350	
delete-literals	**0.848**	0.000	**0.848**	0.000	
twiddle-default-negations	**0.754**	0.049	*0.738*	0.148	
twiddle-double-negations	**1.000**	0.000	**1.000**	0.000	
positive-double-negations	0.464	0.000	0.464	0.000	
twiddle-strong-negations	0.518	0.089	0.500	0.268	
rename-predicates	0.579	0.079	*0.620*	0.153	
wronguarde	*0.646*	0.046	*0.662*	0.077	
advanced-arithmetics	*0.708*	0.000	**0.917**	0.000	
twiddle-bounds	*0.615*	0.038	*0.615*	0.038	
off-by-one	0.526	0.162	*0.620*	0.132	
transpose-arguments	*0.625*	0.125	*0.729*	0.104	
constant-variables	0.570	0.090	*0.713*	0.150	
replace-variables	*0.633*	0.086	*0.710*	0.133	
variable-constants	**0.810**	0.000	*0.714*	0.190	
replace-constants	*0.700*	0.000	0.500	0.100	

- The *Knight Tour* benchmark sees a vastly higher mutation score from the small scope. It is the only one that also meets the target score (Table 9).

   While numbers vary between the individual benchmarks, we find that delete-literals and twiddle-default-negations yield the mutants that are killed most often, whereas others have more varied effects. In some benchmarks, certain operators appear to have no influence, such as advanced-arithmetics in graph colouring or transpose-arguments in the maximum-clique benchmarks. There also appears to be some correlation between generated and selected instances: oftentimes, they hit the same maximum, and even if they don't, mutation scores tend to obey a similar ordering w.r.t. the most killed mutants.

   It may come as a surprise, that our values differ so much from [13]—in particular, that for two benchmarks they were very far apart. We believe, that this difference is best explained by our setup, i.e. the fact that we do use test scripts to find flaws that can be detected in the program as-is. Closely related is the actual choice of the small scope, as highlighted in *Graph colouring*: simply choosing values within some defined limit of parameters may ignore structural properties of the program.

Table 9. Results for the Knight Tour benchmark. Note the high mutation score for the generated inputs.

mutants	generated		selected		target [13]
	s	f	s	f	
all	**0.836**	0.000	0.231	0.000	**0.78**
delete-rules	**0.923**	0.000	0.192	0.000	
delete-literals	**0.966**	0.000	*0.655*	0.000	
twiddle-default-negations	**1.000**	0.000	0.340	0.000	
twiddle-double-negations	**1.000**	0.000	0.333	0.000	
positive-double-negations	*0.681*	0.000	0.319	0.000	
twiddle-strong-negations	**0.938**	0.000	0.250	0.000	
rename-predicates	**0.842**	0.000	0.172	0.000	
wronguarde	*0.743*	0.000	0.086	0.000	
advanced-arithmetics	**0.977**	0.000	0.023	0.000	
twiddle-bounds	**1.000**	0.000	0.286	0.000	
off-by-one	**0.829**	0.000	0.136	0.000	
transpose-arguments	**0.788**	0.000	0.047	0.000	
constant-variables	**0.827**	0.000	0.189	0.000	
replace-variables	**0.802**	0.000	0.337	0.000	
variable-constants	**1.000**	0.000	**0.833**	0.000	
replace-constants	**1.000**	0.000	*0.600*	0.000	

In summary, we see a great variance between the scores derived from particular mutation operators. This variance is in line with state-of-the-art research in mutation testing suggesting that the mutation score depends strongly on the underlying tooling and its implementation of mutation operators [1]. Thus, selective mutation [14], at least with respect to selected operators, is likely to suffer as an approach unless care is taken to ensure that the given operator has no valid semantics anyway. Other techniques for improving mutation testing (cf. [18]) would still need to be applied—or adapted—to answer set programming.

5 Threats to Validity

In this section, we discuss potential flaws that could impact our findings.
Threats to internal validity We only perform our analysis on a subset of the benchmarks found in the 2014 ASP competition. Our analysis is limited twofold

1. to benchmarks for which we found a suitable input generator,
2. to a subset of the above, which would fit within the available space.

There is a risk that our findings are biased toward peculiarities within this subset.

Table 10. Results for the Permutation Pattern Matching benchmark

mutants	generated		selected	
	s	f	s	f
all	**0.945**	0.000	**0.931**	0.000
delete-rules	**1.000**	0.000	**1.000**	0.000
delete-literals	**0.867**	0.000	**0.867**	0.000
twiddle-default-negations	**1.000**	0.000	**1.000**	0.000
positive-double-negations	*0.632*	0.000	*0.632*	0.000
twiddle-strong-negations	**1.000**	0.000	**1.000**	0.000
rename-predicates	**0.944**	0.000	**0.889**	0.000
wronguarde	**0.886**	0.000	**0.857**	0.000
advanced-arithmetics	**1.000**	0.000	**0.875**	0.000
twiddle-bounds	**0.929**	0.000	**0.786**	0.000
transpose-arguments	**1.000**	0.000	**1.000**	0.000
constant-variables	**1.000**	0.000	**0.971**	0.000
replace-variables	**0.986**	0.000	**0.993**	0.000
variable-constants	**0.800**	0.000	**0.800**	0.000

The use of timeouts and parallel execution also carries a risk of hurting reproducibility—in particular, timeouts might lead to a lower reported mutant score if a mutant times out rather than being killed. Mutants with significantly worse performance characteristics are unintuitively labelled as DONTKNOW in our scheme.

There is also a risk, that subsumed mutants inflate our mutation scores [15]. However, our mutation model is similar enough to that of [13], so mutation operators do not simulate each other—while this is not strong enough to rule out subsumption, it does weaken the effect to an extent.

Threats to External Validity. In our work, we only consider a subset of answer set programs for which both a test oracle and an instance generator are known. This set of requirements is similar to other known testing systems, like Harvey [8] or QuickCheck[5] [9], which we haven't evaluated. It may well be that either strategy is better suited to testing answer set programs than exhaustive testing on small scopes.

We notably also do not produce any claim as to how well the method presented in [13] would be at producing output that can be verified to fail under a known oracle.

---

[5] QuickCheck would need to be adapted to answer set programming and also require a "shrinker", as, unlike Harvey, it starts with large instances and then shrinks them if a bug is found.

6 Conclusion

We have reevaluated the small-scope testing hypothesis on the answer set problems [13] with data obtained from running "real-world" test scripts on all mutations of given benchmarks. We find that testing on small scopes may beat other forms of test selection, but is not necessarily applicable to all benchmarks and also may fail to achieve chosen metrics based on the mutation score. Future work could expand our findings or use them to guide the development of practical mutation testing tools for answer set programming.

Acknowledgments. This paper is part of the AI4CSM project that has received funding within the ECSEL JU in collaboration with the European Union's H2020 Framework Programme (H2020/2014-2020) and National Authorities, under grant agreement No. 101007326. The work was partially funded by the Austrian Federal Ministry of Climate Action, Environment, Energy, Mobility, Innovation and Technology (BMK) under the program "ICT of the Future" project 877587.

Disclosure of Interests. The authors have no competing interests to declare relevant to this article's content.

References

1. Alblwi, S., Ayad, A., Mili, A.: Mutation coverage is not strongly correlated with mutation coverage. In: Proceedings of the 5th ACM/IEEE International Conference on Automation of Software Test (AST 2024), AST 2024, pp. 1–11. Association for Computing Machinery, New York (2024). https://doi.org/10.1145/3644032.3644442
2. Amendola, G., Berei, T., Ricca, F.: Testing in ASP: revisited language and programming environment. In: Faber, W., Friedrich, G., Gebser, M., Morak, M. (eds.) JELIA 2021. LNCS (LNAI), vol. 12678, pp. 362–376. Springer, Cham (2021). https://doi.org/10.1007/978-3-030-75775-5_24
3. Calimeri, F., Gebser, M., Maratea, M., Ricca, F.: Design and results of the fifth answer set programming competition. Artif. Intell. **231**, 151–181 (2016). https://doi.org/10.1016/j.artint.2015.09.008
4. DeMillo, R., Lipton, R., Sayward, F.: Hints on test data selection: help for the practicing programmer. Computer **11**(4), 34–41 (1978). https://doi.org/10.1109/C-M.1978.218136
5. Febbraro, O., Leone, N., Reale, K., Ricca, F.: Unit testing in *ASPIDE*. In: Tompits, H., et al. (eds.) INAP/WLP -2011. LNCS (LNAI), vol. 7773, pp. 345–364. Springer, Heidelberg (2013). https://doi.org/10.1007/978-3-642-41524-1_21
6. Gebser, M., Harrison, A., Kaminski, R., Lifschitz, V., Schaub, T.: Abstract gringo. Theory Pract. Logic Program. **15**(4–5), 449–463 (2015). https://doi.org/10.1017/S1471068415000150
7. Gebser, M., Kaminski, R., Kaufmann, B., Schaub, T.: Multi-shot asp solving with Clingo. Theory Pract. Logic Program. **19**(1), 27–82 (2019). https://doi.org/10.1017/S1471068418000054

8. Greßler, A., Oetsch, J., Tompits, H.: Harvey: a system for random testing in ASP. In: Balduccini, M., Janhunen, T. (eds.) LPNMR 2017. LNCS (LNAI), vol. 10377, pp. 229–235. Springer, Cham (2017). https://doi.org/10.1007/978-3-319-61660-5_21

9. Hughes, J.: QuickCheck testing for fun and profit. In: Hanus, M. (ed.) Practical Aspects of Declarative Languages, pp. 1–32. Springer, Heidelberg (2007)

10. Jackson, D., Damon, C.A.: Elements of style: analyzing a software design feature with a counterexample detector. ACM SIGSOFT Softw. Eng. Notes **21**(3), 239–249 (1996).https://doi.org/10.1145/226295.226322

11. Janhunen, T., Niemelä, I., Oetsch, J., Pührer, J., Tompits, H.: On testing answer-set programs. In: Coelho, H., Studer, R., Wooldridge, M.J. (eds.) ECAI 2010 - 19th European Conference on Artificial Intelligence, Lisbon, Portugal, 16–20 August 2010. Frontiers in Artificial Intelligence and Applications, vol. 215, pp. 951–956. IOS Press (2010). https://doi.org/10.3233/978-1-60750-606-5-951

12. Janhunen, T., Niemelä, I., Oetsch, J., Pührer, J., Tompits, H.: Random vs. structure-based testing of answer-set programs: an experimental comparison. In: Delgrande, J.P., Faber, W. (eds.) LPNMR 2011. LNCS (LNAI), vol. 6645, pp. 242–247. Springer, Heidelberg (2011). https://doi.org/10.1007/978-3-642-20895-9_26

13. Oetsch, J., Prischink, M., Pührer, J., Schwengerer, M., Tompits, H.: On the small-scope hypothesis for testing answer-set programs. In: Brewka, G., Eiter, T., McIlraith, S.A. (eds.) Principles of Knowledge Representation and Reasoning: Proceedings of the Thirteenth International Conference, KR 2012, Rome, Italy, 10–14 June 2012. AAAI Press (2012). http://www.aaai.org/ocs/index.php/KR/KR12/paper/view/4550

14. Offutt, A., Rothermel, G., Zapf, C.: An experimental evaluation of selective mutation. In: Proceedings of 1993 15th International Conference on Software Engineering, pp. 100–107 (1993). https://doi.org/10.1109/ICSE.1993.346062

15. Papadakis, M., Henard, C., Harman, M., Jia, Y., Le Traon, Y.: Threats to the validity of mutation-based test assessment. In: Proceedings of the 25th International Symposium on Software Testing and Analysis, ISSTA 2016, pp. 354–365. Association for Computing Machinery, New York (2016). https://doi.org/10.1145/2931037.2931040

16. Rosa, A.: On certain valuations of the vertices of a graph. In: Theory of Graphs, International Symposium, pp. 349–355. Gordon and Breach (1966)

17. Tange, O.: GNU Parallel 20240222 (2024). https://doi.org/10.5281/zenodo.10719803. GNU Parallel is a general parallelizer to run multiple serial command line programs in parallel without changing them

18. Viola Pizzoleto, A., Cutigi Ferrari, F., Offutt, J., Fernandes, L., Ribeiro, M.: A systematic literature review of techniques and metrics to reduce the cost of mutation testing. J. Syst. Softw. **157**, 110388 (2019). https://doi.org/10.1016/j.jss.2019.07.100

19. Wotawa, F., Tazl, O.: On the verification of diagnosis models. In: Industrial Artificial Intelligence Technologies and Applications, pp. 189–203 (2022). https://doi.org/10.13052/rp-9788770227902

Advancing Code Vulnerability Detection

Enhancing Vulnerability Detection with Domain Knowledge: A Comparison of Different Mechanisms

Alessandro Marchetto$^{(\boxtimes)}$ and Rosmaël Zidane Lekeufack Foulefack

University of Trento, Trento, Italy
{alessandro.marchetto,rz.lekeufack}@unitn.it

Abstract. Existing software vulnerability detection methods based on deep-learning and large language models are effective in the identification of vulnerable source code snippets. Their effectiveness, however, decreases when applied to localize the vulnerability-related statements, i.e., those statements in code snippets that lead to the vulnerabilities.

In this paper, we document an exploratory comparison of different mechanisms that can be applied to enhance such existing vulnerability detection methods with domain knowledge information. To this aim, a transformer-based vulnerability detection method has been enhanced with several mechanisms and an experiment has been conducted on a real-life dataset. Results show that the domain knowledge information used is more relevant than the used enhancement mechanism.

Keywords: Software vulnerability detection · Deep Learning · Source code

1 Introduction

Security testing is a specific type of software testing that studies methods and tools for detecting vulnerabilities that can be exploited by attackers for compromising systems and steal data and information. Cyber-attacks that start by exploiting vulnerabilities of connected software systems are nowadays increasing[1], thus approaches for their early detection are more and more needed. The MITRE[2] system provides the Common Weakness Enumeration (CWE), a list of common software security code weaknesses, patterns of source code known to lead to security issues. MITRE uniquely identifies and characterizes such code weaknesses by means of a description, code examples, and possible impact and mitigation strategies, among the other information. Static vulnerability detection techniques (SAST) are shown to be effective in detecting such code weaknesses. Such techniques do not require the system execution but rather use code

---

[1] https://www.forbes.com/advisor/education/it-and-tech/cybersecurity-statistics.
[2] https://cwe.mitre.org.

© IFIP International Federation for Information Processing 2025
Published by Springer Nature Switzerland AG 2025
H. D. Menéndez et al. (Eds.): ICTSS 2024, LNCS 15383, pp. 95–113, 2025.
https://doi.org/10.1007/978-3-031-80889-0_7

parsing, pattern matching, data and control-flow analysis to recognize the weaknesses. SASTs are fast and easy to apply, but they produce a large number of false positive alarms. To limit the developers' intervention, deep-learning and large language models can be applied [28]. These methods require *code snippets* (fragments of source code such as functions) labeled as vulnerable and non-vulnerable as input dataset. The code snippets are tokenized, and then the generated token-based vectors are fed into learning algorithms for the training phase. The algorithms output a model that classifies new code snippets as vulnerable or non-vulnerable.

These learning-based methods show promising results but have also some limits that hamper their adoption in real scenarios [3,20]. First of all, their effectiveness strongly depend on the available training dataset. Several datasets exist (e.g., BigVul, ProjectKB)[3] but most of them are related to C/C++, are strongly imbalanced, and contain spurious information such as wrong labels, irrelevant and duplicated information. Secondly, such methods have a limited capability of capturing and working with semantics and deep-structure characteristics of source code and vulnerabilities. Last but not least, the existing vulnerability detection methods have only a limited understanding of what they are looking for (code weaknesses and vulnerabilities). In other terms, they have a quite limited access to domain knowledge information, and they simply look at the code snippets for identifying (explicit or implicit) characteristics and patterns that could be used to identify the presence of vulnerable code.

In this paper, we document an investigation conducted to compare different mechanisms that can be used to enhance existing vulnerability detection methods with domain knowledge information. In a previous work [21], we observed that vulnerability detection methods enhanced with domain-knowledge can achieve promising results. In this work, we systematically compare different methods to inject domain-specific knowledge information into an existing transformer-based vulnerability detection method named VDet [19], based on JavaBert [25]. We opted for VDet since it achieved promising results without [19,20] and with [21] the use of domain knowledge for different datasets.

2   Transformer-Based Vulnerability Detection

JavaBert. [25] is a BERT-based system specialized for Java. BERT is a learning algorithm typically applied in natural language processing (NLP) tasks and based on a specific type of neural network, named Bidirectional Encoder Representation from the Transformer architecture. JavaBert uses a tokenizer to split in tokens the source code of Java functions. Such tokens are then encoded by means of a vectorized representation of the embeddings (sequences of tokens and their positions). Three special tokens (i.e., $[MASK]$, $[UNK]$, and $[PAD]$) are used to: (i) mask tokens used for improving the model prediction performance in

---

[3] {https://github.com/} ZeoVan/MSR_20_Code_vulnerability_CSV_Dataset, SAP/ project-kb.

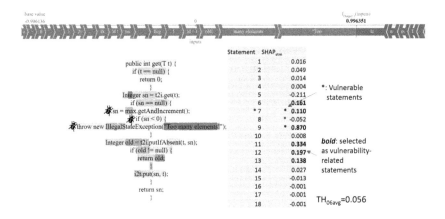

Fig. 1. Example of SHAP applied to a Java function code

token-prediction tasks; (ii) mask unknown tokens; and (iii) fill short sequences of tokens (longer sequences are split into chunks). The resulting vectors are fed to a 12 layers structure of transformers that implements the sequence-to-sequence transformation. Thanks to the attention blocks, this structure can take into account contextual information of each token, thus capturing the token dependencies. JavaBert outputs a classification prediction of the labels for the input code, with a probability value between 0 and 1. This prediction corresponds to the likelihood of the input sample belonging to a label (class). JavaBert uses the Binary Cross-Entropy Loss (BCE) with Logits Loss function, a combination of a sigmoid layer and the binary-cross-entropy loss, to measure the distance between the predicted probability distribution and the true labels. VDet [19] is a JavaBert model fine tuned for detecting vulnerable source code. VDet can classify code snippets (Java functions) as vulnerable or non-vulnerable (binary classification) or it can predict the presence of a specific CWE (multi-label classification [18]).

Explainable AI. [1] provides information about the set of key features used by an AI model. Several explainability methods exist to capture relevant features (in our case, code tokens) used by the model to make decisions (in our case, code classification) [24]. *SHAP* is a *model-agnostic* explainability method that approximates the decision function of the AI model with a surrogate function. SHAP computes the so-called SHAP values (from -1 to 1) for estimating the impact of each feature on the model's decisions. The absolute SHAP value estimates the impact of a feature, and the sign indicates whether the feature impacts positively or negatively on the decisions. The prioritization of the features according to the SHAP values can be used to identify the most relevant ones. The SHAP values are computed by starting from a base value obtained by masking all input tokens with $[MASK]$, i.e., the value without features. Then, the features are iteratively added and the SHAP values computed, with the aim of estimating the contribution of each feature into the value changes. Figure 1 shows a Java function in which tokens have been highlighted according to their

SHAP value (intense red represents higher positive SHAP value, while blue are negative values). For instance, the features *"Too"* and *"many elements"* have a positive contribution on the classification of the function as vulnerable, while "$(sn < 0)$" has a negative contribution.

We used SHAP on top of VDet (named **SVDet**) for localizing the vulnerability-related code statements (lines with bugs and '*' in Fig. 1) [20]. SHAP values are computed for each code statement of the snippet, and the ones with positive SHAP values higher than a **selection threshold** (TH) are identified as the ones related to the vulnerability. For each code snippet, **TH** and the vulnerability-related statements are identified as in [20]: (1) a statement-level SHAP value ($SHAP_{stm}$) is computed for each statement, by summing the values obtained for all tokens of the statement and dividing by the number of tokens; (2) $SHAP_{stm-avg}$ is computed as the average value of the $SHAP_{stm}$ of the entire snippet; (3) vulnerability-related statements are selected as the ones with $SHAP_{stm}$ higher than or equal to 60% of $SHAP_{stm-avg}$. Additional details can be found in our previous work [20].

3   Domain Knowledge Information for Vulnerability Detection

Domain-specific knowledge refers to the knowledge concerning a specific field or discipline. A domain expert is a person with an extensive experience and special knowledge in a specific field such as engineering and computer science. The expert can identify relevant problems and risks in a given field, as well as solutions to such problems. An expert in vulnerability management has experience in identifying, assessing, and prioritizing software security vulnerabilities. For instance, the expert can define strategies to prevent and identify software weaknesses, thus avoiding their exploitation from attackers. *A code "weakness" is a condition in a software that, under certain circumstances, could contribute to the introduction of vulnerabilities.*[4] For example, the code in Fig. 1 is an instance of CWE-119 (*Improper Restriction of Operations within the Bounds of a Memory Buffer*) indicating that the code reads from or writes to a memory location outside the intended memory boundary (in the example, the function "getAndDecrement()" can write into an unexpected memory location), thus resulting in an operation that could be linked to other variables or data. Each MITRE CWE is uniquely defined, tied to attack patterns that can exploit it (listed in the CAPEC[5] collection), and tied to observed real vulnerabilities (listed in the CVE[6] collection). Each CWE corresponds to a specific condition of the code that can lead to a security vulnerability exploited by an attacker. Hence, the knowledge of the CWEs and the capability of identifying them in the code are crucial to drive the developers in removing them.

---

[4] https://cwe.mitre.org/about/index.html.
[5] https://capec.mitre.org.
[6] https://www.cve.org.

CWEs in MITRE are also characterized by relationships among them such as for instance: CWE-x is *ParentOf* CWE-y, CWE-y is *ChildOf* CWE-x, and CWE-y is *PeerOf* CWE-z. The first property means that CWE-x is of the same type, but less specific, than CWE-y. Symmetrically, the second property means that CWE-y is more-specific than CWE-x. The last property means that CWE-y and CWE-z are in the same level of the CWE hierarchy. For instance, CWE-119 is a weakness of the same type but more specific than CWE-118 (*Incorrect Access of Indexable Resource - Range Error*), i.e., CWE-119 is *ChildOf* CWE-118. Moreover, CWE-119 is less specific than CWE-125 (*Out-of-bounds Read*), i.e., CWE-119 is *ParentOf* CWE-125.

These relationships create a CWE hierarchy[7]. This hierarchy can be represented with a Directed Acyclic Graph (DAG) having a neutral root node (i.e., node 1000 from MITRE). For instance, Fig. 2 shows a fragment of the CWE hierarchy used in this work and extracted from the ProjectKB dataset [23]. The DAG is composed of 5 layers for a total of 85 nodes (CWEs) connected by 84 edges (CWEs' relationships). In the DAG, green nodes represent CWEs in the dataset, while gray nodes represent CWEs that are not in the ProjectKB dataset, but that are in relationship with the CWEs in the dataset.

DAG nodes can be enriched with additional domain information about the CWE they represent. In this work, we consider the frequency of the CWE in the ProjectKB dataset and we use this information to estimate the interdependence relationship of each CWE with the others. To this aim:

- (step 1) For each CWE, we measure the number of code snippets in the dataset labelled with that CWE (blue box in Fig. 2) and we compute the inverse frequency, that is 1 minus the ratio between the frequency and the number of code snippets.
- (step 2) For each CWE c in the dataset, are identified all the DAG paths starting from the DAG root, passing through c, and reaching the leaves of the DAG.
- (step 3) we weigh c with 1 plus the sum of the inverse frequency of all CWEs/nodes in the identified paths of c, normalized over the maximun sum obtained on the identified paths.

As an example, Fig. 2 shows our CWE hierarchy with the frequency of the CWEs in the ProjectKB dataset for the Java code snippet in Fig. 1 (CWE-119). To simplify our illustrative example, we consider only a (small) set of CWEs such as: CWE-74, CWE-77, CWE-78, CWE-119, CWE-327, and CWE-787. According to the steps can compute described above:

- (step 1) we compute the frequency for CWE-119, which is 147, and, considering 581 code snippets, the inverse frequency is 0.75 (i.e., 1-147/581=0.75).
- (step 2) we identify the paths in the CWE hierarchy from the root to the leaves that pass through the node 119. An example of these paths is the one depicted with dashed nodes in Fig. 2, that is: CWE-664, CWE-118, CWE-119, and CWE-787.

---

[7] https://cwe.mitre.org/data/slices/1000.html.

– (step 3) we compute the weights for the CWEs in such an identified path: 1 for CWE-664 and CWE-118 (we consider a fixed value of 1 for each gray node in the DAG), 0.75 for CWE-119, and 0.99 for CWE-787. The obtained sum for the example path is: 3.74, which normalized over the maximum sum is, e.g., 2.11. It represents the computed weight of the inter-dependence relationships for CWE-119.

The built DAG-based representation of the ProjectKB CWE hierarchy, enriched with information based on the CWE frequency, represents the domain-specific knowledge we consider in the enhanced SVDet tool (named **eSVDet**) used in this paper.

4   Domain Knowledge Enhancement of Vulnerability Detection

This work documents an exploratory study to compare four domain-knowledge enhancement mechanisms implemented by **eSVDet** and named: Multi-label (Mu), CWE hierarchy for the loss function (CWEh), Multi-label as input (InMu), and CWE hierarchy as input (InCWEh).

Figure 3 presents an overall view of the **eSVDet** architecture that implements such mechanisms by highlighting their data flow. While [19,20] first explored *Mu* and [21] presented *CWEh, InMu* and *InCWEh* are explored in this work for the first time. Differently from *Mu* and *CWEh*, with *InMu* and *InCWEh* we assume to know the CWEs implemented in the Java snippets code in input, while we have to detect the vulnerable ones. Future work will be devoted to predict the presence of CWE(s) in a code, thus also supporting this phase.

Mu. As a baseline for domain enhancement, we consider a multi-label classifier that for labeling each input snippet predicts whether it is vulnerable or not and the specific implemented CWE, if any. The information about the CWE is encoded by means of the one-hot encoding representation, in which the length of the vector corresponds to the number of CWEs.

CWEh. As a further mechanism to add domain knowledge we consider the weighted CWEs hierarchy (Sect. 3). It leverages the information from the CWE hierarchy to weigh the probabilities predicted by **eSVDet** for each CWE in each iteration of the tool and uses it for the computation of the loss function. We weigh the CWE's predictions according to the position of the predicted CWE with respect to the actual one, in the CWE hierarchy. In detail, when running the **eSVDet** learning algorithm, we weigh the probabilities according to the weights computed in Step 2 (Sect. 3) so as to increase the relevance of the CWE's prediction that are "close" to the actual CWE. For instance, let us assume that the original predicted probabilities in the example of Fig. 2 are the ones reported in the second row at the box at the bottom right, that is: 0.2 for CWE-74, 0 for CWE-77, 0.03 for CWE-78, 0.16 for CWE-119, 0.4 for CWE-327, 0.01 for CWE-787. Let us assume also that the weights related to the

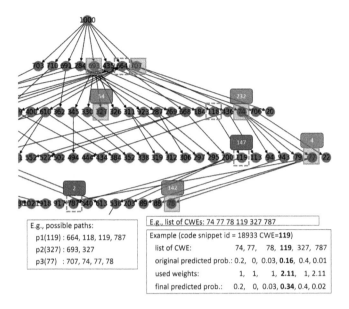

Fig. 2. Fragment of the CWE hierarchy

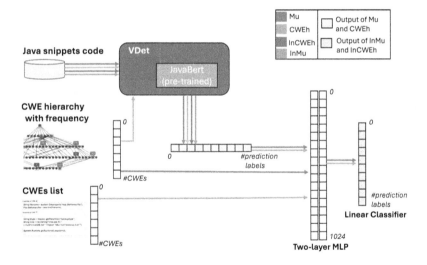

Fig. 3. eSVDet architecture

CWE-119 (our actual one), computed according to the steps 3 (Sect. 3) are the ones reported in the second row of the box at the bottom right of Fig. 2. The new probabilities in the example are: 0.34 for CWE-119 and 0.02 for CWE-787, while the other predicted probabilities remain unchanged since they are not in any paths related to CWE-119. The new probabilities aim at favor the prediction of CWEs that are "closer" to the actual CWE-119. *CWEh* finally we uses these new probabilities to compute the loss function that drives the method evolution.

InMu. Inspired from the existing literature that studies knowledge injection strategies for deep-learning and large language models [2,22], we extend **eSVDet** with a separate step for (pre-)processing the non-code features, i.e., the CWE information in our case. Such a CWE information is represented as a multi-dimensional vector (the dimension corresponds to the number of CWEs). Such a vector is then concatenated with the classification output produced by **eSVDet** and fed into a two-layer multilayer perceptron (MLP) composed of 1024 units for each layer and a Rectified Linear Activation Function (ReLu) activation function. During the training, this two-layer MLP learns a non-linear combination of the input representations that is then passed into the final (linear) classifier. The dimension of this last classifier depends on the number of classes to predict, i.e., in case of *InMu*: the presence of vulnerable code or not and optionally the possible CWEs (used only for checking purpose).

InCWEh. This last mechanism is a combination of *CWEh* and *InMu*. We, in fact, consider the same domain information considered in *CWEh*, and derived from the CWE hierarchy (Sect. 3). For each snippet code used in the training phase, we weigh the actual CWE (the one extracted from the dataset, and not the predicted CWE, as done in *CWEh*) and we encode this information as a multi-dimensional vector then passed into the same two-layer MLP architecture used the *InMu* method. *InCWEh* aims at providing to **eSVDet** the snippets code and the CWE they implement, if any, enriched with the weight computed by considering the position of the CWE in the hierarchy and its frequency in the used dataset, that is the connectivity-degree of the CWE with respect to other CWEs, assuming that a more connected CWE is easer to predict.

5   Evaluation

Our goal is to compare the different domain enhancement mechanisms implemented into **eSVDet** for detecting and localizing vulnerable code. To this aim, we consider (1) *Bin*, binary classifier, as our baseline corresponding to **eSVDet** without any enhancement, and four **eSVDet** variants: (2) **Mu**, (3) **InMu**, (4) **CWEh**, (5) **InCWEh**. The research questions we aim at investigating are:

- **RQ1** *What is the impact of the domain knowledge enhancement mechanisms on the detection of vulnerable code snippets?* RQ1 aims at evaluating the effectiveness of the different enhancement mechanisms used with the deep-learning method to detect vulnerable code snippets. To answer RQ1, we measure the performance of our baseline and of **eSVDet** variants in the identification of vulnerable code snippets (Java functions).
- **RQ2** *What is the impact of the domain knowledge enhancement mechanisms on the localization of the code statements related to vulnerabilities?* RQ2 aims

at evaluating the effectiveness of the different enhancement mechanisms to localize vulnerability-related code statements inside the vulnerable snippets. To answer RQ2, we measure the performance of our baseline *Bin* and of the **eSVDet** variants in the identification of vulnerable code statements.

5.1   Metrics

For RQ1, we compared the obtained output with the ground truth from the dataset, and we calculated the following metrics based on TP (true positive), FP (false positive), TN (true negative), and FN (false negative).

- Balanced accuracy $bAcc = \frac{(Sensitivity+Specificity)}{2}$ represents the number of correctly classified code snippets; it is often used with imbalanced datasets, and it is computed starting from sensitivity and specificity;
- Sensitivity $Sen = \frac{TP}{TP+FN}$ represents the portion of vulnerable code snippets correctly identified.
- Specificity $Spec = \frac{TN}{TN+FN}$ represents the portion of non-vulnerable code snippets identified.
- Normalized Matthews Correlation Coefficient $nMCC = (MCC + 1)/2$ summarizes the trend of the data by considering at the same time TP, FP, TN, and FN, in fact, $MCC = \frac{TP*TN-FP*FN}{\sqrt{(TP+FP)*(TP+FN)*(TN+FP)*(TN*FN)}}$. $nMCC$ it is often used with imbalanced datasets instead of F1-scores (harmonic mean of precision and recall) since it is less sensitive to the result of the majority class [4].

For RQ2, we calculated the same metrics but at the statement-level. The gold standard has been defined by analyzing the commits of the source code in the dataset. According to [11], we adopted a conservative approach in which all statements that have been removed for fixing a vulnerability have been considered as vulnerability-related statements. For all metrics, we used the macro-average [10] by averaging the metric scores of individual measures. The macro-average (high metrics values close to 1 are desired) is often used with imbalanced datasets since it is less influenced by the number of items in the dataset classes with respect to other measures (e.g., micro-average).

5.2   Object

ProjectKB is the used vulnerability dataset. ProjectKB is composed of manually curated security-relevant commits extracted from real-world Java software. The dataset provides: the CVE, the vulnerable code, and the fixed code. ProjectKB contains: (i) 3770 Java files with 1.3M/1.4M lines of code respectively before/after the vulnerability fixes; (ii) 20155 Java functions; (iii) of which 2467 are vulnerable (12.2%) and (iv) related to 496 CVEs that refer to 64 CWEs. The most frequent CWEs are: CWE-20 "Improper Input Validation" (11.9% of the snippets), and CWE-22 "Improper Limitation of a Pathname to a Restricted

Directory (Path Traversal)" (8.8% of the snippets). Respectively 18.8% and 5.1% of the snippets of type CWE-20 and CWE-22 are vulnerable. Other CWEs achieve a frequency around or lower than 6% each one.

5.3 Process

1. We randomly shuffled and splitted the Java functions in training (80%), validation (10%), and test set (10%) – each one with about 12% of vulnerable functions.
2. We used train and validation sets for building the AI models considered. In detail, we used the following configuration: epoch: 4 and 10; input vector length: 512; Loss Function: BCE with logits loss; Optimizer: Adamax; Recurrent Activation: sigmoid; Vocabular Size: 30522 (JavaBert); Training steps: size(input)*epoch; Hidden layers: 12; and Batch size: 12. We, finally, obtained ten AI models.
3. We provided our test set of 2014 Java functions to the built AI models for classifying them, and we repeated the classification 10 times.
4. We computed the performance metrics for answering RQ1 on the classified functions
5. We then ran SHAP on top of the 10 AI models to identify the vulnerable functions and the vulnerability-related statements for a subset of 300 randomly selected functions from our test set.
6. On the obtained results, we computed the performance metrics for RQ2

5.4 Threats to Validity

The most relevant threat to the validity of our study concerns the adoption of only one dataset and one AI method. About the dataset, we used a real-world dataset that lets us apply the methods in real-life conditions. For instance, the dataset is imbalanced but in the real-life it is a common scenario to have large portions of code with only few lines that contain bugs. By using a more balanced dataset, on the one side, could lead to better results but, on the other side, could resort to an unrealistic case. About the used AI method, we used a transformer-based vulnerability detection method since it achieves reasonable and representative results according to the existing literature. In the investigated appraches, the used CWE information is derived from the dataset, this can be a threat to that could limit the generalizability of the presented study, we will repeat the experiment by considering other datasets. Another threat is related to the setup of the experiment, e.g., the split among training and test set functions, the used test functions, and the used configurations of the AI methods and variants. Different experiment configurations will be considered in our future work.

6 Results

RQ1. Table 1 reports the average and median values for $bAcc$ and $nMCC$, and Fig. 4 shows the distribution boxplots. We can observe that by injecting domain knowledge information, we increase the variability of the results with respect to *Bin*. In detail, *Mu* and *CWEh* obtained results comparable to the ones of *Bin*, slightly better but also variable for epochs 10. Instead, *InMu* and *InCWEh* tend to be worse than the other mechanisms, in particular, by considering epochs 4. Their results have a quite large variability and their average/median values for both *bAcc* and *nMCC* are lower than others. For instance, the average *bAcc* is 0.80 for *InMu*, with respect to 0.87 of *Bin* and 0.83 of *CWEh*. By considering epochs 10, the results of other mechanisms remain almost stable, while the results' variability of *InMu* and *InCWEh* decreases and their results become comparable to the other **eSVDet** variants. These results can indicate that *InMu* and *InCWEh* seem to be not enough able to learn relevant features for characterizing the CWEs in the code. However, increasing the epochs their results improve, while the other mechanisms remain almost stable, we can argue that more epochs can improve them again. This has been confirmed by some execution with we did with epochs 20. We have seen that while other mechanisms still remain stable, *InMu* and *InCWEh* achieved respectively the average 0.85 (median 0.92) and 0.84 (median 0.90) for *bAcc* and 0.84 (median 0.90) and 0.89 (median 0.92) for *nMCC*.

RQ1 The experiment shows that *Mu* and *CWEh* can achieve classification performance comparable to the binary classifier, but slightly variable. Conversely, *InMu* and *InCWEh* require a more extensive learning phase to achieve comparable results.

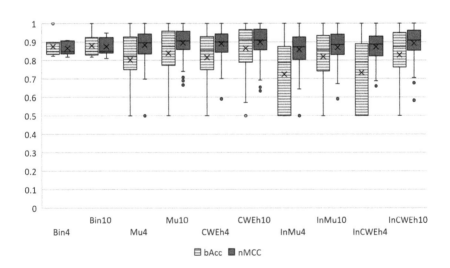

Fig. 4. RQ1: boxplots of *bAcc* and *nMCC* (epochs 4 and 10)

RQ2. Table 1 reports the average and median values for *bAcc* and *nMCC*, and Fig. 5 shows the distribution boxplots. We can observe that all domain knowledge enhanced mechanisms outperform the binary classifier, for epoch 4. In fact,

Table 1. RQ1 and RQ2: average and median values of $bAcc$ and $nMCC$

	RQ1								RQ2							
	epochs = 4				epochs = 10				epochs = 4				epochs = 10			
	bAcc		nMCC		bAcc		nMCC		bAcc		nMCC		bAcc		nMCC	
	avg	med	avg	med	avg	med	avg	med	avg	med	avg	med	avg	med	avg	med
Bin	**0.87**	0.84	0.86	0.84	**0.87**	0.84	0.87	0.84	0.46	0.29	0.46	0.37	**0.56**	0.6	**0.54**	**0.57**
Mu	0.83	**0.91**	**0.88**	**0.93**	0.83	**0.90**	**0.88**	**0.93**	0.55	0.5	**0.54**	0.5	0.48	0.4	0.47	0.44
CWEh	0.83	0.89	0.87	0.92	0.84	**0.90**	**0.88**	**0.93**	0.52	0.5	0.52	0.5	0.52	**0.64**	0.50	0.55
InMu	0.80	0.89	0.86	0.92	0.82	0.88	0.87	0.91	0.50	0.4	0.49	0.45	**0.56**	0.59	0.53	**0.57**
InCWEh	0.81	0.88	0.86	0.92	0.82	0.88	**0.88**	0.91	0.51	**0.56**	0.50	**0.55**	0.52	**0.64**	0.53	0.56

the value of the metrics of the enhanced **eSVDet** variants are almost all greater than 0.5, while the binary classifier's values are lower than 0.5. Conversely, by increasing the number of epochs to 10, the result is not so obvious as expected. In fact, *Bin* largely improves the performance (on average, +10% and +8% for $bAcc$ and $nMCC$). *InMu*, *CWEh*, and *InCWEh* slightly increase their performance (on average, +2.3% and +3% for $bAcc$ and $nMCC$), preserving slightly better or comparable results than *Bin*. In a few cases, *InMu* achieved very promising results but, on average, *CWEh* and *InCWEh* tend to achieve better results with respect to *Bin* and the other enhancement mechanisms. Furthermore, we can notice that when increasing the epochs, *Mu* decreases the performance (on average, -7% for $bAcc$ and $nMCC$), thus highlighting a case of overfitting.

Overall, we observe that on average the domain enhancement variants of **eSVDet** (expect *Mu*) achieve results comparable or better than *Bin*, and that the more informative domain knowledge information derived from the CWE hierarchy seems to be more impacting than the simple information about the CWE. For all the cases, the boxplots show a quite large variability of the metrics, even increasing the epochs. This could be due to the used imbalanced dataset, in terms of vulnerable Java functions and statements. However, we argue that this did not compromise our goal of exploratory evaluating different mechanisms to add domain knowledge information to a transformer-based vulnerability detection method.

> **RQ2** The experiment shows that domain-enhanced methods can achieve results comparable or slightly better than the ones of the binary classifier. In particular, *CWEh* and *InCWEh* slightly overcome other mechanisms. This indicates that there is no a most effective mechanism to inject domain knowledge information, but rather it seems to be more relevant the type of the domain knowledge information considered.

7   Further Analysis and Discussion

We conducted two further analysis in the collected data, for better comprehending the achieved results.

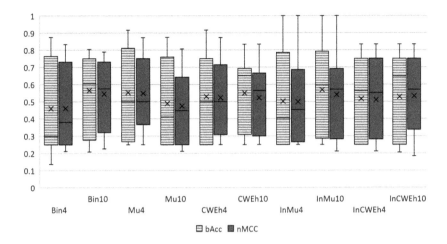

Fig. 5. RQ2: boxplots of $bAcc$ and $nMCC$ (epochs 4 and 10)

Table 2. Impact of the CWE's distribution: average value of $bAcc$ and $nMCC$

	Epochs	function-level						statement-level					
		all		top5		top3		all		top5		top3	
		$bAcc$	$nMCC$	$bAcc$	$nMCC$	$bAcc$	$nMCC$	$bAcc$	$nMCC$	$bAcc$	$nMCC$	$bAcc$	$nMCC$
Mu	4	**0.86**	0.81	**0.83**	**0.88**	**0.85**	**0.90**	**0.55**	**0.54**	0.55	**0.56**	0.51	**0.52**
$CWEh$	4	0.81	**0.83**	0.80	0.83	0.81	0.84	0.52	0.52	0.52	0.52	0.48	0.47
$InMu$	4	0.69	0.67	0.75	0.80	0.75	0.80	0.5	0.49	0.41	0.45	0.36	0.41
$InCWEh$	4	0.69	0.67	0.80	0.85	0.82	0.87	0.51	0.5	**0.64**	0.51	**0.66**	0.49
Mu	10	**0.84**	**0.84**	0.803	0.83	0.814	0.845	0.48	0.47	0.55	**0.56**	0.38	0.39
$CWEh$	10	**0.84**	0.84	**0.84**	0.83	0.815	0.84	0.52	0.5	0.52	0.52	0.46	0.457
$InMu$	10	0.69	0.67	0.808	0.85	0.82	0.87	**0.56**	0.53	0.41	0.45	0.45	0.458
$InCWEh$	10	0.69	0.67	**0.817**	**0.887**	**0.827**	**0.89**	0.52	**0.53**	0.64	0.51	**0.54**	**0.52**

Impact of the CWE's Distribution and Frequency on the Vulnerability Detection Performance. We hypothesize that the CWE's distribution and frequency within the dataset can influence the capability of **eSVDet** to detect vulnerable code snippets. As a further analysis, we computed the performance metrics by focusing only on the most frequently vulnerable CWEs.

Table 2 shows the average metrics calculated for vulnerable functions and code statements by considering *all* CWEs, *top5* and *top3* (epochs 4 and 10), for the set of 300 functions considered in RQ2. Figure 6 shows an example of boxplots for the statement-level prediction of *top3*, epochs 4. We can observe that for *top5* and *top3*: (i) *InCWEh* improves the prediction performance with respect to *all* (i.e., function-level) and to the results collected for RQ2 (Table 1 statement-level); (ii) *InMu* improves the performance with respect to *all* (function-level) but not to RQ2 (statement-level); (iii) *CWEh* obtains comparable results with respect to both *all* (function-level) and RQ2 (statement-level, even if *top3* slightly decreases for RQ2); and (iv) *Mu* tends to decrease the performance with respect to *all* (function-level), while it becomes more stable for RQ2

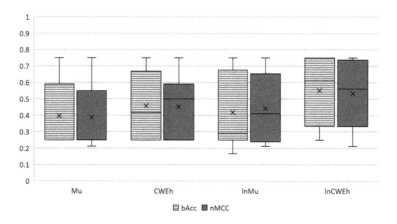

Fig. 6. Impact of the CWE's distribution in $bAcc$ and $nMCC$ at statement-level (*top3* epochs 10)

(statement-level). These results indicate that *Mu* and *CWEh* are more robust with respect to the CWEs' distribution in the dataset, while *InMu* and *InCWEh* are more sensitive. However, *InCWEh* overcomes the other mechanisms for RQ2 (statement-level), whether the CWEs are "enough" frequent in the dataset (e.g., the frequency of the CWEs in *top5* and *top3* is greater then 5%).

Impact of the CWE's Granularity on the Vulnerability Detection Performance. We hypothesize that the CWE granularity can influence the vulnerability detection performance. As a further analysis, we identified the most frequent CWEs and we splitted the top six ones in two groups (named *Low* and *High*), by considering their position in the *layers* of the CWE hierarchy (i.e., the *granularity*). *Low* groups the code snippets with CWEs of a lower granularity than the ones of the code snippets in *High* (i.e., higher distance from the hierarchy's root). We built the two groups also by balancing the number of the code snippets in the groups, as well as the frequency of the vulnerable code snippets.

Table 3 shows the average metrics calculated for vulnerable functions and code statements, by considering *Low* and *High* (epochs 4 and 10), for the set of 300 functions considered in RQ2. As an example, Fig. 7 shows the boxplots of *Low* and *High*, epochs 10, statement-level. At the function-level, almost all mechanisms achieve better performance with the *Low* group, at epochs 4, viceversa if we increase to epochs 10 (apart *CWEh* for which the group *Low* always achieved better performance). This is only partially confirmed at statement-level, for which all methods tend to achieve better performance within the *Low* group, nevertheless the epochs (apart *CWEh* for which *Low* better performs only with epochs 4). These results indicate that CWEs having lower granularity can be better interpreted and classified from **eSVDet** with few epochs, while by increasing the epochs the difference becomes less impacting.

Table 3. CWEs granularity: average value of $bAcc$ and $nMCC$ for Low/High granularity at Function and Statement level

	Epochs	Function-level				Statement-level			
		Low granularity		High granularity		Low granularity		High granularity	
		$bAcc$	$nMCC$	$bAcc$	$nMCC$	$bAcc$	$nMCC$	$bAcc$	$nMCC$
Mu	4	*1*	**1**	**0.9**	0.86	0.52	**0.59**	0.51	0.59
CWEh	4	**1**	**1**	0.64	0.89	0.46	0.56	**0.61**	**0.81**
InMu	4	0.83	**1**	0.64	**0.94**	**0.59**	0.54	0.48	0.56
InCWEh	4	0.83	**1**	0.72	0.86	0.49	0.52	0.5	0.45
Mu	10	0.75	**1**	0.97	0.91	0.57	0.59	0.52	**0.57**
CWEh	10	**1**	**1**	0.90	0.86	**0.63**	**0.65**	0.51	0.55
InMu	10	0.7	0.95	0.90	0.86	0.58	0.55	**0.6**	**0.57**
InCWEh	10	0.83	**1**	**1**	**1**	0.54	0.56	0.52	0.48

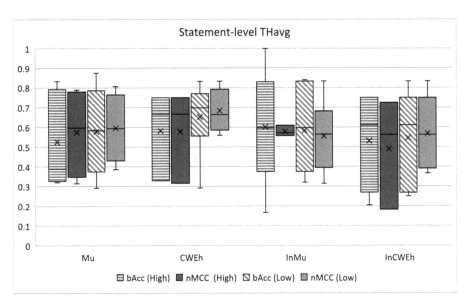

Fig. 7. Impact of the CWE's granularity: boxplots of $bAcc$ and $nMCC$ at statement-level for Low and High -level granularity, epochs 10

The experiment shows that the domain-enhancement mechanisms achieves promising results but they can be sensitive to the code snippets distribution in the different CWEs, and (partially) to the granularity. *InMu* and *InCWEh*, that use the domain information as input to the learning phase, seem to be more sensitive but can also achieve better detection performance.

8   Related Work

Several works investigate the use of learning methods for detecting vulnerabilities [28]. For instance, VulDeePecker [14] and SySeVR [13] are two pioneer works on vulnerabilities detection with deep-learning methods. [14] applies Bidirectional Long Short-Term Memory to code "gadgets" (semantically-related code statements) encoded into fixed-length vectors of symbols. [13] extended VulDeePecker by using Bidirectional Recurrent Neural Networks, with the aim of capturing the semantic relationships among code statements within a gadget. VDet [19] and LineVul [7] use transformer structures to detect vulnerability in Java code by considering the token context. IVDetect [11] and Funded [26] use graph-based code representations (e.g., abstract syntax trees) and graph-based learning architectures to capture code semantics and deep-structure.

Some effort has been spent by the community to adopt domain knowledge in vulnerability detection. For instance, [16] uses learning algorithms to study the cross-domain issues that often hamper the vulnerability detection. [5] proposes a transformer-based approach to map CVE described in natural-language to their related CWEs. [17] uses two learning algorithms to detect code vulnerabilities by combining local and global information of code snippets in a dataset. [8] uses a graph and transformer-based learning model to detect vulnerabilities by considering source code, data-flow information, and natural-language descriptions of code commits. [12] proposes the use of commit-level code changes, represented by graph-based structure, fed into Graph Convolution Network, for detecting vulnerabilities. [27] uses statistic features (e.g., number of changed statements) to capture code changes, then used to detect vulnerabilities with a machine-learning method. [6] considers the similarity among code snippets neighbors to classify new snippets. [15] enhances a vulnerability prediction learning algorithm with external knowledge aiming at combining the information from the source code and from natural-language descriptions of CVEs (i.e., semantic features to search). More similar to our work, [9] presented the first attempt to use a probabilistic model that integrates the domain knowledge derived from the CWEs into a transformer-based vulnerabilities prediction method.

This work documents an exploratory investigation of several mechanisms to enhance a transformer-based vulnerability detection method with domain-knowledge [19,20]. By starting from the promising results we achieved in a previous work [21], we extended it by comparing and deeply investigating the performance of several domain information injection mechanisms. We, in fact, considered the most representative mechanisms from [21] and compared them with new methods in which the domain-specific information is provided as input to the learning phase. We tried to identify the most promising enhancement mechanisms and the most relevant domain-information to be used.

9   Conclusions

We documented an exploratory comparison of mechanisms to enhance a vulnerability method with domain-specific information. We observed that by adding some extra information, with respect to the sole source code, we overcome the traditional detection methods but the added information play a fundamental role by amplifying or hampering the results.

More investigation is still required to corroborate and generalize the observed results, hence, our future work will be devoted to extend the study by considering additional datasets and other learning methods to be enhanced with domain knowledge information. We will also go beyond this investigation by considering different types of domain-specific knowledge information that can be used for increasing the detection performance.

Acknowledgments. The work was partially supported by the European Union Horizon Europe Research and Innovation Programme under Grant 101120393 (Sec4Ai4Sec) and partially by project SERICS (PE00000014) under the MUR National Recovery and Resilience Plan funded by the European Union - NextGenerationEU.

References

1. Burkart, N., Huber, M.F.: A survey on the explainability of supervised machine learning. J. Artif. Intell. Res. **70**, 245–317 (2021)
2. Cadeddu, et al.: A comparative analysis of knowledge injection strategies for large language models in the scholarly domain. Eng. Appl. Artif. Intell. **133**(133) (2024)
3. Chakraborty, S., Krishna, R., Ding, Y., Ray, B.: Deep learning based vulnerability detection: are we there yet? IEEE Trans. Softw. Eng. **48**(09), 3280–3296 (2022)
4. Chicco, D.: Ten quick tips for machine learning in computational biology. BioData Min. **10**(35) (2017)
5. Das, S.S., Serra, E., Halappanavar, M., Pothen, A., Al-Shaer, E.: V2W-BERT: a framework for effective hierarchical multiclass classification of software vulnerabilities. In: Proceedings of IEEE International Conference on Data Science and Advanced Analytics (DSAA), pp. 1–12 (2021)
6. Du, Q., Kuang, X., Zhao, G.: Code vulnerability detection via nearest neighbor mechanism. In: Proceedings of International Conference on Empirical Methods in Natural Language Processing (EMNLP) (2022)
7. Fu, M., Tantithamthavorn, C.: LineVul: a transformer-based line-level vulnerability prediction. In: Proceedings of International Conference on Mining Software Repositories, pp. 608-620. ACM (2022)
8. Guo, D., et al.: GraphCodeBERT: pre-training code representations with data flow. In: Proceedings of International Conference on Learning Representations, ICLR 2021, Virtual Event, Austria, 3-7 May 2021. OpenReview.net (2021)
9. Jeong, S.: Integrating domain knowledge into transformer-based approaches to vulnerability detection. Master's thesis, Ludwig-Maximilians-Universität München, Ge (2023)
10. Kanae, T., Kouji, Y., Aya, K., Tatsuki, K.: Confidence interval for micro-averaged F1 and macro-averaged F1 scores. Appl. Intell. **52**(5), 4961–4972 (2022)
11. Li, Y., Wang, S., Nguyen, T.N.: Vulnerability detection with fine-grained interpretations. In: Proceedings of ACM Joint Meeting on European Software Engineering Conf. and Symposium on the Foundations of Software Engineering, pp. 292-303. ESEC/FSE 2021. Association for Computing Machinery, USA (2021)

12. Li, Y., Yadavally, A., Zhang, J., Wang, S., Nguyen, T.N.: Commit-level, neural vulnerability detection and assessment. In: Proceedings of ACM Joint European Software Engineering Conf. and Symposium on the Foundations of Software Engineering (ESEC/FSE), pp. 1024-1036. Association for Computing Machinery, New York (2023)
13. Li, Z., Zou, D., Xu, S., Jin, H., Zhu, Y., Chen, Z.: SySeVr: a framework for using deep learning to detect software vulnerabilities. IEEE Trans. Dependable Secure Comput. **19**(04), 2244–2258 (2022)
14. Li, Z., et al.: VulDeePecker: a deep learning-based system for vulnerability detection. In: Proceedings of Network and Distributed System Security Symposium. Internet Society, San Diego (2018)
15. Liu, J., Ai, J., Lu, M., Wang, J., Shi, H.: Semantic feature learning for software defect prediction from source code and external knowledge. J. Syst. Softw. **204**(C) (2023)
16. Liu, S., et al.: CD-Vuld: cross-domain vulnerability discovery based on deep domain adaptation. IEEE Trans. Dependable Secure Comput. **19**(1), 438–451 (2022)
17. Lu, Z., Du, P., Nie, J.-Y.: VGCN-BERT: augmenting BERT with graph embedding for text classification. In: Jose, J.M., et al. (eds.) ECIR 2020. LNCS, vol. 12035, pp. 369–382. Springer, Cham (2020). https://doi.org/10.1007/978-3-030-45439-5_25
18. Mamede, C., Pinconschi, E., Abreu, R., Campos, J.: Exploring transformers for multi-label classification of Java vulnerabilities. In: Proceedings of IEEE International Conference on Software Quality, Reliability and Security (QRS), pp. 43–52 (2022)
19. Mamede, C., Pinconschi, E., Abreu, R.: A transformer-based ide plugin for vulnerability detection. In: Proceedings of International Conference on Automated Software Engineering. ASE, ACM (2023)
20. Marchetto, A.: Can explainability and deep-learning be used for localizing vulnerabilities in source code? In: Proceedings of International Conference on Automation of Software Test (2024)
21. Marchetto, A., Foulefack, R.Z.: Towards the use of domain knowledge to enhance transformer-based vulnerability detection. In: Proceedings of International Conference the Quality of Information and Communications Technology. Springer (2024)
22. Ostendorff, M., Bourgonje, P., Berger, M., Moreno-Schneider, J., Rehm, G., Gipp, B.: Enriching BERT with knowledge graph embeddings for document classification. In: Proceedings of International Conference on Natural Language Processing (KONVENS), pp. 156–162 (2019)
23. Ponta, S.E., Plate, H., Sabetta, A., Bezzi, M., Dangremont, C.: A manually-curated dataset of fixes to vulnerabilities of open-source software, pp. 383-387. MSR, IEEE Press (2019)
24. Sotgiu, A., Pintor, M., Biggio, B.: Explainability-based debugging of machine learning for vulnerability discovery. In: Proceedings of International Conference on Availability, Reliability and Security. ARES, ACM, USA (2022)
25. Sousa, N.D., Hasselbring, W.: JavaBERT: training a transformer-based model for the java programming language. In: Proceedings of International Conference on Automated Software Engineering Workshops (ASEW), pp. 90–95. IEEE, USA (2021)
26. Wang, H., et al.: Combining graph-based learning with automated data collection for code vulnerability detection. IEEE Trans. Inf. Forensics Secur. **16**, 1943–1958 (2021)

27. Wang, X., Sun, K., Batcheller, A., Jajodia, S.: Detecting 0-day vulnerability: an empirical study of secret security patch in OSS. In: Proceedings of IEEE/IFIP International Conference International Conference on Dependable Systems and Networks (DSN) (2019)
28. Zeng, P., Lin, G., Pan, L., Tai, Y., Zhang, J.: Software vulnerability analysis and discovery using deep learning techniques: a survey. IEEE Access **8** (2020)

LLMs Can Check Their Own Results to Mitigate Hallucinations in Traffic Understanding Tasks

Malsha Ashani Mahawatta Dona[1]([✉])[iD], Beatriz Cabrero-Daniel[1][iD], Yinan Yu[2][iD], and Christian Berger[1][iD]

[1] University of Gothenburg, Gothenburg, Sweden
{malsha.mahawatta,beatriz.cabrero-daniel,christian.berger}@gu.se
[2] Chalmers University of Technology, Gothenburg, Sweden
yinan@chalmers.se

Abstract. Today's Large Language Models (LLMs) have showcased exemplary capabilities, ranging from simple text generation to advanced image processing. Such models are currently being explored for in-vehicle services such as supporting perception tasks in Advanced Driver Assistance Systems (ADAS) or Autonomous Driving (AD) systems, given the LLMs' capabilities to process multi-modal data. However, LLMs often generate nonsensical or unfaithful information, known as "hallucinations": a notable issue that needs to be mitigated. In this paper, we systematically explore the adoption of SelfCheckGPT to spot hallucinations by three state-of-the-art LLMs (GPT-4o, LLaVA, and Llama3) when analysing visual automotive data from two sources: Waymo Open Dataset, from the US, and PREPER CITY dataset, from Sweden. Our results show that GPT-4o is better at generating faithful image captions than LLaVA, whereas the former demonstrated leniency in mislabeling non-hallucinated content as hallucinations compared to the latter. Furthermore, the analysis of the performance metrics revealed that the dataset type (Waymo or PREPER CITY) did not significantly affect the quality of the captions or the effectiveness of hallucination detection. However, the models showed better performance rates over images captured during daytime, compared to during dawn, dusk or night. Overall, the results show that SelfCheckGPT and its adaptation can be used to filter hallucinations in generated traffic-related image captions for state-of-the-art LLMs.

Keywords: hallucination detection · safety-critical systems · multi-modal data · perception systems · automotive · large language models

1 Introduction

State-of-the-art Large Language Models (LLMs) have demonstrated remarkable capabilities in performing generative tasks. Nowadays, such generative tasks have

© IFIP International Federation for Information Processing 2025
Published by Springer Nature Switzerland AG 2025
H. D. Menéndez et al. (Eds.): ICTSS 2024, LNCS 15383, pp. 114–130, 2025.
https://doi.org/10.1007/978-3-031-80889-0_8

progressed from simple text generation to advanced image generation involving multi-modal data. The usage of LLMs has been positively increased up to a level, where even standardized knowledge tests are already questioned [23]. Hence, LLMs such as Pre-trained Transformers (GPT) are adopted in many domains given their exceptional capabilities in language understanding and generation [3].

1.1 Problem Domain and Motivation

The proprietary LLMs such as GPT-4o introduced in May 2024 [2] and open source models such as Large Language-and-Vision Assistant (LLaVA) [16] have been trained on a large corpus that contains text and image-based data. ome automotive Original Equipment Manufacturers (OEMs) are already experimenting with potential application scenarios where LLMS are used within vehicles to provide better services to their passengers by engaging in natural language-based conversations [1,19]. As LLMs show great potential in image description tasks where the retrieved image captions are often well composed, it is not surprising that such LLMs could be even considered to improve perception systems for Advanced Driver Assistance Systems (ADAS) or Autonomous Driving (AD).

However, tackling the impact of LLM's stochasticity remains a challenge due to a notable issue known as hallucinations, which refers to the tendency of LLMs generating nonsensical information [13]. Hallucinations caused by LLMs are unacceptable regardless of their usage scenario. Therefore many researchers have focused on hallucination detection and mitigation techniques [22] that depend on different approaches such as (a) combinations of retrieval-augmented generation (RAG) [8,25], (b) comparing the generated response with the given ground truth [10,12], (c) evaluating the LLM's own consistency in the generated responses [18], or (d) systematically assessing whether excerpts of an LLM's generated answer can be substantiated with other responses obtained from it for the same prompt [17].

1.2 Research Goal and Research Questions

Manakul et al. [17] have evaluated and extended a technique to spot hallucinations called SelfCheckGPT on a text corpus based on the information extracted from Wikibio dataset [15]. However, the application and adoption of SelfCheckGPT for usage scenarios covering multi-modal data such as images and text are currently the subject of ongoing research as outlined in Sect. 2. Hence, the goal of our research is to (a) adopt the SelfCheckGPT approach for multi-modal data from the automotive context that is relevant for ADAS and AD, and (b) to assess its performance across three state-of-the-art LLMs, namely GPT-4o, LLaVA, and Llama3, by using our datasets' labels as ground truth for reference. We derive the following research questions:

RQ-1 To what extent can the SelfCheckGPT approach be adopted to spot potential hallucinations when using state-of-the-art LLMs for image captioning tasks for automotive usage scenarios?

RQ-2 What is the performance of the adopted SelfCheckGPT approach on two state-of-the-art automotive datasets (Waymo covering traffic scenarios in the US, and PREPER CITY covering traffic scenarios in Sweden)?

RQ-3 To what extent is the performance of SelfCheckGPT affected by environmental conditions such as light or weather?

1.3 Contributions and Scope

We explore the adoption of SelfCheckGPT as the first study that aims at spotting potential hallucinations for automotive usage scenarios relevant for ADAS and AD. Our main contribution is the systematic performance evaluation of SelfCheckGPT and its adaptation to spot the hallucinations on two datasets from two geographical regions covering urban and suburban areas in the US and Sweden, normalized wrt. the traffic scenarios covered in the respective datasets. Furthermore, the potential impact of the time of the day on the performance of SelfCheckGPT was assessed. We limited the captioning capabilities on vehicles, pedestrians, and cyclists for experimental reasons; allowing an LLM to freely describe everything it *sees* in an image would maybe unveil more insights but would limit the scalability of the experimental setup. We propose an adaptation of SelfCheckGPT and its extension CrossCheckGPT [20] to identify hallucinations in automotive usage scenarios.

1.4 Structure of the Paper

The remainder of the paper is organized as follows: Sect. 2 reviews existing hallucination detection and mitigation strategies. Section 3 provides the overview and details of our research methodology. Sections 4 and 5 present the results of the experiments and its analysis and discussion. Section 6 concludes the paper.

2 Related Work

We reviewed adoptions and usage scenarios of SelfCheckGPT [17], which presents a self-correction hallucination detection mechanism for text-based data. Existing hallucination detection and mitigation strategies consider SelfCheckGPT as the baseline.

Sun et al. [20] present CrossCheckGPT that assesses the responses generated by a multi-modal LLM using the evidence responses that are generated by a different set of such LLMs. This method is slightly different from SelfCheck-GPT, which assesses the consistency of the generated response using the same model. The proposed method has been validated for image-to-text data using the MHaluBench benchmark [4], which contains 1143 image captioning data records. The said captions and the images are not focused on the automotive domain and, therefore, may not include labels relevant for perception-related tasks in the automotive discipline. Deng et al. [6] propose a hallucination mitigation technique that evaluates the LLM-generated responses against captions generated by a CLIP model. The CLIP Score has been used to evaluate the primary response and the candidate sentences. Elaraby et al. [7] also present an adoption of SelfCheckGPT called HaloCheck that demonstrates better estimations of the severity of the hallucinations by using knowledge injection. This method requires fine-tuning the model with domain-specific knowledge to gain better performance and that limits the applicability of HaloCheck for LLMs in general.

The studies such as Hartvigsen et al. [12], Guan et al. [10], Es et al. [8], and Yu et al. [25] propose different adaptations of SelfCheckGPT that use the concept of Retrieval Augmented Generation (RAG) by passing context to the LLM along with the question. Guan et al. [10] use knowledge graphs created based on a selected dataset to retrieve the context related to the query. Even though the main research goal of [12] is not hallucination detection and mitigation, they propose an adaptation of SelfCheckGPT that requires correct sentences from Wikipedia to mitigate potential hallucinations. Similarly, [8] also uses a custom-made dataset called WikiEval that covers data retrieved from 50 Wikipedia pages to generate context for RAG. [25] proposes prompting the same LLM with the initial primary response together with the context taken from the retrieved documents to reduce hallucinations by refining the response. All aforementioned RAG-based SelfCheckGPT adaptations require additional information sources that are referred to as context, which is difficult to retrieve in the automotive domain especially related to perception-related tasks.

In addition to that, there are more recent studies conducted focusing on both factuality and consistency of the responses. Ji et al. [14] propose a hallucination mitigation technique for question-and-answer systems, where multiple prompting is involved. Under this approach, the factuality of the initial primary response is assessed by a scorer and the response will be continuously refined until it reaches the threshold value. A similar approach will then be applied to assess the consistency of the response. Wu et al. [24] also present a new technique to mitigate the hallucinations by understanding the logical consistency of the primary response. This method requires prompting the LLM twice with questions regarding the attributes and objects in the primary response. These actuality and consistency checking mechanisms demonstrate promising results focusing on text-based generic data.

Cole et al. [5] address the "ambiguous questions" problem in the domain of LLMs, a very common issue that occurs in text-based processing applications. Even though the main goal of the study is tightly coupled with handling ambiguous questions, the proposed approach can be applied to mitigate hallucinations caused by LLMs. The authors have presented the idea of using another or the same LLM to validate the initial responses with boolean answers.

3   Methodology

We aim to address the following research objectives with our study:

1. Adopting SelfCheckGPT for multi-modal, automotive data,

2. Designing an experimental setup that addresses the issue of determining the correctness of a sentence s_i (cf. aspect (a) mentioned before) that does not require additional data such as the dataset ground truth for image captioning tasks for automotive usage,
3. Assessing the performance of different combinations of LLMs to effectively spot hallucinations, and
4. Evaluating SelfCheckGPT's and the proposed adaptation's sensitivity to external influences such as light and weather conditions.

As we adopt SelfCheckGPT for our setup, we describe its core principles in the following. The general idea behind SelfCheckGPT as depicted in Fig. 1 is to sample a given LLM $n + 1$ times for a specific prompt P. Then, the initial response R_1 provided by the LLM is divided into separate chunks of texts, for instance, separate sentences $s_1 \cdots s_n$ from R_1. The consistency of SelfCheck-GPT is measured using five variants including BERTScore, question-answering, n-gram, Natural Language Inference (NLI), and LLM prompting. We focus on the fifth variant "SelfCheckGPT with LLM prompting", given the effectiveness of LLMs in information assessing tasks [11]. This variant uses an LLM to determine whether the subsequent responses $R_2, \cdots, R_{n+1}$ support the individual sentences $s_1 \cdots s_n$, respectively. For each s_i from the initial response R_1, the same or a different LLM is prompted to check whether s_i is supported by R_{i+1}. This is done by obtaining a yes or no reply for each check. The results from these individual consistency checks are aggregated to a joint score to spot potential hallucinations. The idea behind this is that either each sentence s_i is not sufficiently supported by a R_{i+1} or that a sufficiently large subset of responses is showing varying or contradicting support of the sentences. While this approach by design can neither provide proof of whether a given sentence s_i is correct or incorrect nor show what part of a complete response is a hallucination, it yet allows to check for self-consistency and uses it as a proxy for detecting hallucinations. Assuming a certain level of internal consistency for the LLM in question, increasing the number of samples n may enhance the likelihood of spotting potential hallucinations.

Our experiments consist of the following components: (A) Multi-modal, automotive datasets, and (B) LLMs that are capable of processing multi-modal prompts (i.e., text and/or images simultaneously) as we presented selected images from different traffic situations with a task to the LLMs. To reduce specific, non-controllable, and potentially unknown influential factors of a given automotive dataset, we decided to use two different datasets: Waymo Open Dataset [21] and PREPER CITY [26]. The Waymo Open Dataset was created in 2021 by Google in metropolitan areas in the US to support and facilitate research around algorithms needed for self-driving technology. The Waymo Open Dataset covers 2,030 segments, each approximately 20 s long. It contains around 390,000 captured video frames that cover five cameras including one forward-facing camera and four side cameras.

As that dataset is US-centric and hence, specific to visual appearance of traffic agents like cars as well as driving styles typical to the US, numerous

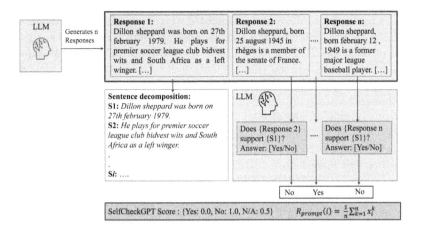

Fig. 1. SelfCheckGPT with LLM prompting. The LLM-generated sentences in a caption are compared against the remaining captions generated by the same LLM for the same prompt. The sentences that are supported by the other captions are considered to be non-hallucinated and this comparison is conducted by LLMs.

other datasets were created and shared over the years covering other regions of the world, featuring other sensors to capture a vehicle's surroundings, focusing other traffic situations. To complement the Waymo Open Dataset as well as to reduce its potential shortcomings, we included PREPER CITYwhich was collected in 2021 in Gothenburg, Sweden, and hence, covers other types of vehicles, metropolitan appearance, and different behavior in traffic from the included traffic actors. It features 114 traffic segments, each approximately 15 min long. It contains more than 1.5 million video frames covering multiple cameras.

3.1 Dataset Curation for Waymo and PREPER CITY

Both datasets contain manually added annotations to foster the research and development of algorithms for ADAS and AD systems. These annotations are necessary to train, test, and evaluate the performance of specifically trained machine learning (ML) components to support a vehicle's perception stack. We use these labels (a) as ground truth to *fact-check* the individual sentences s_i from a generated response R_j to assess the quality of initial answers from an LLM by comparing with the ground truth (for instance, if the labels state `car` and `truck`, but the LLM described `car` and `bike`; here, the LLM hallucinated the `bike` and it also overlooked the `truck`); furthermore, (b) we also used the ground truth to get an overview of the typical distribution of scenarios covered in the two datasets so that we sample similar traffic situations from both datasets; and finally, (c) we used the different label categories such as `car`, `truck`, `pedestrian`, `cyclist`, dots to consolidate a common super-set of keywords that we allowed the LLMs to use for its description.

The consolidation of keywords enabled the comparison of the generated responses with the ground truth for the two datasets. We heuristically determined a prompt for GPT-4o and LLaVA that allowed them to be as expressive as possible while constraining the description of traffic actors to be identified to match with our consolidated list of annotations that are valid on both datasets, which allowed to scale the number of different traffic situations in our experiments while relying on the ground truth labels for fact-checking.

Eventually, we conducted our experiments with the following curated subset of traffic scenarios: We selected 920 images from the Waymo Open Dataset, and another 920 images from PREPER CITY showing different combinations of traffic agents. 617 (PREPER CITY) and 619 (WAYMO) images contain only vehicles, whereas 10 (PREPER CITY) and 5 (WAYMO) images contain only pedestrians. 4 images from PREPER CITY contain only cyclists. Similarly, 165 (PREPER CITY) and 198 (WAYMO) images contain both vehicles and pedestrians whereas it is 31 (PREPER CITY) images for vehicles and cyclists and 6 (PREPER CITY) images for pedestrians and cyclists. 87 (PREPER CITY) and 98 (WAYMO) images contain all three traffic agents. The label `vehicle` dominates the traffic scenarios captured in both datasets.

3.2   Experimental Setup

We depicted our experimental setup in Fig. 2. For both multi-modal LLMs, GPT-4o (gpt-4o-2024-05-13 version) and LLaVA (latest 8dd30f6b0cb1 version), we fed every image 5 times using the following prompt as shown by step (A):

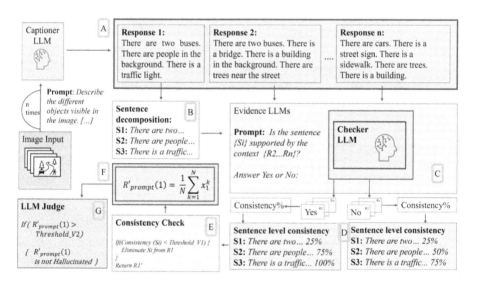

Fig. 2. The experimental setup that depicts the adaptation of SelfCheckGPT. The LLM-generated sentences in a caption are compared with the remaining captions to identify the hallucinated sentences. Based on the sentence level consistency check, the sentences in the caption are filtered to create a refined version of the caption. Different checker and captioner LLMs are used in this setup.

```
Describe the different objects visible in the image. Please write
very simple and clear sentences. Use the format: ''There are
[object].'' For example, ''There are cars. There are people. There
are cyclists.''
Look carefully and make sure to mention all types of objects you
see, especially people. There are multiple types of objects in
the image, provide a separate sentence for each type.
```

For each response R_i, we recorded the response itself for post-processing and the actual processing time per frame. Next, we broke down the first response R_1 into the individual sentences $s_{1...n}$ as portrayed by step (B) in Fig. 2. For each sentence s_i, we extracted the first noun/noun and determinant block and checked whether it matches the ground truth labels for that given image. This way, we could determine the sensitivity and specificity of an LLM's response: TP (non-hallucinations, not flagged as hallucinations), TN (hallucinations flagged as hallucinations), FP (hallucinations, not flagged as hallucinations), and FN (non-hallucinations, flagged as hallucinations).

Next, we applied the fifth variant of the SelfCheckGPT approach to determine for every sentence s_i from R_1, whether it is supported by $R_{2...n}$. This step is depicted by step (C) in the Fig. 2. For each sentence s_i and for each response R_j, we used the following prompt to obtain the Yes or No answer to calculate the potential hallucination score:

```
Context: {{CONTEXT}}  Sentence: {{SENTENCE}}
Is the sentence supported by the context above? Answer Yes or No:
```

After calculating the sentence level consistency percentage for all sentences in R_1, the sentences with lower consistency levels were eliminated from the R_1, providing the opportunity to return a refined version of R_1 denoted by R'_1. These steps are showcased by steps (D) and (E) in Fig. 2. In this experimental setup, we calculated the average consistency level for the caption by considering the average of the sentence level consistencies generated at step (D) based on the refined R_1. The caption level consistency percentage was used in step (G), where the LLM uses a threshold value to determine whether the refined R_1 is hallucinated or not.

We also studied the performance of the hallucination score computations by combining permutations of different LLMs for the self-consistency checking. In any case, GPT-4o and LLaVA were used as origin for the responses $R_{1...n}$, but applying the SelfCheckGPT approach was conducted in various permutations involving GPT-4o, LLaVA, and Llama3 : GPT-4o to check GPT-4o and LLaVA generated captions, and Llama3 to check GPT-4o and LLaVA generated captions. For the original use case scenario as motivated in our introduction, in particular, the combination LLaVA to feed Llama3 is of interest as it could be executed entirely offline, i.e., with no access to a cloud back-end infrastructure, as well as the models are not proprietary in that sense that traceability concerning what model and which version is in use is possible in contrast to GPT-4o.

4   Results

We report the results based on two categories as mentioned in the Sect. 4.1 and in Sect. 4.2 considering different perspectives. Section 4.1 focuses on the concept of hallucination detection and, therefore, defines the correctness as not having non-sensical traffic agents present in the answer compared to the input image. This method identifies the hallucinated traffic agents in the LLM-generated response, but may not include details about all traffic agents in the image. However, when it comes to the automotive domain, it is adamant that we learn about all traffic agents present in the area through the perception system to make the automated decision-making process more accurate. Therefore, not overlooking the traffic agents present in the area is crucial for perception-based tasks in ADAS/AD.

Considering the importance of not overlooking traffic agents, we report results under Sect. 4.2 defining the correctness as not overlooking traffic agents in the caption compared to the input image. However, this approach does not apply to the sentence level consistency check as a single sentence may not contain information about all the objects.

We conducted some further analysis to understand the impact made by each dataset on hallucination detection and how the time of the day impacted hallucination detection. Sections 4.3 and 4.4, respectively, contain results for the two categories and the two definitions of correctness mentioned above. Table 1 shows a sequence of images taken from the PREPER CITY dataset together with sample captions to illustrate the two different definitions of correctness and the consistency check between the captions.

Table 1. Example of captions, correctness checks, and consistency checks for a sequence.

Timestamp	t_0	t_1	t_2	t_3	t_4	t_5	t_6	t_7
Images								
Manual annotation	{pedestrian}	{pedestrian}	{pedestrian}	{pedestrian}	{pedestrian}	{pedestrian}	{pedestrian}	{pedestrian}
Caption 1	There is a pedestrian	There is a pedestrian and a vehicle	There is a tree	There is a vehicle	There is a pedestrian	There is a pedestrian and a vehicle	There is a tree	There is a vehicle
Complimentary captions for check	There is a vehicle	There is a vehicle	There is a vehicle	There is a pedestrian	There is a pedestrian	There is a pedestrian and a vehicle	There is a tree	There is a vehicle
Captions consistent	✗	✗	✗	✗	✓	✓	✓	✓
Caption 1 - No hallucinations	-	✓	✗	✓	✗	✓	✗	✓	✗
Caption 1 - No overlooking	-	✓	✓	✗	✗	✓	✓	✗	✗

The rest of the tables follow these definitions and show the performance metrics recorded for the original R_1 (the image caption before applying sentence filtering) and for the fixed response R'_1 (after applying sentence and caption filtering). For this, the sentence level consistency threshold has been arbitrarily fixed as 50%. The metrics precision, recall, specificity, and F1 score help to understand the performance of the systems whereas the Matthews correlation coefficient helps to interpret more complex insights such as class imbalances and the performances of the models on minor classes. The results are recorded for both GPT-4o and Llama3 as checker LLMs considering the captions generated by LLaVA and GPT-4o as captioner LLMs.

4.1   Detecting Hallucinated Traffic Agents

The LLM-generated responses were checked against the ground truth annotations with the intention of hallucination detection as the baseline. Out of the captions generated by LLaVA and GPT-4o, 76.39% and 94.51%, respectively, were correct without any hallucinated content about the present traffic agents. These statistics are used as the baseline to evaluate the performances of the adapted methodology, which is reported in Table 2.

Table 2. Performance for hallucination detection using Llama3 and GPT-4o for the captions generated by GPT-4o and LLaVA. Caption correctness is defined as not hallucinating traffic agents. The performances are compared for the original response R_1, before filtering sentences, and for the fixed response, R_1'.

	Fixed response R_1'				Original response R_1			
Captioner LLM	LLaVA	**GPT4o**	LLaVA	**GPT4o**	LLaVA	**GPT4o**	LLaVA	**GPT4o**
Checker LLM	Llama3	**Llama3**	GPT4o	**GPT4o**	Llama3	**Llama3**	GPT4o	**GPT4o**
Precision (correct over consistent)	86.23%	**96.38%**	92.89%	**96.92%**	86.23%	**96.38%**	87.63%	**96.46%**
Recall (consistent over correct)	98.53%	**99.68%**	78.21%	**93.78%**	98.53%	**99.68%**	80.1%	**93.99%**
Specificity (flagged hallucinations)	0.0%	**0.0%**	13.85%	**2.08%**	0.0%	**0.0%**	29.86%	**8.47%**
F1 Score	91.97%	**98.0%**	84.92%	**95.32%**	91.97%	**98.0%**	83.7%	**95.21%**
Matthews Correlation Coefficient	−0.0450	**−0.0107**	−0.0478	**−0.0292**	−0.0450	**−0.0107**	0.0841	**0.0193**

4.2   Trusting Captions: Detecting Overlooked Traffic Agents

Considering the correctness based on not overlooking traffic agents, the LLaVA and GPT4o-generated captions were again checked against the ground truth annotations to use as a baseline. 75.1% of the captions in the GPT4o-generated captions were reported as correct whereas the correct percentage was 76.95% for the LLaVA-generated captions. Table 3 contains the performance metrics for the adapted methodology "Not overlooking traffic agents" that can be compared against the above correct percentages as a baseline.

4.3   Dataset Effect on Hallucination Detection

This section presents the results based on each dataset considering the two approaches to understand a dataset's impact on the hallucination detection process in perception tasks targeting ADAS and AD. Firstly, we define correct captions as those not containing any traffic agents that are not mentioned by the manual labels. Table 4 includes the performance metrics recorded for the images retrieved from the Waymo dataset following the correctness definition of "detecting Hallucinations". Table 5 includes the performance metrics recorded for the PREPER CITY dataset images.

Table 3. Performance of spotting overlooking traffic agents using Llama3 and GPT-4o in the captions generated by GPT-4o and LLaVA. Correctness is defined as not overlooking traffic agents in the captions. The performances are compared for the original response R_1, before filtering sentences, and for the fixed response R'_1.

	Fixed response R'_1				Original response R_1			
Captioner LLM	LLaVA	**GPT4o**	LLaVA	**GPT4o**	LLaVA	**GPT4o**	LLaVA	**GPT4o**
Checker LLM	Llama3	**Llama3**	GPT4o	**GPT4o**	Llama3	**Llama3**	GPT4o	**GPT4o**
Precision (correct over consistent)	72.78%	**73.59%**	72.65%	**72.72%**	72.78%	**73.59%**	72.65%	**72.72%**
Recall (consistent over correct)	99.47%	**100.0%**	87.81%	**97.71%**	98.43%	**99.75%**	78.1%	**93.82%**
Specificity (flagged hallucinations)	3.2%	**1.15%**	38.25%	**14.93%**	0.47%	**0.46%**	19.59%	**5.88%**
F1 Score	84.06%	**84.78%**	79.51%	**83.38%**	83.68%	**84.69%**	75.28%	**81.94%**
Matthews Correlation Coefficient	0.1069	**0.0919**	0.3034	**0.2423**	−0.0434	**0.0170**	−0.0249	**−0.0054**

Table 4. Performance of Hallucination detection using Llama3 and GPT-4o for the captions generated by GPT-4o and LLaVA for Waymo images. Correctness is defined as not hallucinating traffic agents. The performances are compared for the original response R_1, before filtering sentences, and for the fixed response R'_1.

Dataset: Waymo	Fixed response R'_1				Original response R_1			
Captioner LLM	LLaVA	**GPT4o**	LLaVA	**GPT4o**	LLaVA	**GPT4o**	LLaVA	**GPT4o**
Checker LLM	Llama3	**Llama3**	GPT4o	**GPT4o**	Llama3	**Llama3**	GPT4o	**GPT4o**
Precision (correct over consistent)	84.51%	**96.8%**	92.64%	**97.31%**	84.38%	**96.8%**	86.95%	**96.93%**
Recall (consistent over correct)	99.2%	**99.75%**	81.2%	**95.0%**	99.2%	**99.75%**	84.12%	**95.22%**
F1 Score	91.27%	**98.25%**	86.54%	**96.14%**	91.19%	**98.25%**	85.51%	**96.07%**
Specificity (flagged hallucinations)	0.0%	**0.0%**	10.94%	**0.0%**	0.0%	**0.0%**	31.29%	**7.69%**
Matthews Correlation Coefficient	−0.03514	**−0.00900**	−0.05107	**−0.03666**	−0.03532	**−0.0090**	0.14448	**0.02369**

Secondly, we consider captions to be correct if they do not overlook any traffic agents that appear in the manual annotations. Table 6 includes the performance metrics recorded for the Waymo images following the correctness definition of "not overlooking traffic agents".

Finally, Table 7 includes the performance metrics recorded for the images retrieved from the PREPER CITY dataset following the correctness definition of "Not overlooking traffic agents".

4.4   Time of Day Effect on Hallucination Detection

The Waymo dataset contains three different labels, 'Day', 'Dawn and dusk', and 'Night' to denote the time of the day each image was captured. These label data were extracted to categorize the hallucination detection results to understand the variations in the performance metrics in terms of the time of the day. This section includes tables that present such categorized results retrieved for Waymo images, under the definition of correctness detecting hallucinations: traffic agents in the generated captions that do not appear in the manual annotations.

Table 5. Performance of Hallucination detection using Llama3 and GPT-4o for the captions generated by GPT-4o and LLaVA for PREPER CITY images. Correctness is defined as not hallucinating traffic agents. The performances are compared for the original response R_1, before filtering sentences, and for the fixed response R_1'.

Dataset: PREPER CITY	Fixed response R_1'				Original response R_1			
Captioner LLM	LLaVA	**GPT4o**	LLaVA	**GPT4o**	LLaVA	**GPT4o**	LLaVA	**GPT4o**
Checker LLM	Llama3	**Llama3**	GPT4o	**GPT4o**	Llama3	**Llama3**	GPT4o	**GPT4o**
Precision (correct over consistent)	87.78%	**95.95%**	93.14%	**96.51%**	87.65%	**95.95%**	88.28%	**95.97%**
Recall (consistent over correct)	97.95%	**99.62%**	75.53%	**92.53%**	98.22%	**99.62%**	76.62%	**92.73%**
F1 Score	92.59%	**97.75%**	83.42%	**94.47%**	92.64%	**97.75%**	82.04%	**94.32%**
Specificity (flagged hallucinations)	0.0%	**0.0%**	16.67%	**3.7%**	1.94%	**0.0%**	28.24%	**9.09%**
Matthews Correlation Coefficient	−0.0500	**−0.0124**	−0.0442	**−0.0260**	0.0039	**−0.0124**	0.0375	**0.0138**

Table 6. Performance of spotting overlooking traffic agents using Llama3 and GPT-4o in the captions generated by GPT-4o and LLaVA using Waymo images. Correctness is defined as not overlooking traffic agents in the captions. The performances are compared for the original response R_1, before filtering sentences, and for the fixed response R_1'.

Dataset: Waymo	Fixed response R_1'				Original response R_1			
Captioner LLM	LLaVA	**GPT4o**	LLaVA	**GPT4o**	LLaVA	**GPT4o**	LLaVA	**GPT4o**
Checker LLM	Llama3	**Llama3**	GPT4o	**GPT4o**	Llama3	**Llama3**	GPT4o	**GPT4o**
Precision (correct over consistent)	71.47%	**71.83%**	68.6%	**68.37%**	71.47%	**71.83%**	68.6%	**68.37%**
Recall (consistent over correct)	99.62%	**100.0%**	88.5%	**96.74%**	99.06%	**99.66%**	79.73%	**93.85%**
F1 Score	83.23%	**83.61%**	77.29%	**80.12%**	83.03%	**83.49%**	73.75%	**79.11%**
Specificity (flagged hallucinations)	1.41%	**0.87%**	29.97%	**8.18%**	0.0%	**0.0%**	13.52%	**1.98%**
Matthews Correlation Coefficient	0.05692	**0.07886**	0.2303	**0.1072**	−0.0518	**−0.0310**	−0.0797	**−0.0892**

Table 7. Performance of spotting overlooking traffic agents using Llama3 and GPT-4o in the captions generated by GPT-4o and LLaVA using PREPER CITY images. Correctness is defined as not overlooking traffic agents in the captions. The performances are compared for the original response R_1, before filtering sentences, and for the fixed response R_1'.

Dataset: PREPER CITY	Fixed response R_1'				Original response R_1			
Captioner LLM	LLaVA	**GPT4o**	LLaVA	**GPT4o**	LLaVA	**GPT4o**	LLaVA	**GPT4o**
Checker LLM	Llama3	**Llama3**	GPT4o	**GPT4o**	Llama3	**Llama3**	GPT4o	**GPT4o**
Precision (correct over consistent)	73.96%	**75.34%**	76.56%	**77.28%**	73.96%	**75.34%**	76.56%	**77.28%**
Recall (consistent over correct)	99.34%	**100.0%**	87.22%	**98.63%**	97.9%	**99.84%**	76.75%	**93.8%**
F1 Score	84.79%	**85.93%**	1.54%	**86.66%**	84.26%	**85.87%**	76.65%	**84.75%**
Specificity (flagged hallucinations)	4.91%	**1.47%**	46.44%	**23.18%**	0.93%	**0.99%**	26.27%	**11.05%**
Matthews Correlation Coefficient	0.1418	**0.1052**	0.3713	**0.3728**	−0.0386	**0.0587**	0.0303	**0.0790**

Table 8 showcases the performances of hallucination detection when the captions are generated only for the images captured during daytime. Table 9 showcases the performances of hallucination detection when the captions are generated for the Waymo images captured during dawn and dusk. Finally, Table 10 showcases the performances of hallucination detection when the captions are generated for the Waymo images captured during nighttime.

Table 8. Performance of hallucination detection using Llama3 and GPT-4o for the captions generated by GPT-4o and LLaVA for Waymo images captured during the daytime. Correctness is defined as not hallucinating traffic agents. The performances are compared for the original response R_1, before filtering sentences, and for R_1'.

Dataset: Waymo	Fixed response R_1'				Original response R_1			
Captioner LLM	LLaVA	GPT4o	LLaVA	GPT4o	LLaVA	GPT4o	LLaVA	GPT4o
Checker LLM	Llama3	Llama3	GPT4o	GPT4o	Llama3	Llama3	GPT4o	GPT4o
Precision (correct over consistent)	81.74%	**93.24%**	91.26%	**93.95%**	81.45%	**93.24%**	83.29%	**93.37%**
Recall (consistent over correct)	99.65%	**99.71%**	84.93%	**95.88%**	99.65%	**99.71%**	88.28%	**96.43%**
F1 Score	89.81%	**96.37%**	87.98%	**94.91%**	89.63%	**96.37%**	85.71%	**94.88%**
Specificity (flagged hallucinations)	0.0%	**0.0%**	8.11%	**0.0%**	0.0%	**0.0%**	26.14%	**8.0%**
Matthews Correlation Coefficient	−0.0254	**−0.0139**	−0.0540	**−0.0499**	−0.0256	**−0.0139**	0.1617	**0.0582**

Table 9. Performance of hallucination detection using Llama3 and GPT-4o for the captions generated by GPT-4o and LLaVA for Waymo images captured during dawn and dusk. Correctness is defined as not hallucinating traffic agents. Performances are compared for the original response R_1, before filtering sentences, and for R_1'.

Dataset: Waymo	Fixed response R_1'				Original response R_1			
Captioner LLM	LLaVA	GPT4o	LLaVA	GPT4o	LLaVA	GPT4o	LLaVA	GPT4o
Checker LLM	Llama3	Llama3	GPT4o	GPT4o	Llama3	Llama3	GPT4o	GPT4o
Precision (correct over consistent)	86.38%	**99.64%**	95.08%	**100.0%**	86.38%	**99.64%**	90.53%	**99.68%**
Recall (consistent over correct)	99.11%	**100.0%**	79.68%	**97.21%**	99.11%	**100.0%**	82.13%	**97.2%**
F1 Score	92.31%	**99.82%**	86.7%	**98.59%**	92.31%	**99.82%**	86.13%	**98.43%**
Specificity (flagged hallucinations)	0.0%	**0.0%**	23.53%	**0.0%**	0.0%	**0.0%**	39.02%	**0.0%**
Matthews Correlation Coefficient	−0.0348	**0.0**	0.0175	**0.0**	−0.0348	**0.0**	0.1724	**−0.0094**

On the other hand, caption correctness can also be defined as not overlooking any traffic agents, as this is critical for safety in the automotive domain. The performance metrics values for other times of the day following this definition of correctness are included in the supplementary materials and discussed in Sect. 5.

Table 10. Performance of hallucination detection using Llama3 and GPT-4o for the captions generated by GPT-4o and LLaVA for Waymo images captured during night time. Correctness is defined as not hallucinating traffic agents. The performances are compared for the original response R_1, before filtering sentences, and for R_1'.

Dataset: Waymo	Fixed response R_1'				Original response R_1			
Captioner LLM	LLaVA	GPT4o	LLaVA	GPT4o	LLaVA	GPT4o	LLaVA	GPT4o
Checker LLM	Llama3	**Llama3**	GPT4o	**GPT4o**	Llama3	**Llama3**	GPT4o	GPT4o
Precision (correct over consistent)	88.06%	**100.0%**	91.74%	**100.0%**	88.06%	**100.0%**	90.91%	**100.0%**
Recall (consistent over correct)	98.33%	**99.41%**	74.0%	**87.59%**	98.33%	**99.41%**	77.46%	**87.59%**
F1 Score	92.91%	**99.71%**	81.92%	**93.39%**	92.91%	**99.71%**	83.65%	**93.39%**
Specificity (flagged hallucinations)	0.0%	**0.0%**	0.0%	**0%**	0.0%	**0.0%**	38.89%	**0%**
Matthews Correlation Coefficient	−0.0446	**0.0**	−0.1465	**0.0**	−0.0446	**0.0**	0.1203	**0.0**

5 Analysis and Discussion

The analysis of the LLM-generated responses revealed that LLaVA and GPT-4o are capable of generating captions consistent with the ground truth labels. Therefore, the application and adaptation of a hallucination detection technique such as SelfCheckGPT was expected to be effective in filtering out errors by the LLM that would be critical in perception-related tasks in the automotive domain. The performance matrices in Tables 2 and 3 show that the SelfCheckGPT-like filtering process is slightly more effective for GPT4o-generated captions than for LLaVA ones. The performance of this filtering process is however quite varied across the captioner- and checker-LLMs at the sentence level.

In general, the higher recall and precision values recorded for Llama3 under the hallucination detection definition indicate that this checker LLM model is better at correctly identifying non-hallucinated content. GPT-4o reports lower recall values for LLaVA-generated captions, indicating that some non-hallucinated content generated by LLaVA may have been flagged incorrectly as hallucinations. This behavior is not impacted by the sentence-level filtering process, which was introduced to reduce incorrectly flagged sentences from the captions resulting in increasing the trustworthiness of the final caption. Also, the same analysis applies to the performances reported in Table 3 following the definition of correction of not overlooking traffic agents. However, the precision for the "not overlooking traffic agents" approach is lower, indicating that the proposed methodology is better at identifying and detecting non-hallucinated content at the expense of missing hallucinations. Hence, the SelfCheckGPT approach and its adaptation can be applied to filter out hallucinations using state-of-the-art LLMs for image captioning tasks for automotive usage scenarios, yet it comes with a price of missing some hallucinations.

The second research question (RQ2) is concerned with the performance differences of SelfCheckGPT and its adaptations based on the two state-of-the-art datasets, given the different traffic scenarios and geographical areas they cover. However, significant deviations were not visible within the recorded results indicating that the main differences in Waymo and PREPER CITY do not pose any impact on the hallucination detection.

The results generated for the Waymo dataset were analyzed separately to answer the third research question (RQ3). The main motivation was to identify to what extent the performance of SelfCheckGPT and its adaptations are affected by light conditions. Based on the recorded results, the daytime captured images show better results compared to dawn and dusk or nighttime captured images. The higher performance matrices are recorded for daytime captured images for both correctness definitions.

We used the study by Feldt and Magazinius (2010) [9] to assess potential threats to the validity of our study. We heuristically designed a specific prompt that aligns with the operational setup of our experiment by restricting the LLMs from generating lengthier sentences. This bears potentially the risk of missing out on an LLM's preferred or more likely way of describing a traffic situation and hence, potentially penalizing an LLM for not spotting a traffic agent even though its synonyms may have spotted them. However, as prompts are still very difficult to systematize, variants may have been more successful. In addition to that, the use of annotations to normalize the distribution of traffic scenarios may not consider the difficulty level, i.e., partially occluded traffic agents for example. Here, we may have unknowingly favored one dataset over the other. Furthermore, as highlighted in the experimental design, vehicles dominate the captured traffic scenarios. This bears potentially the risk that more vulnerable road users such as pedestrians and cyclists are insufficiently represented in the experimental sample. Hence, the performance of the adopted SelfCheckGPT approach may vary if a dataset contains many more traffic scenarios with such vulnerable road users. The use of GPT-4o was considered an industrial gold standard. However, at the same time, this LLM is proprietary and hence, may have undergone unnoticed and non-controllable updates during or after our experimentation. This would potentially affect the robustness of our findings. Furthermore, we had no control over the manual annotations of the objects in the Waymo dataset as we directly used the labels provided by the dataset creators, given that some scenarios with inaccurate labels were identified while randomly checking image samples.

6   Conclusion and Future Work

We have adopted SelfCheckGPT for an automotive application scenario that is relevant for improving perception stacks for ADAS and AD when they may incorporate LLMs or more specific Foundational Models (FMs). We have compared the performance of SelfCheckGPT and its adaptation to spot potential hallucinations and filter them out from the generated description of the vehicle surroundings. This experimental setup was designed and evaluated using the proprietary, cloud-based LLM GPT-4o, and an offline open-source LLM LLaVA. Both LLMs show exemplary performances on image description tasks when prompted thoroughly. We found that GPT-4o was lenient in finding mismatches with many of the captions demonstrating a tendency to flag more captions as hallucinated, which did improve the overall hallucination detection process, but at a large expense of mislabelling non-hallucinated content. The trade-off between precision and recall should be researched further to fine-tune the proposed methodology by reducing the occurrence of mislabelling. Overall, the SelfCheckGPT setup and its adaptation with sentence level filtering improved the overall performance, however the improvement was marginal.

As highlighted in the previous section, thorough attention needs to be given to vulnerable road users such as pedestrians or cyclists. Similarly, it is very important to reduce the amount of overlooked traffic participants in a given usage scenario, which helps in mitigating the risk of potential collisions. Hence, future studies should focus thereon to identifying specifically challenging scenarios for the SelfCheckGPT approach to improve its potential suitability for automotive perception systems.

Acknowledgments. This work has been supported by the Swedish Foundation for Strategic Research (SSF), Grant Number FUS21-0004 SAICOM and the Wallenberg AI, Autonomous Systems and Software Program (WASP) funded by the Knut and Alice Wallenberg Foundation. This research has been partially supported by the Swedish Research Council (Diarienummer: 2024–2028).

References

1. BMW intelligent personal assistant powered by the Alexa large language model (LLM) (2024). https://tinyurl.com/BMWweb. Accessed 26 Feb 2024
2. Hello GPT-4o (2024). https://openai.com/index/hello-gpt-4o/. Accessed 15 May 2024
3. Brown, T., et al.: Language models are few-shot learners. In: Larochelle, H., Ranzato, M., Hadsell, R., Balcan, M., Lin, H. (eds.) Advances in Neural Information Processing Systems, vol. 33, pp. 1877–1901. Curran Associates, Inc. (2020). https://proceedings.neurips.cc/paper_files/paper/2020/file/1457c0d6bfcb4967418bfb8ac142f64a-Paper.pdf
4. Chen, X., et al.: Unified hallucination detection for multimodal large language models. arXiv preprint: arXiv:2402.03190 (2024)
5. Cole, J.R., Zhang, M.J., Gillick, D., Eisenschlos, J.M., Dhingra, B., Eisenstein, J.: Selectively answering ambiguous questions. arXiv preprint: arXiv:2305.14613 (2023)
6. Deng, A., Chen, Z., Hooi, B.: Seeing is believing: mitigating hallucination in large vision-language models via clip-guided decoding. arXiv:2402.15300 (2024)
7. Elaraby, M., Lu, M., Dunn, J., Zhang, X., Wang, Y., Liu, S.: Halo: estimation and reduction of hallucinations in open-source weak large language models. arXiv preprint: arXiv:2308.11764 (2023)
8. Es, S., James, J., Espinosa-Anke, L., Schockaert, S.: RAGAS: automated evaluation of retrieval augmented generation. arXiv preprint: arXiv:2309.15217 (2023)
9. Feldt, R., Magazinius, A.: Validity threats in empirical software engineering research - an initial survey, pp. 374–379 (2010)
10. Guan, X., et al.: Mitigating large language model hallucinations via autonomous knowledge graph-based retrofitting. In: Proceedings of the AAAI Conference on Artificial Intelligence, vol. 38, pp. 18126–18134 (2024)
11. Guo, Z., et al.: Evaluating large language models: a comprehensive survey (2023). https://arxiv.org/abs/2310.19736

12. Hartvigsen, T., Sankaranarayanan, S., Palangi, H., Kim, Y., Ghassemi, M.: Aging with grace: lifelong model editing with discrete key-value adaptors. In: Advances in Neural Information Processing Systems, vol. 36 (2024)
13. Huang, L., et al.: A survey on hallucination in large language models: principles, taxonomy, challenges, and open questions (2023)
14. Ji, Z., Yu, T., Xu, Y., Lee, N., Ishii, E., Fung, P.: Towards mitigating LLM hallucination via self reflection. In: Findings of the Association for Computational Linguistics: EMNLP 2023, pp. 1827–1843 (2023)
15. Lebret, R., Grangier, D., Auli, M.: Neural text generation from structured data with application to the biography domain (2016). https://arxiv.org/abs/1603.07771
16. Liu, H., Li, C., Wu, Q., Lee, Y.J.: Visual instruction tuning. In: Oh, A., Naumann, T., Globerson, A., Saenko, K., Hardt, M., Levine, S. (eds.) Advances in Neural Information Processing Systems, vol. 36, pp. 34892–34916. Curran Associates, Inc. (2023). https://proceedings.neurips.cc/paper_files/paper/2023/file/6dcf277ea32ce3288914faf369fe6de0-Paper-Conference.pdf
17. Manakul, P., Liusie, A., Gales, M.J.: SELFCHECKGPT: zero-resource black-box hallucination detection for generative large language models. arXiv:2303.08896 (2023)
18. Ronanki, K., Cabrero-Daniel, B., Berger, C.: Chatgpt as a tool for user story quality evaluation: trustworthy out of the box? In: International Conference on Agile Software Development, pp. 173–181. Springer (2022)
19. Rony, M.R.A.H., et al.: CarExpert: leveraging large language models for in-car conversational question answering (2023)
20. Sun, G., et al.: CrossCheckGPT: universal hallucination ranking for multimodal foundation models. arXiv preprint: arXiv:2405.13684 (2024)
21. Sun, P., et al.: Scalability in perception for autonomous driving: Waymo open dataset. In: Proceedings of the IEEE/CVF Conference on Computer Vision and Pattern Recognition (CVPR) (2020)
22. Tonmoy, S.M.T.I., et al.: A comprehensive survey of hallucination mitigation techniques in large language models (2024). https://arxiv.org/abs/2401.01313
23. Wang, S., et al.: Large language models for education: a survey and outlook. arXiv:2403.18105 (2024)
24. Wu, J., et al.: Logical closed loop: uncovering object hallucinations in large vision-language models. arXiv preprint: arXiv:2402.11622 (2024)
25. Yu, W., Zhang, Z., Liang, Z., Jiang, M., Sabharwal, A.: Improving language models via plug-and-play retrieval feedback. arXiv preprint: arXiv:2305.14002 (2023)
26. Yu, Y., Scheidegger, S., Bakker, J.: Safety-driven data labelling platform to enable safe and responsible AI (2021). https://trid.trb.org/View/1948943

Enhanced Graph Neural Networks for Vulnerability Detection in Java via Advanced Subgraph Construction

Rosmaël Zidane Lekeufack Foulefack$^{(\boxtimes)}$ and Alessandro Marchetto

University of Trento, Trento, Italy
{rz.lekeufack,alessandro.marchetto}@unitn.it

Abstract. Software vulnerability detection (SVD) in source code remains a significant challenge, capturing the attention of researchers due to its critical importance. Numerous automated detection techniques have emerged, leveraging deep learning and large language models. Graph Neural Network models have been used for SVD and have shown promising results. However, graph-based models often struggle to capture long-term dependencies within code snippets due to simplistic hop neighborhood encoding.

This study explores the potential of enhancing graph neural networks by capturing both local and global complex code structures through node and edge embeddings. By generating contextualised embeddings using Node2vec model, we aim to enrich the model's understanding of source code through an advanced subgraph construction. Our results demonstrate an improvement in the detection capabilities of graph neural networks for identifying vulnerabilities at the statement level in Java source code. Specifically, the proposed approach has achieved a detection precision of up to 82.08% (i.e., improvement of 11.33%), enhancing the model's noise robustness and detection capability.

Keywords: Vulnebility detection · Deep learning · Graph neural Networks · Java Source code · Embedding

1 Introduction

Testing software before its release is a crucial step in the development process, despite being time-consuming and requesting expert knowledge. Testing, which became more demanding while moving from small to large code-based projects, aims to identify and evaluate potential vulnerabilities, thereby reducing the risk of attacks from malicious agents [6]. Automated software testing methodologies are broadly categorised into two types: the traditional approach known as static and dynamic analysis, and the data-driving one. Conventional analysis, which relies on predefined rules, often suffers from a high rate of false positive alarms; consequently motivating researchers to dedicate their focus to data-driving solutions.

© IFIP International Federation for Information Processing 2025
Published by Springer Nature Switzerland AG 2025
H. D. Menéndez et al. (Eds.): ICTSS 2024, LNCS 15383, pp. 131–148, 2025.
https://doi.org/10.1007/978-3-031-80889-0_9

Data-driving solutions, which leverage data mining solutions to predict the presence of vulnerability [8], involve the use of techniques such as deep learning and machine learning. This approach primarily requires training a classifier using a training data sample and using the trained component to classify unseen samples as either vulnerable or benign. It can be categorised into two main classes based on the type of learning algorithm used: (1) sequence-based, which transforms programming data such as source code into a sequence of vectors; and (2) graph-based, which applies graph theory and machine learning techniques to comprehend source code efficiently [22].

A sequence-based model leverages learning algorithms such as recurrent neural networks, transformers, and long-short-term memory (LSTM). For instance, Fu et al. [5] proposed LineVul, a sequential-based model using a transformer architecture for detecting vulnerable functions and statements within a C/C++ code snippet. These models do not require parsing the source code, which might not be well written or wrongly handled during the pre-processing step, thus making them non-compilable and leading the proposed architecture to learn from the wrong code syntax.

On the other hand, Graph-based learning algorithms consider converting source code into graph representations by extracting properties such as Abstract Syntax Tree (AST), Control Flow Graph (CFG), Program Dependency Graph (PDG), Code Property Graph (CPG), and more. The graph is then created with nodes representing programming elements such as functions, variables, or statements, and edges showing the relationships between these elements like control flow or data dependencies [12,20]. Graph-based model leverages suitable deep learning for graph data, such as graph neural networks (GNN), graph convolutional neural networks, and graph attention networks (GAN). They have proven to be effective in vulnerability detection, considering code semantics and syntactic [21,22]. David et al. [9] introduced LineVD, a novel deep-learning model for software vulnerability detection at the statement level. This model frames the detection problem as a node classification task and uses Control Dependence Graphs (CDG) and Programme Dependence Graphs (PDG) to build training features. It improves the F1 score compared to the state-of-the-art IVdetect [13] on Bigvul dataset [3]. Whilst FUNDED [21] utilises GNNs to represent programme source code as graphs, capturing control, data, and call dependencies for function-level granularity detection.

Despite considerable advancements in the literature for sequential and graph-based models, most proposed solutions are still limited in predicting vulnerabilities at various source data granularity levels, such as file, function, slice, and rarely at the statement level. Additionally, proposed software vulnerability detection (SVD) mostly applied to the C/C++ datasets [15,16], thus hampering their adoption with data from other programming languages.

This research addresses these limitations by focusing on statement-level vulnerability detection in Java source code and enhancing model robustness through an advanced subgraph construction process. Unlike existing approaches that leverage neighbourhood relationships through one- or two-hop encoding, this study explores capturing more complex relationships within subgraphs by embedding nodes and edges, applying random walks using Node2vec. This method aims to improve the representation of long-term code dependencies within subgraphs, thereby enriching the GNN learning process with contextualized embeddings. In summary, this study makes the following contributions:

- This study adapts an existing graph-based vulnerability detection model, LineVD, initially designed for C/C++ source code, for use with Java. The adapted model demonstrates significant vulnerability detection capabilities in Java, achieving a detection precision of 70.75%, comparable to its performance with C/C++.
- Furthermore, this study introduces an advanced subgraph construction methodology that captures both local and global neighbourhood information through contextualized embeddings generated by Node2vec[1] model. This enriched approach enhances the model's understanding of vulnerability-related code structure, improving detection precision by approximately 11%.
- Our investigation also reveals that focusing solely on either local (closest) or global neighbourhoods does not significantly enhance the learning algorithm's capabilities. Instead, an optimal balance between local and global neighbourhood embedding information maintains and even enhances the model's effectiveness in detecting vulnerabilities in source code, improving the model's robustness to noise.

The rest of the paper is organized as follows: Sect. 2 presents key concepts in graph neural networks, Sect. 3 details the methodology process, and Sect. 4 describes the experimental setup. Subsequently, Sect. 5 presents the obtained results, Sect. 6 reviews related work and the paper concludes with Sect. 7, which outlines potential future investigations.

2   Background

2.1   Source Code Embedding

Representing text-related sources of information in an understandable format for a learning algorithm is a crucial step in the deep neural networks (DNN) training cycle. This process involves converting the text into numerical variables that the learning algorithm can process directly. Starting with tokenization, which involves breaking a text sequence into smaller units known as tokens, several embedding approaches exist. These approaches provide embeddings from a given corpus at different levels, such as words, sentences, or documents.

For source code, several software vulnerability detection approaches have utilized embedding techniques such as GloVe[2], Doc2vec[3], Word2vec[4], CodeBERT[5]

---

[1] https://snap.stanford.edu/node2vec.
[2] https://stanford.edu/projects/glove/.
[3] https://github.com/jhlau/doc2vec.
[4] https://code.google.com/archive/p/word2vec/.
[5] https://github.com/microsoft/CodeBERT.

to generate pre-trained vectors for individual tokens. For example, [21] used Word2Vec for source code embedding, while [13] employed GloVe. [9,17] experimented with different embedding tools and the reported results proved that model performance also depends on the embedding method used, highlighting the variation in model effectiveness.

Despite producing embedding at different levels, these methods differ significantly in the type of embedding they produce. Techniques like Word2vec, GloVe, and FastText[6] generate static embedding (i.e. embed the same word into the same vector, no matter the context), whereas CodeBERT and Doc2vec produce contextual embedding. In contextualised embedding from models like BERT and GPT[7], tokens are differently represented based on the surrounding context. Therefore, we utilized the CodeBERT model to extract features for our study (see Fig. 1(c)). However, these approaches are mostly based on the linear structure of the text (i.e., consider the text as a linear sequence) and do not account for the nonlinear structure of code, as methods like Node2vec recently proposed for graph-based architecture. Node2vec generates contextualised embedding that captures complex relationships with its neighbours, potentially enhancing the learning algorithm's understanding of the source feature's topological structure.

2.2 Graph Neural Networks

Different from sequence-based models that consider source code only as text, graph neural networks have shown promising performance at mining graph data from several code-related tasks, including code clone detection [11] and source code classification [5,13], while considering complex semantic and syntactic code structures. To this end, source code is parsed to extract code property graphs (i.e., a data structure designed to analyse large codebases[8]) to build the graph data, in which nodes could represent functions or lines, while edges represent programme dependence. The graph representation $G = (v, \varepsilon)$, where v is the set of nodes and ε is the set of edges, allowing easy source code manipulation. The embedding code text is added to the graph as nodes and edges features, allowing a GNN model to learn latent relationships within the source data.

Figure 1 presents a piece of code (a) and its corresponding graph (b) extracted and constructed using DGL[9] and NetworkX[10] libraries, where nodes represent the code lines from the code snippet. An embedded function (CodeBERT output) is added to the graph as one of the node features (c).

---

[6] https://github.com/benathi/multisense-prob-fasttext.
[7] https://github.com/Muennighoff/sgpt.
[8] https://docs.joern.io/code-property-graph/.
[9] https://docs.dgl.ai/.
[10] https://networkx.org/.

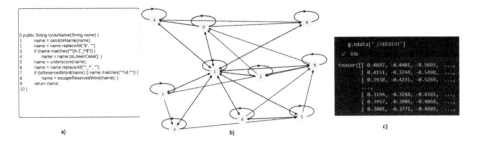

Fig. 1. Representation of Code Snippet as a Graph: (a) Original code snippet, (b) Graph representation with nodes representing lines of code, (c) Contextual embedding

3 Methodology

In this study, we address the challenge of identifying vulnerabilities in Java source code. Our methodology involves converting a state-of-the-art model originally designed for C/C++ programming languages to be applicable for detecting vulnerabilities in Java code, and improve it. Specifically, we chose LineVD since it has achieved promising performance for C/C++ in predicting vulnerabilities at the line-level granularity, which isn't the same as other approaches that mostly proposed functional-level prediction. This conversion is crucial since existing DNN detection algorithms are often tailored specifically for C/C++ and do not effectively generalize to other programming languages such as Java.

3.1 Problem Description

Following LineVD [9] problem's description, in this work, the problem of identifying vulnerable statements in a Java function is formulated as a binary node classification problem. Considering a data $(V_i, Y_i)|V_i \in v, Y_i \in \{0,1\}$ where V_i and Y_i represent respectively the set of statements and corresponding label, where 0 represents the non-vulnerable statement while 1 is the vulnerable one. $i = (1, 2, 3, \ldots, n)$, where n is the number of nodes in the dataset. The learning algorithm can then be summarized as a mapping function f of the statement V_i to a label Y_i:

$$f : V \longrightarrow Y \tag{1}$$

where V is the set of node and $Y = \{0, 1\}$ the set of labels. The learning process of f consists of minimizing the cross entropy (C) loss function:

$$min \sum_{i=1}^{n} C(f(G_i, Y_i|V_i)) \tag{2}$$

where G is a graph.

3.2   Approach

The LineVD methodology for C/C++ vulnerability detection consists of three main components: feature extraction, graph construction and the classifier. We first adopted the LineVD methodology, by applying it to Java code (instead of C/C++ like the original one). Subsequently, we enhanced the graph construction process by incorporating node embedding from Node2vec, aiming to capture the local and global topological structure of the source code graph. Figure 2 presents the proposed architecture.

Feature Extraction: Generating a detailed and comprehensive representation of source code is crucial for effectively building subsequent models. LineVD is a method specifically designed to extract code features, leveraging a transformer-based approach. This is considered an effective strategy for source code-related tasks, particularly when employing self-supervised learning objectives. It takes a single function as raw input. The method first tokenises each individual statement V_i within the given function using the pre-trained Byte-Pair Encoding (BPE) tokeniser from CodeBERT. After collecting the set of statements $V = \{V_1, V_2, ..., V_n\}$, the entire function and its constituent statements are then passed through the CodeBERT model to obtain contextualized embedding. CodeBERT is a pre-trained transformer model specifically designed for programming languages, which leverages a large corpus of code and natural language pairs to generate high-quality embedding for code understanding, natural language code search and code documentation generation tasks [4].

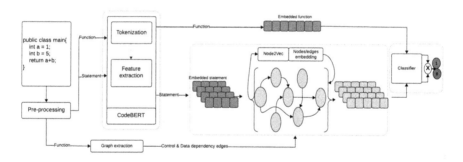

Fig. 2. Graph-based Java vulnerability detection approach overview

In order to effectively process Java functions, we implemented several key modifications to the feature extraction process, such as migrating the extraction process from C/C++ source code to Java. These changes were necessary to ensure we could properly extract the relevant code features and representations. This refined approach allowed us to more accurately and comprehensively capture the important characteristics of the Java functions for further analysis.

Graph Construction: Based on the methodology described in [9], the graph construction process focuses on data and control dependency information, utilising a Graph Attention Networks (GAT) model. The GNN-based model architecture leverages information diffusion mechanisms to learn from graph-structured data, unlike traditional models that rely on a single flat vector representation of source data. That enables the model to update node states according to graph connectivity, thereby preserving crucial information. To this end, Joern[11] program [23] (version 2.0.331) is used to extract comprehensive graph information from source code, including nodes and edges related to data and control dependencies. It is designed for robust analysis of source code, bytecode, and binary code by generating code property graphs (CPGs). These CPGs provide a detailed and unified representation of the code, facilitating advanced cross-language code analysis, vulnerability detection, and other static analysis tasks. Joern's capability to handle different programming languages and code formats makes it an essential tool for thorough and scalable code analysis [23].

Additionally, we introduce the novel use of Node2vec [7] in our graph construction process. Node2vec is a model designed to generate contextualized node embeddings by simulating random walks on the graph, effectively capturing the local and global topological structure of the graph (snippet code). By embedding nodes and edge features in the graph, we enrich each subgraph with detailed information about its neighboring nodes and edge relationships. This integration significantly enhances a GNN model's robustness to noise and missing edges, improving its ability to accurately detect vulnerabilities in the source code. The enriched subgraphs provide a more comprehensive representation of the source code, enabling the learning algorithm to learn more effectively from the structural nuances of the code.

This comprehensive graph construction and embedding process ensures that the GNN-based model captures the intricate dependencies within the source code, leading to more accurate and reliable analysis.

Classifier: We apply LineDV's classification methodology that provides both function and statement-level prediction using a multi-layer perceptron (MLP). The detection process assumes an equal contribution from function-level and statement-level code snippets to the prediction outcomes. This involves constructing a shared architecture that consists of linear and dropout layers that process function-level embeddings from CodeBERT and statement embeddings from the GAT layer.

The Classifier maintains prediction consistency through wise-element multiplication of the statement and function-level output classes, which can be either one or zero, respectively, for non-vulnerable and vulnerable. This mechanism ensures that a vulnerable statement can influence the function's vulnerability status while leveraging function-level information for training. The operation subsequently balances conflicting outputs between function-level and statement-level embeddings, ensuring that if the function-level output class is zero, all statement-level outputs are also zero since a non-vulnerable function cannot contain a vulnerable statement.

---

[11] https://docs.joern.io/.

4   Experimental Setup

This section provides an overview of the experimental setup, detailing the key components related to the dataset and the evaluation process. We describe the dataset used for training and testing, outline the evaluation metrics with respect to research questions, and discuss the procedures implemented to assess the performance and effectiveness of our methodology.

4.1   Datasets

With the first objective of highlighting vulnerabilities in Java source code, the SVD tool presented in this study employs the ProjectKB dataset [19]. ProjectKB is a vulnerability database that compiles a set of security-relevant commits, which are extracted and manually curated from real-world Java software and GitHub. The dataset provides comprehensive information, including the vulnerable code, the type of vulnerabilities (categorized according to the National Vulnerability Database – NVD – and Common Vulnerabilities and Exposures – CVE), and the corresponding fixed code.

The dataset consists of the following:

- **Java Files:** A total of 3770 Java files, containing over 1.3 million lines of code before vulnerability fixes and 1.4 million lines of code after fixes, including statements and comments.
- **Java Functions:** The dataset includes 20.155 Java functions, of which 12% are labeled as vulnerable. These vulnerable functions contain at least one statement related to one of the 496 CVEs, spanning 64 different Common Weakness Enumerations (CWEs).

4.2   Data Preparation

We extracted a sample of 19784 functions (before and after), with a subset of 2433 functions labelled as vulnerable and the remainder as non-vulnerable. The preprocessing steps involved several critical steps to ensure the integrity and quality of the data. First, comments were removed from the code to eliminate non-executable elements that could negatively impact the analysis. Subsequently, missing data was appropriately handled to prevent gaps that could affect model training and evaluation. Due to the non-compilable status of certain functions, a minor number of functions were lost as they could not be processed by the graph extractor.

Given that the data is labelled at the function level, we derived the ground-truth labels for vulnerable and non-vulnerable lines by adhering to established assertions in the literature [9]. Specifically, (i) lines removed in a vulnerability-fixing commit are considered indicators of vulnerability, and (ii) all lines that are control or data dependent on the added lines are also labelled as vulnerable.

The dataset is then divided into three distinct subsets to facilitate robust deep learning model development and evaluation. Specifically, 80% of the data was allocated to the training set, 10% to the validation set, and the remaining 10% to the testing set. This stratified division guarantees that the model has enough data to learn from during training while supplying independent datasets for validation and testing, allowing reliable assessment of the model's performance and generalisation capabilities.

This rigorous pre-processing and data partitioning are essential for constructing accurate models capable of classifying vulnerable and non-vulnerable code, hence contributing to the progress of automated SVD approaches in Java.

4.3   Evaluation Methodology

In accordance with the literature, we report several classification performance metrics, including accuracy, F1-score, precision, AUROC (Area Under the Receiver Operating Characteristic Curve), and the Matthews Correlation Coefficient (MCC) for our binary classification task. These metrics provide a comprehensive evaluation of the proposed framework's ability to differentiate between vulnerable and non-vulnerable code.

- Accuracy measures the overall correctness of the model, indicating how well it distinguishes between vulnerable and non-vulnerable snippet codes.

$$Accuracy = \frac{TP + TN}{TP + TN + FP + FN} \tag{3}$$

- F1-score is the harmonic mean of precision and recall, offering a balanced measure between precision and recall.

$$F1_{Score} = \frac{2TP}{2TP + FP + FN} \tag{4}$$

- Precision is the ratio of correctly predicted positive observations to the total predicted positives, reflecting the correctness of positive predictions.

$$Precision = \frac{TP}{TP + FP} \tag{5}$$

- AUROC evaluates the model's ability to discriminate between positive and negative classes across all possible threshold values, providing insight into the model's discriminatory power.
- MCC is a correlation coefficient that considers true and false positives and negatives, offering a balanced evaluation even in the presence of class imbalance.

$$MCC = \frac{(TP * TN - FP * FN)}{\sqrt{(TP + FP)(TP + FN)(TN + FP)(TN + FN)}}. \tag{6}$$

- Recall, also known as the true positive rate, measures the percentage of data samples correctly identified.

$$Recall = \frac{TP}{TP + FN} \tag{7}$$

Where True Positives (TP) represent the number of statements correctly classified as vulnerable, while True Negatives (TN) denote the number of statements accurately identified as non-vulnerable. False Positives (FP) refer to the number of statements incorrectly classified as vulnerable when they are actually non-vulnerable, and False Negatives (FN) indicate statements incorrectly classified as non-vulnerable when they are, in fact, vulnerable. The statement-level predictions used to compute these metrics for performance evaluation are derived through an element-wise multiplication of function-level predictions and the corresponding line-level predictions, ensuring that a non-vulnerable function cannot contain a vulnerable line.

Traditional accuracy can be misleading when dealing with imbalanced datasets like ProjectBK, as it may be disproportionately high due to the model's effectiveness in predicting the majority class while failing to accurately predict the minority class, i.e., the vulnerable class, which is the most important in our case. The other metrics above (F1-score, MCC, AUROC, and precision) provide more nuanced insights [1].

Further metrics such as N@5, MRR, and MFR are also considered to assess the model's effectiveness. N@5 measures the proportion of cases where the correct item is ranked within the top 5 predictions. While MRR is the average of the reciprocal ranks of the correct answers in a list of ranked predictions, MFR is the average rank at which the first relevant item appears in the ranked list.

4.4   Research Question

We seek to investigate the impact of capturing contextualized node and edge relationships to enhance the subgraph construction process, with the goal of improving the performance of GNN in detecting statement-level vulnerabilities within Java source code. This study addresses the following research questions, utilizing the evaluation metrics outlined in Sect. 4.3.

RQ1: *How effectively does the converted LineVD model perform in detecting vulnerabilities in Java source code compared to its performance in C/C++ source code?* This question aims to evaluate the adaptability and performance of the LineVD model when applied to Java source code. We seek to determine if the model retains its effectiveness and accuracy after being adapted from C/C++ to Java.

RQ2: *How does the integration of Node2vec embeddings impact the accuracy and effectiveness of graph-based vulnerability detection in Java source code?* We aim to assess whether the enrichment of subgraph construction with Node2vec embeddings leads to measurable improvements in vulnerability detection accuracy and effectiveness.

RQ3: *What are the comparative advantages of using Node2vec-enhanced subgraphs over traditional subgraph construction methods in the context of source code vulnerability detection?* This question aims to explore the specific benefits of Node2vec embeddings by comparing the performance of the enhanced model while considering different embedding configurations.

To address these research questions (see Sect. 5), we will compute the evaluation metrics described in Sect. 4.3 at node (statement) level predictions. For **RQ1**, we will calculate these metrics for the converted LineVD (named **JLineVD**) model applied to Java source code vulnerability detection. Subsequently, we plan to integrate the advanced subgraph construction process into the new variant and computed the same metrics for evaluation, referring to this enhanced model as **JLineVD+** for **RQ2**. Finally, we will systematically vary the Node2Vec settings to assess the benefits of embeddings for Java vulnerability detection for **RQ3**.

4.5   Parameter Selection and Implementation

The model hyperparameters were tuned using the fine-tuning Python library Ray Tune [14] through a randomized grid search, ensuring a thorough exploration of the hyperparameter space.

To effectively capture the local relationships within each subgraph, we used the number of nodes within the subgraph as the *walk_length* and the number of edges as the *num_walks* for generating node and edge embeddings with the Node2vec model. This choice ensures that the random walks fully explore the local topology of each subgraph, leading to more informative embeddings. Furthermore, we selected a *window size* of 5, based on the typical function length in our dataset, and the dimension equal to the embedding length produced by the CodeBERT model for homogeneity. Given that functions are generally not long enough to form graphs with more than 200 nodes, a window size of 5 provides an optimal balance between capturing local context and maintaining computational efficiency. This approach enhances the model's ability to detect vulnerabilities by leveraging both the syntactic and semantic structure of the source code.

4.6   Threats to Validity

We acknowledge that using a single imbalanced dataset with limited vulnerable samples may restrict the generalizability of our results. However, this dataset is derived from real-world projects, allowing us to apply the methods under authentic conditions. Another potential limitation arises from using Joern as a graph feature extractor, as different versions of Joern can lead to varying model performance, as demonstrated by previous automated SVD graph-based research. We selected the LineVD methodology due to its rare graph-based architecture that offers clear instructions for replication. We recognize that incorporating more datasets and methods could enhance our findings, and we plan to expand our experimentation in future work.

5   Results

RQ1: After training, we tested the GNN model on a dataset comprising $1,795$ functions, which achieved significant results as summarised in Table 1. The table also reports LineVD's results of the original experiments for C/C+ [9]. The model attains a statement-level accuracy of 97.20%, indicating that it correctly predicts vulnerabilities in 97.20% of the cases. Additionally, the model's precision of 70.75% and the recall rate of 58.04%. The F1-score, which balances precision and recall, is 61.36%, and the Matthews Correlation Coefficient (MCC) is 0.2583.

Table 1. Macro Metrics Performance in Response to RQ1. JLineVD results are related to the ProjectKB dataset. While LineVD results are related to the original C++ dataset [9]

	Accuracy	Precision	F1-Score	AUROC	MCC	Rec
JLineVD	0.9720	0.7075	0.6135	0.5803	0.2583	0.5804
LineVD [9]	\	0.271	0,36	0.913	\	0.533

To further evaluate the model's effectiveness, we compute additional metrics such as N@5, MRR, and MFR. The N@5 value of 0.9860 indicates that nearly all relevant vulnerabilities are found within the top 5 predictions, demonstrating the model's capability to prioritize critical vulnerabilities effectively. The Mean Reciprocal Rank is 1.0, showing that the first relevant vulnerability is consistently ranked first, highlighting the model's excellent ranking performance. The Mean First Rank of 1.028 reinforces this.

These results suggest that the converted LineVD model (**JLineVD**) is particularly effective at detecting line-level vulnerabilities in Java source code, even better than the original case applied to a C/C++ dataset.

RQ2: We retrain the model with the same parameters as in RQ1, enriching the sub-graphs with corresponding node and edge embeddings. Table 2 shows the obtained results. From the table, we observe that, while the changes in results are not drastic, the model has gained confidence in detecting vulnerabilities in Java source code. This is evident from the improvement in precision, which has increased from 70.75% to 80.48%. The F1-score has also improved, rising from 61.35 to 66.24, and accuracy has slightly increased from 97.20% to 97.42%. However, unexpected behaviour is observed in the MCC and AUROC, which decreased respectively by 0.0429 and 0.05 units, raising the point of finding the best configuration in the Node2vec model' setting. These results indicate the possible positive impact that capturing contextualized neighbourhood information can have on enhancing the model's knowledge for vulnerability detection.

RQ3: We systematically varied the Node2vec model's hyperparameters, including the number of walks, walk length, and window size. Starting with initial values for these hyperparameters, we systematically increased/decreased each

Table 2. Macro Metrics Performance in Response to RQ2

	Accuracy	Precision	F1-Score	AUROC	MCC	Recall
JLineVD+	**0.974**	**0.804**	**0.662**	0.538	0.215	0.538
JLineVD	0.972	0.707	0.6135	**0.58**	**0.258**	**0.580**

value based on the model's performance in detecting vulnerabilities from source code. Figure 3 illustrates the sensitivity of the metric after some trials, while Table 3 details the different model settings, and the corresponding values are presented in Table 4.

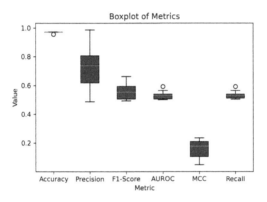

Fig. 3. Performance Variation in Different Node2Vec Settings

The analysis reveals that the optimal model performance is achieved with a walk length of 5, a number of walks set to 10, and a window size of 8. This configuration suggests an ideal balance between capturing local and global structural information within the subgraphs. Specifically, a walk length of 5 ensures that the random walks are long enough to capture local neighbourhood structures without introducing excessive noise. Setting the number of walks to 10 allows for sufficient graph sampling, facilitating comprehensive node representations by exploring different parts of the graph multiple times. The window size of 8 in the Skip-gram model provides an appropriate context range, enabling the understanding of the local context of each node by considering nearby nodes within an 8-hop distance, a significant departure from the common 1-hop consideration in the literature.

Table 3. Parameters of the embedding model: Node2vec

	Walk length	number of walks	window
1	1	1	1
2	1	3	1
3	1	10	1
4	1	2*(nodes)	1
5	3	6	1
6	nodes	edges	5
7	5	10	3
8	**5**	**10**	**8**
9	5	10	10
10	7	7	7
11	10	10	3
12	nodes	edges	8

Table 4. Corresponding evaluation metrics with different settings of Table 3

	Accuracy	Precision	F1-Score	AUROC	MCC	Recall
1	0.9733	0.4867	0.4932	0.5000	0.0478	0.5000
2	0.9725	0.7135	0.5962	0.5647	**0.235**	0.5647
3	0.9733	0.7375	0.5534	0.5333	0.1778	0.5332
4	0.9563	0.5880	0.5902	**0.5925**	0.1805	**0.5926**
5	0.9740	0.7877	0.5627	0.5395	0.2130	0.5394
6	0.9717	0.8047	**0.6624**	**0.5380**	0.2154	0.5380
7	0.9738	0.8072	0.5377	0.5235	0.1697	0.5234
8	**0.9742**	**0.8208**	0.6530	0.5322	0.1697	0.5234
9	0.9723	0.6004	0.5070	0.5067	0.0520	0.5067
10	0.9726	0.6704	0.5231	0.5155	0.1031	0.5156
11	0.9729	0.6368	0.5018	0.5042	0.0478	0.5041
12	0.9736	**0.9868**	0.5050	0.5059	0.1077	0.5059
mean	0.9717	0.7200	0.5571	0.5296	0.1432	0.5289

The performance appears to be sensitive to the number of nodes (i.e., the mean code lines per function is 9 in our datasets, approximately the selected number of walks) within each input graph. We observed a significant performance decrease when using excessively large hyperparameters for the embedding model; this might be subject to increasing noise due to the repeating process that a high random walk may generate.

Furthermore, we individually assessed the impact of each setting on the final model performance using a t-test statistic. The test considers $(X, Y) \approx$

(*setting*, *metric*) and defines the null hypothesis (H_0) that these values do not positively impact model performance. The reported t-values and p-values in Table 5 demonstrate that these settings significantly contribute to model performance variation, as illustrated in Fig. 3. This is evidenced by the reported p-values being less than the $\alpha = 0.05$ confidence interval.

Table 5. Statistical Effect of Node2Vec Settings on Evaluation Metrics

	window					
	Accuracy	Precision	F1-Score	AUROC	MCC	Recall
t-statistic	2.7798	3.0666	3.1956	3.2111	4.0180	3.6390
p-value	0.0194	0.0119	0.0095	0.0093	0.0020	0.0038
	number of walks					
t-statistic	5.2543	5.4500	5.5429	5.5508	5.9165	5.6896
p-value	0.0003	0.0002	0.0002	0.0002	0.0001	0.0001
	Walk length					
t-statistic	3.3539	3.6483	3.7520	3.76276	4.4997	4.1437
p-value	0.0073	0.0044	0.0037	0.0037	0.0009	0.0016

RQ1: The experimental results indicate that JLineVD's performance on the ProjectKB dataset is comparable or even better to the results achieved by LineVD on the BigVul dataset (C/C++). This demonstrates the successful adaptation of LineVD to JLineVD, thereby reinforcing the relevance of SVD across different programming languages.

RQ2: The comparison between JLineVD+ and JLineVD shows the advantages of using an appropriate embedding method, such as Node2Vec, to capture both local and global relationships within the code through node and edge embedding. This enhancement improves the model's ability to accurately classify vulnerable lines of code from non-vulnerable ones.

RQ3: Further analysis suggests that focusing exclusively on either local or global neighbourhood embeddings does not significantly improve the learning algorithm's performance. This underscores the importance of finding an optimal balance between local and global embedding information to maximize the model's classification capabilities.

However, the observed limited improvement in metrics such as AUROC and MCC remains unexplained and could be attributed to additional hyperparameters not investigated in this study and the highly imbalanced nature of our dataset. We will further investigate this in our future work.

6   Related Work

The domain of vulnerability detection has witnessed significant progress in recent years [12, 25]. The application of artificial intelligence methods is transforming code testing, vulnerability discovery, and various other programming tasks from time-intensive, expert-driven analysis to automated processes.

Researchers have proposed detection models for accurately identifying vulnerabilities across different programming languages. For instance, [18, 24] introduced a graph-based model for detecting vulnerabilities in C/C++ source code at the functional level. Similarly, Wang et al. [21] proposed FUNDED framework, which extends graph-based approach to multiple languages, including C/C++, Java, Swift, and PHP, by leveraging graph neural networks (GNNs) to represent programme source code as graphs. These graphs capture control, data, and call dependencies and automatically gather high-quality training samples from open-source projects, thereby enhancing model performance.

However, these proposed detection architectures often contend with issues such as high false-positive rates and instability in detection. To address these shortcomings, Chen et al. [2] proposed iGnnVD, which integrates graph neural networks to improve detection accuracy. Their method integrates the results of three base detectors using a voting strategy for the final analysis but is limited to function-level detection. Additionally, [10] introduced a quantum convolutional neural network with self-attentive pooling for Java source code, also at the function level. Despite these advancements, the interpretability of model predictions remains a significant challenge for developers, particularly given the potential complexity of functions with numerous lines of code.

For more precise granularity detection, [5] and [9, 13] have proposed transformer-based and graph-based models, respectively, for automated vulnerability detection at the line level in C/C++ source code. However, the applicability of these models to other programming languages remains an open question, underscoring the need for further research into line-level detection for a broader range of languages.

In this work we investigated the potential of capturing local information within a subgraph by the means of node and edge embedding, enhancing the subgraph construction process to enrich the model with contextualized neighbourhood information. We used Node2vec model to generate nodes and edges embedding, which are then added to the corresponding subgraph as a node and edge feature to make the model learn both local and global structure of the source code through appropriate n-hop encoding overcoming the limitation of the literature that mostly consider the closest neighbor (1-hop).

7   Conclusion

Software vulnerability detection remains one of the most critical issues in security testing, as it is a time-consuming task that requires expert knowledge, especially given the complexity and size of the projects to be analyzed. This study proposed an approach to enhancing the subgraph construction process for graph-based vulnerability detection in source code. Our method involves generating node and edge embeddings to enrich the model's capability of capturing both local and global relationships within the input function. The results demonstrate that this approach enhances the model's robustness in understanding source code, leading to improved statement-level detection metrics. Notably, the model's precision increased, reflecting its ability to effectively capture contextualized code structure for precise detection. Although evaluated with an unbalanced dataset, we plan to gather more real-world data to generalize our findings further and potentially expand the model's ability to detect and classify vulnerabilities across different programming languages.

Acknowledgements. The work was partially supported by the European Union Horizon Europe Research and Innovation Programme under Grant 101120393 (Sec4Ai4Sec) and partially by project SERICS (PE00000014) under the MUR National Recovery and Resilience Plan funded by the European Union - NextGenerationEU.

References

1. Bekkar, M., Djemaa, H.K., Alitouche, T.A.: Evaluation measures for models assessment over imbalanced data sets. J. Inf. Eng. Appl. **3**(10) (2013)
2. Chen, J., Yin, Y., Cai, S., Wang, W., Wang, S., Chen, J.: iGnnVD: a novel software vulnerability detection model based on integrated graph neural networks. Sci. Comput. Program. 103156 (2024)
3. Fan, J., Li, Y., Wang, S., Nguyen, T.N.: AC/C++ code vulnerability dataset with code changes and CVE summaries. In: Proceedings of the 17th International Conference on Mining Software Repositories, pp. 508–512 (2020)
4. Feng, Z., et al.: Codebert: a pre-trained model for programming and natural languages. arXiv preprint arXiv:2002.08155 (2020)
5. Fu, M., Tantithamthavorn, C.: Linevul: a transformer-based line-level vulnerability prediction. In: Proceedings of the 19th International Conference on Mining Software Repositories, pp. 608–620 (2022)
6. Ghaffarian, S.M., Shahriari, H.R.: Software vulnerability analysis and discovery using machine-learning and data-mining techniques: a survey. ACM Comput. Surv. (CSUR) **50**(4), 1–36 (2017)
7. Grover, A., Leskovec, J.: node2vec: scalable feature learning for networks. In: Proceedings of the 22nd ACM SIGKDD International Conference on Knowledge Discovery and Data Mining, pp. 855–864 (2016)
8. Hanif, H., Nasir, M.H.N.M., Ab Razak, M.F., Firdaus, A., Anuar, N.B.: The rise of software vulnerability: taxonomy of software vulnerabilities detection and machine learning approaches. J. Netw. Comput. Appl. **179**, 103009 (2021)
9. Hin, D., Kan, Λ., Chen, H., Babar, M.A.: Linevd: statement-level vulnerability detection using graph neural networks. In: Proceedings of the 19th International Conference on Mining Software Repositories, pp. 596–607 (2022)
10. Hussain, S., et al.: Vulnerability detection in java source code using a quantum convolutional neural network with self-attentive pooling, deep sequence, and graph-based hybrid feature extraction. Sci. Rep. **14**(1), 7406 (2024)

11. Ji, X., Liu, L., Zhu, J.: Code clone detection with hierarchical attentive graph embedding. Int. J. Software Eng. Knowl. Eng. **31**(06), 837–861 (2021)
12. Lekeufack Foulefack, R.Z., Marchetto, A.: A rapid review on graph-based learning vulnerability detection. In: International Conference on the Quality of Information and Communications Technology, pp. 355–372. Springer, Cham (2024)
13. Li, Y., Wang, S., Nguyen, T.N.: Vulnerability detection with fine-grained interpretations. In: Proceedings of the 29th ACM Joint Meeting on European Software Engineering Conference and Symposium on the Foundations of Software Engineering, pp. 292–303 (2021)
14. Liaw, R., Liang, E., Nishihara, R., Moritz, P., Gonzalez, J.E., Stoica, I.: Tune: a research platform for distributed model selection and training. arXiv preprint arXiv:1807.05118 (2018)
15. Lin, G., Xiao, W., Zhang, J., Xiang, Y.: Deep learning-based vulnerable function detection: a benchmark. In: Zhou, J., Luo, X., Shen, Q., Xu, Z. (eds.) ICICS 2019. LNCS, vol. 11999, pp. 219–232. Springer, Cham (2020). https://doi.org/10.1007/978-3-030-41579-2_13
16. Lu, S., et al.: Codexglue: a machine learning benchmark dataset for code understanding and generation. arXiv preprint arXiv:2102.04664 (2021)
17. Nguyen, H.V., Zheng, J., Inomata, A., Uehara, T.: Code aggregate graph: effective representation for graph neural networks to detect vulnerable code. IEEE Access **10**, 123786–123800 (2022)
18. Ni, C., Guo, X., Zhu, Y., Xu, X., Yang, X.: Function-level vulnerability detection through fusing multi-modal knowledge. In: 2023 38th IEEE/ACM International Conference on Automated Software Engineering (ASE), pp. 1911–1918. IEEE (2023)
19. Ponta, S.E., Plate, H., Sabetta, A., Bezzi, M., Dangremont, C.: A manually-curated dataset of fixes to vulnerabilities of open-source software. In: Proceedings of the 16th International Conference on Mining Software Repositories (2019)
20. Vagavolu, D., Swarna, K.C., Chimalakonda, S.: A mocktail of source code representations. In: 2021 36th IEEE/ACM International Conference on Automated Software Engineering (ASE), pp. 1296–1300 (2021)
21. Wang, H., et al.: Combining graph-based learning with automated data collection for code vulnerability detection. IEEE Trans. Inf. Forensics Secur. **16**, 1943–1958 (2020)
22. Wu, B., Zou, F.: Code vulnerability detection based on deep sequence and graph models: a survey. Secur. Commun. Netw. **2022**(1), 1176898 (2022)
23. Yamaguchi, F., Golde, N., Arp, D., Rieck, K.: Modeling and discovering vulnerabilities with code property graphs. In: 2014 IEEE Symposium on Security and Privacy, pp. 590–604. IEEE (2014)
24. Zhou, Y., Liu, S., Siow, J., Du, X., Liu, Y.: Devign: effective vulnerability identification by learning comprehensive program semantics via graph neural networks. In: Advances in Neural Information Processing Systems, vol. 32 (2019)
25. Zuo, F., Rhee, J.: Vulnerability discovery based on source code patch commit mining: a systematic literature review. Int. J. Inf. Secur. **23**(2), 1513–1526 (2024)

Short Papers

Mutating Clingo's AST with `clingabomino`

Liliana Marie Prikler$^{(\boxtimes)}$ and Franz Wotawa

Institute of Software Technology, Graz University of Technology, 8010 Graz, Austria
{liliana.prikler,wotawa}@ist.tugraz.at

Abstract. Although answer set programming has been a tried way of problem-solving for over thirty years, few tools and methodologies exist today to test it rigorously. Previous research suggests that mutation testing is able to uncover flaws even with small inputs. In this paper, we introduce `clingabomino`, a mutant generator implemented in C++ that directly operates on the abstract syntax tree of the Clingo solver. Our tool consists of a command-line application that implements commonly useful mutation operators as well as a library to aid in the development of domain-specific mutation operators.

Keywords: Answer set programming · Mutation testing · Mutant generation

1 Introduction

In software engineering, testing is indispensable for assuring that the software under development meets its specified quality criteria. While testing aims to detect faults, it does not guarantee that there exists no fault when none are found—such bugs will remain part of the software after deployment and might be revealed during operation. To avoid missing critical bugs, a test suite must be "good enough", where coverage criteria or mutation scores [10] are used to evaluate the test suite quality.

Typical coverage criteria focus on the number of statements under various conditions executed using a test suite, whereas the mutation score measures the degree of introduced defects, i.e., the mutants, that can be revealed using the test suite. Both test suite quality criteria are important to judge testing activities and are used in practice when developing ordinary software. However, there is limited research work dealing with such criteria when the software relies on methods from artificial intelligence and, in particular, knowledge-based systems.

In this short paper, we contribute to the application of mutation testing to one particular class of knowledge-based systems, particularly systems relying on answer set programming (ASP) [1,8]. ASP is a declarative programming scheme with applications, e.g., in model-based reasoning [7] and diagnosis [15] among others. For such applications, the need to verify the underlying logic representations of knowledge has been identified (see, e.g., [16]). In ASP, this representation is usually concise, but unfortunately, methods for validating and

© IFIP International Federation for Information Processing 2025
Published by Springer Nature Switzerland AG 2025
H. D. Menéndez et al. (Eds.): ICTSS 2024, LNCS 15383, pp. 151–158, 2025.
https://doi.org/10.1007/978-3-031-80889-0_10

verifying answer set programs are still rare. Coverage rules [6] and a basic mutation model [9] started being described only in the last decade, whereas a variety
of well-integrated tools exists for other languages (e.g., PIT [2] for Java).

This paper introduces a new tool for generating mutations of ASP programs.
Our tool, `clingabomino`, is built on top of the Clingo ASP solver [5] and is
freely available for others[1]. We describe the input language handled by our tool
in Sect. 2, the implementation in Sect. 3, and provide a usage example in Sect. 4.
Finally, we conclude the paper in Sect. 5.

2   Clingo's Input Language and Syntax Tree

Clingo reads answer set programs in the abstract Gringo notation [4], which can
historically be traced back to Prolog. While the syntax is oftentimes strikingly
close, there are edge cases, which have a different meaning between the two
languages, and even expressions that are valid in one language but not so in the
other.

An answer set program consists of *rules* of the form

$$H \leftarrow B_1 \wedge \cdots \wedge B_m,$$

where the literals B_i constitute the body of the rule and H is the head of the
rule[2]. Typically, the head will itself be a symbolic or arithmetic literal, but it
may also be a disjunction, choice expression, or aggregate.

Literal expressions are built from the ground up, starting with *terms*, which
are defined recursively as

- numeric or symbolic constants
- variables
- functions $f(t_1, \ldots, t_n)$ with f a symbolic constant and t_i terms
- operations $t_1 \star t_2$ with $\star \in \{+, -, \times, /, ..\}$ and t_1, t_2 terms
- tuples $(t_1, \ldots, t_n)$ with t_i terms

An *atom* is an expression of the form $p(P)$ or $\neg p(P)$ with p a symbolic constant and P a pool—i.e. a possibly empty sequence—of terms. As a shorthand,
p is equivalent to $p()$ so that symbolic constants can also be viewed as atoms.

For atoms A, A_1, A_2 and $\prec \in \{=, \neq, <, >, \geq, \leq\}$, the expressions A, **not** A,
and **not not** A are *symbolic literals*, and the expression $A_1 \prec A_2$ is an *arithmetic literal*, and $\{A\}$ is a *choice expression*.

At a higher level, conditional and aggregate literals may be formed from symbolic and arithmetic literals. Conditional literals have the form $L : C_1, \ldots, C_n$,
with L and C_i symbolic or arithmetic literals, and expand to all L for which
$C_1, \ldots, C_n$ holds—if none, then they expand to $\top$. To delimit literals correctly

[1] https://git.ist.tugraz.at/clingabomino/clingabomino.
[2] The $\leftarrow$ is represented by :- like in Prolog, but the $\wedge$ may be represented by both ;
and , almost interchangeably.

when conditional literals appear in the body, the semicolon may be used as $\wedge$. Aggregate literals have the form

$$s_1 \prec_1 f\{t_1 : L_1; \ldots; t_n : L_n\} \prec_2 s_2,$$

with s_1, s_2 terms, $\prec_{1,2} \in \{=, \neq, <, >, \geq, \leq\}$, $f \in \{\mathtt{count}, \mathtt{sum}, \mathtt{sum+}, \mathtt{min}, \mathtt{max}\}$, t_i terms and L_i a comma-separated sequence of symbolic or arithmetic literals (if the aggregate appears in the body) or a conditional literal (if the aggregate appears in the head).

Clingo exposes all these syntactical constructs to the C programmer as an `clingo_ast_t *`, and to the C++ programmer as an `Clingo::AST::Node`. The nodes in this abstract syntax tree may refer to other nodes and data via named attributes, some of which are shown in Table 1. Clingo has functions for retrieving and setting named attributes of a node, which are nicely abstracted as `Clingo::AST::Node::get` and `Clingo::AST::Node::set` in the C++ interface, using a `NodeValue` (similar to `std::variant`) to abstract over the various data types.[3]

3   Implementation

We choose C++ as our implementation language, as it allows us to reuse existing programming interfaces to read and write answer set programs rather than implementing our own parser. This has the advantage that our system can (in theory) handle all the syntax supported by Clingo, but at the same time, requires a stable API with respect to the various nodes and attributes in the syntax tree.[4]

Our implementation consists of a library and a command line application. In terms of dependencies, we make use of Clingo's C++ API, and `fmt` [17] in the library, and additionally use Immer [12] and CLI11 [13] in the application. We use Meson [11] for building the library and application and support reproducible builds through GNU Guix [3].[5]

The library defines a concept for mutations: in C++ terms, they are regularly invocable, copy- and move-constructible types, whose `operator ()` can be applied to a single `const T &` argument to get a `T`. Using these primitive mutations, the library then further provides templates that can be used to formulate

---

[3] The C++ API notably also includes methods to visit and transform the AST, but these methods apply the same transformation to all nodes reachable from the node they were called on. These methods are therefore not well-suited generating subtle changes (i.e., mutants).

[4] The structure of this syntax tree may change with minor releases of Clingo, as has been observed between Clingo 5.5 and Clingo 5.6. However, as long as a program remains readable by older versions of Clingo, this is not a problem—though obviously, if one wanted to compile `clingabomino` itself against a newer Clingo version with a different syntax tree, one would have to adjust the affected mutations accordingly.

[5] We also have a Homebrew recipe for Mac, but can make no positive statement w.r.t. reproducibility for this recipe yet.

Table 1. Some node types in Clingo's AST (assuming Clingo 5.6) and their attributes. In C, attributes are snake_case rather than lower case, and different functions need to be used to distinguish between data types. In C++, a uniform get<T> method can be used. Namespaces were stripped to reduce space.

Node type	Attribute	Data type
Rule	Head	Node
	Body	NodeVector
ConditionalLiteral	Literal	Node
	Condition	NodeVector
Literal	Sign	int
	Atom	Node
BooleanConstant	Value	int
SymbolicAtom	Symbol	Node
Comparison	Guards	NodeVector
Guard	Comparison	int
	Term	Node
SymbolicTerm	Symbol	Symbol
Variable	Name	const char *
UnaryOperation	OperatorType	int
	Argument	Node
BinaryOperation	OperatorType	int
	Left	Node
	Right	Node

a "super-set"[6] of the mutation operators laid out in Table 2. We formulate these templates to be more or less agnostic of data types and instead, use concepts to model container types.

The application finally instantiates the templated mutation operators and hooks them up with command line parsing logic. The application is configured through command-line arguments that enable (or respectively disable) particular mutation operators. This effectively implements *constrained mutation* (cf. [14]), with the default operators (marked with a + in Table 2) being selected because they are the least subtle and thus ought to be easy to kill.

As can also be seen in Table 2, we group similar operators into one operation (e.g. delete-rules and delete-literals) and restrict others in their effect. At present, our tool complements [9] rather than serving as a complete replacement: while it additionally deals with double negations, it only deletes literals in disjunctive and aggregate (rather than all) heads.

---

[6] Our implementation contains a "do anything" template that can trivially be used to carry these out. More practically, we define named templates for most mutations, but some descriptions provided by [9] were unclear. For instance, we only consider adjacent terms in term swapping instead of all possible permutations.

Table 2. Mutation operators for ASP, adapted from [9].

Operation	Original Rules	Examples Mutant
delete proper rule[dr,+]	`p(X) :- q(X). q(X) :- r(X).`	`p(X) :- q(X).`
delete constraint[dr,+]	`good(x-men). :- good(X),evil(X).`	`good(x-men).`
delete fact[dr,+]	`good(x-men). :- good(X),evil(X).`	`:- good(X), evil(X).`
delete body literal[dl,+]	`norm(X) :- p(X), not ab(X).`	`norm(X) :- p(X).`
delete head literal[dl,+,†]	`norm(X) :- p(X), not ab(X).`	`:- p(X),not ab(X).`
add default negation[°]	`p :- q(X,Y), t(Y).`	`p :- q(X,Y), not t(Y).`
remove default negation[°]	`p :- q(X,Y), not r(X).`	`p :- q(X,Y), r(X).`
add double negation[*,°]	`p :- q(X,Y), t(Y).`	`p :- q(X,Y), not not t(Y).`
remove double negation[*,°]	`p :- q(X,Y), not not t(Y).`	`p :- q(X,Y), t(Y).`
add strong negation[°]	`person(X) :- mutant(X).`	`person(X) :- -mutant(X).`
remove strong negation[°]	`norm(X) :- -mutant(X).`	`norm(X) :- mutant(X).`
rename predicate	`r(X,Y):- e(X,Y). :- e(a,b).`	`r(X,Y):- e(X,Y). :- r(a,b).`
replace comparison relation	`:- succ(X,Y), Y > X.`	`:- succ(X,Y), Y >= X.`
replace arithmetic operator	`next(X,Y) :- r(X;Y),Y=X+1.`	`next(X,Y) :- r(X;Y),Y=X*1.`
twiddle variable domain	`:- s(X,Y), X==(Y+X)*2.`	`:- s(X,Y), X==((Y+1)+X)*2.`
twiddle aggregate bound[±1]	`1 {guess(X)} N :- max(N).`	`1 {guess(X)} (N-1) :- max(N).`
twiddle aggregate weight[±1]	`ok :- 2 #sum {V: val(P,V)} 8.`	`ok :- 2 #sum {V+1: val(P,V)} 8.`
swap terms in literals[tp,+]	`less(X,Y) :- n(X,Y),X < Y.`	`less(Y,X) :- n(X,Y),X < Y.`
change variable to constant	`p(a;b). fail :- p(X).`	`p(a;b). fail :- p(a).`
rename variable	`first(X) :- rel(X,Y).`	`first(Y) :- rel(X,Y).`
change constant to variable	`ok :- exit(1,Y),grid(X,Y).`	`ok :- exit(X,Y), grid(X,Y).`
rename constant	`first(alpha). last(omega).`	`first(omega). last(omega).`

[+] Enabled by default.
[dr] Grouped into a single `delete-rules` mutation.
[dl] Grouped into a single `delete-literals` mutation.
[†] Only applies to disjunctions and aggregated headers in `clingabomino`. Clingo internally uses the boolean constant ⊥ (written as `#false`) to represent constraints.
[°] Add and remove grouped into a single mutation.
[*] Not present in [9].
[±1] Errors are exactly off by one.
[tp] Only adjacent terms are swapped ("transposed").

4 Example Usage

In this section, we quickly demonstrate `clingabomino`, on a common problem in artificial intelligence, namely that of the penguin Tweety. Normally, birds may fly, but to the extent that humans have enumerated them, penguins do not. Listing 1.1 shows one possible encoding for this problem, where we obtain the answer as for whether a given bird may fly through *brave reasoning*. That is, if `flies(B)` holds in any answer set, B may fly.

Listing 1.1. An encoding for the Tweety problem.

```
{ flies(B) } :- bird(B).
  bird(B) :- penguin(B).
  #false :- flies(B), penguin(B).
```

The fact `bird(tweety).` is one instance of this program, another would be `penguin(tweety).` or similar rules for birds that may or may not be penguins.[7]

Listing 1.2. Two out of six mutants of Listing 1.1, using the default options of clingabomino. In the first mutant (before `%<-- cut here -->%`), the first rule of the program has been dropped, making all birds flightless. In the last mutant, the transformation of `#false :- flies(B), penguin(B).` to `#false :- flies(B).` similarly makes all birds flightless. Note, that the programs are written *as read by Clingo*, including hidden literals and statements.

```
#program base.
bird(B) :- penguin(B).
#false :- flies(B); penguin(B).
  [more mutants ...]
  #program base.
{ flies(B) } :- bird(B).
bird(B) :- penguin(B).
#false :- flies(B).
```

If we delete any single rule in Listing 1.1, we may find that birds are not able to fly, that penguins aren't birds (or don't exist), or that penguins can actually fly. Our tool can generate these mutants as well as other, more subtle mutants and prints them either with a separator as in Listing 1.2 or, when provided an output directory, one mutant per file.

5   Conclusion

We have presented a tool for generating mutants of answer set programs based directly on `clingo` with few additional dependencies. For its implementation, we have defined general mutation testing concepts and refined them through templates and template instantiation. Our tool is—just like its inspiration—limited to answer set programs in abstract Gringo.

Acknowledgments. This paper is part of the AI4CSM project that has received funding within the ECSEL JU in collaboration with the European Union's H2020 Framework Programme (H2020/2014-2020) and National Authorities, under grant agreement No.101007326. The work was partially funded by the Austrian Federal Ministry of Climate Action, Environment, Energy, Mobility, Innovation and Technology (BMK) under the program "ICT of the Future" project 877587.

Disclosure of Interests. The authors have no competing interests to declare relevant to this article's content.

---

[7] One might also want to consider other flightless birds, as well as injured birds that require medical attention before being able to fly again.

References

1. Brewka, G., Eiter, T., Truszczyński, M.: Answer set programming at a glance. Commun. ACM **54**(12), 92–103 (2011). https://doi.org/10.1145/2043174.2043195
2. Coles, H., Laurent, T., Henard, C., Papadakis, M., Ventresque, A.: Pit: a practical mutation testing tool for java (demo). In: Proceedings of the 25th International Symposium on Software Testing and Analysis, ISSTA 2016, pp. 449–452. Association for Computing Machinery, New York (2016). https://doi.org/10.1145/2931037.2948707
3. Courtès, L.: Déploiements reproductibles dans le temps avec GNU Guix. GNU/Linux Magazine (2021). https://inria.hal.science/hal-03418210
4. Gebser, M., Harrison, A., Kaminski, R., Lifschitz, V., Schaub, T.: Abstract gringo. Theory Pract. Logic Program. **15**(4–5), 449–463 (2015). https://doi.org/10.1017/S1471068415000150
5. Gebser, M., Kaminski, R., Kaufmann, B., Schaub, T.: Multi-shot ASP solving with clingo. TPLP **19**(1), 27–82 (2019)
6. Janhunen, T., Niemelä, I., Oetsch, J., Pührer, J., Tompits, H.: On testing answer-set programs. In: Coelho, H., Studer, R., Wooldridge, M.J. (eds.) ECAI 2010 - 19th European Conference on Artificial Intelligence, Lisbon, Portugal, 16–20 August 2010, Proceedings. Frontiers in Artificial Intelligence and Applications, vol. 215, pp. 951–956. IOS Press (2010). https://doi.org/10.3233/978-1-60750-606-5-951
7. Kaufmann, D., Nica, I., Wotawa, F.: Intelligent agents diagnostics - enhancing cyber-physical systems with self-diagnostic capabilities. Adv. Intell. Syst. **3**(5), 2000218 (2021). https://doi.org/10.1002/AISY.202000218
8. Lifschitz, V.: Answer Set Programming. Springer (2019). https://doi.org/10.1007/978-3-030-24658-7
9. Oetsch, J., Prischink, M., Pührer, J., Schwengerer, M., Tompits, H.: On the small-scope hypothesis for testing answer-set programs. In: Brewka, G., Eiter, T., McIlraith, S.A. (eds.) Principles of Knowledge Representation and Reasoning: Proceedings of the Thirteenth International Conference, KR 2012, Rome, Italy, 10–14 June 2012. AAAI Press (2012). http://www.aaai.org/ocs/index.php/KR/KR12/paper/view/4550
10. Offutt, J.: A mutation carol: past, present and future. Inf. Softw. Technol. **53**(10), 1098–1107 (2011). https://doi.org/10.1016/j.infsof.2011.03.007. Special Section on Mutation Testing
11. Pakkanen, J.: The meson build system. https://mesonbuild.com/
12. Puente, J.P.B.: Persistence for the masses: RRB-vectors in a systems language. Proc. ACM Program. Lang. **1**(ICFP) (2017). https://doi.org/10.1145/3110260
13. Schreiner, H., et al.: CLI11: Version 2.3.2, Zenodo (2023). https://doi.org/10.5281/zenodo.7502818. CLI11 is a header-only command line parser with no external requirements
14. Viola Pizzoleto, A., Cutigi Ferrari, F., Offutt, J., Fernandes, L., Ribeiro, M.: A systematic literature review of techniques and metrics to reduce the cost of mutation testing. J. Syst. Softw. **157**, 110388 (2019). https://doi.org/10.1016/j.jss.2019.07.100
15. Wotawa, F., Kaufmann, D.: Model-based reasoning using answer set programming. Appl. Intell. **52**(15), 16993–17011 (2022). https://doi.org/10.1007/S10489-022-03272-2

16. Wotawa, F., Tazl, O.: On the verification of diagnosis models. In: Vermesan, O., Wotawa, F., Nava, M.D., Debaillie, B. (eds.) Industrial Artificial Intelligence Technologies and Applications, pp. 189–203. River Publishers Series in Communications and Networking (2022). https://doi.org/10.13052/rp-9788770227902
17. Zverovich, V.: fmt 9.1.0 (2022). https://fmt.dev/. fmt is a formatting library, providing a fast and safe alternative to C stdio and C++ iostreams

Towards a Knowledge Graph Based Approach for Vulnerable Code Weaknesses Identification

Martina Vecellio Reane, Daniele Dall'Anese, Rosmaël Z. L. Foulefack[ID],
and Alessandro Marchetto[✉][ID]

University of Trento, Trento, Italy
{m.vecellioreane,daniele.dallanese}@studenti.unitn.it,
{rz.lekeufack,alessandro.marchetto}@unitn.it

Abstract. A large literature exists that investigates the use of learning models for vulnerabilities detection. Even if it is well-recognized that the presence of code weaknesses (CWEs) in code fragments can make them vulnerable, most of the effort has been spent to propose new models and methods for the early detection of vulnerable code in a dataset of code fragments. This paper reports a preliminary study conducted to adopt Knowledge Graphs (KGs) for detecting the presence of CWEs in the code. The proposed approach has been evaluated on two datasets and has shown interesting results.

Keywords: Software vulnerability detection · Deep Learning · Source code

1 Introduction

Security testing is becoming more and more relevant since a large number of recent cyber-attacks exploits the vulnerabilities of connected software systems to penetrate and corrupt them.[1] The **Common Weakness Enumeration** (CWE) is an ordered list of common software security code weaknesses, by MITRE[2]. Each CWE is defined by means of: (i) a unique identifier, (ii) a natural language description, (iii) a list of code examples in different languages, (iv) mitigation strategies, (v) CAPEC[3]-specific attack patterns, and (vi) observed vulnerabilities expressed as Common Vulnerability and Exposures (CVE)[4]. For instance, the CWE-78 "Improper Neutralization of Special Elements used in an OS Command - OS Command Injection" concerns not neutralized or incorrectly neutralized input elements that could modify the input (OS) command. Each CWE corresponds to a specific condition of the code that can lead to a security vulnerability. To identify the presence of a CWE in a code fragment can be a crucial

---

[1] https://www.forbes.com/advisor/education/it-and-tech/cybersecurity-statistics.
[2] https://cwe.mitre.org.
[3] https://capec.mitre.org.
[4] https://www.cve.org.

© IFIP International Federation for Information Processing 2025
Published by Springer Nature Switzerland AG 2025
H. D. Menéndez et al. (Eds.): ICTSS 2024, LNCS 15383, pp. 159–166, 2025.
https://doi.org/10.1007/978-3-031-80889-0_11

step to limit the code vulnerabilities. However, it is also evident that not all CWEs lead to vulnerabilities.

The CWEs are hierarchically[5] organized by means of properties such as: CWE-x is *ParentOf* CWE-y, CWE-y is *ChildOf* CWE-x, and CWE-y is *PeerOf* CWE-z. *ParentOf* means that CWE-x is of the same type, but less specific than CWE-y. *ChildOf* means that CWE-y is more-specific than CWE-x. *PeerOf* means that CWE-y and CWE-z are at the same level of the hierarchy. For instance, CWE-78 is *ChildOf* CWE-77 "Improper Neutralization of Special Elements used in a Command - Command Injection", i.e., CWE-78 is of the same type but more specific than CWE-77.

Existing security testing techniques often use deep-learning (DL) and large language (LLM) models to identify vulnerable code, i.e., predict if a code snippet is vulnerable [15]. To this aim, AI architectures (e.g., neural networks, transformers) are trained on large datasets of labeled code fragments to learn models that can classify new code fragments as vulnerable (or non-vulnerable). These learning-based methods have shown promising results under specific conditions [4,7]. For instance, Bert-like models showed promising results in identifying vulnerable code functions, but their capability of identifying the vulnerable statements, i.e., those statements that make a function vulnerable, is limited [7]. Graph-based approaches also achieve interesting results, but they show difficulties with large and complex code fragments [5]. Furthermore, existing datasets are often imbalanced and contain noise (e.g., wrongly classified code fragments), hampering their adoption [4]. We observed that the CWE-based domain-knowledge can be used to enhance existing vulnerability detection methods [8]. However, while most of the existing works focus on the identification of vulnerable code, only a limited number of works focuses on how AI methods can identify, in a code fragment, the presence of CWE(s) that make it vulnerable. We argue that this could be due to the fact that identifying the CWEs that make a code vulnerable is a complex task such as to identify the statements that make a code fragment vulnerable. Conversely, several works (e.g., [1]) classify the natural-language descriptions of the CVEs according to the CWEs. More similarly to our work, [10] and [9] present two approaches for identifying the CWE for fragments of source code. [10] presents a technique that extracts an Abstract Syntax Trees (AST) from the source code, converts it into a textual representation (by traversing the built AST), encodes such a representation in a vector space, and analyzes it for identifying security weaknesses. [9] presents an approach for the identification of the CWE for security patches (code before and after the fix) provided with known CVEs. [9] expresses the CWE identification task as a hierarchical multi-label classification task. Hence, given the CWE hierarchy and the code of security patches, it traverses the hierarchy for extracting appropriate paths (sequence of nodes from the root to the leaves, up to a maximum of depth-3), which are then used to identify the CWEs' patches. The experimental results of both papers show that the CWE identification for a code fragment is a complex task that can be strongly influenced by: (i) the

---

[5] https://cwe.mitre.org/data/slices/1000.html.

number of samples per CWE, and (ii) level of the CWE(s) in the hierarchy (i.e., their granularity).

This paper investigates the use of a Knowledge Graph (KG), that embeds domain-specific knowledge about the CWE hierarchy, to identify the presence of CWEs in code fragments. Differently from [10], we do not extract any kind of intermediate representation from the source code. Differently from [9], we consider only the code that actually contains the vulnerability and we aim at predicting the implemented CWE. We built a KG starting from the CWE hierarchy and a training set of vulnerable code fragments. We then represent entities and relations of the KG in a vector space by applying a knowledge graph embedding model, named **TransE** [3]. We conducted a preliminary experiment for comparing the achieved results with the ones of two baselines. Results are promising, but they also confirm how the used datasets can play a pivotal role, hampering or amplifying the CWE identification capabilities.

2 Knowledge Graph CWE Identification

Knowledge Graph Construction. A Knowledge Graph (KG) is a semantic network that aims at capturing and describing entities, concepts, and the semantic relations among them. Domain-specific KGs focus on the knowledge of a specific field. For instance, cybersecurity KGs [6,11] capture cybersecurity entities such as vulnerabilities, attack patterns, threats actors, and exploitation strategies, as well as their relationships. A knowledge graph is built from a dataset consisting of triples of the form (h, r, t), as defined by the Resource Description Framework.[6] Each triple represents a factual statement in the graph where h (head) and t (tail) are entities and r (relation) is the relationship between them.

In this work, we build a KG where the entities are CWEs and vulnerable code fragments (e.g., C++ and/or Java functions), while the relationships reproduce the MITRE's CWE hierarchy and link each code fragment to its own CWE(s). Each KG is built by means of a three-step approach: (i) a set of triples is extracted from the input dataset of labeled code fragments; (ii) two dictionaries (*Entity to Id* and *Relation to Id*)

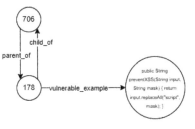

Fig. 1. Fragment of a built KG

created to map entities and relations to unique identifiers; (iii) the identified triples are converted to ID-based representations by using the created dictionaries; each triple is represented as (*entity id head, relation id, entity id tail*). The built KG can be represented as a directed graph where nodes are entities and edges are relations. This kind of graph forms the basis for the embedding and the prediction activity. Figure 1 shows the graphical representation of a small example from a built KG, composed of two CWEs and a fragment of code linked to one of the CWEs.

---

[6] https://www.w3.org/TR/rdf11-primer/.

KG Embedding Using TransE. KGs are used to represent structured data potentially coming from different sources. A Knowledge Graph Embedding (KGE) aims at learning how to represent entities and relationships of a KG into continuous vectors in a lower-dimensional space, so that AI algorithms can use them for prediction and recommendation tasks. In our case, KG entities are code fragments and CWEs. By working with the embeddings of code fragments, instead of only focusing on the pure code, we are representing the code in a latent space, thus allowing us to work with learned patterns of behavior and relationships, rather than relying only on the syntactic aspect of code. This, however, implies that the quality of the embeddings and training data can influence the effectiveness of the whole approach. Several KGE approaches exist, e.g., translation-based, tensor factorization-based, and neural network-based [14]. The choice of the approach depends on the specific requirements of the task to conduct, the available data, and computational resources. For instance, inspired from tools such as Word2vec[7], TransE (Translating Embeddings) [3,13] is one of the most used *translational distance model* that learns how to represent KGs in vector spaces. TansE represents both KG's entities and relations embedding vectors in the same geometric space. A translational distance model uses a scoring function that evaluates the plausibility of a triple by measuring the distance in the vector space (vectors' translation). The model relies on the fact that when the embedding of *head* is added to the embedding of *relation*, the result corresponds to the embedding of *tail*. In fact, the key idea behind TransE is that relations are represented as translations in the embedding space. More formally, for the KG triple (h, r, t), TransE aims to learn embeddings so that $\mathbf{h} + \mathbf{r} \approx \mathbf{t}$, where $\mathbf{h}$ is the embedding of the head entity, $\mathbf{r}$ is the embedding of the relation, and $\mathbf{t}$ is the embedding of the tail entity. The model is trained to minimize the ranking loss based on the margins between positive triples (i.e., true facts) and negative triples (i.e., factually incorrect triples) sampled from the input data, during the training. The optimization goal is expressed in terms of:

$$\mathcal{L} = \sum_{(h,r,t)\in \text{pos\_triples}} \sum_{(h',r,t')\in \text{neg\_triples}} \max(0, \gamma + d(\mathbf{h} + \mathbf{r}, \mathbf{t}) - d(\mathbf{h}' + \mathbf{r}, \mathbf{t}')) \quad (1)$$

where $d(\mathbf{a}, \mathbf{b})$ is the distance between vectors $\mathbf{a}$ and $\mathbf{b}$, typically *L1* or *L2* norm distance, γ is a margin hyperparameter, *pos_triples* are true triples, and *neg_triples* are triples generated by corrupting the positive triples. The optimization goal hence requires that $\mathcal{L}$ should tend to 0, i.e., the distance between the embeddings of the head entity, the relation entity, and the tail entity must be minimized. In other terms, given a valid triple (h, r, t), $\mathbf{h}$ (embedding of the head entity), when translated by $\mathbf{r}$ (the relation vector), must be close to $\mathbf{t}$ (embedding of the tail entity).

---

[7] https://code.google.com/archive/p/word2vec.

Link Prediction. By means of their embedding representation, KGs can be used for predictions, e.g., entity classification and link prediction, and recommendation purposes. We focus on link prediction to predict the existence of a link between two KG's entities, i.e., in our case the relation between a code fragment and CWE. For learning how to predict new links, during the training phase, the TransE model is trained on positive triples and their negative counterparts, and positive (correct) triples are assigned higher scores than the other ones. In such a way, the model can predict (missing) links by inferring relationships between non-explicitly defined entities. During the testing phase, for each triple of test for which the relationship is missing, the model predicts the probability of the correct relationship by scoring potential relationships using learned embeddings and selecting the relationship that maximizes the score: $\text{Score}(h, r, t) = -\|\mathbf{h}+\mathbf{r}-\mathbf{t}\|_1$ where $\|\cdot\|_1$ denotes the *L1* norm. We define the problem of detecting the CWE implemented in a fragment of vulnerable code, as a link prediction problem by focusing only on the head-batch in the testing phase, i.e., we focus on the heads, representing the information related to the CWEs, rather than on the tails, representing the information related to the source code. Our goal, in fact, is only to classify the new code fragments on the CWEs in the KG. Hence, we train the TransE model for learning how to identify such associations of entities of code fragments with their CWEs. For each input code fragment, the produced output is a set of probabilities computed to estimate the probability that a specific CWE is implemented in the code.

3   Preliminary Results

We applied KG_{pred} in the following process for preliminarily evaluating whether KGEs and link prediction can identify CWEs in code fragments.

1. We used two datasets: ProjectKB[8] and PrimeVul[9]. ProjectKB is a manually curated dataset of 20k Java functions, of which 1.8k are vulnerable and related to 64 CWEs. PrimeVul is a dataset of 10k C/C++ functions, of which 2.4k are vulnerable and related to 36 CWEs. For both datasets, we considered the original version (*AllCWEs*) and a second version (*FewCWEs*) in which we re-classified the functions by considering a small set of CWEs (the ones at a high level in the CWE hierarchy). We obtained datasets with a larger and more balanced number code fragments per CWE. We hence considered 13 CWEs for ProjectKB and 10 CWEs for PrimeVul.
2. We splitted each dataset in: 80% training, 10% validation, and 10% testing.
3. We built a KG for each dataset. The built KGs contain more than 1.9k/1.8k entities (CWEs and code functions) for ProjectKB, for *All-CWEs/FewCWEs* respectively, and 2.5k/2.4k for PrimeVul.
4. For each KG, we trained the KGE with TransE, with the following configuration: negative sample size: 256; batch: 1024; hidden dimension: 1000; gamma:

---

[8] https://sap.github.io/project-kb.
[9] https://github.com/DLVulDet/PrimeVul.

24.0; alpha: 1.0; learning rate: 0.0001; test batch: 16; max steps: 200k. We chose the values for these parameters by experimenting different configurations and selecting the values that lead to representative results (avoiding outlier results).

5. We applied the 4 built link prediction models, one per dataset, to predict the CWEs of the functions in each test set. We then measured the prediction metrics.

We measured the Mean Reciprocal Rank (MRR), the Mean Rank (MR) and Hits@K ($H@K$) as prediction metrics, since they are largely used for evaluating ranking systems [2]. MRR is the arithmetic mean of reciprocal ranks. It ranges between 0 and 1 (values closed to 1 are preferred), and it is computed as the inverse of the harmonic mean of ranks. MR computes the arithmetic mean over all individual ranks. It ranges in the interval $[1, \infty)$, where lower is better. $H@K$ describes the fraction of correctly classified items in the first k positions of the sorted ranking (we considered 1, 3, and 5 as k). $H@K$ ranges in the interval $(0, 1]$, where closer to 1 is better.

With the aim of preliminarily comparing KG_{pred} with existing learning-based prediction models, we adopted BERT and Phy2 as baselines. These models are representative of the learning models often applied for vulnerability detection in source code [12] and we executed and tuned them in a local server. Instead of predicting the presence of vulnerabilities in the source code, we applied them as multiclass predictors, where the predicted classes are the possible CWEs of the datasets. To this aim, we fine-tuned both BERT and Phy2 with our four datasets, by applying the following configurations: epoch: 2; input vector length: 512; loss function: BCE with logits loss; Optimizer: Adamax; training steps: size(input)*epoch; learning rate: 1e-04, weight decay: 0.01, gradient accumulation steps: 4. We selected these values by considering the most frequently used values and by experimenting different configurations, aiming at selecting the ones that allow us to collect representative results (i.e., avoiding outliers). We separated each dataset in training, validation, and testing sets, and used both training and validation sets for fine-tuning each model, i.e., for specializing the generic BERT and Phy2 models for our task of identifying CWEs in code fragments. We obtained 8 models, then used to predict the CWEs of the functions in the test sets, and compute prediction metrics.

Table 1 reports the collected results. KG_{pred} overcomes BERT in both ProjectKB datasets, and Phy2 in the ProjectKB version *FewCWEs*. In PrimeVul, KG_{pred} achieves slightly worse (in *AllCWEs*) or comparable (in *FewCWEs*) results with respect to both BERT and Phy2. We observe that: (i) KG_{pred} requires an adequate number of execution steps to achieve relevant results (200k steps); (ii) KG_{pred} achieves better results if the code functions in the dataset are better distributed over the CWEs (i.e., *FewCWEs*); and (iii) overall, the results in PrimeVul are worse than the ones in ProjectKB. We argue that this is mainly due to the fact that PrimeVul is composed of several large and complex C/C++ functions, not well-processed from KG_{pred} and the other learning-based methods.

Table 1. Performance metrics for the CWE prediction

	ProjectKB						PrimeVul					
	AllCWEs			FewCWEs			AllCWEs			FewCWEs		
	KG_{pred}	BERT	Phy2	KG_{pred}	BERT	Phy2	KG_{pred}	BERT	Phy2	KG_{pred}	BERT	Phy2
MRR	0.62	0.28	**0.77**	**0.83**	0.5	0.65	0.49	0.49	**0.54**	0.51	0.52	**0.54**
MR	19	19.28	**6.3**	4.2	3.8	**2.3**	4.8	3.7	**3.5**	3	**2.8**	**2.8**
HITS@1	0.5	0.15	**0.73**	**0.76**	0.28	0.65	0.29	0.29	**0.36**	0.27	0.27	**0.3**
HITS@3	0.69	0.31	**0.79**	**0.89**	0.62	0.8	0.58	0.61	**0.64**	0.71	**0.73**	0.71
HITS@5	0.74	0.4	**0.81**	**0.93**	0.8	0.87	0.82	**0.83**	**0.83**	0.87	**0.89**	**0.89**

4   Discussion and Conclusions

This study shows that KGs can detect CWEs in the code, but several factors can negatively impact the results. For instance, the datasets used to build the KG play a crucial role. We observed that a cleaned and rich dataset helps build an effective KG. Moreover, the KG needs to contain a representative code samples for each CWE, otherwise it is difficult to map new code fragments to the entities of the KG. Another possible limit is that the code samples have been considered as "plain text"., while the adoption of an intermediate representation could help in better capturing the underlying code structure, thus better characterizing the code of the CWEs. In our future work, we will extend the experimentation with additional datasets and baselines. Moreover, we will investigate the use of intermediate representations for the code, and the scalability of the approach by increasing the size of datasets and KGs.

Acknowledgments. The work was partially supported by the European Union Horizon Europe Research and Innovation Programme under Grant 101120393 (Sec4Ai4Sec) and by SERICS (PE00000014) under the MUR National Recovery and Resilience Plan funded by the European Union - NextGenerationEU.

References

1. Aota, M., Ban, T., Takahashi, T., Murata, N.: Multi-label positive and unlabeled learning and its application to common vulnerabilities and exposure categorization. In: Proceedings of IEEE/ACM International Conference on Trust, Security and Privacy in Computing and Communication (TrustCom) (2021)
2. Berrendorf, M., Faerman, E., Vermue, L., Tresp, V.: Interpretable and fair comparison of link prediction or entity alignment methods. In: Proceedings of International Joint Conference on Web Intelligence and Intelligent Agent Technology (2020). https://doi.org/10.1109/WIIAT50758.2020.00053
3. Bordes, A., Usunier, N., Garcia-Durán, A., Weston, J., Yakhnenko, O.: Translating embeddings for modeling multi-relational data. In: Proceedings of International Conference on Neural Information Processing Systems. Curran Associates Inc. (2013)

4. Chakraborty, S., Krishna, R., Ding, Y., Ray, B.: Deep learning based vulnerability detection: are we there yet? IEEE Trans. Softw. Eng. **48**(09), 3280–3296 (2022)
5. Foulefack, R.Z.L., Marchetto, A.: A rapid review on graph-based learning vulnerability detection. In: Proceedings of International Conference on Quality of Information and Communications Technology. Springer (2024)
6. Li, H., Shi, Z., Pan, C., Zhao, D., Sun, N.: Cybersecurity knowledge graphs construction and quality assessment. Complex Intell. Syst. **10** (2024)
7. Marchetto, A.: Can explainability and deep-learning be used for localizing vulnerabilities in source code? In: Proceedings of International Conference on Automation of Software Test (2024)
8. Marchetto, A., Foulefack, R.Z.: Towards the use of domain knowledge to enhance transformer-based vulnerability detection. In: Proceedings of International Conference on Quality of Information and Communications Technology. Springer (2024)
9. Pan, S., Bao, L., Xia, X., Lo, D., Li, S.: Fine-grained commit-level vulnerability type prediction by CWE tree structure. In: Proceedings of IEEE/ACM International Conference on Software Engineering (ICSE) (2023)
10. Saletta, M., Ferretti, C.: A neural embedding for source code: Security analysis and CWE lists. In: Proceedings of IEEE International Conference on Dependable, Autonomic and Secure Computing (2020)
11. Sikos, L.: Cybersecurity knowledge graphs. Knowl. Inf. Syst. **65**, 3511–3531 (2023)
12. Steenhoek, B., Rahman, M.M., Roy, M.K., Alam, M.S., Barr, E.T., Le, W.: A comprehensive study of the capabilities of large language models for vulnerability detection. CoRR abs/2403.17218 (2024)
13. Sun, Z., Deng, Z.H., Nie, J.Y., Tang, J.: Rotate: knowledge graph embedding by relational rotation in complex space. In: Proceedings of International Conference on Learning Representations (2019)
14. Wang, Q., Mao, Z., Wang, B., Guo, L.: Knowledge graph embedding: a survey of approaches and applications. IEEE Trans. Knowl. Data Eng. **29**(12), 2724–2743 (2017)
15. Zeng, P., Lin, G., Pan, L., Tai, Y., Zhang, J.: Software vulnerability analysis and discovery using deep learning techniques: a survey. IEEE Access **8** (2020)

Tutorial

Automatic Summarization Evaluation: Methods and Practices

Héctor D. Menéndez$^{(\boxtimes)}$ and Aidan Dakhama

Department of Informatics, King's College London, London, UK
{hector.menendez,aidan.dakhama}@kcl.ac.uk

Abstract. Automatic summarization systems extract relevant information from documents to provide concise summaries that maintain the same information. Traditionally a human task, automatic summarization has been a challenge since the 1950s and continues to evolve with the advent of large language models (LLMs). The main techniques used in summarization are statistical and fall into two categories: extractive and abstractive summarization. Extractive summarization involves selecting relevant sections of the original text to form the summary, while abstractive summarization creates an entirely new text based on the information in the original document. Evaluation methods for these techniques have evolved from traditional metrics like ROUGE and BLEU to the use of advanced LLMs that assess summary quality in terms of writing, completeness, conciseness, and factuality. This tutorial introduces various summarization techniques and explores both historical and contemporary approaches to their evaluation.

Keywords: Summarization · Extractive · Abstractive · Evaluation

1 Introduction

The interest in summarization systems has grown since their introduction in the 1950s [12]. Summaries provide concise information from documents and are used in various applications, such as search engines, news aggregation, and document analysis. Summarization techniques are mainly statistical and fall into two primary categories: extractive and abstractive summarization [28,29]. Extractive summarization involves selecting relevant sections from the original text to form a summary, while abstractive summarization generates new text based on the original document's information.

Extractive summarization is typically divided into two steps: sentence selection and sentence ordering. Sentence selection identifies the most important sentences in the original text, while sentence ordering arranges the selected sentences coherently. Notable methodologies in extractive summarization include TextRank [30] and LexRank [10], which utilize graph-based algorithms to represent text as a graph and apply ranking algorithms to identify key sentences. Other techniques, like Latent Semantic Analysis (LSA) [32], use matrix factorization and linear algebra to select essential sentences.

© IFIP International Federation for Information Processing 2025
Published by Springer Nature Switzerland AG 2025
H. D. Menéndez et al. (Eds.): ICTSS 2024, LNCS 15383, pp. 169–181, 2025.
https://doi.org/10.1007/978-3-031-80889-0_12

Abstractive summarization, which requires generating new text, is more challenging than extractive summarization. Noteworthy methodologies include seq2seq models [36] and transformer models [18], both based on neural networks trained on extensive datasets. Seq2seq models use recurrent neural networks to produce new text, while transformer models rely on attention mechanisms. Transformer models such as BERT and GPT have achieved state-of-the-art performance on summarization tasks [14].

Summarization can be applied across different domains, including single-document, multi-document, and cross-lingual summarization [9]. Single-document summarization condenses information from one document, multi-document summarization synthesizes information from multiple documents, and cross-lingual summarization produces summaries in different languages [3]. Summarization systems can also be monolingual, handling documents in a single language, or multilingual, summarizing documents across various languages [19].

Popular datasets for summarization include WikiLingua [25], CrossSum [9], XSUM [19], OPUS Parallel Corpora [39], AMI Meeting Corpus [23], SAMSUM [16], and DIALOGSUM [6]. These datasets span various languages and domains, enabling training and evaluation of summarization systems. Additionally, popular libraries like NLTK, Gensim, Scikit-learn, SpaCy, Summa, TensorFlow, Keras, PyTorch, and HuggingFace offer implementations of summarization algorithms, aiding the development and assessment of summarization systems.

Evaluating summarization systems is crucial for assessing their performance. Traditional metrics, such as ROUGE and BLEU, measure overlap between the generated and reference summaries [17]. These metrics are based on n-gram overlap and widely used in summarization research. METEOR [2] enhances these capabilities by incorporating harmonic mean calculations. Despite their utility, these metrics may fall short in evaluating writing quality, coherence, and factuality. BERTScore [42] addresses these gaps by using semantic similarity and contextual embeddings, providing better alignment with human judgments of summary quality. Recently, large language models (LLMs) have been used to evaluate summarization quality in dimensions such as coherence, accuracy, factuality, completeness, comprehension, and density [37]. These metrics enable more nuanced evaluations of summarization systems' strengths and weaknesses.

This tutorial introduces various summarization techniques, covering both historical and modern evaluation approaches. We will discuss the primary techniques in summarization, including extractive and abstractive methods, and examine the field's challenges and opportunities. Additionally, we will review popular datasets and libraries for summarization, providing examples of how to develop and evaluate summarization systems. Finally, we will explore the latest evaluation metrics, discussing their utility in assessing summary quality in terms of writing, coherence, and factuality.

2   Summarization Strategies

Summarization techniques, or summarizers, aim to extract the most relevant information from a text, reducing its content while highlighting key topics. Current automatic summarization methods fall into three main categories: extractive techniques (focused on selecting the most relevant sentences from the text), abstractive techniques (focused on synthesizing content into new formulations), and hybrid models that combine both approaches.

Summarization techniques face several limitations, the most notable being the difficulty in establishing a definitive ground truth, as multiple valid summaries can exist for the same text [15]. Human evaluations are also complex due to their subjective, time-intensive nature [11], and model randomness, influenced by their statistical basis, can impact consistency [7]. Since humans typically create more abstract summaries, it is important to consider creativity and fluency when evaluating abstractive techniques, which requires a deeper understanding of language and content [20].

Summarization techniques must also contend with challenges associated with different languages and summarization strategies. Techniques that generate summaries in multiple languages are referred to as multilingual summarization, while those that create summaries in a different language from the original text are known as cross-lingual summarization. Common issues in both multilingual and cross-lingual summarization include the following [40]:

- **Lack of faithfulness**, where the summary includes inconsistent or unrepresented content relative to the source document. This issue is especially pertinent with generative models, which can produce factual errors [21]. Studies by Kryściński et al. [24] and Wang et al. [40] highlight that this limitation is prevalent in neural-based models.
- **Redundant information or missing key content** in the summary, both of which remain significant challenges in summarization [22].
- **Inclusion of foreign words**, which can relate to code-switching issues in multilingual contexts [33].

During the tutorial, we will begin by cataloging some extractive summarization models based on sentence extraction [11], graph-based methods [29], and machine learning [15]. This catalog will be extended to cover abstractive approaches, including statistical machine translation [20], sequence-to-sequence models [41], reinforcement learning [31], and large language models (LLMs) [1]. Additionally, there exist hybrid approaches [35], where some are focused on multilingual [22] and cross-lingual [25] summarization methods.

2.1 Extractive and Abstractive Summarization

Extractive summarization is a technique that selects the most important sentences from the original text to construct a summary [30]. These techniques operate under the assumption that the most critical information is already contained in the text, making it possible to form a summary by identifying and extracting the most relevant sentences [34]. Extractive summarization is widely used for summarizing news articles, scientific papers, and other documents where key points are explicitly presented.

Several methods can be employed for extractive summarization, including TextRank [30], LexRank [10], Latent Semantic Analysis (LSA) [32], and Term Frequency–Inverse Document Frequency (TF-IDF) [11]. TextRank is a graph-based algorithm that represents the text as a graph, applying graph-ranking algorithms to select the most significant sentences. LexRank, an extension of TextRank, uses lexical similarity to improve sentence ranking. LSA applies matrix factorization, representing the text as a matrix and using linear algebra to identify important sentences. TF-IDF, a statistical method, assigns weights to words based on their frequency in the text, utilizing these weights to select sentences with the highest relevance.

Abstractive summarization, on the other hand, involves generating new text based on the information in the original document [36]. This approach is more complex than extractive summarization, as it requires the model to comprehend the content of the text and generate novel sentences that convey the main ideas. Abstractive summarization is commonly applied in chatbots, question-answering systems, and other contexts where generating new text is essential. Popular models for abstractive summarization include sequence-to-sequence (seq2seq) models, transformer-based models [18], and BERT. Seq2seq models [36] use recurrent neural networks (RNNs) to produce new text, while transformer models leverage attention mechanisms for text generation. BERT, a pre-trained language model, can be fine-tuned for specific summarization tasks, enhancing its adaptability to various applications.

3   Summarization Scenarios

Depending on the domain and document type, summarization can be applied in different contexts. Common scenarios include single-document summarization, multi-document summarization, and cross-lingual summarization. Single-document summarization refers to generating a summary from one document, while multi-document summarization synthesizes information from multiple documents [19]. Cross-lingual summarization creates summaries in one language based on documents written in another language [3]. Each scenario presents unique challenges and requires specialized techniques for effective summarization.

3.1   Single and Multi-document Summarization

Single-document summarization focuses on summarizing a single document. This approach is widely used for news articles, scientific papers, and other document types where main ideas are contained within a single source. Summarization for a single document can be performed using either extractive or abstractive techniques, depending on document complexity and task requirements. Extractive techniques are often favored for single-document summarization due to their simplicity and computational efficiency [9]. Popular datasets for single-document summarization include the CNN/Daily Mail, Newsroom, and PubMed datasets.

Multi-document summarization, in contrast, involves summarizing content from multiple documents. This scenario is commonly used in applications like news aggregation and comprehensive document summarization, where information from various sources needs to be combined. Like single-document summarization, multi-document summarization can use extractive or abstractive methods, although extractive techniques are generally more efficient for handling multiple documents [9]. Common datasets for multi-document summarization include the DUC, TAC, and MultiNews datasets.

3.2 Monolingual, Multilingual, and Cross-Lingual Summarization

Summarization tasks can also be categorized based on language: monolingual, multilingual, and cross-lingual summarization. Monolingual summarization generates summaries in the same language as the source document, while multilingual summarization produces summaries for documents in various languages. Cross-lingual summarization generates summaries in a different language than the original document [3], commonly used in applications such as machine translation and cross-lingual information retrieval.

Cross-lingual summarization can utilize either extractive or abstractive techniques, with extractive methods often preferred for their efficiency and simplicity. Popular datasets supporting cross-lingual summarization include WikiLingua, CrossSum, and XSUM.

3.3 Benchmark Datasets

Benchmark datasets are essential for training and evaluating summarization models across different domains. Popular datasets used in general-purpose, multilingual, and cross-lingual contexts include:

- **WikiLingua** [25]: A large cross-lingual dataset involving 18 languages and covering 306 (18×17) cross-lingual directions, each containing approximately 18,000 cross-lingual summarization (CLS) samples. WikiLingua also provides summaries in the original language.
- **CrossSum** [19]: A substantial cross-lingual dataset featuring more than 1,500 language pairs.
- **XSUM Dataset** [19]: Spanning 44 languages, XSUM supports extensive multilingual summarization.
- **OPUS Parallel Corpora** [39]: Covering over 200 languages, OPUS is valuable for multilingual and cross-lingual summarization tasks.

In addition, several datasets are specifically designed for summarization of conversational data:

- **AMI Meeting Corpus** [23]: Contains 100 h of recorded meeting conversations, ideal for summarizing structured discussions.
- **SAMSum Dataset** [16]: Features various mobile-based dialogues, providing realistic data for chat summarization.

- **DialogSum Dataset** [6]: Consists of 16,000 online chat logs and corresponding summaries, useful for summarizing informal conversations.

These datasets span a wide range of domains and languages, making them well-suited for training and evaluating diverse summarization models. They enable the assessment of different summarization techniques and facilitate performance comparisons across various approaches.

4   Evaluation Techniques

Evaluating summarization systems is a crucial task for measuring system performance. Summaries can be evaluated against a human-derived ground truth, such as an abstract when summarizing a paper [29], or through a reference-free approach that does not rely on human judgments [1]. Examples of reference-free metrics include:

- **Perplexity** [13]: Measures the probability of the generated text according to a language model; lower perplexity generally indicates better fluency and coherence.
- **Factuality checks** [24]: Verifies the accuracy of factual information in the summary using external knowledge sources.
- **Consistency checks** [5]: Assesses the internal coherence of the generated text.
- **Readability metrics** [4]: Evaluates the readability of the text using metrics like the Flesch-Kincaid or Gunning-Fog index.

In evaluating reference-based methods, several traditional and modern techniques have been widely applied in the literature.

4.1   Traditional Metrics

Traditional evaluation metrics for summarization, such as BLEU, ROUGE, and METEOR, measure the overlap between the generated summary and a reference summary [11]. These metrics rely on n-gram overlap and have been widely adopted in the summarization community. However, they have limitations, as they may not fully capture summary quality aspects such as writing style, coherence, and factual accuracy.

BERTScore is a more recent metric that addresses some of these limitations by using contextual embeddings to evaluate summary quality [43]. BERTScore has shown stronger correlations with human judgments of summary quality. Additionally, large language models (LLMs) can now be employed to assess summary quality along multiple dimensions, including coherence, accuracy, factuality, completeness, comprehensibility, and information density [26]. These newer methods provide a more fine-grained evaluation, helping us better understand the strengths and weaknesses of a summarization system.

Many traditional metrics use a reference summary R to evaluate the generated summary S through an n-gram approach. This approach divides the text into units, typically words, and calculates the probability of various n-gram combinations. For example, a 2-gram (bigram) approach calculates the probabilities of two-word combinations. Metrics such as ROUGE and BLEU are rooted in n-gram analysis [17].

ROUGE (Recall-Oriented Understudy for Gisting Evaluation) is a set of n-gram based metrics that are used to evaluate automatic summarization and machine translation. The most commonly used variants are ROUGE-N (N-gram recall), ROUGE-L (Longest Common Subsequence), and ROUGE-S (Skip-bigram). These metrics are defined as:

$$\text{ROUGE-N} = \frac{\sum_{S\in\{\text{References}\}} \sum_{\text{gram}_n \in \{S\}} \text{Count}_{\text{match}}(\text{gram}_n)}{\sum_{S\in\{\text{References}\}} \sum_{\text{gram}_n \in \{S\}} \text{Count}(\text{gram}_n)} \tag{1}$$

where $\text{Count}_{\text{match}}(\text{gram}_n)$ is the maximum number of n-grams co-occurring in a candidate and a set of reference sentences, and $\text{Count}(\text{gram}_n)$ is the number of n-grams in the reference.

$$\text{ROUGE-L} = \frac{LCS(\text{candidate}, \text{reference})}{\text{length of reference}} \tag{2}$$

where $LCS(\text{candidate}, \text{reference})$ is the length of the longest common subsequence between the candidate and the reference.

BLEU (Bilingual Evaluation Understudy) is a precision-based metric originally developed for machine translation but also used for text generation tasks. It measures the overlap between n-grams in the generated text and the reference text.

$$\text{BLEU} = \text{BP} \cdot \exp\left(\sum_{n=1}^{N} w_n \log p_n\right) \tag{3}$$

where BP is the brevity penalty, p_n is the precision for n-grams, and w_n is the weight for n-grams, typically $w_n = \frac{1}{N}$. The brevity penalty (BP) is calculated as:

$$\text{BP} = \begin{cases} 1 & \text{if } c > r \\ e^{(1-r/c)} & \text{if } c \leq r \end{cases} \tag{4}$$

METEOR (Metric for Evaluation of Translation with Explicit ORdering) evaluates translations by aligning them to the reference translation using exact matches, stemming, and synonymy. It calculates precision, recall, and a penalty for incorrect word order.

$$\text{METEOR} = F_{\text{mean}} \cdot (1 - \text{Penalty}) \tag{5}$$

where F_{mean} is the harmonic mean of precision P and recall R:

$$F_{\text{mean}} = \frac{10 \cdot P \cdot R}{R + 9P} \tag{6}$$

and the penalty is calculated based on the number of chunks ch and the number of matches m:

$$\text{Penalty} = \gamma \left(\frac{ch}{m}\right)^{\theta} \tag{7}$$

with γ and θ being parameters typically set to 0.5.

The main challenges in evaluating abstractive summarization methods are the diversity of outputs and the level of system creativity [11]. These problems and potential difficulties make it difficult to create a comprehensive evaluation framework that considers multiple dimensions. Additionally, domain-specific challenges arise, as different domains (e.g., news, scientific articles) may require different evaluation criteria.

Techniques like BERTScore [43] and SummaC [27] can evaluate the consistency of the summary with respect to the original document by simple matching similarities between relevant sentences extracted for both the main document and the summary.

BERTScore is based on cosine similarity between contextual embeddings of tokens in the generated summary and the reference summary. Let S be the generated summary and R the reference summary, with $\mathbf{x}_i$ representing the embedding of the i-th token in S and $\mathbf{y}_j$ the embedding of the j-th token in R. The BERTScore formula is:

$$\text{BERTScore} = \frac{1}{|S|} \sum_{i=1}^{|S|} \max_{j} \cos(\mathbf{x}_i, \mathbf{y}_j) \tag{8}$$

where:

- $|S|$ is the length of the generated summary,
- $\cos(\mathbf{x}_i, \mathbf{y}_j) = \frac{\mathbf{x}_i \cdot \mathbf{y}_j}{\|\mathbf{x}_i\| \|\mathbf{y}_j\|}$ is the cosine similarity between embeddings $\mathbf{x}_i$ and $\mathbf{y}_j$,
- $\max_{j}$ finds the most similar reference token embedding for each token in the generated summary.

For better alignment, BERTScore is typically calculated in three ways: *Precision*, *Recall*, and *F1-score*, similar to traditional evaluation metrics.

SummaC is a metric based on natural language inference (NLI) for measuring factual consistency by comparing segments of the summary and the source document. It uses a pre-trained NLI model to evaluate entailment probabilities.

Given a set of sentences in the source document $\{s_1, s_2, \ldots, s_m\}$ and sentences in the generated summary $\{t_1, t_2, \ldots, t_n\}$, the SummaC metric is calculated as:

$$\text{SummaC} = \frac{1}{n} \sum_{i=1}^{n} \max_{j} \text{NLI}(t_i, s_j) \tag{9}$$

where:

- NLI(t_i, s_j) represents the probability of entailment between the summary sentence t_i and each source sentence s_j,
- $\max_j$ finds the maximum entailment score for each summary sentence t_i,
- n is the number of sentences in the summary.

SummaC thus provides a score based on the maximum entailment probability for each summary sentence with respect to the source document, giving an overall measure of factual alignment.

Although these approaches can measure similarity to the original text, modern approaches aim to understand semantic aspects of the summary.

4.2 Modern Approaches

Different authors are employing LLMs to create both reference-based and reference-free evaluations of summaries. For instance, Liu et al. [26] use GPT-4 to extract different aspects of summarization quality.

In evaluating factual content, modern approaches define ways to assess the presence of facts in both the reference and the generated summary. Some notable techniques evaluate summary quality in terms of criteria such as factuality, completeness, conciseness, and accuracy [8,37].

Factuality: This measures the alignment between facts in the original text (or reference summary) and those in the generated summary. The process involves: 1) extracting a list of facts with LLMs, 2) calculating the match between facts from the original (f) and the summary (g). Using a similarity metric, we determine the maximum correspondence between f_i and g_j to form pairs $p_k \in P$, where P represents all possible pairs. Factuality is calculated as:

$$\frac{1}{|P|} \sum_{p \in P} \mathrm{sim}(p)$$

Facts f can be aggregated to enhance similarity.

Completeness: This counts the number of facts f_i from the original that are included in the summary. For this, we set a similarity threshold τ, counting only pairs with similarity above the threshold:

$$\frac{1}{|F|} \sum_{p} \lceil \mathrm{sim}(p) - \tau \rceil$$

Conciseness: This metric is similar to completeness but focuses on counting relevant facts g_i in the summary. Using a threshold τ, only pairs with similarity above the threshold are counted:

$$\frac{1}{|G|} \sum_{p} \lceil \mathrm{sim}(p) - \tau \rceil$$

Accuracy: This metric evaluates sentence-by-sentence similarity between the reference and generated summary, identifying fits (sentences included in both) and misses (sentences missing from the generated summary). Accuracy is then calculated as:

$$ACC = \frac{TP_{fit} + TN_{miss}}{TP_{fit} + TN_{miss} + FP_{fit} + FN_{miss}}$$

Although these metrics provide a deeper semantic understanding of summaries, more efforts are needed to understand semantic equivalence when facts are defined in different forms.

In terms of evaluating summaries generated by LLMs, it is also essential to consider LLM limitations such as hallucinations and factual errors [11]. Metrics like CoCo [44] and FIB [38] can be used to evaluate the factual consistency of the summary, helping to identify hallucinations and factual inaccuracies and providing feedback to improve system performance. Additionally, it is important to consider biases in the summary, such as stereotypes and representation bias.

5   Conclusions

Although summarization techniques have advanced significantly in recent years, many challenges remain. Effective evaluation of summarization systems requires a comprehensive understanding of their strengths and weaknesses. Traditional evaluation metrics like ROUGE and BLEU have notable limitations, as they do not fully capture summary quality in terms of writing style, coherence, and factual accuracy. Moreover, newer metrics must contend with the complexity and variability of different solutions and diverse outputs. Evaluating abstractive summarization methods is particularly challenging due to the inherent creativity of these systems and the range of potential outputs they produce.

Domain-specific challenges also arise, as evaluation criteria may vary widely depending on the field. To address these issues, it is essential to develop new evaluation metrics that can assess qualities such as coherence, accuracy, factuality, completeness, comprehension, and density. These metrics can provide valuable insights into the strengths and limitations of a summarization system and offer constructive feedback to enhance its performance. By creating more sophisticated evaluation metrics and techniques, we can further the field of summarization and build more effective summarization systems.

Acknowledgments. The support of the UKRI Trustworthy Autonomous Systems Hub (reference EP/V00784X/1) and Trustworthy Autonomous Systems Node in Verifiability (reference EP/V026801/2) and the Alan Turing grant G2027 - MuSE is gratefully acknowledged.

References

1. Akkasi, A., Fraser, K.C., Komeili, M.: Reference-free summarization evaluation with large language models. In: Proceedings of the 4th Workshop on Evaluation and Comparison of NLP Systems, pp. 193–201 (2023)

2. Banerjee, S., Lavie, A.: Meteor: an automatic metric for MT evaluation with improved correlation with human judgments. In: Proceedings of the ACL Workshop on Intrinsic and Extrinsic Evaluation Measures for Machine Translation and/or Summarization, pp. 65–72 (2005)
3. Bhattacharjee, A., Hasan, T., Ahmad, W.U., Li, Y.F., Kang, Y.B., Shahriyar, R.: Crosssum: beyond English-centric cross-lingual summarization for 1,500+ language pairs. arXiv preprint arXiv:2112.08804 (2021)
4. Brewer, J.C.: Measuring text readability using reading level. In: Advanced Methodologies and Technologies in Modern Education Delivery, pp. 93–103. IGI Global (2019)
5. Chen, Y., Liu, P., Qiu, X.: Are factuality checkers reliable? Adversarial meta-evaluation of factuality in summarization. In: Findings of the Association for Computational Linguistics: EMNLP 2021, pp. 2082–2095 (2021)
6. Chen, Y., Liu, Y., Chen, L., Zhang, Y.: Dialogsum: a real-life scenario dialogue summarization dataset. arXiv preprint arXiv:2105.06762 (2021)
7. Deutsch, D., Dror, R., Roth, D.: A statistical analysis of summarization evaluation metrics using resampling methods. Trans. Assoc. Comput. Linguist. **9**, 1132–1146 (2021)
8. Dierickx, L., Van Dalen, A., Opdahl, A.L., Lindén, C.G.: Striking the balance in using LLMs for fact-checking: a narrative literature review. In: Multidisciplinary International Symposium on Disinformation in Open Online Media, pp. 1–15. Springer (2024)
9. El-Kassas, W.S., Salama, C.R., Rafea, A.A., Mohamed, H.K.: Automatic text summarization: a comprehensive survey. Expert Syst. Appl. **165**, 113679 (2021)
10. Erkan, G., Radev, D.R.: Lexrank: graph-based lexical centrality as salience in text summarization. J. Artif. Intell. Res. **22**, 457–479 (2004)
11. Ermakova, L., Cossu, J.V., Mothe, J.: A survey on evaluation of summarization methods. Inf. Process. Manag. **56**(5), 1794–1814 (2019)
12. Gambhir, M., Gupta, V.: Recent automatic text summarization techniques: a survey. Artif. Intell. Rev. **47**(1), 1–66 (2017)
13. Garimella, A., Sancheti, A., Aggarwal, V., Ganesh, A., Chhaya, N., Kambhatla, N.: Text simplification for legal domain: {i}nsights and challenges. In: Proceedings of the Natural Legal Language Processing Workshop 2022, pp. 296–304 (2022)
14. Ghojogh, B., Ghodsi, A.: Attention mechanism, transformers, BERT, and GPT: tutorial and survey (2020)
15. Gholamrezazadeh, S., Salehi, M.A., Gholamzadeh, B.: A comprehensive survey on text summarization systems. In: 2009 2nd International Conference on Computer Science and its Applications, pp. 1–6. IEEE (2009)
16. Gliwa, B., Mochol, I., Biesek, M., Wawer, A.: Samsum corpus: a human-annotated dialogue dataset for abstractive summarization. arXiv preprint arXiv:1911.12237 (2019)
17. Graham, Y.: Re-evaluating automatic summarization with bleu and 192 shades of rouge. In: Proceedings of the 2015 Conference on Empirical Methods in Natural Language Processing, pp. 128–137 (2015)
18. Gupta, A., Chugh, D., Anjum, Katarya, R.: Automated news summarization using transformers. In: Sustainable Advanced Computing: Select Proceedings of ICSAC 2021, pp. 249–259. Springer (2022)
19. Hasan, T., et al.: XL-sum: large-scale multilingual abstractive summarization for 44 languages. arXiv preprint arXiv:2106.13822 (2021)

20. ter Hoeve, M., Kiseleva, J., de Rijke, M., et al.: What makes a good summary? Reconsidering the focus of automatic summarization. arXiv preprint arXiv:2012.07619 (2020)
21. Huang, Y., Feng, X., Feng, X., Qin, B.: The factual inconsistency problem in abstractive text summarization: a survey. arXiv preprint arXiv:2104.14839 (2021)
22. Johner, T., Jana, A., Biemann, C.: Error analysis of using bart for multi-document summarization: a study for English and German language. In: Proceedings of the 23rd Nordic Conference on Computational Linguistics (NoDaLiDa), pp. 391–397 (2021)
23. Kraaij, W., Hain, T., Lincoln, M., Post, W.: The AMI meeting corpus. In: Proceedings of the International Conference on Methods and Techniques in Behavioral Research, pp. 1–4 (2005)
24. Kryściński, W., McCann, B., Xiong, C., Socher, R.: Evaluating the factual consistency of abstractive text summarization. arXiv preprint arXiv:1910.12840 (2019)
25. Ladhak, F., Durmus, E., Cardie, C., McKeown, K.: Wikilingua: a new benchmark dataset for cross-lingual abstractive summarization. arXiv preprint arXiv:2010.03093 (2020)
26. Liu, Y., Iter, D., Xu, Y., Wang, S., Xu, R., Zhu, C.: G-eval: NLG evaluation using GPT-4 with better human alignment. arXiv preprint arXiv:2303.16634 (2023)
27. Mani, I., Klein, G., House, D., Hirschman, L., Firmin, T., Sundheim, B.: Summac: a text summarization evaluation. Nat. Lang. Eng. $8(1)$, 43–68 (2002)
28. Menéndez, H.D., Plaza, L., Camacho, D.: A genetic graph-based clustering approach to biomedical summarization. In: Proceedings of the 3rd International Conference on Web Intelligence, Mining and Semantics, pp. 1–8 (2013)
29. Menéndez, H.D., Plaza, L., Camacho, D.: Combining graph connectivity and genetic clustering to improve biomedical summarization. In: 2014 IEEE Congress on Evolutionary Computation (CEC), pp. 2740–2747. IEEE (2014)
30. Mihalcea, R., Tarau, P.: TextRank: bringing order into text. In: Proceedings of the 2004 Conference on Empirical Methods in Natural Language Processing, pp. 404–411 (2004)
31. Narayan, S., Cohen, S.B., Lapata, M.: Ranking sentences for extractive summarization with reinforcement learning. arXiv preprint arXiv:1802.08636 (2018)
32. Ozsoy, M.G., Alpaslan, F.N., Cicekli, I.: Text summarization using latent semantic analysis. J. Inf. Sci. $37(4)$, 405–417 (2011)
33. Pfaff, C.W.: Constraints on language mixing: intrasentential code-switching and borrowing in Spanish/English. Language 291–318 (1979)
34. Qazvinian, V., et al.: Generating extractive summaries of scientific paradigms. J. Artif. Intell. Res. 46, 165–201 (2013)
35. Sahoo, D., Bhoi, A., Balabantaray, R.C.: Hybrid approach to abstractive summarization. Procedia Comput. Sci. 132, 1228–1237 (2018)
36. Shi, T., Keneshloo, Y., Ramakrishnan, N., Reddy, C.K.: Neural abstractive text summarization with sequence-to-sequence models. ACM Trans. Data Sci. $2(1)$, 1–37 (2021)
37. Song, H., Su, H., Shalyminov, I., Cai, J., Mansour, S.: Finesure: fine-grained summarization evaluation using LLMs. arXiv preprint arXiv:2407.00908 (2024)
38. Tam, D., Mascarenhas, A., Zhang, S., Kwan, S., Bansal, M., Raffel, C.: Evaluating the factual consistency of large language models through summarization. arXiv preprint arXiv:2211.08412 (2022)
39. Tiedemann, J., Thottingal, S.: Opus-MT–building open translation services for the world. In: Proceedings of the 22nd Annual Conference of the European Association for Machine Translation, pp. 479–480 (2020)

40. Wang, J., Meng, F., Zheng, D., Liang, Y., Li, Z., Qu, J., Zhou, J.: Towards unifying multi-lingual and cross-lingual summarization. arXiv preprint arXiv:2305.09220 (2023)
41. Xue, L.: MT5: a massively multilingual pre-trained text-to-text transformer. arXiv preprint arXiv:2010.11934 (2020)
42. Zeyad, A.M.A., Biradar, A.: Advancements in the efficacy of flan-t5 for abstractive text summarization: a multi-dataset evaluation using rouge and bertscore. In: 2024 International Conference on Advancements in Power, Communication and Intelligent Systems (APCI), pp. 1–5. IEEE (2024)
43. Zhang, T., Kishore, V., Wu, F., Weinberger, K.Q., Artzi, Y.: Bertscore: evaluating text generation with BERT. arXiv preprint arXiv:1904.09675 (2019)
44. Zhou, Y., et al.: Analyzing and mitigating object hallucination in large vision-language models. arXiv preprint arXiv:2310.00754 (2023)

Journal First

Summary of ObfSec: Measuring the Security of Obfuscations from a Testing Perspective

Héctor D. Menéndez[1]([✉])[iD] and Guillermo Suárez-Tangil[2][iD]

[1] Department of Informatics, King's College London, London, UK
`hector.menendez@kcl.ac.uk`
[2] IMDEA Networks Institute, Madrid, Spain
`guillermo.suarez-tangil@imdea.org`

Abstract. Code obfuscation is a widely used technique to protect the intellectual property of software by altering its structure to make it harder to understand or reverse-engineer. However, these modifications to the control flow and data flow can inadvertently compromise the security of the software. With a broad range of obfuscation methods available, each altering the program's structure differently, these changes can introduce new bugs or exacerbate existing ones, potentially increasing the risk of vulnerabilities.

In this context, we introduce ObfSec (Obfuscation Security), a novel approach to evaluate the security implications of software obfuscation. ObfSec systematically detects pre-existing errors in software and analyzes how obfuscation can alter the nature of these errors, particularly focusing on transformations that might convert benign bugs into exploitable vulnerabilities. Our study, conducted on a corpus of approximately 70,000 programs subjected to various obfuscation techniques, demonstrates that obfuscation can indeed degrade the security of software.

Keywords: Obfuscations · Security · Testing

Journal First Paper: Menéndez, H. D., & Suárez-Tangil, G. (2022). *ObfSec: Measuring the security of obfuscations from a testing perspective.* Expert Systems with Applications, 210, 118298. https://doi.org/10.1016/j.eswa.2022.118298.

1 Introduction

Code obfuscation is a widely used technique to protect software intellectual property by making programs more difficult to analyze or reverse-engineer [2,5,7]. While effective in safeguarding code [9–11], obfuscation can also negatively impact software quality by introducing new bugs or exacerbating existing ones. The transformations applied during obfuscation can alter the control and data flow of a program [1,4], potentially turning non-exploitable bugs into serious vulnerabilities. Although past research has focused on the strength of obfuscation engines against de-obfuscation [8,13], there has been limited exploration of the impact of obfuscation on software reliability, particularly from a testing perspective.

This paper introduces ObfSec [12], a novel framework designed to evaluate the security implications of obfuscation by measuring a program's security before and after obfuscation. ObfSec employs four key metrics: resistance, exploitability, stability, and complementarity, to assess how obfuscation affects software vulnerability and testability. The study examines 20 state-of-the-art obfuscation techniques across 70,137 programs, analyzing over 646,000 crashes. The findings reveal that obfuscation can be leveraged as a testability transformation [6], contrary to the expectation that it complicates the testing process. Additionally, the research introduces a triage system for prioritizing crash analysis, demonstrating that certain obfuscation methods are more likely to result in exploitable vulnerabilities.

2   ObfSec: The Security of Obfuscation

ObfSec [12] provides a comprehensive framework to quantify the security impact of code obfuscation. Notably, it enables the identification of fundamental flaws within obfuscation systems.

ObfSec integrates four key measures into a seamless processing pipeline, focusing on both independent properties of obfuscated programs and their relationship to the original code. First, it assesses: a) the effort required to discover crashes through fuzzing [14] (`fuzzibility`), and b) the likelihood that an obfuscation will introduce vulnerabilities (`exploitability`). While `fuzzibility` evaluates how prone an obfuscation is to generating crashes, `exploitability` measures the severity of those crashes. These metrics provide complementary perspectives on the reliability of an obfuscation engine.

Additionally, ObfSec introduces two comparative measures: c) the transferability of observations between the original and obfuscated programs (`stability`), and d) the extent to which obfuscation aids in uncovering new crashes and exploits beyond what is detectable in the original program (`complementarity`). The latter relates to the concept of testability transformation [6], where program modifications enhance the testing process.

The processing pipeline of ObfSec operates in three stages: *generation*, *triage*, and *cross-testing*, as illustrated in Fig. 1. Initially, obfuscations of a program are generated using various algorithms, treating both the original and obfuscated versions as Subjects Under Test (SUTs). A fuzzing system then produces test suites for each SUT, identifying inputs that trigger crashes. The *triage* stage evaluates the severity of these crashes using heuristics that consider crash types (e.g., segmentation faults) to estimate exploitability. Finally, the *cross-testing* phase compares the original and obfuscated programs, allowing ObfSec to calculate `stability` and `complementarity`. This approach enables developers to prioritize fixes based on their specific obfuscation needs.

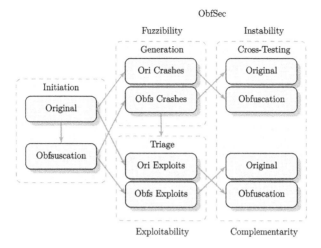

Fig. 1. ObfSec process. It is divided in three phases: the generation, triage and the cross-testing.

3   Experiments

For the evaluation of our ObfSec methodology, we selected four obfuscation engines. These engines exhibit diverse properties and strategies, although some commonalities exist, such as literal modifications and arithmetic transformations.

To conduct our experiments, we considered four state-of-the-art obfuscation tools for C commonly employed in related research [2]: `Tigress`, LLVM-O, the commercial `Stunnix` (CXX), and the system tool `CObfusc`. Given our focus on C code, we prioritized established tools. We compared the obfuscation engines across compilers, using `Clang` for LLVM-based obfuscations and `GCC` for the others.

In total, we explored 20 different transformations from the four engines. `Tigress`, offered several obfuscation strategies: 1) Injection of unreachable predicates (`InitOp`), 2) Utilization of system-specific variations (`UpOp`), 3) Virtualization (`Virtu`), 4) Implicit flow obfuscation (`ImplFl`), 5) Entropy manipulation (`InitEn`), 6) Branch manipulation (`InitBr`), 7) Anti-branch analysis countermeasures (`AntiBr`), 8) Anti-taint analysis countermeasures (`AntiTa`), 9) Anti-alias analysis countermeasures (`AntiAl`), 10) Literal encoding (`EncLit`), and 11) Arithmetic operation encoding (`EncAri`).

The system tool `C-OBFUSC` manipulated literals using numbers (`CobfsNum`) or words (`CObfsWord`). The commercial tool `Stunnix` provided the following obfuscations: 1) Shortened names (`cxxobfShortest`), 2) Hexadecimal string encoding (`cxxhexchar`), and 3) Constant transformation into sums of three elements (`cxxobfSum3`).

Finally, `LLVM-Obfuscation` offered four transformations: 1) Arithmetic instruction replacement (`llvmsub`), 2) Control flow graph flattening (`llvmfla`),

3) Basic block splitting (`llvmsplit`) and 4) Bogus control flow insertion before function calls with opaque predicates (`llvmbcf`).

Our selection of transformations aimed to cover a wide spectrum of techniques as described by Collberg et al. in [3], encompassing both open-source and commercial tools.

4 Main Outcomes

ObfSec is effective across different obfuscations and compilers, as it does not disrupt the fuzzing process. On average, the fuzzer identifies at least four crashes per program efficiently, demonstrating the viability of the `fuzzibility` metric.

Obfuscations influence a program's exploitability, reducing it by up to 50% with `AntiAl` or increasing it by 27% with `EncAri`. ObfSec reveals how errors evolve under various obfuscations, with some crashes disappearing, particularly with `AntiAl` and `InitBr`, while most obfuscations remain stable in terms of error detection by fuzzers.

Obfuscation can serve as a `testability transformation`, unmasking errors, especially with `Virtu` and LLVM-Fla. For instance, `Virtu` exposes new Floating Point Exception errors that are harder to detect in the original program. ObfSec also highlights the sensitivity of exploits to obfuscation, with inverse instability increasing significantly, particularly with `Virtu`, `InitBr`, `InitOp`, `IpOp`, and LLVM obfuscations like `BCF` or `Split`, altering the nature of the exploits.

Moreover, ObfSec demonstrates that the quality of obfuscation extends to detecting novel exploits beyond crashes. For example, the `complementarity` of `Virtu` reaches a factor of 28.74, and specific vulnerabilities, such as the BadInstruction vulnerability, are uncovered differently depending on the compiler, with `UpOp` revealing it in GCC and `BCF` in Clang.

Obfuscations cause transitions between crashes and errors, revealing patterns, with SegmentationFault being the most severe crash type, capable of evolving into nearly any other crash type. For vulnerabilities, DestAv, SegFaultOnPC, and StackCorruption are particularly significant, all related to stack manipulation.

5 Conclusions

ObfSec employs four novel metrics across three phases: `fuzzibility` measures how obfuscation affects fuzzing resistance, `exploitability` assesses the severity of crashes, `instability` examines testing divergence between the original and obfuscated programs, and `complementarity` evaluates the added value of these divergences. Our study on 70,137 programs using 20 obfuscation algorithms revealed how obfuscation impacts software reliability. Future work will extend ObfSec to guide fuzzification, improve testability, and rank problematic obfuscations.

Acknowledgments. The support of the UKRI Trustworthy Autonomous Systems Hub (reference EP/V00784X/1) and Trustworthy Autonomous Systems Node in Verifiability (reference EP/V026801/2) and the Alan Turing grant G2027 - MuSE is gratefully acknowledged.

References

1. Banescu, S., Collberg, C.S., Ganesh, V., Newsham, Z., Pretschner, A.: Code obfuscation against symbolic execution attacks. In: Proceedings of the 32nd Annual Conference on Computer Security Applications, ACSAC 2016, Los Angeles, CA, USA, 5–9 December 2016, pp. 189–200 (2016). http://dl.acm.org/citation.cfm?id=2991114
2. Chen, T.Y., et al.: Metamorphic testing for cybersecurity. Computer **49**(6), 48–55 (2016)
3. Collberg, C., Thomborson, C., Low, D.: A taxonomy of obfuscating transformations. Technical report, Department of Computer Science, The University of Auckland, New Zealand (1997)
4. Garg, S., Gentry, C., Halevi, S., Raykova, M., Sahai, A., Waters, B.: Candidate indistinguishability obfuscation and functional encryption for all circuits. SIAM J. Comput. **45**(3), 882–929 (2016)
5. Güler, E., Aschermann, C., Abbasi, A., Holz, T.: Antifuzz: impeding fuzzing audits of binary executables. In: 28th USENIX Security Symposium (USENIX Security 2019), pp. 1931–1947 (2019)
6. Harman, M., et al.: Testability transformation. IEEE Trans. Software Eng. **30**(1), 3–16 (2004)
7. Jung, J., Hu, H., Solodukhin, D., Pagan, D., Lee, K.H., Kim, T.: Fuzzification: anti-fuzzing techniques. In: 28th USENIX Security Symposium (USENIX Security 2019), pp. 1913–1930 (2019)
8. Ma, H., Ma, X., Liu, W., Huang, Z., Gao, D., Jia, C.: Control flow obfuscation using neural network to fight concolic testing. In: International Conference on Security and Privacy in Communication Systems, pp. 287–304. Springer (2014)
9. Martin, A., Menéndez, H.D., Camacho, D.: Genetic boosting classification for malware detection. In: 2016 IEEE Congress on Evolutionary Computation (CEC), pp. 1030–1037. IEEE (2016)
10. Menéndez, H.D.: Malware: the never-ending arms race. Open J. Cybersecur. **1**(1), 1–25 (2021)
11. Menéndez, H.D., Llorente, J.L.: Mimicking anti-viruses with machine learning and entropy profiles. Entropy **21**(5), 513 (2019)
12. Menéndez, H.D., Suárez-Tangil, G.: Obfsec: measuring the security of obfuscations from a testing perspective. Expert Syst. Appl. **210**, 118298 (2022)
13. Wang, P., et al.: Software protection on the go: a large-scale empirical study on mobile app obfuscation. In: Proceedings of the 40th International Conference on Software Engineering (ICSE 2018) (2018)
14. Zalewski, M.: American fuzzy lop (2019). http://lcamtuf.coredump.cx/afl/

Health Track

A Trusted Friend in the Middle of the Night: End-User Perspectives on Artificial Intelligence Informed Software Systems as a Decision-Making Aid for Patients and Clinicians Navigating Uncertainty in Kidney Transplant

Laura R. Wingfield[1]($\boxtimes$) ⓘ, Katie Wainwright[2], Simon Knight[1] ⓘ, and Helena Webb[3] ⓘ

[1] Nuffield Department of Surgical Sciences, University of Oxford, Oxford, UK
Laura.Wingfield@ox.ac.uk, simon.knight@nds.ox.ac.uk
[2] School of Medicine, University of Nottingham, Nottingham, UK
[3] School of Computer Science, University of Nottingham, Nottingham, UK
helena.Webb@nottingham.ac.uk

Abstract. Deceased donor kidney transplantation is often the only treatment for patients in end-stage renal disease and other life-threatening conditions. Kidney transplant processes can be fraught with uncertainty for both clinicians making critical decisions about whether to transplant an organ and the kidney recipients. There is potential for AI-informed software-based systems to support the activities of information-giving, decision-making, and waiting. This study analyses qualitative interviews to explore the user perspectives including those of both clinicians and transplant patients regarding this kind of decision making aid. Fourteen kidney transplant recipients and ten clinicians were recruited in a U.K transplant centre clinic. Data was collected via face-to-face and video-recorded semi-structured interviews and was analysed using a modified grounded-theory approach. Two patient themes were generated: 'The murky waters of AI' and 'AI-driven tools could help transplant patients.' The clinician themes included: 'Understanding AI and the general perception around this technology,' and 'AI can be a friend to call on.' The results highlight the possibility of an AI software programme to explain complex ideas to patients, by providing visual and graphical representations of AI-powered, individualised survival calculations or organ wait list times. The design and implementation of such tools must centre around trust in AI technology for clinicians and patients. The balance of staying on the waiting list or accepting an organ involves many complex factors but using AI-informed technology would be welcomed by patients and clinicians.

Keywords: End-user Testing · Artificial Intelligence · Semi-structured interviews · Kidney Transplant · Modified Grounded Theory

© IFIP International Federation for Information Processing 2025
Published by Springer Nature Switzerland AG 2025
H. D. Menéndez et al. (Eds.): ICTSS 2024, LNCS 15383, pp. 193–209, 2025.
https://doi.org/10.1007/978-3-031-80889-0_14

1   Introduction

Kidney transplantation is usually considered the optimum treatment for patients with end-stage renal disease who are fit enough to undergo surgery [1, 2]. In addition to better patient survival with transplantation, patients also experience a better quality of life following their kidney transplant [3]. However, although approximately 2,500 deceased donor kidney transplants are performed in the UK each year, there are around 5,000 patients on the kidney transplant waiting list at any one time. This disparity between supply and demand means that many patients waiting for a kidney transplant become too unwell for surgery or die while on the waiting list [4]. Uncertainty about short and long-term post-transplant outcomes for these donor organs leads to variability in organ offer decline rates between kidney transplant centres as well as individual clinicians [5].

Decisions to accept or decline an organ offer are made by the transplant team based upon information about the donor, recipient and the organ that they have available at the time of the offer. Clinicians use their experience to make these often complex decisions, but currently do not have tools to help them predict what could happen if they chose to accept or decline an offer and wait for the next one. The few computer-based tools that are available have limited capabilities and generally use regression-based models, which do not allow for the complex non-linear relationships seen between donor and recipient variables and clinical outcomes.

Previous research using Artificial Intelligence (AI)-based predictive models shows promise, including the ability of models to better predict kidney graft survival times when compared to traditional models used in clinical practice. The models that have been created thus far have been successful in predicting kidney transplant data from various global transplant registry data sets. However, very few of these tools have been actually implemented in a real-world, clinical environment [6, 7].

AI-based models can lack transparency and may be perceived to lack moral judgement, which may therefore result in a lack of trust towards the use of AI in surgery [8]. Despite these concerns, research has suggested that patients are indeed open to the use of an AI-informed tool due to the significant benefits that it may have on providing further insight into surgical decision making and greater patient-centred planning particularly in the transplant process [9]. Research has also made clear that patients are more comfortable with the use of AI when under the supervision of a doctor, using the system as an advisory tool rather than having overall control of the course of treatment [10].

Clinicians have also shown support for implementing potential AI models, acknowledging the benefits that improved accuracy and efficiency may have. They have however noted the need for a significant amount of research and testing in order to prove the effectiveness and reliability of the AI, before putting this into practice [9]. Research amongst medical professionals reveals they have raised concerns around the lack of clarity and transparency in AI, further highlighting the desire for explainable models [11]. In agreement with patients, medical professionals have made clear the desire for AI-informed systems to be implemented as an advisory tool, whilst ensuring ease of use and integration with existing systems [12, 13].

Possibly the most prominent barrier to the use of AI in transplant surgery, is the lack of previous testing and understanding of its implementation in the specific setting. Whilst doctors have expressed their acceptance of such a model, it is key that these concerns are accounted for [14]. Additionally, the lack of official guidance, both ethical and practical, on how AI should be implemented in the transplant setting has further hindered its adoption. Whilst some guidance has now been published by Vasey *et al.,* this must be adopted on a wide-scale basis in order to ensure proper regulation in the development of AI-based tools in a clinical setting [15, 16]. This study uses qualitative interviews to elicit context specific clinician and patient perspectives around AI-informed software systems to answer the question: can a clinician decision making tool be used in kidney transplant to help patients and clinicians understand the risk associated with specific patient-allocated organs?

2   Methods

Kidney transplant patients (n = 14) were directly recruited from a transplant centre outpatient clinic at an NHS hospital in the UK. Inclusion criteria included both men and women over the age of 16 years old who had received a deceased donor kidney transplant in the last three years. Further criteria included participants were willing and able to give informed consent for participation in the study and were willing to participate in a 30-min interview. All ethnic backgrounds were included within the study. Study participants ranged in age from 28–81 years old. Additional patient characteristics are shown in Table 1.

Clinician participants (n = 10) were recruited from a kidney transplant centre at an NHS hospital in the UK. The inclusion criteria included those currently working as a consultant surgeon or nephrologist, fellow or specialist registrar in transplantation or nephrology. Participants needed to be willing and able to participate in a 30-min interview. Both men and women were included as were all ethnic backgrounds. Self-reported clinical years of experience ranged from 7–40 years. Additional clinical participant characteristics are shown in Table 2.

Table 1. Patient Study Participant Characteristics

Participant number	Participant	Age	Sex	Ethnicity	Patient reported reason for transplant	Patient reported comorbidities
1	Amit	81	M	Asian	Hypertension	N/A
2	Connor	63	M	White British	Anti-GMB	Hypertension
3	Edward	78	M	Black	Hypertension	Asthma, angina, arthritis

(continued)

Table 1. (*continued*)

Participant number	Participant	Age	Sex	Ethnicity	Patient reported reason for transplant	Patient reported comorbidities
4	Gerry	52	M	White British	Diabetes	Asthma, retinopathy, macular oedema, peripheral neuropathy and ischemic damage phalanges
5	Izzy	28	F	White British	Diabetes	N/A
6	Karen	77	F	White British	Chronic Kidney Disease	Bipolar disease
7	Manuel	56	M	White British	Polycystic kidney disease	Mitral valve replacement
8	Oliver	32	M	White British	Ig Nephropathy	N/A
9	Rachel	42	F	White British	Diabetes	Bilateral central retinal detachment, hypothyroidism, transient ischaemic attack, post-traumatic stress disorder
10	Tina	30	F	White British	Unknown autoimmune disease	Type I diabetes
11	Vivian	59	F	White British	Glomerulonephritis	Ulcerative Colitis, diverticulitis
12	Carl	49	M	White British	Diabetes	DVT, high cholesterol, previous eye surgery
13	Ethan	74	M	White British	Kidney cancer	Hypertension
14	Glen	58	M	White British	Diabetes	Charcot's foot, peripheral neuropathy, visual impairment

Table 2. Clinician Study Participant Characteristics

Participant number	Participant	Sex	Job Title	Years of experience
1	Aaron	M	Consultant Transplant Surgeon	15
2	Carmen	F	Transplant Surgery Fellow	7
3	Erik	M	Consultant Nephrologist	24
4	Gurpreet	M	Consultant Transplant Surgeon	29
5	Ian	M	Consultant Transplant Surgeon	12
6	Kieran	M	Consultant Transplant Surgeon	10
7	Mary	F	Consultant Transplant Surgeon	26
8	Oliver	M	Consultant Nephrologist	10
9	Quintin	M	Consultant Nephrologist	40
10	Sarah	F	Consultant Nephrologist	24

2.1 Procedure

The recruitment for the study was carried out by one of the researchers prior to patient routine appointments. Informed consent was taken in writing prior to all interviews. Semi-structured, in-depth interview format was used to collect data. Fourteen face-to-face patient interviews were carried out by from April 2022 to October 2022 and clinical participants were similarly recruited during the same time. LW was the sole interviewer for both patient and clinician participants to ensure consistency in the process and data collection. The recruitment of patients and clinicians was carried out until data saturation was achieved [17]. Patient interview questions covered the following topics: demographic details and introductory questions, decision making around the transplant process, general AI/Machine Learning (ML) themed questions, and questions around an AI driven clinical tool. The clinician questions included similar themes such as demographic questions and length of transplant experience, general AI/ML themed questions, and questions around the clinicians' thoughts about an AI software tool being used in their clinical practice. (see appendix). This study received favourable ethical opinion from the Southeast Scotland Research Ethics Committee (reference: 22/SS/0008). All research carried out within this study followed the World Medical Association Declaration of Helsinki. All participants provided written informed consent prior to enrolment in the study.

3 Data Analysis

All interviews were audio-recorded and semi-structured interviews were utilised as the data collection method of choice. Short interview guides were created that include opening, central and closing questions with a focus on open-ended questions to allow for greater consistency in the data collection process [18]. As part of a theoretical sampling approach to data collection, the researchers jointly collected, coded, and analysed the data in a cyclical process in order to develop emerging themes. As themes emerged during the data collection, the team collected further data to either confirm or deny concepts. The participants were continuously recruited throughout the data collection process until data saturation was achieved [19]. Saturation was determined via a grounded theory approach as data was continuously being coded and collected as new participants entered the study. When no new themes were emerging from the data, a discussion between researchers LW and HW was conducted and participant recruitment was then ended. Coding and theme generation was initially completed by LW and then discussed with HW for creation of the final set of codes. The process of coding was an iterative process and occurred continuously during the data collection process [20].

4 Results

Both the clinicians and patients discussed a range of understanding and engagement with AI-informed systems. Clinicians described their understanding of the technology and overall positive perception of how it may be used in real-world terms. Patients described how they did not need an in-depth understanding of AI to see useful application of it during their transplant journey. The main themes evident within the patient data included: 'The murky water of AI: understanding what AI actually is' and 'AI-driven tools could help transplant patients.' The main themes which immerged within the clinician data included: 'Understanding AI and the general perception around this technology' and 'AI can be a friend to call on.' The names for both clinicians and patients are pseudonyms to protect anonymity.

4.1 Theme 1 Patients: The Murky Waters of AI, Understanding What AI Actually is

All patients interviewed for this study had heard of AI to some extent; either in the media, television, film or connected with their occupation. Younger patients tended to have a connection or understanding of AI due to ways it was used within their professional spheres. Some of the elderly patients admitted to not knowing a great deal regarding AI, but they had heard of the concept most commonly on news programmes discussing the technology. Many of the patient participants admitted to feeling confused or unsure of what the technology was, citing that they believed it had something to do with robotics and computing combined. However, despite some participants believing that the field was very challenging to understand, several participants were able to provide very clear definitions of what AI technology entailed including,

"I think of it as an assisting tool that is supervised by human beings…And by that I mean human beings who actually know what the results are meant to say, and yes and understand it, not just an IT person who's making sure the programs work. And then I think they can be very useful…" (Edward).

Furthermore, for the participants who were able to grasp the concept of AI, several of them were able to understand why it could be helpful in general, citing enhanced processing speeds. Further participants went on to express the widespread applicability of the technology.

"I think it's [AI] a huge step forward in terms of speed and accuracy…" (Manuel).

"AI is interesting. I see that it has good applications." (Gerry).

Although the patients generally perceived AI in a neutral or positive light, a few patients with more specific awareness highlighted certain ethical issues around AI-informed systems. One patient stated, "… That machine [AI] might make the wrong decision, right?" (Edward).

Overall, although some of the patients expressed difficulties in navigating the vernacular of AI technology even when discussed in films or the news or expressed some minor concern with the technology, they still regarded AI as overwhelmingly positive.

4.2 Theme 2 Patients: AI-Driven Tools Could Help Transplant Patients

Although most patients interviewed had limited in-depth knowledge of AI or experience using AI-based systems themselves, many of them saw AI as a positive tool to be potentially used with transplant patients. Furthermore, most patients could make the link between AI being similar to advanced computer programmes. This understanding could be extremely important in establishing trust between patients and any type of AI used in clinical practice.

"I mean… Hang on, hang on, to me basically It's sort of saying this is just computing on steroids [AI]. Because you know it just works with what, if any, computer comes up and out, but it's much faster and much more powerful than uh, when we use it. So yeah, there's a risk of things like… I know biases, it so that you know happens anyway, people or computing…" (Oliver).

Additionally, patients could see the technology being used specifically in their transplant waiting list journey. They often noted that personalising the information being given to them would be useful and were excited at the prospect of such mechanisms being utlised.

"No, no, no, I definitely I definitely would love to know that [organ waiting list times]. I think that in that sense AI would act as a tool as any other tool, yeah? Yeah, so as long as the medical professional know exactly the parameters of that tools, uh so he or she yeah could uh, look at those results and then make a final conclusion of that." (Manuel).

Participants made connections to how the information from AI predictions used in transplant would directly affect them during their transplant patient journey. It was especially clear that the road to receiving a transplant was often long and plagued with emotional stresses for patients. They described having AI-driven information about how long they would need to wait for their transplant as very helpful.

"Yeah, yeah, it's just nice to know where the end of the tunnel is because we were just waiting every day you know. Initially we didn't think about waiting for the kidney. And once we had that first time to come in, then because the fact that we've declined it [declined a kidney organ offer], you think, oh I wonder how long we're gonna wait now… "(Carl).

4.3   Theme 1 Clinicians: Understanding AI and the General Perception Around This Technology

All of the clinicians interviewed had heard of AI and were aware of some of the basic principles behind it. Interestingly, amongst the clinicians, there were several participants with a very high level of understanding of AI including those who had learned how to programme basic machine learning algorithms. Other clinicians, although not directly involved in AI, had been so interested in the subject that they were reading books about AI in their spare time.

"Yeah, I think basic. I've gone so far as to have bought the book called, 'Hello World.' An introduction to AI stats, it's beside my bed and I've not read it yet. But the thought of using AI, I think it's just brilliant. Yeah, I think it'll be such… it's such a bonus because the alternative is us going.. uh, on a WhatsApp group going, 'I've got this offer [organ offer], what do people think?' We've got the data out there. We need to use it so I am an enthusiast." (Carmen).

All of the clinicians involved in the study either saw AI as neutral or positive. No one interviewed felt that it was negative (overall) or expressed generalised distrust of the use of AI. Clinicians were very quick to point out the potential benefits of AI-informed systems and without being prompted often mentioned how they could be included in their day-to-day clinical experiences and how they may improve patient outcomes.

"I think I'm very positive about the role of AI. I'm still mindful that sometimes a human being making the ultimate decision is probably best and I wouldn't think that AI should just take over…. Yeah, just the sum of so many brains in one machine so I'm sure that people think that's a good idea. I think that probably, especially unless it would be in medicine, a lot of it will be a conversation between AI, the clinicians and the patient." (Mary).

Ultimately, the clinicians were very enthusiastic about the use of AI in various fields, especial the medical one. None of the cohort interviewed specifically mentioned that they felt the technology was negative in general or should not be used. Not unsurprisingly, as many of those interviewed were involved in medical research, they had a very good grasp of AI and basic principles behind how it worked. This was in contrast to the patient population interviewed where a number of the group were unsure of the principles behind AI and could not clearly explain how AI-informed systems work or how they could be implemented in a clinical setting.

4.4 Theme 2 Clinician: AI Can Be a Friend to Call on

A key theme that emerged from interviews with clinicians was that they viewed AI similarly to a friend or trusted colleague that they could call on in the middle of the night if they needed urgent advice on an organ transplant. Some of the clinicians even gave potential AI solutions a 'human-like' description and noted that they were hopefully that they would come up with the correct solutions in the middle of the night.

"I'm optimistic that that there are potential solutions if we understand the multivariate factors that go into it and create appropriate algorithms, then I think the machine will come up with the right deductions sometimes at 3:00 o'clock in the morning, the night or morning that the human mind might fail to take into account. Yeah, so I could see the potential benefit of it, yes." (Gurpreet).

Furthermore, clinicians described it as a great, complementary tool to have in their arsenal to provide consent-based information during the pre-operative process.

"That when you're consenting a patient, if you were to have that to say, the model says, I think it's good for you, but also the numbers. The model says this you are likely 90% to survive one year, five years X. And the average survival is this and this is gonna give you X, think that would be amazing." (Mary).

Finally, the clinicians within this study, seemed to describe a high level of trust in the technology with the assumption that anything used in clinical practice had been adequately tested: "Uh, yeah, the assumption I would make, rightly or wrongly, is that, um, is that if something makes it if a particular technology makes it into clinical practice, but it's been well tested and it's been peer reviewed by AI Scientists, as well as clinicians, so I would sort of assume that it… is the limitations are acknowledged and that the information you're getting is to a greater degree accurate, and so I wouldn't any hesitation in using that information, uh, in the field." (Kieran).

5 Discussion

To date, there has been scarce research into transplantation and this current analysis can provide insight into an area that needs urgent exploration. As AI is becoming more advanced, researchers and clinicians seem eager to implement it in clinical settings; however, before this step is materialised, it is essential to capture the perspectives and practical needs of both patients and clinicians, and to ensure they are accommodated in the design and implementation of AI-informed software systems.

Although the majority of patients did not possess expert knowledge on AI, almost all of them saw the potential benefits to such a technology being used in transplant medicine. Overall, patients inherently trusted tools that their transplant clinicians would use and integrated the trust of the clinician with the trust of technology the clinician may elect to use as part of their clinical practice. Many of the patients noted that clinicians were already using resources such as statistics and online information so they would not have an issue trusting the AI technology being used as it would be yet another resource.

The clinicians interviewed as part of this study both understood the basics of AI and saw the importance of implementing AI-informed technologies in the near future. They were aware of such technologies being used by colleagues in other areas of medicine and were excited and enthusiastic about implementing equivalent tools within their own department. Despite their optimism about AI, the majority of those interviewed wanted any AI-informed software system that was developed to both validated and equitable to their patient cohorts. Some key concerns that were discussed included the integrity of inputted data, which if inputted incorrectly could have significant ramifications. Similarly to other research on the viewpoints of clinicians and AI, the participants here wanted to understand as much as possible the way the technology worked while also admitting that it was unlikely they would fully grasp some of its intricacies [21].

5.1 Evaluation of the Research

The study takes a vital user-centred approach: engaging with future-end users at this early stage ensures that user needs are captured and can be attended to in the eventual design and implementation of software tools to aid decision-making in transplant settings. This user-centred approach also identifies potential features for such tools, such as mechanisms to personalise decision-making to specific scenarios such as transplant recipient age, comorbidities etc. and consent-taking processes. These findings also address a direct gap in the current field of transplant medicine as previous tools have been basic and do not allow for this kind of personalisation.

The evaluation of this study involved ensuring that the methodology was thorough and able to be replicated. Standard semi-structured interview methodology was used, making this study replicable on a larger scale in the future at different U.K. transplant centres. Our inclusion and exclusion criteria for both the clinicians and transplant recipients was robust, as detailed in our methodology section. This both aids in the reproducibility of the study and the generality of the findings.

5.2 Clinical Implications of this Study

This study highlights the possibility of AI-informed tools being used in the clinic or bedside to explain often complex ideas to patients, by providing visual and graphical representations of AI-powered, individualised survival calculations or organ wait list times [22]. As previously mentioned, the clinical implementation of such tools, especially in the medical environment, must centre around trust in the AI technology for both clinicians and patients. The key components of a 'trusting relationship' that were mentioned within both clinician and patient interviews focused on the transparency of the technology (when possible), knowledge of those building the tool, and a cycle of building trust in AI-based tools.

5.3 Challenges to Implementation

Although the majority of both patients and clinicians saw AI in a positive way and could realise the benefits of it being implemented, there are a number of challenges to incorporating AI-informed software systems into a healthcare setting. Barriers to implementation cited by innovators in the NHS include IT infrastructure difficulty and language clarity. Solutions suggested within the research include education strategies and the creation of innovation champions within each healthcare organisation [23]. Within the UK, further implementation hurdles lie in the classification of AI as a medical device by the Medicines and Healthcare products Regulatory Agency (MHRA). Clinicians, data scientists and software developers may lack the experience necessary to navigate a long, time-consuming regulatory process to embed AI-informed tools to assist transplant patients in real clinical practice [24]. Further challenges include difficulties in the integration of AI-informed tools with existing electronic health records [25, 26]. This is a vital hurdle that healthcare systems must address as an increasing number of transplant centres rely on electronic patient data when transplanting a kidney.

Another challenge for clinicians and researchers is the 'Black-Box Phenomenon,' where due to the nature of AI techniques, especially Machine Learning, the exact mechanism of how computations are derived are opaque. AI algorithms may provide clinicians, for example, a recommendation to 'accept this organ for patient x,' but with no explanations or justifications provided for how the results were derived [27, 28]. This opacity can affect trust in the system. Additionally, patients may experience further trust-related concerns. As reflected in our findings, research has shown that there is often limited public literacy about AI and the extent that it 'makes' decisions independently. Patients may feel – and mistrust – AI-informed systems will decide their treatment options autonomously from their clinicians.

Finally, machine learning bias possess a threat to both clinician and patient trust within the transplant decision tool. This algorithm design challenge can result in a tool that may favour or cause negative consequences to certain (often underrepresented) groups. Often this occurs when the system itself is designed based on biased data sets or when data scientists creating the models may have some inherit bias. These concerns are especially worrying in the context of tools delivering medical solutions to patients and clinicians where in extreme cases life and death decisions are being formulated.

5.4 Study Limitations

All clinicians and patients who agreed to participate in this study may have exhibited some self-selection of those interested or knowledgeable about AI in transplantation. Additionally, participants were recruited from a transplant clinic for post-transplant follow-up. This allowed somewhat recent transplant recipients to participate in the research project to ensure they remembered the information given during their transplant. Finally, both patient and doctor interviews were limited to a single-transplant centre in the UK.

6 Conclusions

The data extracted from the clinicians and patients from this study can be generalisable to a wider audience in the implementation of AI-informed clinical tools. A potential tool could be developed as a web-based, end-user interface tool that would enable the user to personalise the displayed data points according to their preferences (i.e. numerical, graphs, or a combination of both). Ideally, such a web-based interface would be integrated with existing transplant programmes found within the hospital setting such as the NHS

Blood and Transplant (NHSBT) Electronic Offering System (EOS), which is used by all transplant centres within the U.K. when an organ offer is made.

Both participant groups for the most part welcomed the use of new technology, such as AI, to help provide tailored information to make the transplant journey easier. The understanding of AI technology including the trust, transparency, and transferability into existing systems must be undertaken to meet this unmet patient and clinician requirement in transplantation. This is further actualised in the need to create user-centred AI tools that take into account the requirements of those that will both utilise the tool in their clinical settings and the patients receiving what is often life-changing information. Ultimately, there is a need for further research in the specific AI tool design, functionality, and transparency factors to ensure the integration of this vital technology in the near future to transplant centres throughout the UK.

Declaration of Conflicting Interests. The authors declare that there is no conflict of interest.

Appendix

Supplementary Material 1: Patient Participant Interview Schedule
Explainable machine learning models for clinical decision support in kidney transplant offering.
[For Internal Use Only]

Demographic details/introductory questions

1. What is your age?
2. What is your ethnicity?
3. When did you receive your kidney transplant?
4. Why did you need a kidney transplant?
5. What medical conditions do you currently suffer from? (i.e. diabetes, COPD, etc.)

Decision making around the transplant process.

1. When you discussed the transplant offering system with your doctor, how much information were you given about the process? Did you feel that you received an option on whether to accept verse decline an offer?
2. How did the clinician give you the information about your offer? Did they simply tell you an offer was made or did you have information on the quality of the organ itself?
3. Did your doctor say you were a difficult to match patient? Or were their discussions around the criteria needed to match you with a suitable donor organ?
4. Did you have any discussions around waiting list times during your transplant journey? If so, were you given estimated times for how long you would have to wait? If not, would you have liked to have this information?
5. Looking back on your transplant experience, how much information about the transplant process would you have liked to have? (i.e. I wished I had received less information at the time, what I received at the time was sufficient, or I wish I had been given more detail)

General Artificial/Machine Learning themed Questions.

Note: researcher to ask the first question to the participant. If the participant does not have any knowledge in AI, the researcher will elaborate and give a basic explanation of AI to include the following:

Artificial Intelligence (AI) is a type of computer programme that mimics human thinking in the way it processes information. It is able to form complex pathways and 'think' like humans. The way that AI works is sometimes understood by computer scientists but there are other instances that AI works in ways we can not explicitly understand. Researchers are using this type of technology to help solve complicated problems in a variety of fields, including medicine.

Additional Note: depending on participant's answers, only Questions 1 and 2 to be asked if no previous knowledge of AI.

1. Do you have any knowledge of Artificial Intelligence (AI)? And what level of knowledge do you have?
2. How much interest in AI do you have? If you are interested in AI, where did you first hear about it? (news programme, article online, etc.)
3. What is your awareness and views on AI in general?
4. What do you think are the positive aspects of AI?
5. Do you think there are any negative aspects of AI?

Difficult to ask questions about AI if patient is unaware of AI in general – may need to relate it to mathematical tool.

Research specific questions and Clinical Decision Support Tool.

1. What aspects of Artificial Intelligence (AI) do you have concerns around? What would stop you from accepting this technology to help make decisions by doctors? (i.e. around transplanted organs)
2. How would you feel about AI technology being used to assist clinicians make a decision about your transplants?
3. How transparent would you need the AI tool (in calculating your organ transplant or waitlist times) to be for you to feel comfortable? (i.e. I would need to know exactly how the AI model calculated the survival, I would only need to know some of the way the model calculated this information, I would not need to know how the tool worked)
4. How would you feel about AI technology helping doctors make predictions on how long your waiting time before an organ may be offered to you?
5. If AI could be used to predict your organ survival as well as waitlist times if you decided not to accept an organ, how would you like to have this information presented to you? (i.e. visual representation, graphs, numeric data)?
6. Is there anything you would like to discuss that we haven't discussed today?

Supplementary Material 2: Clinician Interview Schedule
Explainable machine learning models for clinical decision support in kidney transplant offering.
[For internal use only]

Demographic details/introductory questions

1. What is your current role?
2. How many years have you been involved in kidney transplants?
3. How long have you worked at the Oxford Transplant Centre?

Decision making around the transplant process

1. When discussing the transplant offering system with a kidney transplant patient, how much information do you tell the patient about the process? Do you ask them how much information they would like to receive?
2. How do you present the information about a potential kidney offer? Do you look through the clinical data first and make a decision about whether this is an appropriate offer or do you involve the patient in the decision-making process?
3. Do you let patients know if they may be a difficult to match patient?
4. Do you discuss the pros and cons of accepting a potential donor organ verse continue to stay on the wait list?
5. Do you tell patients how long they may have to wait on the waiting list? (even if this is an estimation)
6. If a marginal kidney is offered, do you let the patient know this information? Do you involve them in the decision-making process to accept/reject such an organ?

General Artificial/Machine Learning themed Questions
Note: researcher to ask the first question to the participant. If the participant does not have any knowledge in AI, the researcher will elaborate and give a basic explanation of AI to include the following:

Artificial Intelligence (AI) is a type of computer programme that aims at providing computer programmes that mimic human thinking in the way they processes information. The way that AI works is sometimes understood by computer scientists but there are other instances that AI works in ways we can not explicitly understand. Researchers are using this type of technology to help solve complicated problems in a variety of fields, including medicine.

One example of AI is in risk prediction scoring. Similar to regression models there are input variables that can be used to determine outcomes. However, in AI we are not always aware of the weighting of each variable in the algorithm.

Additional Note: depending on participant's answers, only Questions 1 and 2 to be asked if no previous knowledge of AI.

1. Do you have any knowledge of Artificial Intelligence (AI)? And what level of knowledge do you have?
2. How much interest in AI do you have? If you are interested in AI, where did you first hear about it? (news programme, article online, etc.)
3. What is your awareness and views on AI in general?
4. What do you think are the positive aspects of AI?
5. Do you think there are any negative aspects of AI?
6. Are you aware of AI being used in clinical practice? If so, what areas?
7. Have you heard of any clinicians or research groups using AI in the transplant decision making process? If so, what did you think about this?

Research specific questions and Clinical Decision Support Tool

1. Do you use any calculators or risk assessment tools in your clinical practice? What do you like/dislike about them?
2. What aspects of Artificial Intelligence (AI) do you have concerns around? What would stop you from accepting this technology to help you make decisions? (i.e. around transplanted organs)
3. How would you feel about AI technology being used to assist you to make a decision about your patients' transplants?
4. How transparent would you need the AI tool (in calculating the organ transplant survival or waitlist times) to be for you to feel comfortable? (i.e. I would need to know exactly how the AI model calculated the survival, I would only need to know some of the way the model calculated this information, I would not need to know how the tool worked)
5. If AI could be used to predict patient organ survival as well as waitlist times if you decided to reject an organ in the form of a clinical decision support tool, how would you like to have this information presented to you? (i.e. visual representation, graphs, numeric data)?
6. How much detail do you think your patients would want from the tool? (i.e. very detailed, somewhat detailed, minimal detail)
7. In what format should the clinical decision support tool take? (i.e. web-based, app-based)
8. Would a tool be useful in the informed consent process? (similar to P-POSSOM score for laparotomy)
9. Is there anything you would like to discuss that we haven't discussed today?

References

1. Edwards, E.B., Bennett, L.E., Cecka, J.M.: Effect of HLA matching on the relative risk of mortality for kidney recipients: a comparison of the mortality risk after transplant to the mortality risk of remaining on the waiting list. Transplantation **64**(9), 1274–1277 (1997). https://doi.org/10.1097/00007890-199711150-00007
2. Wolfe, R.A., et al.: Comparison of mortality in all patients on dialysis, patients on dialysis awaiting transplantation, and recipients of a first cadaveric transplant. N. Engl. J. Med. **341**(23), 1725–1730 (1999). https://doi.org/10.1056/NEJM199912023412303
3. Ogutmen, B., et al.: Health-related quality of life after kidney transplantation in comparison with intermittent hemodialysis, peritoneal dialysis, and normal controls. Transpl. Proc. **38**(2), 419–421 (2006). https://doi.org/10.1016/j.transproceed.2006.01.016
4. Section-5-kidney-activity.pdf. (n.d.). https://nhsbtdbe.blob.core.windows.net/umbraco-assets-corp/27118/section-5-kidney-activity.pdf. Accessed 22 Nov 2022
5. Variation_in_organ_decline_rates.pdf. (n.d.). http://odt.nhs.uk/pdf/advisory_group_papers/KAG/Variation_in_organ_decline_rates.pdf. Accessed 22 Nov 2022
6. Seyahi, N., Ozcan, S.G.: Artificial intelligence and kidney transplantation. World J. Transplant. **11**(7), 277–289 (2021). https://doi.org/10.5500/wjt.v11.i7.277
7. Wingfield, L.R., Ceresa, C., Thorogood, S., Fleuriot, J., Knight, S.: Using artificial intelligence for predicting survival of individual grafts in liver transplantation: A systematic review. Liver Transpl. **26**(7), 922–934 (2020). https://doi.org/10.1002/lt.25772

8. Asan, O., Bayrak, A.E., Choudhury, A.: Artificial intelligence and human trust in healthcare: focus on clinicians. J. Med. Internet Res. **22**(6), e15154 (2020). https://doi.org/10.2196/15154

9. Murray, T., McCarthy, M.: Perceptions of AI in healthcare: insights from a national survey. J. Healthc. Manag. **66**(2), 115–126 (2021). https://doi.org/10.1097/JHM-D-20-00179

10. Palmisciano, P., Jamjoom, A.A., Taylor, D., Stoyanov, D., Marcus, H.J.: Attitudes of patients and their relatives toward artificial intelligence in neurosurgery. World Neurosurg. **138**, e627–e633 (2020). https://doi.org/10.1016/j.wneu.2020.03.029

11. Ghassemi, M., Oakden-Rayner, L., Beam, A.L.: The false hope of current approaches to explainable artificial intelligence in health care. Lancet Digit. Health **3**(11), e745–e750 (2021). https://doi.org/10.1016/S2589-7500(21)00208-9

12. Gumbs, A.A., et al.: White paper: definitions of artificial intelligence and autonomous actions in clinical surgery. Artif. Intell. Surg. **2**, 93–100 (2022). https://doi.org/10.20517/ais.2022.10

13. Hassan, N., Slight, R., Slight, S.: Healthcare staff perceptions on using artificial intelligence predictive tools: a qualitative study. BMJ Health Care Inform. **29**(Suppl 1), A4–A5 (2022). https://doi.org/10.1136/bmjhci-2022-FCIASC.7

14. Horsfall, H.L., et al.: Attitudes of the surgical team toward artificial intelligence in neurosurgery: international 2-stage cross-sectional survey. World Neurosurg. **146**, e724–e730 (2021). https://doi.org/10.1016/j.wneu.2020.10.171

15. Vollmer, M.A.: Ethical considerations in artificial intelligence applications in healthcare: perspectives from patients and practitioners. Ethics Med. **36**(4), 233–245 (2020). https://doi.org/10.1177/1388888X20949787

16. Vasey, B., et al.: Reporting guideline for the early stage clinical evaluation of decision support systems driven by artificial intelligence: DECIDE-AI. BMJ e070904 (2022). https://doi.org/10.1136/bmj-2022-070904

17. Francis, J.J., et al.: What is an adequate sample size? Operationalising data saturation for theory-based interview studies. Psychol. Health **25**(10), 1229–1245 (2010). https://doi.org/10.1080/08870440903194015

18. Foley, G., Timonen, V.: Using grounded theory method to capture and analyze health care experiences. Health Serv. Res. **50**(4), 1195–1210 (2015). https://doi.org/10.1111/1475-6773.12275

19. Bryant, A., Charmaz, K.: The SAGE Handbook of Grounded Theory. SAGE Publications Ltd. (2007). https://doi.org/10.4135/9781848607941

20. Vollstedt, M., Rezat, S.: An introduction to grounded theory with a special focus on axial coding and the coding paradigm. In: Kaiser, G., Presmeg, N. (eds.) Compendium for Early Career Researchers in Mathematics Education, pp. 81–100. Springer (2019). https://doi.org/10.1007/978-3-030-15636-7_4

21. Strauss, A.T., et al.: Hepatol. Commun. **7**(10), e0239 (2023)

22. Clement, J., Maldonado, A.Q.: Augmenting the transplant team with artificial intelligence: toward meaningful AI use in solid organ transplant. Front. Immunol. **12** (2021)

23. Morrison, K.: Artificial intelligence and the NHS: a qualitative exploration of the factors influencing adoption. Future Healthcare J. **8**(3), e648–e654 (2021). https://doi.org/10.7861/fhj.2020-0258

24. Software and AI as a Medical Device Change Programme—Roadmap. (n.d.). GOV.UK. https://www.gov.uk/government/publications/software-and-ai-as-a-medical-device-change-programme/software-and-ai-as-a-medical-device-change-programme-roadmap. Accessed 22 Nov 2022

25. Davenport, T., Kalakota, R.: The potential for artificial intelligence in healthcare. Future Healthcare J. **6**(2), 94–98 (2019). https://doi.org/10.7861/futurehosp.6-2-94

26. Kelly, C.J., Karthikesalingam, A., Suleyman, M., Corrado, G., King, D.: Key challenges for delivering clinical impact with artificial intelligence. BMC Med. **17**(1), 195 (2019). https://doi.org/10.1186/s12916-019-1426-2

27. Burrell, J.: How the machine 'thinks': understanding opacity in machine learning algorithms. Big Data Soc. **3**(1), 2053951715622512 (2016). https://doi.org/10.1177/2053951715622512
28. Price, W.N.: Big data and black-box medical algorithms. Sci. Transl. Med. **10**(471), eaao5333 (2018). https://doi.org/10.1126/scitranslmed.aao5333

Binary Classification Optimisation with AI-Generated Data

Manuel Jesús Cerezo Mazón[1], Ricardo Moya García[1], Ekaitz Arriola García[1], Miguel Herencia García del Castillo[1], and Guillermo Iglesias[2]($\boxtimes$)

[1] Ainovis, Colquide 6, 28231 Las Rozas, Madrid, Spain
info@ainovis.health
[2] Universidad Politécnica de Madrid, Madrid, Spain
guillermo.iglesias@upm.es

Abstract. In the field of machine learning, obtaining sufficient and high-quality data is a persistent challenge. This report explores the innovative solution of using synthetic data generated from existing datasets to overcome this limitation. By employing synthetic data, we not only increase the quantity of available information but also maintain the integrity and essential characteristics of natural data. This methodology allows the application of conventional data augmentation techniques, ensuring a more robust and efficient learning process. The study is based on a dataset provided by the International Skin Imaging Collaboration (ISIC), consisting of 3,323 cases divided equally between melanomas and Basal Cell Carcinoma (BCC). Using Generative Adversarial Networks (GANs), specifically StyleGAN2 with transfer learning from the Flickr-Faces-HQ (FFHQ) model, synthetic images were generated, expanding the dataset fourfold to a total of 26,584 synthetic records. The quality of the synthetic images was ensured using the Frechet Inception Distance (FID) metric [5], with BCC obtaining 22.2534 and melanomas obtaining 20.4577 according to this metric. Models trained with a hybrid approach using both real and synthetic data showed improved performance metrics (F1 0.71 to 0.79), highlighting the effectiveness of this method in enhancing binary classification tasks in medical imaging. The source code for all the research, along with the generated dataset is publicly available.

Keywords: Machine Learning · Synthetic Data · GAN · Skin Lesion Classification · Data Augmentation · FID · ISIC · Medical Imaging

1 Introduction

In the field of machine learning, the availability of sufficient and high-quality data is a constant challenge that limits the effectiveness of predictive models [1]. This challenge is particularly pronounced in the domain of medical imaging, where the acquisition of large annotated datasets is often infeasible due to privacy concerns, the need for expert annotations, and the inherent rarity of certain conditions. To address these issues, researchers have turned to synthetic

H. D. Menéndez et al. (Eds.): ICTSS 2024, LNCS 15383, pp. 210–216, 2025.
https://doi.org/10.1007/978-3-031-80889-0_15

data generation techniques, which have shown promise in augmenting existing datasets and improving model performance [13].

This study focuses on the binary classification of skin lesions, specifically melanoma and BCC, using a dataset provided by the ISIC. The dataset consists of 3,323 images, divided equally between the two types of skin lesions. However, the limited size of this dataset poses a significant challenge in the training of robust machine learning models. To mitigate this issue, we employ synthetic data generation using Generative Adversarial Networks (GANs).

Using StyleGAN2 [8] with transfer learning from the FFHQ pretrained model [7], we generated high-quality synthetic images to augment the original dataset. The augmented dataset significantly increased the amount of training data available, enabling the training of more robust classification models. The quality of the synthetic images was evaluated using the Frechet Inception Distance (FID) metric [5], with scores that indicate high fidelity to the real images.

The enhanced dataset was used to train two separate models for skin lesion classification, employing the ResNet-18 architecture [4]. The integration of synthetic data led to improvements in precision, recall, and overall classification accuracy, demonstrating the potential for GAN-based data enhancement in medical imaging.

Overall, this study highlights the effectiveness of synthetic data generation in overcoming data limitations and improving the performance of machine learning models in the medical domain. The use of high-quality synthetic data can address the challenges posed by limited datasets and improve diagnostic performance in medical applications.

The source code[1] and the dataset[2] are available in open repositories.

2   Background

Data augmentation is a common technique used to increase the amount and diversity of data available for training machine learning models. Techniques such as rotation, flipping, and cropping have been widely used to enhance the robustness of models by artificially increasing the size of the dataset [11]. However, these methods are often insufficient for tasks that require high-quality, diverse data, such as medical image classification.

GANs, introduced by Goodfellow et al. [3], have revolutionized data augmentation by enabling the generation of high-fidelity synthetic data. GANs consist of two neural networks, a generator and a discriminator, that are trained simultaneously through adversarial processes. This approach has been successfully applied in various fields, including the synthesis of medical images.

---

[1] https://github.com/Ekaitz723/Skin-lesion-clasif-GDA.
[2] Ainovis. (2024). Synthetic Datasets for "Binary Classification Optimisation with AI-Generated Data" [Data set]. 36th International Conference on Testing Software and Systems (ICTSS), London, United Kingdom.

Previous works have demonstrated the effectiveness of GANs in enlarging medical datasets. For example, Frid-Adar et al. [2] used GANs to generate synthetic liver lesion images, significantly improving the performance of a liver lesion classification model. Similarly, Shin et al. [10] showed that GAN-generated data could enhance the performance of deep learning models in the classification of brain tumors. In this study, we used StyleGAN2 [8] with transfer learning from the FFHQ model [7] to generate synthetic images for skin lesion classification.

The FID metric, introduced by Heusel et al. [5], is used to evaluate the quality of the generated images. The FID score is calculated by comparing the feature distributions of real and generated images. Lower FID scores indicate that the generated images are more similar to the real images. However, the effectiveness of the FID metric is highly dependent on the dataset used. In addition to that, many works that use generative models for Data Augmentation use FID to evaluate the quality of the synthetic samples [6,12].

3   Experimental Setup

3.1   Original Data

The present study is based on a data set provided by ISIC[3]. This dataset consists of 3,323 images, evenly divided between two main types of skin cancer: melanoma and BCC. The images are in RGB format, but their sizes vary. To ensure consistency, all images were resized to 512×512 pixels during the preprocessing stage.

The preprocessing process involved several key steps to prepare the images for the classification model:

- **Resizing:** All images were resized to 512×512 pixels to maintain uniformity in input dimensions.
- **Normalization:** The images were normalized scaling individual samples to have unit norm values following the *l2* norm, ensuring that the model could learn more effectively.
- **Data Augmentation:** Color jittering, variation in brightness, contrast, saturation, and hue, where applied to the training dataset, enhancing the robustness of the model by providing a diverse set of training examples.

These preprocessing steps ensured that the input data was properly processed and standardized for the classification task, facilitating effective training of the model.

3.2   Artificial Intelligence Generated Data

To address the problem of data sparsity and improve the robustness of the classification model, GANs was used to generate synthetic data. Specifically,

---

[3] https://www.isic-archive.com.

StyleGAN2 [8] was used, with transfer learning applied from the FFHQ 512×512 pretrained model[4] [7] to ensure high-quality generation of skin lesion images.

The training of the StyleGAN2 model involved the following hyperparameters:

- **Batch Size:** 150
- **Generator Learning Rate (glr):** 0.003
- **Discriminator Learning Rate (dlr):** 0.003
- **Gamma:** Initially set to 6.2, then adjusted to 5.5, 3.2, and finally 0.5 during the training course.
- **Epochs:** 260 epochs for melanoma and 310 epochs for BCC.

These parameters were chosen to optimize the quality of the generated images and to ensure that the synthetic data maintained high fidelity to the original dataset. The FID for the BCC synthetic images was 22.2534, while that for the Melanoma (MEL) synthetic images was 20.4577. According to Heusel et al., FID scores below 50 are generally considered good for medical image synthesis [5]. Once a satisfactory level of quality was reached, the dataset was expanded eight times, resulting in a total of 26,584 synthetic images (Fig. 1).

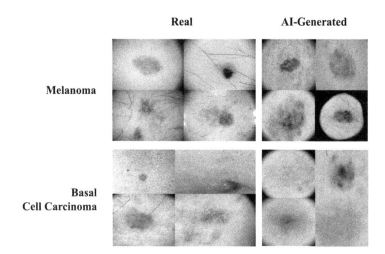

Fig. 1. Comparison between Real and Artificial Intelligence-Generated images

4   Data Assessment

4.1   Architecture of the Model

To implement the classification model, we used the ResNet-18 architecture [4]. ResNet-18 consists of 18 layers, including convolutional layers, pooling layers,

---

[4] https://catalog.ngc.nvidia.com/orgs/nvidia/teams/research/models/stylegan2/files.

and fully connected layers. This architecture is renowned for its ability to address the problem of vanishing gradients by incorporating residual connections. However, we altered the ResNet architecture to better suit the classification task and ensure appropriate handling of the input data. Specifically, the first convolutional layer, was replaced by a new convolutional layer with a kernel size of 7, a *stride* of 2, and a *padding* of 3. This alteration was made to better process the input data. The final fully connected layer was replaced by a sequence including a *dropout* layer and a linear layer ending with a *softmax* function for classification.

These alterations were made to optimize the network for the specific characteristics of the skin lesion images and improve the overall performance of the classification model.

The model has a total of 11,177,538 trainable parameters. ResNet-18's relatively shallow depth compared to other variants in the ResNet family strikes a balance between computational efficiency and model performance.

The training process was carried out using 4 A40 model graphics processing units (GPUs). Consistent hyperparameters were used for all experiments to ensure that the only variable that affected the performance of the model was the amount of synthetic data. These hyperparameters included 250 epochs, a batch size of 95 per GPU, a dropout rate of 0.15, a learning rate of 0.0005, and a weight decay of 0.01. The optimizer used was Adam [9].

5   Results

The models developed were evaluated using an entirely independent test set, composed exclusively of real images. This test set was not exposed to the models during training or validation phases, ensuring the impartiality and relevance of the evaluation results.

To systematically assess the impact of synthetic data on model performance, a series of experiments were conducted where the number of synthetic images in the training dataset was incrementally increased. The baseline model was trained using 5,400 real images. In subsequent experiments, 1,000 synthetic images were incrementally added to the training dataset. This resulted in a series of models trained on datasets containing 5,400 real images plus an increasing number of synthetic images, up to a maximum of 15,400 synthetic images.

The initial experiments, which used a lower percentage of synthetic data, yielded more favorable results in the metrics evaluated. A notable enhancement in precision, recall, F1 score, and accuracy was observed when the proportion of synthetic data was lower than that of real data. However, this improvement was not sustained in later experiments, in which the amount of synthetic data exceeded that of real data. This indicates that although synthetic data is beneficial for augmenting the quantity of data available for training, there is an optimal balance between synthetic and real data, beyond which the quality of classification is negatively affected.

Figure 2 illustrates how the evaluation metrics evolve with the number of synthetic images.

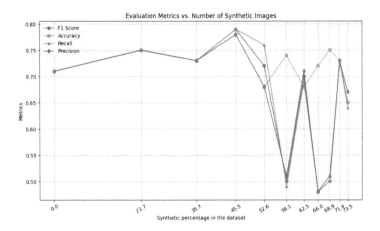

Fig. 2. Evaluation Metrics vs. Number of Synthetic Images

6   Discussion

The use of Artificial Intelligence-generated data allowed for multiple training iterations without the risk of overfitting, a common concern when working with small datasets. By artificially increasing the size of the dataset, the model can be trained on a wider diversity of examples, which improves its ability to generalize to new data not seen during training.

The inclusion of a large amount of synthetic data significantly increased the diversity of the training set. This is crucial in the context of skin lesion classification, where variations in images can be subtle but clinically and statistically significant. By exposing the model to a wider range of features and patterns present in skin lesion images, the model's ability to correctly identify both common and atypical lesions is improved.

7   Conclusions

The use of synthetic data generated by GANs has proven to be an effective solution to overcome data limitations in skin lesion classification. The integration of synthetic data not only increases the amount of data available for training but also improves the performance of the model in terms of accuracy, generalizability, and robustness [10]. The synthetic dataset used in the research is publicly available, along with the source code used for the development.

Optimal performance is found by using 45.5% synthetic data. Beyond this equilibrium point, recall and precision decline, and therefore the F1 score drops, while accuracy remains relatively unchanged without considerable drops. This suggests that while synthetic data is highly beneficial, there is an optimal balance between synthetic and real data that maximizes classification performance. This methodology can be applied to other areas of medicine and machine learning where data availability is a constant challenge.

References

1. Althnian, A., et al.: Impact of dataset size on classification performance: an empirical evaluation in the medical domain. Appl. Sci. **11**(2), 796 (2021). https://doi.org/10.3390/app11020796
2. Frid-Adar, M., Diamant, I., Klang, E., Amitai, M., Goldberger, J., Greenspan, H.: Gan-based synthetic medical image augmentation for increased CNN performance in liver lesion classification. Neurocomputing **321**, 321–331 (2018). https://doi.org/10.1016/j.neucom.2018.09.013
3. Goodfellow, I.J., et al.: Generative adversarial networks (2014). https://arxiv.org/abs/1406.2661
4. He, K., Zhang, X., Ren, S., Sun, J.: Deep residual learning for image recognition. In: Proceedings of the IEEE Conference on Computer Vision and Pattern Recognition, pp. 770–778 (2016). https://arxiv.org/abs/1512.03385
5. Heusel, M., Ramsauer, H., Unterthiner, T., Nessler, B., Hochreiter, S.: GANs trained by a two time-scale update rule converge to a local Nash equilibrium (2018). https://arxiv.org/abs/1706.08500
6. Jiménez-Gaona, Y., Carrión-Figueroa, D., Lakshminarayanan, V., Rodríguez-Álvarez, M.J.: GAN-based data augmentation to improve breast ultrasound and mammography mass classification. Biomed. Signal Process. Control **94**, 106255 (2024). https://doi.org/10.1016/j.bspc.2024.106255. https://www.sciencedirect.com/science/article/pii/S1746809424003136
7. Karras, T., Laine, S., Aila, T.: A style-based generator architecture for generative adversarial networks (2019). https://arxiv.org/abs/1812.04948
8. Karras, T., Laine, S., Aittala, M., Hellsten, J., Lehtinen, J., Aila, T.: Analyzing and improving the image quality of stylegan (2020). https://arxiv.org/abs/1912.04958
9. Kingma, D.P., Ba, J.: Adam: a method for stochastic optimization (2017). https://arxiv.org/abs/1412.6980
10. Shin, H.C., et al.: Medical image synthesis for data augmentation and anonymization using generative adversarial networks (2018). https://arxiv.org/abs/1807.10225
11. Shorten, C., Khoshgoftaar, T.M.: A survey on image data augmentation for deep learning. J. Big Data **6**(1), 1–48 (2019). https://doi.org/10.1186/s40537-019-0197-0
12. Tran, N.T., Tran, V.H., Nguyen, N.B., Nguyen, T.K., Cheung, N.M.: On data augmentation for GAN training. IEEE Trans. Image Process. **30**, 1882–1897 (2021). https://doi.org/10.1109/tip.2021.3049346
13. Yi, X., Walia, E., Babyn, P.: Generative adversarial network in medical imaging: a review. Med. Image Anal. **58**, 101552 (2019)

Responsible MLOps Design Methodology for an Auditing System for AI-Based Clinical Decision Support Systems

Pepita Barnard[1] , John Robert Bautista[2] , Aidan Dakhama[3] ,
Arya Farahi[4] , Kazim Laos[5] , Anqi Liu[6] , and Héctor D. Menéndez[3(✉)]

[1] School of Computer Science, University of Nottingham, Nottingham, UK
`pepita.barnard@nottingham.ac.uk`
[2] Sinclair School of Nursing, University of Missouri-Columbia, Columbia, USA
`jbautista@missouri.edu`
[3] Department of Informatics, King's College London, London, UK
`{aidan.dakhama,hector.menendez}@kcl.ac.uk`
[4] University of Texas at Austin, Austin, USA
`arya.farahi@austin.utexas.edu`
[5] Computer Science and Electronic Engineering, Solent University London, London, UK
[6] Department of Computer Science, Johns Hopkins University, Baltimore, USA
`aliu@cs.jhu.edu`

Abstract. The responsibility of making clinical diagnoses and treatment decisions will fall on clinicians regardless of whether an AI system is used. Ensuring trust in such systems is challenging given the fast paced development of AI technologies. In this paper, we present a methodology for designing appropriate auditing strategies and mechanisms involved in the life cycle of AI-based clinical decision support systems. The methodology is based on MLOps and responsible AI design principles. To ensure clinicians are involved in the MLOps process, we propose a Medical-MLOps process that includes clinicians in the design and deployment of an auditing extension for the MLighter tool. MLighter is designed to provide with the necessary information to understand the system's limitations and make informed decisions about its outcomes. MLighter is holistic, interpretable, and easy-to-use. The design decisions and requirements are derived from interviews with 20 clinicians in the UK and US. This information, along with input from developers and QA testers, enables us to define a set of auditing requirements. This work outlines the steps we followed during requirement extraction, the architecture we designed to adapt the tool, and the various workflows we established for different user types to ensure a holistic experience.

Keywords: Responsible Artificial Intelligence · Auditing AI · Clinical Decision Support System · MLighter

H. D. Menéndez et al. (Eds.): ICTSS 2024, LNCS 15383, pp. 217–236, 2025.
https://doi.org/10.1007/978-3-031-80889-0_16

1   Introduction

The new era of artificial intelligence (AI) has revolutionized the healthcare industry, with AI-based clinical decision support systems (AI-CDSS) offering the potential to enhance diagnostic accuracy and efficiency. However, the deployment of AI-based tools in clinical settings has raised concerns regarding the reliability and trustworthiness of these systems [10, 22, 29]. To address these concerns, we developed a machine learning-enhanced evaluation system for AI-based medical diagnostic tools. This system enables clinicians to evaluate AI models, ensuring that diagnostic recommendations are reliable and trustworthy. By integrating clinicians into the operational loop, we aim to enhance the trustworthiness of AI-CDSS tools and improve the overall quality of patient care.

Using questionnaires, we gathered information from clinicians regarding their preferences for system auditing features (Sect. 3). This information guided our design to ensure the auditing system included features that build and enhance medical professionals' trust in the AI-CDSS. Additionally, we integrated features that simplify deployment, testing, and management, facilitating future iterations of the system (Sect. 4).

In MLOps [14], a primary strategy to ensure efficiency throughout the software life-cycle is rigorous testing. Testing is essential to verify that the system meets the specified requirements provided by the stakeholders [19]. However, this becomes a complex task when the stakeholders are operating machine learning systems [20]. The inherent challenges include deciphering the internal workings of the models and establishing trust among the operators, particularly within the healthcare ecosystem. To address these challenges, we developed a tool that is accessible and understandable to various domain experts.

The initial step in our process involved collecting a comprehensive set of requirements from the operators, which detail how they intend to conduct testing. These requirements were translated into various potential interfaces within the tool we developed for auditing purposes. Thus, operators have the opportunity to interact directly with the models, posing queries relevant to diagnostic evaluations to ensure model coherence and integrity. Our focus was also extended to creating multiple interfaces for the operators, enabling us to assess which ones are most effective. This aims to create an AI-Human collaboration tool that can enhance trust in AI-CDSS among the medical professionals. By involving clinicians in the MLOps process, we obtained feedback from operators that guided our comparison of these interfaces, culminating in recommendations tailored to optimize data presentation for different users.

The main contributions of this paper are:

- We adapted MLOps design mechanisms to include clinicians during the AI-CDSS development life-cycle (Sect. 2).
- We created a set of questionnaires to collect information from 20 clinicians in the UK and the US to establish the most relevant audit requirements (Sect. 3).
- We extended the MLighter [20] tool's architecture to include the technical needs for the auditing process (Sect. 4).

– We defined multiple workflows for different stakeholders in the AI-CDSS life-cycle (Sect. 5) and match clinical requirements with these specific workflows (Sect. 6).

The extended version of the MLigther tool is publicly available here: https://github.com/hdg7/mlighter.   ,

2   The Medical Context of Machine Learning Operators (MLOps)

MLOps is a DevOps specification, especially focused on machine learning applications [14]. DevOps (or Developers/Operators) are the set of practises and tools involving different ways for developers, who create the software, and operators, who use it, to communicate and work together during the software life-cycle. The main goal is to optimize the development process, improve software security and performance, and maintain functionality to the required ones.

One of the main problems of MLOps in the medical context is that clinicians working in specialized areas will operate the machine learning system having little or no knowledge about how it is constructed [2]. This can lead to a lack of trust in the system and also to a lack of understanding of the system's limitations. Lack of understanding on system's limitations is problematic, for example, when the system is used in a different medical context than the one for which it was trained.

Within the context of medical domain, the MLOps process can be divided into three main stages: developing, operating and monitoring. The development stage is where the machine learning model is trained and tested. The operating stage is where the model is used in the real world, and the monitoring stage is where the model is evaluated and adjusted by the clinicians.

Figure 1 shows the main strategies for DevOps that easily generalize to MLOps. The process begins with a plan that outlines the tasks for the developers. The developers then build the software, which is subsequently tested by the continuous integration system. After testing, the software is deployed by the continuous deployment system. Once deployed, operators manage and monitor the software, providing feedback to the developers. Together, they design a new plan for adjustments, and the cycle begins again.

MLOps performs operations similarly to DevOps, but with some key differences [14]. One of the most important differences is the necessity of training and testing phases for the machine learning model. An ML implementation changes its outcomes by changing the training and test data that create the model. This, in turn, impacts the testing process, where outcomes depend not just on the implementation but also on the data and algorithms chosen.

During the integration phase, the models must be properly tested and validated by expert data scientist, in contrast to DevOps, where there are no models. The deployment phase is also different, as the model must be deployed in a way that is easy to use by the operators.

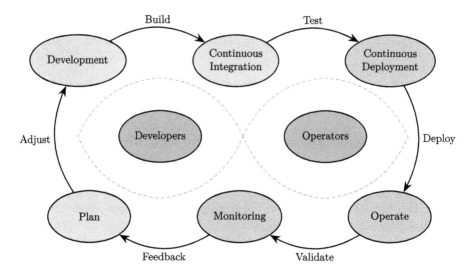

Fig. 1. The DevOps process loop.

This led us to identify three different actors in the MLOps process: developers, operators (clinicians), and data scientist, which we define as quality assurance (QA) testers. Developers are responsible for building the software, operators are responsible for operating the software, and data scientist are responsible for training and testing the machine learning models. Our tool, MLighter, is designed to assist these three roles in implementing testing strategies during the MLOps testing phase.

3   Interviews

The development of any health information technology requires input from potential end-users that would benefit from its use [25]. It is also an essential step to develop features that are responsive to the identified needs of end-users, thus, enhancing the trustworthiness and adoption of the resulting technology. To help us guide the development of our auditing system, we performed needs assessment interviews with clinicians in the UK ($n = 9$, September 2023 to May 2024) and the US ($n = 11$, August to October 2023). Conducting interviews in two countries is beneficial because it would allow us to design both general (i.e., features that could be useful in both countries) and context-specific (i.e., country-specific features) versions of the auditing tool.

We initially used network sampling to reach potential interviewees within our professional network. To enhance the qualitative findings' trustworthiness, rigor, and transferability, a maximum variation sampling [30] was utilized by recruiting diverse participants across professions (medical doctors and nurses), positions (clinicians and administrators), genders, and races. Interviews were conducted in line with interviewee preferences (i.e., in-person or online; with or without audio recording). Participants were asked questions about their work background (e.g., profession, years of informatics experience, and role in present institution), insights about AI as part of CDSS (e.g., familiarity, experiences, and concerns with AI-CDSS), and features of an auditing system that could display AI-CDSS audit results (e.g., what information should the auditing system display and who will be the potential users?). We also asked questions exploring participants' trust in AI-CDSS and how an auditing tool could influence that. Transcripts were automatically generated through Microsoft MS Teams or Zoom for audio-recorded interviews. The initial transcripts were checked for consistency with the audio recording. All personally identifiable details were deleted from the transcripts to uphold confidentiality. The verified transcripts were uploaded to MAXQDA 24 for thematic and content analyses.

3.1   Interview's Results

Preliminary results show that most participants were familiar with AI-based clinical decision support systems (AI-CDSS). Although most were working in health facilities that had not yet implemented AI-CDSS, a few had the opportunity to use them as part of their clinical work. Here, we present a case that exemplifies the need for an auditing system that health facilities can use. One example of a routinely used AI-CDSS is an ML-based risk score based on a constellation of data in the patient's electronic health record (EHR). The risk score highlights the severity of the patient's condition and is often used by clinicians as a guide when choosing interventions to address the patient's condition. Since the risk score is embedded in the EHR, it is typically a module developed by the health facility's EHR vendor and customized by the hospital's clinical/medical informatics team. If asked whether the clinical team audited the AI-CDSS, participants noted that they did not do this.

The main reason is that the EHR vendor considers the dataset and algorithm of the AI-CDSS as proprietary. Thus, confidence in the AI-CDSS is based on the EHR vendor's assurance when it was offered and its performance during pilot testing (e.g., the extent to which it correctly predicts patients with adverse conditions). Ideally, the components of the AI-CDSS should be inspected before pilot testing through an audit. However, even if the EHR vendor provides all the information for an audit, the team does not have a system to allow them to undertake such an audit. Thus, there is a perceived need to develop an auditing system for AI-CDSS.

Participants noted a wide range of information that an AI-CDSS auditing system should show. First, it should provide descriptions of the dataset or algorithm used to develop the AI-CDSS. These include their origin (e.g., which country it came from? what kind of health facility did the data come from? who released the dataset? where is the dataset hosted?), timeline (e.g., when were data first and last collected? when was the dataset released for use? what is the release version?), and utility (was this used in a specific population group? what other AI-CDSS were derived from it?). Second, it should provide evidence of its accreditation, approval, or certification by a government (e.g., US FDA or British Standards Institution) or non-government (e.g., ISO) organization. Third, it should provide information on the AI-CDSS' performance based on multiple parameters (e.g., accuracy, specificity, sensitivity, AUROC, and F1 score) under different conditions (e.g., when using other datasets). Overall, the interview findings provide us with insights into developing an auditing system for AI-CDSS.

3.2 System's Features

In Table 1 we summarize the technical requirements extracted from the interviews. These requirements are essential for the design of the auditing system. The priority for each feature aims to highlight the relevance, where 0 is the lowest priority and 10 is the highest. The features are based on the interview comments and the priority is based on the number of interviewees that indicated the feature and its importance. The table shows that the most relevant features that needed to be implemented for clinicians to be able to use the auditing system were: Clinician Workflow Integration, Transparency & Explainability, Avoiding Bias, User Interface (UI) Design, Benchmarking & Error Rates, User Needs & Dashboard Complexity, and Levels of User Needs. These features were critical for the development of the system. Considering these aspects, the system and its interface prioritized the following features:

- **Clinician Workflow Integration:** The tool was seamlessly integrated into the clinician's workflow to avoid disruption. It provides actionable insights and is easy to use. It employs a simple input/output interface to facilitate the integration of the tool into the clinician's workflow.
- **Transparency & Explainability:** The system provides clear explanations of the underlying training data, LLM functionality, and the model's strengths/weaknesses and limitations. It employs well-known visualization techniques to explain the model's predictions and provides a clear explanation of the model's functionality.
- **User Interface (UI) Design:** The system has a clean and intuitive UI design with minimal clicks.
- **Benchmarking & Error Rates:** The system compares LLMs. By integrating this option in the interface, the user is able to compare different models and see the different outputs they produce.
- **User Needs & Dashboard Complexity:** The system accommodates varying user complexities, providing a simple interface for clinicians and an in-depth interface for auditors. It addresses the specific needs of each user group, offering ease of use and actionable insights for clinicians, and detailed metrics for auditors. The interface clearly distinguishes between user types, ensuring each group receives the necessary information tailored to their requirements.
- **Levels of User Needs:** The system caters to varying information needs of the different user groups (clinicians: core findings, IT/informatics: detailed audit info). It also adapts its language to the specific group that it is addressing, for example, the system uses technical language for IT/informatics and simple language for clinicians.

Table 1. Summary of technical requirements extracted from the interviews. This information extracts the main topics that affected the tool design. The priority for each feature highlights their relevance (0 is low and 10 is the highest).

Feature & Priority	Interview Comments
Clinician Workflow Integration (Priority: 10)	Several interviews emphasized seamless integration to avoid disruption (critical)
Transparency & Explainability (Priority: 10)	The majority highlighted the importance of explaining the underlying training data; emphasized clear LLM explanations, and transparency in comparing LLM to gold standard methods; prioritized transparency about strengths/weaknesses and limitations (critical)
User Interface (UI) Design (Priority: 9)	Significant cases emphasized a clean and intuitive UI design with minimal clicks (high)
Benchmarking & Error Rates (Priority: 9)	A strong number suggested comparing LLMs (highly important)
User Needs & Dashboard Complexity (Priority: 9)	Several emphasized catering to different user complexities (clinicians: simple, auditors: in-depth), keeping a simple detailed interface for clinicians (very important)
Levels of User Needs (Priority: 9)	Several interviewees highlighted catering to different user groups with varying information needs (clinicians: core findings, IT/informatics: detailed audit info) (very important)
Clinician vs. Auditing Needs (Priority: 9)	Several highlighted catering to different groups with separate needs (clinicians: ease and actionable; auditors: detailed metrics) (very important)
Avoiding Bias (Priority: 8)	Some interviewees highlighted avoiding bias in data presentation, also exposing potential biases in the model (important)
Target Audience (Priority: 7)	A few defined two audiences: clinicians (decision support) and external stakeholders (oversight) (medium)
Visualization (Priority: 7)	A few suggested clear visualizations like traffic light systems, they highlighted charts and graphs (medium)
Customizable Views (Priority: 7)	Some cases suggested catering to different user roles with customizable information (medium)
Condition-Specific Information (Priority: 7)	One interview suggested filtering information by medical condition (medium)
Technical Details & Usability (Priority: 7)	Some clinicians suggested clear visuals alongside technical details (medium)
Patient Needs Focus (Priority: 6)	A few cases emphasized presenting risks clearly for patients (medium)
Context-Specific Evaluation (Priority: 6)	Some of interviewees suggested allowing filtering by medical condition (somewhat important)
External Platform (Priority: 5)	One case suggested a platform for researchers and regulators to share data (somewhat important)
Data Provenance (Priority: 2)	One case emphasized showing the data origin (low)

4   MLighter's Architecture

MLigther's architecture provides testing resources to facilitate both developers and operators to employ the same tool for evaluating machine learning systems [20]. It enables a holistic testing environment. Developers are able to identify different vulnerabilities at the low level of their machine learning pipeline implementation, and design testing strategies at different levels of abstraction, while operators are able to employ adapted interfaces to analyse machine learning models and detect incoherence among them. This is performed at a level of abstraction suitable for a QA tester, and at a level of abstraction to suit a clinician.

4.1   The Low-Level Infrastructure

To facilitate continuous and simple deployment, MLighter employs an architecture, based on containers or micro-services, that allows operators to deploy the system in a single command. The architecture is based on Docker [4], an open-source software platform to build, share, run, and verify applications with containers. We considered QA testers as operators while designing the original version of the tool. This work focuses on simplifying the testing experience to also allow clinicians to perform user-friendly testing at a higher level of abstraction.

Figure 2 presents the whole system architecture. A container installs the operating system (Linux-based) and sets the developing language, concretely Python and R. To identify which libraries are affected by different test cases and cover the majority of the interpreters of these languages, MLigther compiles the interpreters using the American Fuzzy Loop instrumentation [11]. This instrumentation facilitates low-level testing and vulnerability detection. The instrumentation covers all the C/C++ code from Python and R and it is also imposed in every installed library, to guarantee that the low-level testing process can be guided.

The main machine learning libraries that the system covers are PyTorch and Keras for deep learning and large language models [8], Sklearn for classical models and MLR for the equivalent models in R [5]. The system in then divided into three different levels of abstraction:

1. **Fuzzing pipelines**: these pipelines are focused on developers and detect whether a specific machine learning implementation might contain a bug. It asks the user to provide the machine learning implementation (its code). The system automatically employs fuzzing to mutate the implementation parameters, utilising the instrumentation to provide feedback about the quality of these mutations. Mutations are better when they cover paths in the interpreter or libraries that previous versions have not covered before as this will provide specific parameters or inputs that can crash or hang the system.
2. **Adversarial ML**: this part focuses on QA testers and aims to provide inputs to specific machine learning models. Considering the different representations of these models, this part tests normal structural models that provides a single class as an output, and those that provide multiple classes. Based on a series

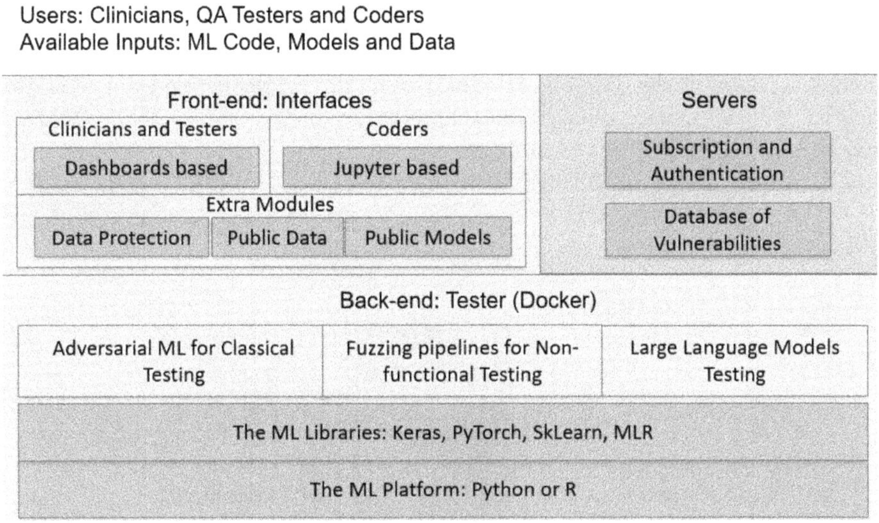

Users: Clinicians, QA Testers and Coders
Available Inputs: ML Code, Models and Data

Front-end: Interfaces		Servers
Clinicians and Testers	Coders	Subscription and Authentication
Dashboards based	Jupyter based	
Extra Modules		Database of Vulnerabilities
Data Protection / Public Data / Public Models		

Back-end: Tester (Docker)		
Adversarial ML for Classical Testing	Fuzzing pipelines for Non-functional Testing	Large Language Models Testing
The ML Libraries: Keras, PyTorch, SkLearn, MLR		
The ML Platform: Python or R		

Fig. 2. MLighter's architecture from low to high level.

of transformations, this methodology will define mutation strategies (blinded or guided by search) to find inputs that are clearly misclassified by simple transformations that made equivalent variants [21].

3. **LLMs** [31]: this part focuses on clinicians intended to test the machine learning system. MLighter easily allows to connect with multiple LLMs and query them. MLighter also evaluates their responses based on a specific ground truth. In the interface, clinicians will provide the questions and the ground truth, and MLighter will identify model's consistency and reliability based on it.

4.2   The High-Level Interfaces

MLighter provides a high-level web-based interface based on Vue. This interface allows users to test machine learning systems through a specific server that contain the required resources for running the models[1]. The web interface allows multiple users to work at the same time remotely with the same server. Different elements follow a model-view-control paradigm to guarantee that the system remains stateless. This will keep the system resting but for specific processing commands. This was constructed following a session model, where different users have independent sessions allowing them to upload files and evaluate their reports independently. These files contain models and data and remain within the session.

---

[1] It is important to highlight that multiple language and generative models employ at least 15 Gb of GPU memory.

5 Workflows to Identify Bugs and Responsibilities

In consideration of the different MLighter users' needs, we defined workflows for each to use. Here, we considered developers, QA testers and clinical operators who will be working with the tool.

MLighter starts with the welcoming page (Fig. 3). This first page is common for every expected user and reflects the general interface by describing user options.

Fig. 3. General Welcome Interface in Vue.

5.1 Developers' Workflow

Based on the way machine learning models are implemented, MLighter facilitates its low level architecture for developers to simply identify bugs and crashes within the code, providing auditing strategies to guarantee that the system has as few vulnerabilities as possible. The interface simplifies this process by allowing the developer to upload their code, an example of an input, and letting the system manipulate the input to identify every possible path in the program. This identification is allowed by the low level architecture which instruments the system to receive feedback about which parts have already been tested. The system then provides testing monitoring, showing how many executions it has run, how many paths have been explored, how many crashes have been identified and how many hangs. It is also able to run these tests and it provides a report of the error including the input that lead to it (Fig. 4).

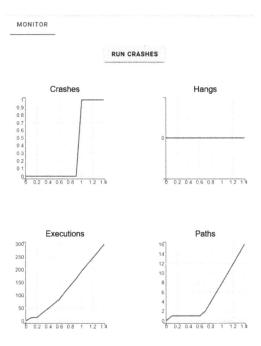

Fig. 4. Code Testing Interface of MLighter.

5.2   Quality Assurance Team's Workflow

QA testers can evaluate complex machine learning models by running the system for specific models fed with structure data. Some of these models can support language models to construct their decisions (e.g. LLMs using Retrieval-Augmented Generation or RAG technology [7]). These models can not be tested by clinicians, considering their background and their capabilities (recorded in Sect. 3). They cannot be expected to have the technical skills to test them.

There are potential biases in machine learning models that need to be tested before clinicians can actually trust their final evaluation. These are related to protected features, such as age, gender and race. MLigther allows to add a machine learning model, an input to the model and let QA tester define specific transformations against the data (Fig. 5). This identifies inconsistencies among the outcomes that depend only on protected inputs (Fig. 6).

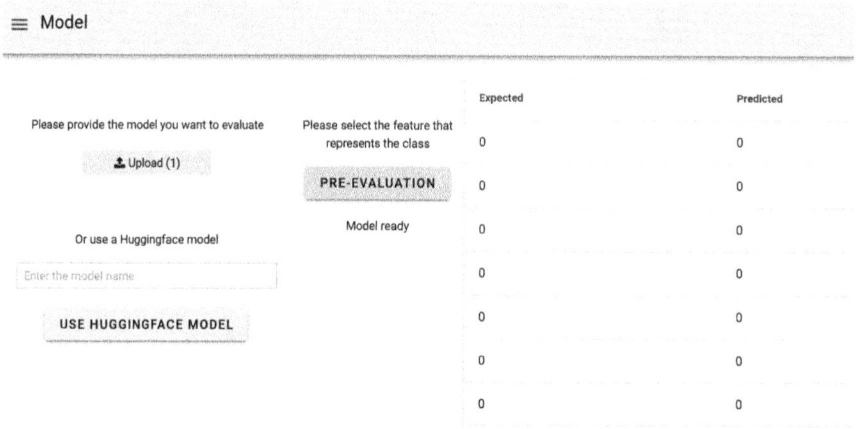

≡ Model

		Expected	Predicted
Please provide the model you want to evaluate	Please select the feature that represents the class	0	0
⬆ Upload (1)	PRE-EVALUATION	0	0
	Model ready	0	0
Or use a Huggingface model		0	0
Enter the model name		0	0
USE HUGGINGFACE MODEL		0	0
		0	0

Fig. 5. Model uploading and pre-evaluation interface for QA Tester.

These inconsistencies are reflected in the way of misclassifications after applying the transformation as an adversarial attack. For example, assume that a clinical report describes features of a patient (male, 28, Caucasian) and a set of flu symptoms. One transformation will manipulate the patient's features within margins that are still reasonable for the symptomatology to apply. The system will simplify the analysis by showing a full report of the misclassification (Fig. 6).

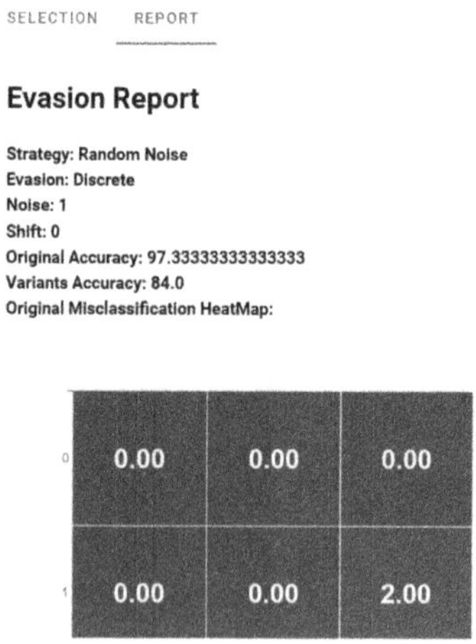

SELECTION   REPORT

Evasion Report

Strategy: Random Noise
Evasion: Discrete
Noise: 1
Shift: 0
Original Accuracy: 97.33333333333333
Variants Accuracy: 84.0
Original Misclassification HeatMap:

Fig. 6. Report interface for the adversarial attack to the ML model. Corpus of questions related to clinical reports uploaded with a specific diagnosis for evaluation.

5.3   Clinician's Workflow

The final workflow focuses on the clinicians. Considering the answers of Sect. 3, we needed to consider clinicians' backgrounds to provide an appropriate way to visualize the machine learning systems' goals with its expected outcomes. We expect clinicians, like other professionals will increasingly interact with LLMs [28]. The first thing that MLighters provides is a familiar chat interface where the clinician can introduce direct questions to test a specific LLM. If any answer brings concerns, the clinicians are allowed to use the question and set a specific answer as a ground truth that they consider as an appropriate answer to that specific question. They can also refine the question provided to the LLM. With the question and answer, clinicians can tests multiple LLMs, comparing their answers among them and with the one provided. Considering the necessity to test multiple different clinical scenarios, the system also allows clinicians to upload a whole corpus of questions and potential answers (or generated answers) if needed.

MLighter allows clinicians to compare answers provided with those offered by alternative language models, which they may want to evaluate. There are multiple gains in this multi-model evaluation: 1) The clinician can identify whether the models are suitable for answering questions in their specific speciality (dermatology, GP, oncology, etc.); 2) The clinician can compare different models to choose the best match for their requirements. 3) The clinicians can select models that optimize resources to accommodate economical needs of their clinical teams.

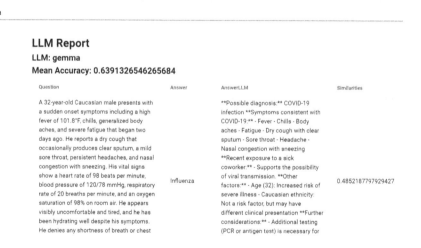

Fig. 7. Outcome of the language models showing the clinician's answer, LLM's answer and the semantic similarity between them.

This flow aims to meet clinicians' needs, including that for a guaranteed responsible evaluation, as well as provide a way to establish AI auditing responsibilities for different users (or/and) at the different levels of the architecture.

6   Requirements Discussion

In Sect. 3.2, we discussed the main requirements of the systems. This section discusses how these requirements are satisfied and what the current limitations are.

– **Clinician Workflow Integration:** Sect. 5 discusses the tool's different workflows, specifying those suitable for clinicians. Given that interviewees provided general rather than specific information about their commonly used workflows and tools, we employed a simple input/output integration system based on tables (which can be easily imported from CSV or Excel files) where clinicians input questions and answers. The rest of the users (auditors or QA testers and ML developers) may employ the system using model and inputs files.
– **Transparency & Explainability:** The system queries the LLMs during the evaluation process. LLMs provide not only the outcome but also an explanation (see Fig. 7). This facilitates clinicians to check whether the system explanation is consistent. Related to the training data, it can only be reported when the LLM itself contains this information. In relation to the models' strengths, weaknesses, and limitations, the system allows different models to be compared to each other, using a similarity metric based on semantic similarity. This comparison allows better understanding of which one may be better under the tested conditions.
– **User Interface (UI) Design:** The user interface depends on the user's expertise (see Fig. 3). For clinicians, the interface employs a simple set of commands that are based on well-known chat interface systems for public LLMs (such as ChatGPT or Gemini). Further evaluation is required to understand the usability of the interface in a clinical environment.
– **Benchmarking & Error Rates:** By allowing clinicians to introduce their ground truth related to the LLM's expected outcome, the system can compare LLMs. We integrated the similarity measure to allow clinicians to compare the different models and understand which one is more suitable, given the ground truth provided (Fig. 7). Further reviews of suitable metrics is needed to understand how this process can be made more accurate.
– **User Needs & Dashboard Complexity:** MLighter deals with different levels of users' knowledge and adapts its complexities (clinicians: simple, auditors or QA tester: models' in-depth, ML developers: code in-depth). It also separates needs (clinicians: ease of use, actionable insights; auditors or QA testers: detailed metrics; ML developers: bugs and crashes).
– **Levels of User Needs:** MLigther provides a set of reports whose language is adapted to the specific user group. For example, the system employs technical

language for reporting bugs for ML developers while it shows the specific outputs for clinicians. Also, clinicians can check outputs against individual patient's reports, e.g. what different LLMs would recommend for the diagnosis of one patient. Further validation of these features is needed to understand their suitability.

Although the features fit with several of the requirements from the different interest groups, it remains important to clearly define responsibilities during the evaluation process in order to guarantee that AI-CDDS systems can successfully contribute as a co-pilot for clinical decisions.

7   Related Work

The most relevant works that connect with this work are AI auditing in health-care; their ethical, legal and social implications; and specific cases for auditing AI-CDSS system.

7.1   AI and Auditing in Healthcare

AI and auditing in healthcare is growing; various studies have explored the implications, challenges, and methodologies of integrating AI systems into clinical settings [2,13,16,24]. Koreff et al. [13] examine the impact of AI-enabled tools and analytics in healthcare audits, revealing that paraprofessional auditors, when guided by AI, often lack the necessary expertise and judgment to conduct effective data-driven audits (e.g. those focused on algorithmic models), raising concerns about over-reliance on AI for such work in sensitive contexts as healthcare audits. MLighter aims to facilitate the involvement of clinicians by simplifying the way they can approach AI-based auditing processes. Similarly, Lu et al. [16] highlight the importance of conducting reliability and fairness audits for predictive models in advance care planning, noting significant challenges such as poor demographic data quality and the extensive resources required for thorough audits. Their work emphasizes the need for verifying data validity and ensuring model performance across diverse demographic groups to prevent biased outcomes. Although data-validity is currently not part of MLighter, the adversarial manipulations for QA testers or auditors aim to facilitate this kind of analysis, which will be extended to clinicians in the future.

Ameen et al. [2] critique the reductionist approach of AI systems in clinical decision-making, particularly in colorectal cancer screening, arguing that these systems often marginalize the nuanced, context-dependent interactions between clinicians and patients. They call for more balanced approaches to the evaluation and deployment of AI systems to mitigate the undesired consequences for patient care. Similarly, Oakden et al. [24] present a comprehensive evaluation of a deep learning model for detecting proximal femoral fractures, demonstrating the model's high performance compared to radiologists but also uncovering limitations that highlight the importance of rigorous pre-clinical evaluations and algorithmic audits to identify unexpected behaviors and ensure safe deployment. For this reason, this work considers AI-based systems as co-pilots instead of fully autonomous and standalone tools. They are support systems, but clinicians share responsibility with the systems.

There is generally a need for thorough and context-aware auditing of AI systems in healthcare to ensure they are reliable, fair, and effectively integrated into clinical practice, without compromising the nuanced expertise of human clinicians or the integrity of patient care.

7.2   Ethical, Legal, and Social Implications of AI in Healthcare

The integration of AI in healthcare necessitates a thorough examination of its ethical, legal, and social implications (ELSI in the USA) or aspects (ELSA in Europe). Cartolovni et al. [6] conducted a comprehensive scoping review, identifying key ELSI/ELSA concerns such as patient safety, algorithmic transparency, regulatory inadequacies, and the impact on the patient-physician relationship. Their findings suggest that while AI holds great promise for improving patient care, its implementation is fraught with complex challenges that must be addressed through approaches like Ethics by Design (EbD) to ensure responsible development and deployment. This fits with our Med-MLOps approach where, by involving clinicians, we can include ethical concerns at different levels of the evaluation of machine learning systems.

Similarly, Munoko et al. [23] discussed the ethical implications of using AI in auditing, emphasizing the need to balance the technological benefits with potential ethical pitfalls. Their aim was to forecast issues such as bias, transparency, and accountability, urging the development of robust policies and governance structures to mitigate these risks. Furthermore, Aldrees et al. [1] focused on auditing algorithms in healthcare to identify and reduce biases in AI systems, particularly by examining the parameters of healthcare datasets that might influence algorithmic outcomes. In contrast with these previous works, MLighter aims to perform auditing by directly querying the system.

Magrabi et al. [17] highlighted the challenges in evaluating AI-enabled clinical decision support systems. They stressed the importance of ongoing and rigorous evaluation to ensure safety and effectiveness, considering the dynamic nature of AI that integrates vast and varied healthcare data. Their review underscores the need for practical evaluation frameworks and continuous monitoring to address the unique challenges posed by AI in clinical settings, which is the main goal of MLighter.

In general, there is a critical need for a balanced and well-regulated approach to integrating AI in healthcare, focusing on transparency, accountability, and ongoing evaluation to navigate the ethical, legal, and social complexities involved. We aim to facilitate the technical steps for regulators to start defining the evaluation processes.

7.3   AI Auditing and Fairness in Clinical Decision Support Systems

The burgeoning field of AI for algorithmic auditing and fairness is gaining traction as researchers explore methods to detect and mitigate biases inherent in machine learning models. Patel et al. [27] contributed a comprehensive overview of techniques used to audit black-box AI systems for bias, emphasizing the importance of transparency and fairness. Their survey highlights various auditing methods, including causality, counterfactual reasoning, and adversarial models, all essential for assessing system behavior and improving fairness through modifications in the training pipeline, model parameters, or post-processing outputs.

James et al. [12] demonstrated the effectiveness of integrating clinical decision support systems (CDSS) with educational outreach and audit feedback to reduce the incidence of acute kidney injury (AKI) in patients undergoing coronary angiography or percutaneous coronary intervention. Their results showed a significant reduction in AKI, highlighting the importance of audit and feedback in improving clinical outcomes. Similarly, Panigutti et al. introduced FairLens [26], a methodology for auditing black-box CDSSs to detect and explain biases. Similarly to MLighter, FairLens focuses its auditing strategy on protected attributes related to fairness. Following similar auditing strategies, Lu et al. [16] studied practical aspects of auditing predictive models for advance care planning, highlighting operational challenges such as poor quality of demographic data and the need for robust subgroup performance analysis.

When constructing auditing frameworks, Landers et al. [15] proposed a framework for evaluating AI predictive models in the context of psychology, focusing on fairness and bias. Landers et al.'s framework, which includes psychological audits, aligns with James et al.'s [12] approach by emphasizing the need for systematic audits to improve AI-driven clinical outcomes. During the MACAIF project [3], Banard et al. aimed to develop interfaces for assessing the fairness of machine learning algorithms in healthcare. Like them, Landers et al. [15] considered imperative the need for stakeholder involvement and continuous feedback, similar to the audit and feedback mechanism in Panigutti's et al. work [26].

Further enriching this discourse, Degrave et al. [9] proposed a framework combining medical expert insights with generative AI to interpret and audit medical-image classifiers. This approach reveals both desirable and undesirable features utilized by classifiers for melanoma detection. The desirable features (lesional pigmentation patterns) were also used by domain experts during their decision-making process. Worryingly, the classifiers used undesirable features such as the background skin and colour balance to complement their decision. This underscores the importance of medical expertise in understanding AI decision-making processes. Mahajan et al. [18] also contributed by presenting an algorithmic audit framework for radiology-AI algorithms, stressing the need for independent validation and real-world deployment testing to ensure clinical utility and safety. Their validation strategies included data validation for new inputs, false positives/negatives analysis and general testing. However, their testing was focused on high-level model testing while MLighter aims to guarantee testing at multiple levels of the machine learning system.

8 Conclusions

When an AI-CDSS system is developed following an MLOps approach, it is important to design testing procedures to include clinicians in the workflow. AI-CDSS systems are not only software systems, but also medical devices that need to be validated and verified. The validation and verification process is a key step in the development of AI-CDSS systems, as it ensures that the system is safe and effective for the intended use. In this paper, we have presented a testing framework for AI-CDSS systems that includes clinician participation in the testing process. The framework, which extends the MLighter framework, is based on the principles of MLOps and includes a set of guidelines for testing AI-CDSS systems. It is designed to be flexible and adaptable to different types of AI-CDSS systems and can be used to guide the testing process from the early stages of development to the deployment of the system in a clinical setting. The framework includes guidelines for defining the testing objectives, selecting the test cases, and evaluating the performance of the system. It also includes guidelines for involving clinicians in the testing process and ensuring that the system meets the requirements of the end users. By following the guidelines presented in this paper, developers can be assured that their AI-CDSS systems are safer and more effective for clinical use.

Future work will focus on evaluating specific AI-CDSS systems using MLighter. We plan to apply it to different types of AI-CDSS systems and evaluate its effectiveness in guiding the testing process. We will refine it based on feedback from the evaluation, and make it more comprehensive and practical for developers, QA testers, and especially clinicians. We believe that MLighter will help developers testing AI-CDSS systems and generally improve patient's care.

Acknowledgments. The support of the UKRI Trustworthy Autonomous Systems Hub (reference EP/V00784X/1) and Trustworthy Autonomous Systems Node in Verifiability (reference EP/V026801/2) and the Alan Turing grant G2027 - MuSE is gratefully acknowledged. We especially thank the TAS Hub International Sandpit, December 2022, for funding this specific piece of research through the Machine-Learning Auditing for Artificial Intelligence Fairness (MACAIF) project.

References

1. Aldrees, A., Poland, C., Sattiraju, N., Irshad, S.A.: Auditing algorithms: determining ethical parameters of artificial intelligence systems in healthcare (2020)
2. Ameen, S., Wong, M.C., Yee, K.C., Turner, P.: Ai and clinical decision making: the limitations and risks of computational reductionism in bowel cancer screening. Appl. Sci. **12**(7), 3341 (2022)
3. Barnard, P., et al.: Macaif: machine learning auditing for clinical AI fairness. In: Proceedings of the First International Symposium on Trustworthy Autonomous Systems, pp. 1–4 (2023)
4. Bernstein, D.: Containers and cloud: from LXC to docker to kubernetes. IEEE Cloud Comput. **1**(3), 81–84 (2014)

5. Bischl, B., et al: MLR: machine learning in R. J. Mach. Learn. Res. **17**(170), 1–5 (2016). https://jmlr.org/papers/v17/15-066.html
6. Čartolovni, A., Tomičić, A., Mosler, E.L.: Ethical, legal, and social considerations of AI-based medical decision-support tools: a scoping review. Int. J. Med. Inform. **161**, 104738 (2022)
7. Chen, J., Lin, H., Han, X., Sun, L.: Benchmarking large language models in retrieval-augmented generation. In: Proceedings of the AAAI Conference on Artificial Intelligence, vol. 38, pp. 17754–17762 (2024)
8. Chollet, F.: Deep learning with Python. Simon and Schuster (2021)
9. DeGrave, A.J., Cai, Z.R., Janizek, J.D., Daneshjou, R., Lee, S.I.: Auditing the inference processes of medical-image classifiers by leveraging generative AI and the expertise of physicians. Nat. Biomed. Eng. 1–13 (2023)
10. Farzaneh, N., Ansari, S., Lee, E., Ward, K.R., Sjoding, M.W.: Collaborative strategies for deploying artificial intelligence to complement physician diagnoses of acute respiratory distress syndrome. NPJ Digit. Med. **6**(1), 62 (2023)
11. Fioraldi, A., Maier, D., Eißfeldt, H., Heuse, M.: {AFL++}: combining incremental steps of fuzzing research. In: 14th USENIX Workshop on Offensive Technologies (WOOT 2020) (2020)
12. James, M.T.: Effect of clinical decision support with audit and feedback on prevention of acute kidney injury in patients undergoing coronary angiography: a randomized clinical trial. JAMA **328**(9), 839–849 (2022)
13. Koreff, J., Baudot, L., Sutton, S.G.: Exploring the impact of technology dominance on audit professionalism through data analytic-driven healthcare audits. J. Inf. Syst. **37**(3), 59–80 (2023)
14. Kreuzberger, D., Kühl, N., Hirschl, S.: Machine learning operations (MLOps): overview, definition, and architecture. IEEE Access (2023)
15. Landers, R.N., Behrend, T.S.: Auditing the AI auditors: a framework for evaluating fairness and bias in high stakes AI predictive models. Am. Psychol. **78**(1), 36 (2023)
16. Lu, J., et al.: Considerations in the reliability and fairness audits of predictive models for advance care planning. Front. Digit. Health **4**, 943768 (2022)
17. Magrabi, F., et al.: Artificial intelligence in clinical decision support: challenges for evaluating AI and practical implications. Yearb. Med. Inform. **28**(01), 128–134 (2019)
18. Mahajan, V., Venugopal, V.K., Murugavel, M., Mahajan, H.: The algorithmic audit: working with vendors to validate radiology-AI algorithms–how we do it. Acad. Radiol. **27**(1), 132–135 (2020)
19. Menendez, H.: Software testing or the bugs' nightmare. Open J. Softw. Eng. **1**(1) (2021)
20. Menéndez, H.D.: Measuring machine learning robustness in front of static and dynamic adversaries. In: 2022 IEEE 34th International Conference on Tools with Artificial Intelligence (ICTAI), pp. 174–181. IEEE (2022)
21. Menéndez, H.D., Clark, D., T. Barr, E.: Getting ahead of the arms race: hothousing the coevolution of virustotal with a packer. Entropy **23**(4), 395 (2021)
22. Mittermaier, M., Raza, M., Kvedar, J.C.: Collaborative strategies for deploying AI-based physician decision support systems: challenges and deployment approaches. NPJ Digit. Med. **6**(1), 137 (2023)
23. Munoko, I., Brown-Liburd, H.L., Vasarhelyi, M.: The ethical implications of using artificial intelligence in auditing. J. Bus. Ethics **167**(2), 209–234 (2020)
24. Oakden-Rayner, L., et al.: Validation and algorithmic audit of a deep learning system for the detection of proximal femoral fractures in patients in the emergency

department: a diagnostic accuracy study. Lancet Digit. Health **4**(5), e351–e358 (2022)

25. Østervang, C., Lassen, A., Schmidt, T., Coyne, E., Dieperink, K.B., Jensen, C.M.: Development of a health information system to promote emergency care pathways: a participatory design study. Digit. Health **8**, 20552076221145856 (2022)

26. Panigutti, C., Perotti, A., Panisson, A., Bajardi, P., Pedreschi, D.: Fairlens: auditing black-box clinical decision support systems. Inf. Process. Manag. **58**(5), 102657 (2021)

27. Patel, P., Uddin, M.N.: AI for algorithmic auditing: mitigating bias and improving fairness in big data systems. Int. J. Soc. Anal. **7**(12), 39–48 (2022)

28. Patil, D.D., Dhotre, D.R., Gawande, G.S., Mate, D.S., Shelke, M.V., Bhoye, T.S.: Transformative trends in generative AI: harnessing large language models for natural language understanding and generation. Int. J. Intell. Syst. Appl. Eng. **12**(4s), 309–319 (2024)

29. Rajpurkar, P., Chen, E., Banerjee, O., Topol, E.J.: AI in health and medicine. Nat. Med. **28**(1), 31–38 (2022)

30. Ridgely, M.S., et al.: The importance of understanding and measuring health system structural, functional, and clinical integration. Health Serv. Res. **55**, 1049–1061 (2020)

31. Thirunavukarasu, A.J., Ting, D.S.J., Elangovan, K., Gutierrez, L., Tan, T.F., Ting, D.S.W.: Large language models in medicine. Nat. Med. **29**(8), 1930–1940 (2023)

Innovations in Software Testing and AI Compliance

Software System Testing Assisted by Large Language Models: An Exploratory Study

Cristian Augusto[1]([⊠]) ⓘ, Jesús Morán[1] ⓘ, Antonia Bertolino[2] ⓘ,
Claudio de la Riva[1] ⓘ, and Javier Tuya[1] ⓘ

[1] Computer Science Department, University of Oviedo, Gijón, Spain
{augustocristian,moranjesus,claudio,tuya}@uniovi.es
[2] ISTI-CNR, Consiglio Nazionale Delle Ricerche, Pisa, Italy
antonia.bertolino@isti.cnr.it

Abstract. Large language models (*LLMs*) based on transformer architecture have revolutionized natural language processing (*NLP*), demonstrating excellent capabilities in understanding and generating human-like text. In Software Engineering, *LLMs* have been applied in code generation, documentation, and report writing tasks, to support the developer and reduce the amount of manual work. In Software Testing, one of the cornerstones of Software Engineering, *LLMs* have been explored for generating test code, test inputs, automating the oracle process or generating test scenarios. However, their application to high-level testing stages such as system testing, in which a deep knowledge of the business and the technological stack is needed, remains largely unexplored. This paper presents an exploratory study about how *LLMs* can support system test development. Given that *LLM* performance depends on input data quality, the study focuses on how to query general purpose *LLMs* to first obtain test scenarios and then derive test cases from them. The study evaluates two popular *LLMs* (*GPT-4o and GPT-4o-mini*), using as a benchmark a European project demonstrator. The study compares two different prompt strategies and employs well-established prompt patterns, showing promising results as well as room for improvement in the application of *LLMs* to support system testing.

Keywords: Large Language Model · Software Testing · System Testing · Test Cases · Test Scenarios

1 Introduction

Large Language Models (onwards referred to as *LLMs*) based on transformer architecture have emerged as one of the biggest technological disruptions of recent years in the field of natural language processing (*NLP*). In a nutshell, *LLMs* are deep neural networks trained on a huge amount of data, from which they acquire an astonishing capability to understand and generate human-like text. State-of-the-art *LLMs* show such "*intelligent and rational*" capabilities in imitating human performances that in a recent experiment they have been able to pass the Turing test with a 50% success rate [1].

© IFIP International Federation for Information Processing 2025
Published by Springer Nature Switzerland AG 2025
H. D. Menéndez et al. (Eds.): ICTSS 2024, LNCS 15383, pp. 239–255, 2025.
https://doi.org/10.1007/978-3-031-80889-0_17

LLMs are rapidly transforming the technological landscape while also attracting increasing attention from the media and raising society expectations on their potential benefits. *LLMs* are already widely employed in industry, especially in healthcare, education and financial services [2]. Typical *LLM* applications include for example the creation of conversational agents (bots), empowered support to user's performing tasks or process automation [3], moving towards the so-called industry 6.0 age [4].

In terms of market expansion, even though the estimated (compound annual) growth rates differ largely (from the 33.2% by MarketsandMarkets [5] up to the 79.8% by Pragma Market Research [6]) the analysts concur in predicting steady growing worldwide impact until 2030.

LLMs have also crashed into *Software Engineering (SE)* [7], hinting at several potential breakthroughs in addressing *SE* challenges that can be reformulated in terms of data, code or text analysis [8]. To date, *LLMs* have achieved quite promising results in assisting the developer to generate code, documentation, and reports [9], in improving the explainability of the code itself or its patches [10], and in other tasks considered repetitive and less valuable (so-called "*toils*" [11]).

In Software Testing, one of the cornerstones of the *SE* field, several works have explored how to use *LLMs* to generate test code [12] or also to generate test scenarios [13]. However, as we discuss in the Related Work section, the focus has been mostly on the Unit Test level: as noticed by Ozkaya in a recent editorial about the application of *LLMs* to *SE* tasks, "*Generating unit tests is one of the tasks where developers shortcut the most.*" [7].

In this work, we aim to investigate the capability of *LLMs* to support software testing at system level. System test cases validate the interaction among the different system components or the user interaction with the application. The system test suite development process is usually expensive because it requires a deep knowledge of the business context of the application and knowledge about the technological stack on which the application relies. Therefore, if *LLMs* could be leveraged to help the generation of effective system test cases, this could bring substantial benefits to the whole testing process. To the best of our knowledge, the application of *LLMs* to support system testing remains largely unexplored: some works have scraped the surface by evaluating *LLM* support to test specific types of applications, or to generate test inputs, e.g., for mobile applications. However, no previous work has used *LLMs* to automate the whole path of deriving system test cases from user requirements.

The approach we experiment here considers two different artifacts related to system testing, namely test scenarios and test cases. The former are taken as an input for the latter, in accordance with the *ISO 29119* standard, in which test scenarios are defined as "*the situations or settings for a test item used as a basis for generating the test cases*" [14]. Thus, in this work we first evaluate the support of *LLMs* for deriving test scenarios, which provide a high-level stepwise description of the system tests; afterwards, we also use the *LLMs* to generate the test cases, i.e., the test code that corresponds to a given test scenario.

While remarking on the excellence of *LLMs* for a wide range of tasks, several authors warn that the *LLM* performance is directly related to the quality of their input [15]. In *LLMs* we differentiate between two types of input data: (1) the training data used during the creation of the model and (2) the query data used to prompt the model. Currently, most approaches employ general-purpose pre-trained *LLMs*, tailored for specific tasks through appropriate query data to *prompt* the model [16]. Therefore, to investigate how *LLMs* perform in assisting the system test process, we need to explore how these general purpose pre-trained *LLMs* should be prompted. To achieve this objective, this article uses both the data of a real-world application and its test suite to evaluate how two of the most popular state-of-the-art pre-trained models (*GPT-4o* and *GPT-4o-mini*), perform when asked to assist the system testing process in generating test scenarios and coding the system test cases.

Although we cannot generalize our conclusions outside the employed evaluation subject, our study provides promising results for both tasks, hinting at the opportunity of leveraging *LLMs* to assist the entire system testing process, from test scenario derivation until test cases development.

In our exploratory study we have observed that the LLMs can support the tester during the E2E system process, facilitating their task. According to our initial evaluation, the LLM test scenario generation covered the user requirements extensively (up to 100%). However, the generation of E2E test code requires to slightly change a few lines of the code (up to 29%).

The rest of the paper is structured as follows: Sect. 2 provides the related work. The exploratory study design is presented in Sect. 3. Section 4 presents the evaluation and results while Sect. 5 presents the threats to validity. Finally, Sect. 6 presents the conclusions and future work.

2   Related Work

In this section we review the literature related to our paper. The related work belongs primarily to two fields: (1) Large Language Models and Prompt Engineering and (2) Large Language Models applied to Software Engineering and Software Testing.

2.1   Large Language Models and Prompt Engineering

Large Language Models (*LLMs*) based on neural networks were introduced in the 80s [17–19] for Natural Language Processing (NLP). Later, the introduction of the transformer architecture [20], triggered an explosion in the number of multi-purpose models with reasoning-like capabilities like *PALM* [21], *Llama* [22], or *GPT-4* [23]. These models follow the "*Pre-train, Prompt and Predict*" [16] paradigm, in which a general purpose *LLM* is adapted to a new concrete task through an adequate *prompt*. Therefore, the process of designing and refining the prompts for a pre-trained model, also known as *prompt engineering*, has attracted the interest of both academia and industry; several authors have proposed patterns to accomplish different related tasks [24, 25], various *prompt* strategies [26–28], as well as development tools and repositories [29].

Our exploratory study draws upon all these works, employing state-of-the-art transformer architecture pretrained models [23], using the *pre-train, prompt and predict* paradigm [16]. As described in Sect. 3.2, we employ state-of-the-art patterns [24] to design and create our *prompts* following the best practices [25], and use the *Few-Shot* [28] and *Chain of Thought* [27] prompt techniques.

2.2 Large Language Models Applied to Software Engineering and Software Testing

In recent years, the increasing popularity of *LLMs* has exploded in a wide range of applications in Software Engineering including code generation, code explainability, and more in general for reducing the manual effort in repetitive tasks or improving/easing difficult processes such as Software Testing. *LLM-assisted* generation of code has been popularized through the inclusion of programming assistants like *Microsoft Copilot* [30]. This type of assistants has attracted the interest of academia, who focused on the impact of its *hallucinations* and the quality and usefulness of its code [30–32]. Code explainability using *LLMs* has been addressed through the explainability of the code itself [33], or the explainability of failures, debugging [34], generating documentation [35], and reports [9, 10]. In Software Testing, part of the effort has been put into unit testing for generating test cases, migrating testing code or generating test scenarios [12, 13, 36, 37]. In other testing levels, like System Testing, the literature has focused on generating test inputs/data for mobile/UI testing, such as the necessary human interaction or text inputs [38] or test inputs for other types of software (e.g., simulators) [39]. In mobile testing LLMs have been applied to generate user UI interactions (testing scripts) with the GUI information, generate the [15] navigation through the application using natural language test cases [40] or [37] generate mobile test code from natural language. In GUI testing, some authors [34] have also applied *LLMs* to migrate test scripts between different platforms and apps.

Finally, other works that explore how to generate reports or models [9, 10, 35] provide us with insights on how to address prompt engineering as well as its evaluation in Software Engineering.

Some works share similarities with our approach: [40] has the same objective but the test cases provided as input, and the outputs are direct descriptions of UI interactions (e.g., *press button "A"*). In [15] the authors propose using the GUI as input, but the output is again a natural language description, e.g., *"Operation: Scroll, Widget: Menu"*. In contrast, our approach uses as input the user requirements, generates scenarios, and from these scenarios with test case examples generates the testing scripts that with slight adjustments can be executed directly against the application.

The closest works to this paper are I) the generation of test scenarios using system requirements proposed by [13] and II) the test script generation based on natural language specifications proposed by [37]. Our work attempts to go a step further by exploring the whole process: we first generate the test scenarios from the user requirements, and then generate the test code from them. In perspective, we aim at a fully supported system testing approach that can benefit from *LLM* assistance, and in this work we take the first steps in this direction.

3 Exploratory Study Design

3.1 Overview

The process followed in our exploratory study, depicted in Fig. 1, consists of two sub-processes: the generation of test scenarios (left side of Fig. 1) and the generation of test cases (right side of Fig. 1). These two subprocesses are described below:

- The generation of test scenarios starts by giving as input the user requirements of the application to generate test scenarios [14]. More precisely, the user requirements (Fig. 1, ①), as well as serving an example of a test scenario, (Fig. 1, ②) are provided to generate the prompts of two different prompt techniques: *Few-Shot-prompting* [41] (Fig. 1, ③) and *Few-Shot + Chain of Thought prompting* (Fig. 1, ④). We generate two different prompts that are given to two *LLMs*: *GPT-4o* and *GPT-4o-mini* to generate the different scenarios (four sets in total) for each *prompt* technique (one different prompt for each technique) and *LLM* model (Fig. 1, ⑤-⑧).
- The generation of test cases uses as input the test scenarios generated in the previous subprocess (Fig. 1, ⑨) and some examples of system test cases (Fig. 1,⑩). We generate two different prompts, again one for each technique: *Few-Shot* and *Few Shot + Chain of Thought*. The *prompts* are provided to the *GPT-4o* and *GPT-4o-mini* models that eventually generate four different sets of test cases (Fig. 1,13–16).

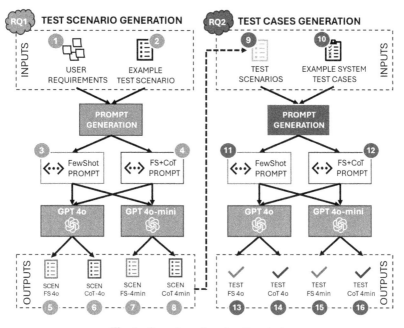

Fig. 1. Overview of exploration study

In accordance with the two subprocesses above described, our exploratory study aims to answer two Research Questions:

RQ1: How do *LLMs* perform in generating system test scenarios from user requirements?

RQ2: How do *LLMs* perform in generating test cases from test scenarios?

In the following subsections, we describe the set-up and the design of our exploratory study.

3.2 Study Subject and Evaluation Set-Up

As an **evaluation subject,** we use the real-world application *FullTeaching* [42], a demonstrator of the Horizon 2020 European project ElasTest [43]. *FullTeaching* is a web application that provides an online teaching platform to impart classes, publish materials, and enable the interaction between teachers and students. Specifically, we employ from this web application:

- The user requirements (translated from Spanish) [44] used during the development of the *FullTeaching* web application and available in the *FullTeaching* project documentation [44]. Precisely, they consist of 39 natural language requirements that cover functionalities such as videocall or course creation.
- The system test suite of this application available in the GIIS repository [45], composed of 21 Java Selenium test cases that cover different test scenarios.

Below is an example of the user requirements, the full list is available in the **replication package** [46]: "*(16) The teacher can add students to a course in different ways: (16.1) using their unique email address, (16.2) using multiple email addresses, or (16.3) using a file (txt, excel, Word, PDF...)."*

In Table 1 below, we provide the user requirements covered (shown in the rows using their original labelling from 1.0 to 16.0) and the different system test cases (shown in the different rows). This user requirement coverage was derived by reaching consensus among the authors. We see that the 21 test cases available from *FullTeaching* cover almost 80% of the 39 user requirements, leaving only uncovered (8) the registration, (7.3) the muting of the teacher audio by the students, (7.7) the cancellation of a requested voice turn, (11) the edition of a class attributes at any time, (12) the profile modification and (14) the captcha test during the registration. This test suite was developed and then extended-migrated to the ElasTest repository. We do not know why the author did not test the whole functionality, we can only guess that this was perhaps due to time constraints.

As a *Large Language Model*, we have studied the current market and decided to select two of the latest models offered by the leader industry *OpenAI* [47], the models concisely are *GPT-4o* (v2024-05-13) and *GPT-4o-mini* (v2024-07-18). We execute the prompts using the *OpenAI* API, setting the *temperature* of the models to 0.2 [48] to improve the repeatability of the results. This parameter controls the model's randomness, a value of 0 selects the highest probability words, while higher temperatures increase creativity and the chance of '*hallucinations*'.

As **evaluation metrics,** concerning RQ1 we consider the test coverage metric: "*number of requirements covered by executed tests*" [14]. We adapt this metric to the case of the *LLM-generated* test scenarios, i.e., we evaluate which and how many user requirements are covered by the *LLM-generated* test scenarios instead of by the executed test cases. This measure of coverage (in percentage) is compared against the requirement coverage achieved by the baseline, i.e., which and how many user requirements are covered by the *FullTeaching* test suite (shown in Table 1). Requirements 1, 2, 3, and 9 covered by most of the test cases correspond to: the user can see the courses enrolled in, the user can access a course, teachers can create a course, and the user can log in to the system, respectively. Concerning RQ2, considering the test cases generated by *LLM*, we measure the effort required to make the generated test code pass (unless we ascertain that they fail because of a bug in the application under test). As a proxy measure of this effort, we use the average number of code changes needed until the test code successfully executes, counting the number of lines of code modified.

In the replication package we provide a series of Java scripts using the *OpenAI API* to query and obtain the answers of the models, the *prompt* templates, strategies, and the findings of our exploratory study. The replication package is available in our *GitHub* repository [46].

Table 1. User Requirements FullTeaching traceability matrix

E2E Test Case	Requirement Covered
oneToOneChatInSessionChrome	1, 2, 6.1, 6.4, 6.5, 6.8, 7.1, 7.4, 7.5,9
courseRestOperations	1, 2, 3, 9, 10
courseInfoRestOperations	1, 2, 3, 9, 10, 13
sessionRestOperations	1, 2, 3, 4.1, 4.2, 4.3, 9
forumRestOperations	1, 2, 3, 4.6, 5.1, 5.2, 9
filesRestOperations	1, 2, 3, 5.5, 5.3, 9
attendersRestOperations	1, 2, 3, 4.4, 9, 16.1
sessionTest	1, 2, 6.1, 6.4, 7.1, 7.4, 9
oneToOneVideoAudioSessionChrome	1, 2, 4.1, 4.2, 4.3, 6.1, 6.2, 6.3, 6.4, 6.6, 6.7, 6.8, 7.1, 7.2, 7.4, 7.6, 7.8, 9
studentCourseMainTest	1, 2, 9, 15
teacherCourseMainTest	1, 2, 9, 15
teacherCreateAndDeleteCourseTest	1, 2, 3, 5.1,9,10, 13
teacherEditCourseValues	1, 2, 3, 9
teacherDeleteCourseTest	1, 2, 9
forumLoadEntriesTest	1, 2, 5.2, 9
forumNewEntryTest	1, 2, 5.2, 9
forumNewCommentTest	1, 2, 5.2, 9
forumNewReply2CommentTest	1, 2, 9
spiderLoggedTest	1, 2, 9
spiderUnLoggedTest	9
loginTest	9

3.3 *Prompt* Creation and Refinement

To create the *prompts* to answer the two research questions we first establish a base *prompt* for *Few-Shot*, and then extend it with the necessary statements to also apply the

Chain-of-Thought prompt technique. *Few-Shot prompting* is a technique that enables in-context learning by providing the *LLM* with examples in the *prompt* (e.g., different assertions in one language if we are asking for a concrete assertion). *Chain of Thought* prompting aims to enable the reasoning capabilities of the model by explicitly requiring the intermediate steps. Precisely, the *prompt* creation was carried out as follows:

Few-Shot Prompts

To generate the test scenarios using *Few-Shot* we create our *prompt* using the *Recipe prompt* pattern [24], as we find that a test scenario has similarities to a recipe: several ordered tasks, an expected output and also incorrect states. The *prompt* structure, as well as the contextual statements to address the test scenario generation, is as follows:

> **I)** *"I would like to generate test scenarios for system testing*
> *I know that I need to fulfill the user requirements: ''Ⓐ{{UserRequirements}}'''*
> *Provide a complete sequence of steps for each scenario and the expected outputs.*
> *Fill in any missing steps*
> *Identify any unnecessary steps.*
> *Examples of a test scenario: ''Ⓑ{{ExampleTestScenario}}''''*

The *prompt* has available two placeholders: (1) *UserRequirements* (**I**, A) contains the application user requirements, while (2) *ExampleTestScenario* (**I**, B) contains from one to several examples of test scenarios.

To generate the system test cases, with the *Few-Shot prompt* technique we use the Context Manager *prompt* pattern [24]. This pattern allows us to delimitate the context of the *LLM*, focusing on the system test cases provided as examples and the test scenarios. The *prompt* is the following:

> **II)** *"When generating system test that covers Ⓐ{{Functionality}}*
> *Please consider the following test scenarios: ''Ⓑ{{TestScenarios}}''''*
> *and the following system test examples: ''Ⓒ{{SystemTestExamples}}''*
> *Don't generate the whole test suite, only the required test case."*

This *prompt* presents three different placeholders: (1) *Functionality* (**II**, A) expects the test functionality to be covered by the generated test case. In the prompt, the *Functionality* placeholder is substituted with a brief, high-level statement that describes what is going to be tested such as: "*User enrolls into a course*" or "*Teacher login and create a course*". In most of the cases, we use the title of the test scenario to be covered, or a summary of it. The (2) *TestScenarios* (**II**, B) placeholder expects all the test scenarios, and finally (3) *SystemTestExamples* (**II**, C) expects the system test cases given as examples to the *LLM*. This *prompt* has been refined based on our experience generating system test code: "*Don't generate the whole test suite, only the required test case*" delimitates the generation of code, avoiding that in some executions the LLM generates more cases than required.

Few-shot + Chain of Thought Prompts

To create the *prompts* for *Chain of Thought*, we extend the *Few-Shot prompts* by adding the phrase *"Let's think step by step"*, which has been proved as a robust *"reasoning enabler"* for instructive outputs [28].

To generate the test scenarios, we include as the first statement the following line:

> **III)** *"Let's think step by step, describe the solution and remark which user requirements are covered"*

To ensure that the reasoning capabilities of the *LLM* are focused on the coverage of the different user requirements, we ask to highlight which user requirements are covered by each test scenario.

For the system test generation, we include the following statements to the *Few-Shot prompt*:

> **IV)** *"Let's think step by step, describe the solution by breaking it down into a task list for then generate the code"*

We add this suggestion to establish the steps of the test case prior to the code generation, as, according to several *prompt* engineering demonstrations and tutorials [46], this improves the expected output.

4   Exploratory Study Execution and Results

The following subsections detail how the exploratory study has been carried out. Section 4.1 and Sect. 4.2 present the evaluation, respectively, for RQ1 and RQ2.

4.1   [RQ1]: Generating Test Scenarios from User Requirements

To answer the first research question, we employ the prompts presented in the previous section, and fulfill the *prompt UserRequirements* (**I**, A) placeholder with the entire *Full-Teaching* user requirements and the *ExampleTestScenario* (**I**, B) with a test scenario of another business context (bank transaction management platform).

We evaluate the results achieved by the *LLMs* using *Few-Shot* and *Chain-of-Thought* for both models (*GPT-4o and GPT-4o-mini*). Thus, we refer to the right side of Fig. 1 in which we obtain four different sets of test scenarios denoted as ⑤-⑧. Moreover, as the results provided by the *LLM* are not deterministic, we execute each thread up to 5 times, thereby obtaining 20 sets of test scenarios in total.

As anticipated, we measure for each set of test scenarios the coverage of user requirements (in percentage), and then we also evaluate the reliability of the test scenario generation approach by comparing for each of the four threads the results of the five executions. Our initial findings between the different executions are that for all the *prompting techniques* and models studied, the test scenarios are quite consistent (even more than we expected, see Table 2).

Table 2. Requirements coverage the different executions, models, and prompt techniques

Prompt Technique	Model	Execution					AVG	MDN	SD
		1	2	3	4	5			
Few-Shot + CoT	GPT-4o	100	100	100	100	100	100	100	0
Few -Shot	GPT-4o	100	100	100	94.9	100	99.0	100	2.3
Few-Shot + CoT	GPT-4o-mini	87.2	97.4	87.2	94.9	92.3	91.8	92.3	4.6
Few-Shot	GPT-4o-mini	94.9	97.4	89.7	97.4	92.3	94.4	94.9	3.3

Small differences among the five sets of test scenarios could include, for instance: one scenario may correspond to the merging between two scenarios of another execution, or it can have different text styles, or be named in a different way: *"User enrollment courses"* vs *"Viewing enrolled courses"*.

In terms of user requirements coverage, the generated test scenarios have a low standard deviation: 2.3 *GPT-4o/Few-Shot*, 0.0 *GPT-4o/CoT*, 3.3 *GPT-4o-mini/Few-Shot* and 4.6 *GPT-4o-mini/CoT*.

Using the *GPT-4o* model with the *Few-Shot prompt* technique, the average in user coverage is 99.0% and the median 100%. With the *Few-Shot + CoT prompt* technique, the average in user coverage is higher (100%) and the median is the same.

Using the *GPT-4mini* model with the *Few-Shot prompt* technique, the average in user requirements coverage is 94.4% and the median 94.9%. With the *Few-Shot + CoT prompt* technique, decreases both the average of coverage (91.8%) and the median (92.3%).

Based on the observed results, we can answer RQ1 as:

> Overall, our findings indicate that model *GPT-4o* slightly outperforms model *GPT-4o-mini* in generating test scenarios. Furthermore, the use of *Few-Shot* with the *Chain of Thought* prompting improves the user requirements coverage in the *GPT-4o-mini* model. Both models achieve better user requirements coverage in all their executions than the baseline 79.46%, generating scenarios that cover functionalities not explored by the *FullTeaching* test suite.

4.2 [RQ2]: Generating System Test Cases from Test Scenarios

To answer RQ2, we employ the above-presented *prompts (II and IV)*, in which we have to fulfill the placeholders: *Functionality*, *TestScenarios* and *SystemTestExamples*.

- With respect to *TestScenarios* (**II**, B), given that five sets were generated for each configuration in the earlier phase of our study, it is now crucial to select one single set from the 20 available test scenarios. To this end, we considered the previously defined test coverage metric over the user requirements, and we opted for the set of test scenarios that achieves the highest coverage; in case of equal coverage value, we prioritize the set with fewer scenarios. Based on these criteria, the selected set of Test

Scenarios was one among the 5 sets produced by the *GPT-4o* model using *Few-Shot + CoT prompt* technique.

- Concerning *SystemTestExamples* (**II**, C), in our study we can use some test cases of those available in the *FullTeaching* test suite (which of course have not been derived from the *LLM* test scenarios). To select which test cases to provide in the prompt, once again we refer to the coverage of the user requirements. Since we have traced the coverage of user requirements by both the test scenarios and the test cases, we can evaluate the relation between a test case and a test scenario comparing their respective coverages. Intuitively, if a test case yields an identical, or very similar, coverage spectrum as a test scenario, we can consider that the test case implements that test scenario. Thus, for each possible pair of a test scenario and a *FullTeaching* test case, we computed their *Levenshtein* distance comparing their respective coverage of the user requirements. We did not consider trivial test cases and scenarios (e.g., login, covered by most of the suite test case). These test cases and scenarios are not considered because the exact code-test methods are provided with all test cases provided by example in the *prompt*, being less challenging for the model. For example, the login test is a simple invocation to *slowLogin (user,password)*, present in all test cases already in the *prompt*. Finally, we selected 4 different test cases as the ones yielding the lowest distance measures from the test scenarios; these 4 test cases, and the 4 test scenarios to which they are close, are referred to as the *Levenshtein* set. We limited the selection to four test cases because we aimed to employ a cross-validation technique, which would have become very costly and time-demanding with a higher number of test cases. The cross-validation technique is described below.
- Concerning *Functionality* (**II**, A), we refer to the titles of the test scenarios in the *Levenshtein* set, and we select one of them according to the cross-validation approach as described below.

In every execution of the LLMs, all the test scenarios in the selected set were used to fulfill the *TestScenarios* (**II**, B) placeholder. Instead, the *Functionality* (**II**, A), and *SystemTestExamples* (**II**, C) take different values according to the cross-validation approach. The cross-validation was performed as follows for each *prompt* technique and model: we remove one test case from the *Levenshtein* set and provide as input the three remaining test cases, asking the LLMs to generate a test case that covers the functionality corresponding to the title of the test scenario closely covered by the one that has been removed.

As anticipated, to assess *LLM* results for the different models and *prompt* techniques, we refer to the effort required to make the test code pass, in terms of the number of lines of code modified. We execute the generated test cases over the *FullTeaching* application, and we manually made the minimal changes to make the test case work/pass. Table 3 shows the number of changes in the code performed, the average, and the percentage in average of lines changed for the different test cases (A-C) with the two models (*4o* and 4o-mini) and two prompting techniques (Few-shot and Few-Shot + CoT):

Table 3. Total and average code changes in the different test cases

Model	Prompt Technique	(A) View Courses	(B) View Classes	(C) Create Course	(D) View Calendar	AVG	% AVG
GPT-4o	Few Shot (FS)	2	5	14	3	6	22.64%
GPT-4o	Few Shot + CoT	6	9	14	4	8.25	31.13%
GPT-4omini	Few Shot	5	7	18 (14H)	6 (1H)	9	31.30%
GPT-4omini	Few Shot + CoT	8 (6H)	10	15 (8H)	4	9.25	34.9%

The results show that using the *GPT-4o* model with the *Few-Shot prompt* technique, the generated test case requires a median of 4 modifications and 6 modifications on average between the different tests generated in the cross validation. Using the *Few-Shot + CoT prompt* technique, the test case requires 7.5 modification in median and 8.25 modifications on average.

Using the *GPT-4mini* model with the *Few-Shot prompt* technique, the generated test case requires 6 modifications in median and 9 modifications on average. Using the *Few-Shot + CoT prompt* technique, the test case requires 7 modifications in median and 9.25 modifications on average.

We have mostly observed two different modification types: in several executions the LLM indicates that it is not sure about a certain value-method and asks the tester for its completion; in other cases, the LLM uses a non-existent method, class, or id (Table 3 (H-*Hallucination*). The slight modifications required are easy to perform, for instance adjusting a UI identifier to its correct value, replacing methods that do not exist with the correct ones, or adding an annotation that was missed by the LLM. Mostly, we observe that up to 77.5% on average of the generated lines code can be directly used.

The *GPT-4o* model is more prone to use those incorrect object identifiers or methods that do not exist (*Hallucination*). On the other hand, the *GPT-4o-mini* requires more modifications, but some of them are required by the model itself (e.g., "*adjust this ID with the submit button id*", "*Set password and user to the correct values*").

Based on the observed results, we can answer RQ2 as:

> In general, our findings indicate that model *GPT-4o* outperforms the *GPT-4o-mini* in generating system test cases from the test scenarios. With reference to the *prompt technique*, *Few-Shot* outperforms the inclusion of *Chain of Thought*, requiring less modifications. In general, the code that needs to be adjusted is around 29% of the total generated code with a standard deviation of 5%.

5   Threats to Validity

Notwithstanding our diligent endeavors, the validity of the findings for the exploratory study described above remains susceptible to various threats. We acknowledge the existence of the following types [49]:

Internal Validity: Threats to internal validity lie in possible biases of our exploratory study such that the properties measured over the observed outcomes are not produced by the *LLMs* but are due to other confounding factors. To mitigate potential internal threats, we employed a test suite and the user requirements of a real system used as a demonstrator in a European project as subject of evaluation. Another possible source of subjectivity is the manual calculation of the test scenarios coverage matrix in the baseline and the RQ1; to mitigate this, two authors originally calculated the traceability of the scenarios over the user requirements and then the coverage table was revised and discussed by all authors until a general consensus was reached.

Construct Validity: The threats to construct validity are concerned with the validity of the settings of our study procedure. The main external threat to validity is the non-determinism of the *LLM* itself, by which the output of the selected model can differ between executions. In the test generation, we tried to mitigate it by repeating the experiments five times and comparing the outputs across the five test scenarios to minimize the impact of the randomness. In the test generation exploratory study, we performed a cross validation and calculated the average of the number of modifications to deal with this not determinism. Another construct threat relies on the data that the *OpenAI* models use for training. It is impossible to know if those models were already pretrained with the *FullTeaching* code or test suite, meaning that the solution could be overfitted or biased.

External Validity: This type of threats refers to the generalizability of the observations. As we only conducted one exploratory study on one subject, we cannot of course make conclusions about the validity of *LLM*-assisted system testing for other differing contexts and applications. While the results are promising, we warn that more experiments are needed to draw more general conclusions. As is well known, the performance of *LLMs* strictly depends on the *prompts* given to them. Thus, even for the *FullTeaching* application, we cannot exclude that different *prompts* provided by different testers could obtain quite different performances. We tried to mitigate this threat by selecting state-of-the-art *prompting* patterns and strategies for the *prompting* creation process, reducing the model temperature to minimize hallucinations, and fix the OpenAI model versions.

Reliability: To tackle this issue and ensure reproducibility by fellow researchers, we provide access to the user execution data, various configurations applied, and the data used as input into a replication package [46]. The replication package also includes the different formatted LLMs outputs and the changes performed into them (RQ2) to make the test cases pass-work.

6   Conclusions and Future Work

LLMs arise as a promising support tool to complement the system test process. This exploratory study has remarked that during the test scenario generation, LLMs can provide an initial set of test scenarios that cover most of the user requirements. The generated test scenarios show room for improvement, for instance by reducing the number of test scenarios by merging several into one (e.g., one test scenario can check the enrolled courses as well as the classes of this course).

Deriving system test cases from the test scenarios poses more challenges. In general, we have observed that the *LLMs* output provides correct test skeleton following the test steps of the scenarios but tend to invent (*hallucinate*) with the identifiers of the web elements or the methods created to support the test cases (e.g., navigate to main menu method). In some cases (mostly the least powerful model) the output explicitly indicates that the tester should tune these parameters, but in other cases the LLM generates method calls or identifiers that do not exist.

Overall, our findings, in line with the community opinion, show that *LLMs* are a great tool to reduce the amount of manual work, but must be supervised by a human tester to reduce the impact of hallucinations.

This is a preliminary work, and several lines of future work have been opened due to the promising results. The most prominent research line entails comparing our approach with the state-of-the-art tools not employing generative AI, as well as evaluating our approach with more models (different to the GPT-based family) with different tunings (e.g., different temperature values or introducing embeddings). We also plan to extend and evaluate the performance of *LLMs* in assisting system testing by improving the preliminary approach employed in this first study. We intend to explore how the *prompting* techniques could be improved to achieve better results in terms of test effectiveness, which has not been covered here. We also need to introduce some approach to assess the efficiency of the LLM-assisted process. Finally, we also intend to explore if and how *LLMs* could support the generation of negative (robustness) test cases.

Acknowledgments. We would like to thank Alessio Ferrari for his help and guidance throughout our first work on this topic. We also want to extend our gratitude to the URJC ElasTest/FullTeaching team for their continuous support, especially Oscar, Pablo, and Patxi. This work was supported in part by the project PID2022-137646OB-C32 under Grant MCIN/ AEI/10.13039/501100011033/FEDER, UE, and in part by the project MASE RDS-PTR_22_24_P2.1 Cybersecurity (Italy).

References

1. Jones, C., Bergen, B.: Does GPT-4 Pass the Turing Test? (2023). http://arxiv.org/abs/2310.20216
2. Raman, S.: The rise of AI-powered applications: large language models in modern business (2023). https://www.computer.org/publications/tech-news/trends/large-language-models-in-modern-business. Accessed 01 Aug 2024
3. Minaee, S., et al.: Large language models: a survey (2024). http://arxiv.org/abs/2402.06196

4. Duggal, A.S., et al.: A sequential roadmap to Industry 6.0: exploring future manufacturing trends. IET Commun. **16**(5), 521–531 (2022). https://doi.org/10.1049/CMU2.12284
5. MarketsandMarkets, "Large Language Model Market Size And Share Report, 2030" (2024). https://www.grandviewresearch.com/industry-analysis/large-language-model-llm-market-report. Accessed 01 Aug 2024
6. P. M. Research, "Global Large Language Model (LLM) Market Size, Share, Growth Drivers, Competitive Analysis, Recent Trends & Developments, and Demand Forecast To 2030" (2024). https://www.pragmamarketresearch.com/reports/121032/large-language-model-llm-market-size. Accessed 01 Aug 2024
7. Ozkaya, I.: Application of large language models to software engineering tasks: opportunities, risks, and implications. IEEE Softw. **40**(3), 4–8 (2023). https://doi.org/10.1109/MS.2023.3248401
8. Hou, X., et al.: Large language models for software engineering: a systematic literature review, vol. X(December), pp. 1–79 (2023). http://arxiv.org/abs/2308.10620
9. Jin, P., et al.: Assess and summarize: improve outage understanding with large language models. In: ESEC/FSE 2023 – Proceedings of 31st ACM Jt. Meet. European Software Engineering Conference Symposium Foundation Software Engineering, pp. 1657–1668 (2023). https://doi.org/10.1145/3611643.3613891
10. Sobania, D., et al.: Evaluating explanations for software patches generated by large language models. In: Lecture Notes Computer Science (including Subser. Lect. Notes Artif. Intell. Lect. Notes Bioinformatics), vol. 14415 LNCS, pp. 147–152 (2024). https://doi.org/10.1007/978-3-031-48796-5_12
11. Betsy, B., Chris, J., Jennifer, P., Niall Richard, M.: Site Reliability Engineering: How Google Runs Production Systems. O'Reilly Media, Inc., (2016)
12. Schafer, M., Nadi, S., Eghbali, A., Tip, F.: An empirical evaluation of using large language models for automated unit test generation. IEEE Trans. Softw. Eng. **50**(1), 85–105 (2024). https://doi.org/10.1109/TSE.2023.3334955
13. Arora, C., Herda, T., Homm, V.: Generating test scenarios from NL requirements using retrieval-augmented LLMs: an industrial study (2024). http://arxiv.org/abs/2404.12772
14. "ISO/IEC/IEEE International Standard - Software and systems engineering --Software testing --Part 1:General concepts," ISO/IEC/IEEE 29119–1:2022(E), pp. 1–60 (2022). https://doi.org/10.1109/IEEESTD.2022.9698145
15. Liu, Z., et al.: Make LLM a testing expert: bringing human-like interaction to mobile GUI testing via functionality-aware decisions, pp. 1–13 (2024). https://doi.org/10.1145/3597503.3639180
16. Liu, P., Yuan, W., Fu, J., Jiang, Z., Hayashi, H., Neubig, G.: Pre-train, prompt, and predict: a systematic survey of prompting methods in natural language processing. ACM Comput. Surv. **55**(9), 1–46 (2023). https://doi.org/10.1145/3560815
17. Rumelhart, D.E., Hinton, G.E., Williams, R.J.: Learning internal representations by error propagation. in readings in cognitive science: a perspective from psychology and artificial intelligence, pp. 399–421 (1985). https://doi.org/10.1016/B978-1-4832-1446-7.50035-2
18. Elman, J.L.: Finding structure in time. Cogn. Sci. **14**(2), 179–211 (1990). https://doi.org/10.1016/0364-0213(90)90002-E
19. Mahoney, M.V.M.: Fast text compression with neural networks. In: Proceedings of AAAI FLAIRS (2000). https://www.aaai.org/Papers/FLAIRS/2000/FLAIRS00-044.pdf
20. Vaswani, A., et al.: Attention is all you need. Adv. Neural Inf. Process. Syst. **2017**(Decem), 5999–6009 (2017). https://arxiv.org/abs/1706.03762v7. Accessed 22 Jul 22 2024
21. Chowdhery, A., et al.: PaLM: scaling language modeling with pathways (2022). http://arxiv.org/abs/2204.02311. Accessed 22 Jul 2024
22. Touvron, H., et al.: LLaMA: open and efficient foundation language models (2023).http://arxiv.org/abs/2302.13971. Accessed 22 July 2024

23. OpenAI *et al.*, "GPT-4 Technical report" (2023). http://arxiv.org/abs/2303.08774
24. White, J., et al.: A prompt pattern catalog to enhance prompt engineering with ChatGPT (2023). http://arxiv.org/abs/2302.11382
25. Zamfirescu-Pereira, J.D., Wong, R.Y., Hartmann, B., Yang, Q.: Why Johnny Can't Prompt: How Non-AI Experts Try (and Fail) to Design LLM Prompts. Conf. Hum. Factors Comput. Syst. - Proc. (2023). https://doi.org/10.1145/3544548.3581388
26. Dang, H., Mecke, L., Lehmann, F., Goller, S., Buschek, D.: How to Prompt? Opportunities and challenges of zero- and few-shot learning for human-ai interaction in creative applications of generative models, vol. 1, no. 1. Association for Computing Machinery (2022). http://arxiv.org/abs/2209.01390
27. Wei, J., et al.: Chain-of-thought prompting elicits reasoning in large language models. Adv. Neural Inf. Process. Syst. **35**(NeurIPS), 1–14 (2022)
28. Kojima, T., Reid, M., Gu, S.S.: Large language models are zero-shot reasoners. Adv. Neural Inf. Process. Syst. **35**(NeurIPS 2022) (2022)
29. Bach, S.H., et al.: PromptSource: an integrated development environment and repository for natural language prompts. In: Proceedings of Annual Meeting of Association of Computer Linguistics, pp. 93–104 (2022). https://doi.org/10.18653/v1/2022.acl-demo.9
30. Microsoft, "GitHub Copilot · Your AI pair programmer" (2022). https://github.com/features/copilot. Accessed 22 July 2024
31. Spiess, C., et al.: Calibration and Correctness of Language Models for Code (2024). http://arxiv.org/abs/2402.02047. Accessed 22 July 2024
32. Liu, F., et al.: Exploring and evaluating hallucinations in LLM-powered code generation (2024). http://arxiv.org/abs/2404.00971. Accessed 22 July 2024
33. Nam, D., Macvean, A., Hellendoorn, V., Vasilescu, B., Myers, B.: Using an LLM to help with code understanding. In: Proceedings of the IEEE/ACM 46th International Conference on Software Engineering, pp. 1–13 (2024). https://doi.org/10.1145/3597503.3639187
34. Wang, J., Huang, Y., Chen, C., Liu, Z., Wang, S., Wang, Q.: Software testing with large language models: survey, landscape, and vision. IEEE Trans. Softw. Eng. **50**(4), 911–936 (2024). https://doi.org/10.1109/TSE.2024.3368208
35. Ferrari, A., Abualhaija, S., Arora, C.: Model generation from requirements with LLMs: an exploratory study. In: 2024 IEEE 32st International Requirements Engineering Conference Workshops (REW), pp. 291–300 (2024). http://arxiv.org/abs/2404.06371
36. Yang, C., Chen, J., Lin, B., Zhou, J., Wang, Z.: Enhancing LLM-based test generation for hard-to-cover branches via program analysis (2024). http://arxiv.org/abs/2404.04966
37. Yu, S., Fang, C., Ling, Y., Wu, C., Chen, Z.: LLM for test script generation and migration: challenges, capabilities, and opportunities. In: IEEE International Conference on Software Quality Reliability and Security QRS, pp. 206–217 (2023). https://doi.org/10.1109/QRS60937.2023.00029
38. Liu, Z., et al.: Fill in the blank: context-aware automated text input generation for mobile GUI testing. In: Proceedings of International Conference on Software Engineering, pp. 1355–1367 (2023). https://doi.org/10.1109/ICSE48619.2023.00119
39. Shrestha, S.L., Csallner, C.: SLGPT: using transfer learning to directly generate simulink model files and find bugs in the simulink toolchain. In: ACM International Conference on Proceeding Series, pp. 260–265 (2021). https://doi.org/10.1145/3463274.3463806
40. D. Zimmermann and A. Koziolek, "Automating GUI-based Software Testing with GPT-3," *Proc. - 2023 IEEE 16th Int. Conf. Softw. Testing, Verif. Valid. Work. ICSTW 2023*, pp. 62–65, 2023, https://doi.org/10.1109/ICSTW58534.2023.00022
41. Ye, X., Durrett, G.: The unreliability of explanations in few-shot prompting for textual reasoning. Adv. Neural Inf. Process. Syst. **35**(NeurIPS), 1–15 (2022)

42. ElasTest EU Project, "Fullteaching: A web application to make teaching online easy." Universidad Rey Juan Carlos (2017). https://github.com/elastest/full-teaching. Accessed 10 Aug 2023
43. Garcia, B., et al.: A proposal to orchestrate test cases. In: Proceedings–2018 International Conference on the Quality of Information and Communications Technology, QUATIC 2018, pp. 38–46 (2018). https://doi.org/10.1109/QUATIC.2018.00016
44. Fuente Pérez, P.: FullTeaching : Aplicación Web de docencia con videoconferencia (2017)
45. Augusto, C., Morán, J., de la Riva, C., Tuya, J.: FullTeaching E2E Test Suite (2023). https://github.com/giis-uniovi/retorch-st-fullteaching
46. Augusto, C., Moran, J., Bertolino, A., De La Riva, C., Tuya, J.: Replication package for 'software system testing assisted by large language models: an exploratory study (2024). https://github.com/giis-uniovi/retorch-llm-rp. Accessed 22 Jul 2024)
47. Krensky, P., et al.: Magic quadrant for data science and machine learning platforms (2020). https://qads.com.br/data-analytics/pdfs/Gartner%0A2018.pdf
48. OpenAI, "Cheat Sheet: Mastering Temperature and Top_p in ChatGPT API - API - OpenAI Developer Forum," OpenAI Documentation (2023). https://community.openai.com/t/cheat-sheet-mastering-temperature-and-top-p-in-chatgpt-api/172683. Accessed 23 July 2024)
49. Wohlin, C., Runeson, P., Höst, M., Ohlsson, M.C., Regnell, B., Wesslén, A.: Experimentation in software engineering, vol. 9783642290 (2012). https://doi.org/10.1007/978-3-642-29044-2

Continuous Auditing Based Conformity Assessment for AI Systems: A Proof-of-Concept Evaluation

Dorian Knoblauch$^{(\boxtimes)}$ and Abhishek Shrestha

Fraunhofer FOKUS, Berlin, Germany
{dorian.knoblauch,abhishek.shrestha}@fokus.fraunhofer.de

Abstract. Continuous Auditing Based Conformity Assessment (CABCA) is a new audit methodology developed to maintain the ongoing compliance of AI systems with various standards and industry-specific regulations. CABCA enables the operationalisation of those high-level requirements into measurable attributes to increase the level of automation. This paper presents CABCA and assesses its effectiveness through a proof-of-concept (PoC) implementation on a Medical Visual Question Answering (MedVQA) system, trained using the Radiology Objects in COntext (ROCO) dataset. In this evaluation, we partially apply guidelines from the "Artificial Intelligence (AI) in medical devices" questionnaire by the IG-NB, illustrating how to evaluate the conformity of an AI system to industry guidelines and standards.

Keywords: Conformity Assessment · AI Compliance · Audit Machine Learning Systems

1 Introduction

In the rapidly evolving landscape of artificial intelligence (AI), where systems are continuously improved and updated throughout the machine learning lifecycle, traditional point-in-time certifications struggle to keep pace. These periodic assessments often fall short of capturing the dynamic nature of AI systems, particularly in domains where compliance and accuracy are critical, such as healthcare.

The Continuous Auditing Based Conformity Assessment (CABCA) methodology addresses these challenges by providing a framework for the ongoing compliance monitoring of AI systems. This approach ensures that AI technologies not only meet standards at a single moment but maintain conformity throughout their operational life. This paper presents CABCA and its application through a proof-of-concept (PoC) evaluation of a Medical Visual Question Answering (MedVQA) system trained using the Radiology Objects in Context (ROCO) dataset.

© IFIP International Federation for Information Processing 2025
Published by Springer Nature Switzerland AG 2025
H. D. Menéndez et al. (Eds.): ICTSS 2024, LNCS 15383, pp. 256–272, 2025.
https://doi.org/10.1007/978-3-031-80889-0_18

Our contributions to the field of AI conformity assessment include:

1. Introducing a novel conformity assessment methodology that supports continuous evaluation, essential for the dynamic nature of AI systems.
2. Demonstrating this methodology through a PoC, highlighting how CABCA can be effectively implemented to continuously monitor and assess a medical AI system.
3. Developing a Medical Data Quality Evaluation Tool to ensure the ROCO dataset's reliability, crucial for the robust performance of the MedVQA system.

The CABCA methodology and the Medical Data Quality Evaluation Tool collectively enhance the compliance and reliability of AI systems, particularly in critical fields like healthcare, thereby supporting safer and more effective AI applications.

2   Related Work

2.1   Conformity Assessment

Conformity assessment is a vital process for verifying that products, systems, and services meet specific standards and regulatory requirements. This is especially critical for AI systems, where ongoing evaluation is necessary due to the rapid evolution of technology and regulatory landscapes.

In our previous work, we developed and evaluated the CABC approach, which leverages automated tools for real-time data assessment against predefined metric thresholds, providing timely insights into an AI system's compliance status [10–12]. This continuous cycle of data collection, analysis, and reporting includes self-assessment, third-party audits, and certification processes, ensuring flexibility and adaptability to the evolving AI and regulatory landscapes.

Möckander et al. [17] and Floridi et al. [5] discuss the European AI Act's proposed enforcement mechanisms, including conformity assessments and post-market monitoring for high-risk AI systems. Their frameworks provide comprehensive auditing guidelines similar to CABCA, which operationalizes these guidelines into continuous, machine-readable metrics for real-time compliance verification.

Sánchez [21] explores the role of measurement accuracy and reliability in conformity assessment, emphasizing their importance in ensuring products, processes, and systems meet established standards. This perspective is crucial for developing reliable and effective conformity assessment methodologies for AI systems.

The KI-Prüfkatalog [20] and AIC4 criteria catalogue [9] offer detailed quality criteria for AI systems, covering aspects such as reliability, safety, robustness, explainability, fairness, and data protection. CABCA builds on these by transforming the criteria into continuous, automated assessments, ensuring ongoing compliance with these standards through its robust monitoring framework.

Recent studies in explainable AI and transparency are vital for effective conformity assessment. Chaudhry et al. [4] propose a Transparency Index Framework for AI in education. Anjomshoae [1] examines context-based explanations, and Anjomshoae [2] explores using Large Language Models for automating legal compliance. These works complement CABCA by enhancing transparency and interpretability necessary for continuous conformity monitoring.

2.2   Conformity Assessment of Medical Devices

The conformity assessment of medical devices, particularly those incorporating AI, presents unique challenges due to the stringent regulatory requirements and the critical nature of these systems. Granlund et al. [6] address the regulatory challenges in developing medical device software, emphasizing the need for compliance processes tailored to software systems. Their approach contrasts with CABCA's continuous, automated monitoring by focusing on manual compliance verification, highlighting CABCA's advantage in dynamic, fast-paced environments.

Pfeiffer et al. [19] propose a standard process for data collection and analysis in Post-Market Surveillance (PMS) within the medical device lifecycle, emphasizing AI support. This aligns with CABCA's principles by enabling ongoing monitoring and evaluation of AI systems' performance and safety, though CABCA extends this by providing continuous, automated assessments.

2.3   Medical VQA Systems, Chatbots, and Datasets

MedVQA systems and chatbots are essential for interpreting medical images and providing accurate, timely information. Recent advancements have leveraged AI and large language models (LLMs) to enhance these capabilities.

MSMedCap [24] employs SAM and CLIP encoders for feature extraction, improving caption quality for medical images using the ROCO dataset. Similarly, PeFoMed [15] fine-tunes multimodal LLMs for Med-VQA, achieving significant performance improvements, particularly on closed-ended questions, also using the ROCO dataset. LLaVA-Med [13] is a vision-language assistant trained to answer open-ended research questions about biomedical images, showing excellent performance on multiple biomedical VQA datasets.

ChatDoctor [14] fine-tunes a large language model using 100,000 patient-doctor dialogues, enhancing its medical advice capabilities. PMC-LLaMA [22] adapts a general-purpose language model using a vast corpus of biomedical papers and textbooks, surpassing models like ChatGPT on medical QA benchmarks.

Regarding datasets, BiomedCLIP [23] introduces a model pre-trained on 15 million scientific image-text pairs, showing significant improvements in biomedical tasks. The PathVQA dataset [7] includes over 30,000 questions created from pathology images and captions, providing a valuable resource for developing AI systems to understand medical images. The ROCO dataset [18] contains over

81,000 radiology images with captions, supporting models for caption and keyword generation, image structuring, and semantic tagging. This dataset is subject to measurements by our Medical Data Quality Evaluation Tool to ensure data file completeness, syntactic accuracy, and label leakage, maintaining the quality of AI systems trained on it.

3 CABCA Methodology

The CABCA methodology is designed for real-time auditing and assessment of AI systems, ensuring they adhere to various standards and regulations throughout their lifecycle. It is based on three core principles: continuous assessment, stakeholder trust, and adaptability.

CABCA continuously monitors compliance using real-time data, which is crucial for AI systems that frequently update. Regular updates on the AI system's compliance status are provided to stakeholders, fostering trust and transparency. The methodology adapts to changes in AI systems, industry standards, and regulatory requirements, ensuring sustained compliance.

CABCA provides multiple modes to suit different needs, including self-assessment, third-party audits, and certification. Self-assessment allows organizations to internally monitor compliance, while third-party audits add credibility to the AI system's compliance status. Certification offers formal recognition from accredited bodies confirming compliance with standards.

Key roles in the CABCA process include the Auditee, Auditing Party, and Conformity Status Publishing Entity. These roles work together to ensure transparency and trust by generating detailed reports that map measurement results to quality dimensions and requirements, facilitating evidence-based audits. This structured approach ensures that AI systems are consistently evaluated against relevant standards and guidelines, maintaining compliance and adaptability in dynamic environments.

4 Operationalization

The operationalization phase in CABCA involves converting high-level Conformity Specifications into practical steps and quantifiable metrics. This phase is essential for ensuring AI systems meet relevant standards consistently and maintain adherence to quality and compliance demands. The outcome is machine-readable documentation that supports automated assessments and is shared with stakeholders for approval, confirming that the operationalization of the Conformity Specifications aligns with their expectations for quality.

4.1 Steps for Operationalization

1. **Identify Quality Dimensions**
   Identifying quality dimensions is crucial for evaluating the AI system's functionality. These dimensions structure the assessment of different system

aspects such as fairness, transparency, reliability, accountability, privacy, and
security. Each dimension is precisely defined and segmented into smaller, manageable parts that align with evolving technology and business needs.

2. **Risk Identification**
   This step involves detailing the risks linked to each quality dimension. Rec-
   ognizing and understanding these risks is essential for developing effective
   mitigation strategies. Each identified risk should be traceable to its respective quality dimension to ensure that mitigation strategies are correctly linked
   to specific risks.

3. **Define Requirements and Suitable Metrics**
   Derived from the risks identified, requirements should be clear, unambiguous,
   and measurable. For every requirement, corresponding metrics are defined
   to quantify compliance. These metrics need to be accurate, relevant, and
   consistently measurable. The frequency of assessing these requirements should
   also be determined.

4. **Implement Measurements**
   A framework for continuous, automated assessment of compliance is established by implementing measurements that correspond to defined metrics.
   To ensure consistency and efficiency, measurements should be as automated
   as possible. The output from measurements should align with the metric's
   specified unit, and results should be systematically collected and stored for
   evidence-based auditing.

4.2   Operationalization Documentation

Documentation is critical in informing stakeholders about operational decisions
and configurations. It functions as a configuration file for automated assessments and supports nested operationalization for systems involving multiple
vendors. This documentation ensures transparency, traceability, and configura-
bility, allowing stakeholders to review and confirm that the operationalization
of conformity specifications meets their quality standards.

The operational documentation is structured hierarchically as follows:

- **Conformity Specification:** A high-level document that specifies required
  types of conformity.
- **Dimensions:** These are subcomponents of the Conformity Specification that
  detail quality dimensions.
- **Requirements:** These are specific criteria derived from quality dimensions
  and associated risks.
- **Metrics:** These are standards established to measure compliance with the
  requirements.
- **Measurements:** Measurements need to be designed as a flexible and extensible framework for measuring various types of data and comparing these
  measurements against specified targets. This system accommodates different
  data types (numeric, ordinal, boolean, string) and supports multiple comparison strategies, enabling a unified and versatile approach for handling diverse

measurement needs. By defining a generic measurement type and implementing specific comparison strategies, the framework ensures that measurement values can be accurately assessed against target values regardless of their underlying data type.

This structured approach provides a comprehensive framework for continuous assessment, accommodating components from third-party vendors where necessary. External assessors may also be involved, with their conformity status accessible via an assessment interface.

Table 1. Attributes of Conformity Specification

Attribute Name	Data Type	Description
Name	String	Name of the Conformity Specification
Comment	String	Provides explanations or additional information
ConfidentialityFlag	Boolean	Indicates if the information is confidential
Assessor	String	Entity responsible for assessing the specification
AssessmentInterface	String	Where to fetch the assessment result if Assessor is not None

Table 2. Attributes of Dimensions

Attribute Name	Data Type	Description
Name	String	Name of the Dimension
Comment	String	Descriptive text regarding the dimension
ConfidentialityFlag	Boolean	Flag to mark if dimension details are confidential
Assessor	String	Entity responsible for assessing the dimension
AssessmentInterface	String	Where to fetch the assessment result if Assessor is not None

Table 3. Attributes of Requirements

Attribute Name	Data Type	Description
Name	String	Name of the Requirement
Comment	String	Explanation or commentary on the requirement
ConfidentialityFlag	Boolean	Indicates confidentiality of the requirement details
Frequency	String	Specifies the frequency of requirement evaluation
Assessor	String	Entity responsible for assessing the requirement
AssessmentInterface	String	Where to fetch the assessment result if Assessor is not None

Tables 1, 2, 3, 4, and 5 depict attributes of each hierarchical elements in the Operationalization Documentation. In all cases, a "None" value in the "Assessor" attribute would mean no external assessor while the "AssessmentInterface" is optional. In Table 5, the "AssessmentInterface" can be a REST endpoint, CLI command, database query, or file location. Similarly, the "ComparisionStrategy" could be "LessThan", "Contains", "GreaterThan", or "EqualTo". "DataType" on

Table 4. Attributes of Metrics

Attribute Name	Data Type	Description
Name	String	Name of the Metric
Comment	String	Provides details about the purpose and use of the metric
ConfidentialityFlag	Boolean	Indicates if the metric includes confidential data
Assessor	String	Entity responsible for assessing the metric
AssessmentInterface	String	Where to fetch the assessment result if Assessor is not None

Table 5. Attributes of Measurements

Attribute Name	Data Type	Description
Name	String	Name of the Measurement
Comment	String	Additional information on how measurements are conducted
ConfidentialityFlag	Boolean	Specifies if measurement details are to be kept confidential
Assessor	String	Entity responsible for performing the measurement
AssessmentInterface	String	Describes how to retrieve the value
ComparisonStrategy	String	The strategy used for comparing values
DataType	Enum	The type of data being measured
TargetValue	Generic	The target value to compare against

the other hand, could be numeric, ordinal, boolean, or string, while the "Target-Value" depends on measurement type.

This hierarchical and comprehensive approach to documentation and operationalization ensures that CABCA can effectively and continuously evaluate AI systems against relevant standards and guidelines. The result is machine-readable documentation that not only facilitates automated assessments but also provides transparency for stakeholders, allowing them to verify that the operationalization aligns with their quality requirements and expectations.

4.3 Measurement Framework

The measurement framework supports various data types to handle diverse measurement needs, including numeric, ordinal, boolean, and string values. Each data type is paired with appropriate comparison strategies to evaluate measurement values against target values effectively. These comparison strategies include methods such as LessThan, GreaterThan, EqualTo, Contains, NotEqualTo, and InRange, providing a flexible and robust system for comparing data. The framework's design ensures accurate assessments regardless of the data type by implementing a generic measurement type that applies the relevant comparison strategy. Pseudocode for the measurement framework outlines its structure and functions, demonstrating how measurements are retrieved, compared, and validated.

The pseudocode below represents the core structure of the measurement framework. It focuses on the interfaces and the function that compares measurement values to target values, illustrating how different components of the measurement system interact within the framework.

```
// Interface for all measurements
interface MeasurementInterface:
    properties:
        Value  // The value of the measurement
        ComparisonStrategy  // Strategy used for comparison
        AssessmentInterface  // Method to retrieve the value
    methods:
        MeetsTarget(targetValue)  // Returns true if the measurement meets
                                  // the target based on the strategy

// Interface for comparison strategies
interface ComparisonStrategy:
    methods:
        Compare(value, targetValue)  // Defines the comparison logic

// Generic method to compare measurement values
function CompareMeasurement(measurement, targetValue):
    return measurement.MeetsTarget(targetValue)
```

The pseudocode begins by defining a `MeasurementInterface` that includes properties for the measurement value, the comparison strategy, and the assessment interface. It also defines a method, `MeetsTarget(targetValue)`, which checks if the measurement meets the specified target value using the comparison strategy. Next, the `ComparisonStrategy` interface is defined, which includes the method `Compare(value, targetValue)` to encapsulate the logic for comparing the measurement value to the target value. Finally, the function `CompareMeasurement(measurement, targetValue)` is provided to facilitate the comparison process. This function invokes the `MeetsTarget` method of the measurement object, which uses the appropriate comparison strategy to determine if the measurement value satisfies the target criteria. This approach ensures flexible, accurate, and consistent measurement and comparison across various data types and scenarios.

5   Continuous Assessment

CABCA is structured to deliver ongoing evaluations of AI systems, ensuring they meet conformity specifications, quality objectives, and effectively manage risks. This section details the steps in the CABCA assessment, with an emphasis on how Operationalization Documentation acts as a configuration tool for the assessment process. Prior to initiating the assessment process, the Operationalization Documentation, which outlines dimensions, requirements, metrics, and measurements, is employed to configure continuous assessment. This documentation facilitates the automatic interpretation of audit criteria, metrics, and corresponding measurements. The frequency of assessments at various levels of operationalization documentation varies based on individual requirements and is specified for each requirement in the configuration file. The assessment process is activated whenever a new model is deployed. During the operation phase, the frequencies for assessments are explicitly defined within the Operationalization Documentation. The Assessment Process:

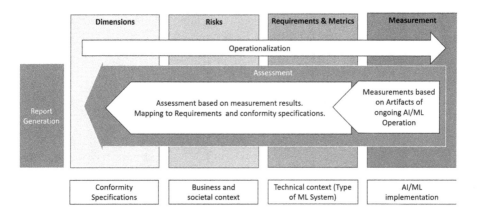

Fig. 1. Assessment Process

1. **Artifacts Production and Usage:**
   Artifacts like log files, model weights, and data samples are generated or utilized at different stages of the ML lifecycle, serving as inputs for the measurements. Some artifacts directly yield measurement results through parsing, while others may require comprehensive test suites to accurately extract data. This step aligns with the "Measurements based on Artifacts of ongoing AI/ML Operation" in Fig. 1.
2. **Measurement Using Artifacts as Inputs:**
   Measurements are performed by analyzing and processing the artifacts. The outcomes of these measurements are then prepared for transmission to the auditing entity. This step allows for real-time or frequency-based evaluations, triggered either following specific cycles such as model deployment or at intervals specified for individual quality requirements. This aligns with the "Measurement" phase in Fig. 1.
3. **Mapping Measurement Results:**
   The measurement data received is automatically evaluated using the Operationalization Documentation as a configuration tool. The evaluation checks against predefined metric thresholds that mirror the quality objectives of the ML system. This automated evaluation ensures the process is not only quick but also consistent with the quality aims outlined in the Conformity Specifications. This step is depicted in the "Mapping to Requirements and Conformity Specifications" in Fig. 1.
4. **Report Generation:**
   The report provides comprehensive details on which quality objectives are achieved by mapping each measurement result to the corresponding parts of the Conformity Specifications, showing how well these specifications are met. It is shared with stakeholders to inform them about the AI system's compliance status. Different versions of the report can be produced with varying levels of detail, suited to the needs of different stakeholders. For example, a high-level overview for executive stakeholders and a more detailed techni-

cal report for engineers and auditors. This final step aligns with the "Report Generation" phase in Fig. 1.

The results of each CABCA assessment are stored persistently for future reference, quality tracking, and for proving compliance during audits. The scope of this persistence includes:

- **Measurement Results:** All metrics, along with their corresponding values, are systematically stored. This includes data on system performance, fairness measures, and other critical indicators essential for evaluating the system's alignment with specified standards.
- **Evaluation Outcomes:** The outcomes of comparisons between metrics and predefined quality goals are archived.
- **Assessment Reports:** The final reports generated after each assessment are saved.

Updating Conformity Status. CABCA highlights the need to regularly update the conformity status of AI-enabled systems. This involves assessing the AI system's compliance with set standards and quality goals. Quality assessments are crucial and include evaluating measurement results from artifacts like log files and model weights against predefined values informed by expert knowledge and risk assessments. If these results match the predefined values, a conformity status is issued, confirming compliance. If they do not, the status is revoked or adjusted, indicating areas for improvement and the need for better risk management. Regularly updating quality requirements is also important, as changes can affect assessment outcomes, reflecting CABCA's adaptability to technological changes.

Transparency is key in CABCA, especially in documenting and communicating assessment outcomes to stakeholders. This includes clear system identification with unambiguous references to the AI system name, type, and additional details for traceability. It also involves documenting the provider's name and address, and providing a statement of the AI system's compliance with relevant standards, regulations, and data protection requirements. Mentioning any relevant standards or specifications used for declaring conformity is also important. This documentation guides the automated assessment process and helps stakeholders understand the conformity measures, ensuring transparent communication of all decisions.

CABCA's communication is clear, consistent, and tailored to different stakeholders. Specific communication channels and their scope are defined to ensure stakeholders receive relevant and up-to-date information. The frequency and detail of communication updates are carefully managed to keep stakeholders informed about the AI system's compliance status without overwhelming them.

6   PoC Medical AI System

6.1   Description of Evaluation Setup

Our hypothetical MedVQA system represents many existing open-source medical AI systems that are fine-tuned on general-purpose VQA models and large language models (LLMs). These systems often use publicly available datasets like the ROCO dataset, which includes over 80,000 medical images and their descriptions. This hypothetical system aims to provide precise answers to medical questions based on both visual and textual data, integrating advanced multimodal large language models fine-tuned on extensive medical datasets to ensure accurate and contextually relevant responses.

Given the critical nature of medical applications, it is crucial to assess these AI systems throughout their entire lifecycle, including rigorous data testing using tools like our Medical Data Quality Evaluation (MD-Eval) Tool. Continuous assessment ensures the reliability, accuracy, and compliance of these systems with industry standards, ultimately safeguarding patient safety and enhancing the quality of medical care. This lifecycle assessment is essential to maintain the high standards required in the medical field and to ensure that AI systems consistently deliver accurate and reliable results.

The hypothetical MedVQA system needs to conform to the "Questionnaire Artificial Intelligence (AI) in medical devices" (Version 5, 15.12.2023). This questionnaire, created by the German Notified Bodies Alliance (IG-NB), provides industry guidelines to ensure the safety and effectiveness of AI-based medical devices through a process-oriented approach.

The document, developed by experts from organizations such as TÜV SÜD, TÜV Rheinland, and others, emphasizes the importance of evaluating all relevant processes throughout the device lifecycle. It draws on the "Guideline for AI for medical devices" by Prof. Christian Johner and Christoph Molnar, and references horizontal standards where specific AI standards are not available.

Key areas include general requirements, product development, and post-development phases. The focus is on best practices, risk management, data management, and continuous validation. Given the dynamic nature of AI models, any significant performance changes due to in-field learning must be reassessed to maintain conformity.

This questionnaire guides our evaluation, ensuring that the MedVQA system adheres to industry standards and maintains safety and reliability throughout its lifecycle. It covers all aspects of product development and operational processes, ensuring comprehensive risk management and ongoing compliance.

6.2   Operationalization Documentation for MedVQA System

In the context of our MedVQA system, we focus on the "Data Management" section of the questionnaire 'Artificial Intelligence (AI) in medical devices'. The section provides the basis for establishing various metrics to evaluate data quality, such as data anonymization, outlier and missing values, and bias among others. For the purpose of the PoC, we select three questions that result in simple metrics that are directly quantifiable from the dataset:

1. **Does the manufacturer specify the number of records and provide justification for its sufficiency? (3.a.1)** According to EN ISO 13485 and ISO/IEC TS 4213, the ROCO dataset should have a specified number of images. We calculate "data file completeness" to ensure the dataset meets this standard:

$$\text{Data file completeness} = \frac{\text{Number of image-caption pairs}}{\text{Number of expected image-caption pairs}} \quad (1)$$

2. **Does the procedure of labeling specify how the correctness of the labels is systematically reviewed? Has the manufacturer documented the choice of this rationale? (3.b.7)** Per BS/AAMI 34971, the correctness of keywords derived from captions is crucial. We compute "syntactic accuracy" to validate the keywords:

$$\text{Syntactic accuracy} = 1 - \left(\frac{\text{Number of images with keyword errors}}{\text{Total number of images with keywords}} \right) \quad (2)$$

3. **Does the manufacturer investigate and rule out the possibility of label leakage? (3.a.11)** In accordance with ISO/IEC TS 4213, possibility of label leakage needs to be evaluated to ensure that the training, validation, and test sets remain independent from each other. To detect this, we use the method proposed in [3], where overlaps in textual information between different splits (training, validation, and test sets) are analyzed.

Listing 1.1 shows the Operationalization Documentation of the questionnaire requirements to the MedVQA system.

Listing 1.1. Conformity Specification and Requirements

```
1   Conformity Specification:
2   - Name: Questionnaire 'Artificial Intelligence (AI) in medical devices' (Version 5, 15.12.2023)
3   - Comment: Ensures safety and effectiveness of AI-based medical devices through a process-oriented
            approach.
4
5   Requirements:
6   1. Requirement:
7      - Name: Data Records Specification
8      - Comment: Does the manufacturer specify the number of records and provide justification for its
            sufficiency? (3.a.1)
9      - Frequency: Triggers Every Lifecycle in the Datapreparation Phase
10
11     Metric:
12     - Name: Data file completeness
13     - Comment: Measures the completeness of the dataset by comparing the number of image-caption pairs
            against the expected total.
14
15     Measurement:
16     - Name: MD-Eval Tool - DataFileCompleteness
17     - Comment: Utilizes the MD-Eval Tool to verify if the dataset has the expected number of image-
            caption pairs.
18     - AssessmentInterface: python app.py data_completeness && jq .data_file_completeness
19     - ComparisonStrategy: GreaterThan
20     - TargetValue: 0.9
21
22  2. Requirement:
23     - Name: Label Correctness Procedure
```

```
24     - Comment: Does the procedure of labeling specify how the correctness of the labels is
                  systematically reviewed? Has the manufacturer documented the choice of this rationale? (3.b
                  .7)
25     - Frequency: Triggers Every Lifecycle in the Datapreparation Phase
26
27     Metric:
28     - Name: Syntactic accuracy
29     - Comment: Evaluates the correctness of keywords derived from captions.
30
31     Measurement:
32     - Name: MD-Eval Tool - SyntacticAccuracy
33     - Comment: Uses the MD-Eval Tool to check the syntactic accuracy of the keywords against standard
                  dictionaries and NLP models.
34     - AssessmentInterface: python app.py syntactic_accuracy && jq .syntactic_accuracy
35     - ComparisonStrategy: GreaterThan
36     - TargetValue: 0.9
37
38  3. Requirement:
39     - Name: Label Leakage Investigation
40     - Comment: Does the manufacturer investigate and rule out the possibility of label leakage? (3.a
                  .11)
41     - Frequency: Triggers Every Lifecycle in the Datapreparation Phase
42
43     Metric:
44     - Name: Label Leakage Probability
45     - Comment: Measures the likelihood of label leakage by evaluating the similarity of textual
                  information between training, validation, and test sets.
46
47     Measurement:
48     - Name: MD-Eval Tool - LabelLeakageProbability
49     - Comment: Utilizes the MD-Eval Tool to compute the cosine similarity between combined textual
                  information from different dataset splits.
50     - AssessmentInterface: python app.py label_leakage && jq .label_leakage_probability
51     - ComparisonStrategy: LessThan
52     - TargetValue: 0.05
```

6.3   Implementation of the Measurements Using MD-Eval Tool

MD-Eval provides systematic checks on the quality of medical datasets. It leverages NLP techniques as well as medical dictionaries to evaluate relevant metrics that help make quality statements about datasets. The tool currently works on the ROCO dataset, which includes images accompanied by textual information such as captions, UMLS (Unified Medical Language System) CUIs (Concept Unique Identifiers), keywords, and UMLS Semantic Types (SemTypes).

The dataset is evaluated against three key metrics: *syntactic accuracy, completeness*, and *label leakage probability*.

Data file completeness is computed by comparing the actual number of image-caption pairs in the dataset to the expected values (Eq. 1). ROCO dataset was derived from PubMedCentral Database after filtering out the compound and non-radiology images. As specified in the original paper [18], the complete dataset should contain 65460 images in training, 8183 in validation, and 8182 in test set. Thus, for our calculation, these numbers serve as the expected number of data points and the dataset is considered incomplete if the corresponding splits do not meet these counts.

Syntactic accuracy is evaluated based on keyword correctness (Eq. 2). Originally, ROCO derives these keywords by applying several preprocessing steps on captions. The correctness of the keywords is important as they are used to fetch UMLS CUIs and SemTypes. To verify the general correctness of spelling, WordNet dictionary [16] is used. Additionally, since the dataset is specialized for the medical domain, the *en_core_sci_sm* NLP model [8] is used to verify the correctness of individual terms. This model resolves minor syntactic errors during analysis; for example, "stenosi", an incorrectly trimmed version of "stenosis", is not detected as a syntactic error. This approach aligns with the methodology used by the authors of ROCO as they use QuickUMLS for deriving CUIs which can resolve these errors as well.

Label leakage occurs when information from the training data leaks into the validation or test data which can lead to overly optimistic performance estimates but poor generalization capability. The tool assesses the potential for label leakage by computing the cosine similarity between all textual information of the images in the training set and those in the test set, as well as between the training and validation sets. High similarity indicates a higher risk of label leakage, while lower similarity suggests a lower risk.

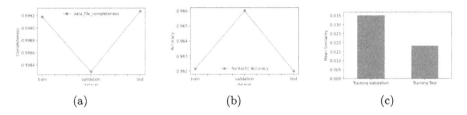

(a)   (b)   (c)

Fig. 2. Data quality evaluation results from MD-Eval for train, test, and validation splits on ROCO, including (a) Data file completeness. (b) Syntactic accuracy. (c) Label leakage probability.

Each run of MD-Eval produces a JSON file containing the evaluation results which includes exact values of computed metrics. Figure 2 shows the results from a single run. The exact values of measurements are then utilized within the operationalization documentation.

6.4   Example Iteration

One iteration of the continuous assessment was executed, where the data preparation phase of the machine learning lifecycle triggered the measurements. This assessment is based on the operationalization documentation, resulting in a conformity status update based on the measurement results:

Listing 1.2. Conformity Specification and Measurements

```
1
2    1. Measurement: MD-Eval Tool - Data File Completeness
3       - Value:
4          - train: 0.99918 > 0.9 True
5          - validation: 0.99829 > 0.9 True
6          - test: 0.99927 > 0.9 True
7       - Metric: Data file completeness
8          - Result: True Conformant
9       - Requirement: Data Records Specification
10          - Result: True Conformant
11
12   2. Measurement: MD-Eval Tool - Syntactic Accuracy
13       - Value:
14          - train: 0.96215 > 0.9 True
15          - validation: 0.96601 > 0.9 True
16          - test: 0.96198 > 0.9 True
17       - Metric: Syntactic accuracy
18          - Result: True Conformant
```

```
19        - Requirement: Label Correctness Procedure
20          - Result: True Conformant
21
22     3. Measurement: MD-Eval Tool - Label Leakage Probability
23        - Value:
24          - Mean similarity Training and Validation dataset: 0.0352 < 0.05 True
25          - Mean similarity Training and Test dataset: 0.01825 < 0.05 True
26        - Metric: Label Leakage Probability
27          - Result: True Conformant
28        - Requirement: Label Leakage Investigation
29          - Result: True Conformant
30
31     Conformity Specification: Questionnaire 'Artificial Intelligence (AI) in medical devices'
32     - Result: True Conformant with the specification → Audit successful for this iteration
```

This conformity status update is communicated to stakeholders in a machine-readable format.

7 Conclusion

This study has successfully demonstrated the CABCA methodology's effectiveness through a proof-of-concept implementation with a Medical Visual Question Answering system. CABCA's continuous assessment capabilities prove crucial for adapting to the evolving nature of AI systems, ensuring ongoing compliance and enhancing system reliability and safety.

8 Outlook

Future research will aim for full coverage of the medical questionnaire for the MedVQA system to ensure comprehensive conformity with all specified guidelines. Additionally, further developments in CABCA will focus on quantifying the extent to which high-level requirements from regulatory documents can be automated. This will involve assessing how effectively the automation captures the essence and intent of these requirements, thus refining the methodology to better serve dynamic AI environments.

Disclosure of Interests. The authors of this paper, Dorian Knoblauch and Abhishek Shrestha, declare the following potential conflicts of interest with respect to the research, authorship, and/or publication of this article:

– The work presented in this paper was partially funded by the German Federal Ministry of Education and Research (BMBF) under grant agreement ITEA-2021-20219-IML4E, as well as by the ITEA4 SmartDelta project, which was funded by the national funding authorities. of the participating countries.

The authors confirm that this work is free from any other potential conflicts of interest.

References

1. Anjomshoae, S.: Context-Based Explanations for Machine Learning Predictions. Ph.D. thesis, Umeå University, Umeå, Sweden (2022). https://www.diva-portal.org/smash/get/diva2:1690986/FULLTEXT02. doctoral Thesis, Department of Computing Science

2. Anjomshoae, S.: Enhancing legal compliance and regulation analysis with large language models. arXiv preprint arXiv:2404.17522v1 (2024). https://arxiv.org/html/2404.17522v1. doctoral Thesis, August 2022, Department of Computing Science, Umeå University, Sweden

3. Apicella, A., Isgrò, F., Prevete, R.: Don't push the button! exploring data leakage risks in machine learning and transfer learning. http://arxiv.org/abs/2401.13796

4. Chaudhry, M.A., Cukurova, M., Luckin, R.: A transparency index framework for AI in education. In: Rodrigo, M.M., Matsuda, N., Cristea, A.I., Dimitrova, V. (eds.) AIED 2022. LNCS, vol. 13356, pp. 195–198. Springer, Cham (2022). https://doi.org/10.1007/978-3-031-11647-6_33

5. Floridi, L., Holweg, M., Taddeo, M., Amaya, J., Mökander, J., Wen, Y.: capai - a procedure for conducting conformity assessment of AI systems in line with the EU artificial intelligence act. SSRN Electron. J. (2022). https://papers.ssrn.com/sol3/papers.cfm?abstract_id=4064091

6. Granlund, T., Mikkonen, T., Stirbu, V.: On medical device software CE compliance and conformity assessment. arXiv preprint arXiv:2103.06815 (2021), https://arxiv.org/pdf/2103.06815

7. He, X., Zhang, Y., Mou, L., Xing, E., Xie, P.: Pathvqa: 30000+ questions for medical visual question answering. arXiv preprint arXiv:2003.10286 (2020). https://arxiv.org/abs/2003.10286

8. Honnibal, M., Montani, I.: spaCy 2: natural language understanding with Bloom embeddings, convolutional neural networks and incremental parsing (2017). https://doi.org/10.5281/zenodo.1212303. to appear

9. for Information Security (BSI), F.O.: Kriterienkatalog für ki-cloud-dienste - aic4 (2021). https://www.bsi.bund.de/SharedDocs/Downloads/EN/BSI/CloudComputing/AIC4/AI-Cloud-Service-Compliance-Criteria-Catalogue_AIC4.pdf?__blob=publicationFile&v=4. Accessed 27 Feb 2023

10. Knoblauch, D., Banse, C.: Reducing implementation efforts in continuous auditing certification via an audit API. In: 2019 IEEE 28th International Conference on Enabling Technologies: Infrastructure for Collaborative Enterprises (WETICE), pp. 88–92. IEEE, IEEE (2019). presented at the International Conference on Enabling Technologies - Infrastructure for Collaborative Enterprises (WETICE) 2019

11. Knoblauch, D., Großmann, J.: Towards a risk-based continuous auditing-based certification for machine learning. Rev. Socionetw. Strat. **17**, 255–273 (2023). https://doi.org/10.1007/s12626-023-00148-w

12. Knoblauch, D., Großmann, J., Strick, L., Pannetrat, A.: Europäisches rahmenwerk für continuous auditing based certification. In: Tagungsband zum 16. IT-Sicherheitskongress des BSI, pp. 495–504. SecuMedia (2019)

13. Li, C., et al.: Llava-med: training a large language-and-vision assistant for biomedicine in one day. arXiv preprint arXiv:2306.00890 (2023). https://arxiv.org/abs/2306.00890

14. Li, Y., Li, Z., Zhang, K., Dan, R., Jiang, S., Zhang, Y.: Chatdoctor: a medical chat model fine-tuned on a large language model meta-ai (llama) using medical domain knowledge. arXiv preprint arXiv:2303.14070 (2023). https://arxiv.org/abs/2303.14070

15. Liu, G., He, J., Li, P., He, G., Chen, Z., Zhong, S.: Pefomed: parameter efficient fine-tuning on multimodal large language models for medical visual question answering. arXiv preprint arXiv:2401.02797 (2024). https://ar5iv.labs.arxiv.org/html/2401.02797

16. Miller, G.A.: Wordnet: a lexical database for English. Commun. ACM **38**(11), 39–41 (1995). https://doi.org/10.1145/219717.219748

17. Mökander, J., Axente, M., Casolari, F., Floridi, L.: Conformity assessments and post-market monitoring: a guide to the role of auditing in the proposed European AI regulation. Minds Mach. **32**, 241–268 (2022). https://link.springer.com/article/10.1007/s11023-021-09577-4

18. Pelka, O., Koitka, S., Rückert, J., Nensa, F., Friedrich, C.M.: Radiology objects in COntext (ROCO): a multimodal image dataset. In: Stoyanov, D., et al. (eds.) LABELS/CVII/STENT -2018. LNCS, vol. 11043, pp. 180–189. Springer, Cham (2018). https://doi.org/10.1007/978-3-030-01364-6_20

19. Pfeiffer, P., Sander, H., Fettke, P., Reisig, W.: Towards a standard process enabling AI-support for safety and conformity of medical devices. In: CEUR Workshop Proceedings, vol. 3264 (2022). https://ceur-ws.org/Vol-3264/HEDA22_paper_2.pdf

20. Poretschkin, D.M., et al.: Ki-pruefkatalog (2021). https://www.iais.fraunhofer.de/content/dam/iais/fb/Kuenstliche_intelligenz/ki-pruefkatalog/202107_KI-Pruefkatalog.pdf. Accessed 27 Feb 2023

21. Sánchez, C.A.: Role of measurement in conformity assessment. In: Handbook of Quality System, Accreditation and Conformity Assessment, pp. 1–15. Springer (2024). https://link.springer.com/referenceworkentry/10.1007/978-3-319-66963-1_141-1

22. Wu, C., Lin, W., Zhang, X., Zhang, Y., Wang, Y., Xie, W.: PMC-llama: towards building open-source language models for medicine. arXiv preprint arXiv:2304.14454 (2023). https://arxiv.org/abs/2304.14454

23. Zhang, S., et al.: Biomedclip: a multimodal biomedical foundation model pretrained from fifteen million scientific image-text pairs. arXiv preprint arXiv:2303.00915 (2023). https://ar5iv.labs.arxiv.org/html/2303.00915

24. Zhang, Z., et al.: Sam-guided enhanced fine-grained encoding with mixed semantic learning for medical image captioning. arXiv preprint arXiv:2311.01004 (2023). https://ar5iv.labs.arxiv.org/html/2311.01004

Improving Software Testing Reliability

Checking Test Suite Efficacy Through Dual-Channel Techniques

Constantin Cezar Petrescu[1]([✉])[iD], Sam Smith[1][iD], Alexis Butler[2][iD], and Santanu Kumar Dash[1][iD]

[1] University of Surrey, Guildford, Surrey, UK
{c.petrescu,s.k.dash}@surrey.ac.uk, sam.edw.smith@proton.me
[2] Royal Holloway, University of London, Egham, Surrey, UK
Alexis.Butler.2023@live.rhul.ac.uk

Abstract. Dynamic Call Graphs trace program execution and are used to model function coverage. They help identify which function calls are missed but do not offer insights on whether those calls are important to cover. We propose a weighted representation of control flow called Natural Call Graphs (NCGs), which can be used to identify important function calls. These weights represent the relevance of the callee to the caller and are computed using information-theoretic reasoning on tokens in the functions. We create a dataset of 1,234 manually verified function calls, containing a mix of relevant and irrelevant functions, from ten Python open-source projects. On this dataset, our approach achieves a peak precision of 78% and a recall of 94% in identifying relevant functions missed by tests.

Keywords: Dual-channel Research · Software Testing · Program Analysis

1 Introduction

Identifying functions that are missed by a test is essential for improving the test, and consequently, function coverage. Developers, who are under time-to-market pressure, rarely aim for full function coverage and can benefit from feedback on which function calls to prioritise during testing [13]. For example, a function call may invoke a logger to log diagnostics and this may not be a part of the software requirement. In this case, testing should prioritise calls that are important for the requirement and deprioritise calls to the logger. While Dynamic Call Graphs can help identify the calls that are missed, they do not offer insights on the importance of missed functions.

We present a technique to rank function calls to establish the relevance of the callee to the caller. Our hypothesis is that a callee would contain tokens similar to those in the caller if it is helping the caller achieve its core objective. On the other hand, it will contain tokens dissimilar to the caller if it is performing distinct tasks from the caller's core objective. These tasks may be either critical and

Published by Springer Nature Switzerland AG 2025
H. D. Menéndez et al. (Eds.): ICTSS 2024, LNCS 15383, pp. 275–291, 2025.
https://doi.org/10.1007/978-3-031-80889-0_19

important or housekeeping tasks, like diagnostic logging, that are less important to the caller. An entropic decision can help to differentiate between essential but diverse functions and fringe housekeeping tasks. Our approach falls under the domain of Dual-Channel Software Engineering [5]. Dual-channel software engineering uses information from both the natural language and algorithmic channels in the code. Information from function tokens has been recently used to improve various software engineering tasks such as program hardening [8] and commit deconflation [16]. We present an extension of Call Graphs called Natural Call Graphs whose edges are weighted based on the importance of the callee to the caller. We show that these weights can be relied on to identify important functions that should be covered in a test but are missed.

Our main contributions are a methodology and a tool (Sect. 3) which can rank function calls, based on their importance, that are missed by a test. We evaluate our tool on a ground truth, which consists of 1,234 manually vetted cases from the Dynamic Call Graphs of 4,004 integration tests from ten open-source projects of varied popularity (683–6.6K stars on GitHub) and size (21K–449K LOC). Our dataset and tool are publicly available[1]. Our tool achieves 78% precision and 94% recall in identifying relevant functions that are missed (Sect. 4). We present a selection of cases in Sect. 4.5 to highlight the capability of the tool to identify functions that should be considered for integration testing.

2   Background

In this section, we discuss a motivating example for our work and introduce key terminology before providing an overview of our approach.

2.1   Motivating Example

Figure 1 presents a motivating example collected from file localdb.py from Conan [6]. Function get_login performs a query on the database to retrieve data, which requires a connection to be established. Function _connect is used to return this connection object, making it highly relevant for function get_login. In addition, it can be seen that a set of tokens (connection, connect, self) from the caller appear also in a high frequency in the callee. This supports our hypothesis that sharing of tokens between functions correlates with the callee being relevant to the caller.

2.2   Our Approach

This section gives an overview of the program representations used to identify important functions that are missed during testing. Details of our approach can be found in Sect. 3. We start by providing key definitions for terms.

Natural Call Graph (NCG). An NCG is a weighted call graph and it can be defined as a tuple $NCG = (V, E)$. V represents the sets of all functions in the

---

[1] https://github.com/Constantin-Petrescu/FindIT/.

```
1 def get_login(self, remote_url):
2
3   with self._connect() as connection:
4     try:
5       statement = connection.cursor()
6       statement.execute('select user, token, refresh_token from ...')
```

Listing 1: Caller

```
1 def _connect(self):
2   connection = sqlite3.connect(self.dbfile)
3   try:
4     yield connection
5   finally:
6     connection.close()
```

Listing 2: Callee

Fig. 1. Motivating example from Conan library. The caller `get_login` runs a query on the database by executing the callee, `_connect`, to receive a database connection object.

program, such that any function f_i that belongs to the program, then $f_i \in V$. E is the set of direct weighted edges representing the function calls between vertices, where the edge weights represent the callee's relevance to the caller. Such that, if $f_1, f_2 \in V$, there is an edge $f_1 \to f_2 \in E$ and the relevance of f_2 to f_1 is defined as the relative importance of f_2 to f_1's objective. We compute relevance using conditional entropy of the tokens in f_2 with respect to f_1.

The NCG contains all methods, and we do not wish to check the relevance of methods that have already been covered by a test. Thus, we end up using two types of NCGs: *Static NCG* (program's NCG) and *Dynamic NCG* 3 (sub-graph of the application's *static NCG* containing only nodes and edges traversed in a test execution). We explore the functions that can be called from the nodes in the *Dynamic NCG* to identify their importance. Based on the relevance scores of the function calls, we classify them as *Core* or *Fringe*, defined below.

Core and Fringe. For a caller f_1 and a callee f_2, the function f_2 is a *core* function for f_1 if the successful completion of f_1's objective depends on it. Otherwise, it is a *fringe* function for f_1.

Cross-Module Calls. While the example in Fig. 1 reinforces our hypothesis, cross-module calls are an exception. Larger requirements are often implemented across multiple modules that use different namespaces and potentially feature varied tokens. To rank function calls in such cases, we need to identify callees that use dissimilar tokens but are an important part of the software that implements the requirement. To identify such methods, we reason over a sequence of function calls instead of a single call. We call this sequence a Candidate Path.

Candidate Path. A Candidate Path is sequence of four functions $f_1 \to f_2 \to f_3 \to f_4$ where $f_1, f_2, f_3 \in Dynamic NCG$. This means that f_1, f_2 and f_3 are already covered by an integration test. The fourth function $f_4 \in Static NCG$ is an untested function at a one-hop distance from f_3 but not covered by a test. f_4 is identified by statically extracting the call graph, and therefore a call to it is represented using the arrow $\xrightarrow{s}$ where s stands for static.

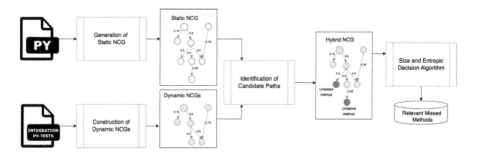

Fig. 2. Tool's software architecture to identify relevant missed methods by tests.

The Candidate Paths allow us to contextualise the relevance score for $\xrightarrow{s}$, by considering the scores for prior calls $f_1 \rightarrow f_2 \rightarrow f_3$, before classifying it as either *core* or *fringe*. An abnormal relevance score could mean a cross-module call.

3   Methodology

This section presents a description of the techniques used by the tool. Our tool is presented in Fig. 2 and it consists of four components: Generation of the Static NCG, Construction of the Dynamic NCGs, Identification of Candidate Paths by mapping the Static and the Dynamic NCGs, and the Decision Algorithm.

3.1   Generation of the Static NCG

Our tool takes any Python project as input and generates a Static NCG. To construct these, we made use of PyCG [20], the most complete tool for Python project Call Graph generation at the time. We extended the PyCG project to collect tokens for both algorithmic and natural language channels by collecting tokens from the function signature, parameters, and body. Conditional entropy [7] is computed between the tokens in the caller and callee and used as edge weights between functions. We store the Static NCG in JSON format.

3.2   Construction of the Dynamic NCGs

For each integration test the tool generates a Dynamic NCG by tracing the integration test execution and mapping the trace output with fully qualified function names. These are then used to identify Candidate Paths.

Initially, the integration tests are executed and traced. Based on the project dependencies, execution of the integration tests is performed using a testing framework such as Pytest [12], Nose [18] or Tox [22]. We experimented with multiple tracing libraries, but the most reliable results came from using the built-in library Trace [21]. Thus, during the execution of an integration test, Trace is used to collect the execution stacks and generate a report with functions calls.

The output files from Trace for each passed integration test contain sets of caller-callee pairs. Since the caller-callee functions have partially qualified names, the tool uses regular expression matching to map to the fully qualified names. With the mapping complete, the edge weights of the Dynamic NCG are set using the entropic information from the project's Static NCG.

3.3   Candidates Paths

The tool identifies sequences of three tested functions from the Dynamic NCG. The initial step is the identification of all pairs of two connected dynamic edges where the last node is a leaf. A function is deemed a leaf when it does not appear as a caller on any edges. The tool performs two passes over the edges: first, all edges with a leaf are identified; second, all edges where the callee is the caller of a leaf node are identified to form a sequence of three tested functions.

The next step is to form possible Candidate Paths by finding a function in the Static NCG that is one-hop away from the leaf dynamic node. This requires an iteration over all the edges from the Static NCG. A potential Candidate Path exists if a static edge is found where the caller coincides with the leaf node from the dynamic edge. The last step is to validate that the potential Candidate Path is an actual Candidate Path: this is done by checking that the static edge is not tested by any integration test.

3.4   Size and Entropic Decision Algorithm

This component provides the mechanism to decide if the statically selected function is *core* or *fringe* for the path. The Decision Algorithm can leverage two potential indicators size and entropy. A Special Method Filter [2] is also applied to identify *fringe* cases. The optimal configuration is decided based on the performance analysis presented in Sect. 4.3.

Size Decision
Size is used as an indicator to mark a Candidate Path as *core* or *fringe*. The Decision Algorithm computes the size of the callee as the percentage size relative to the caller. Usually, a small callee can be viewed as a function with only one goal and few instructions. Some examples of such cases are wrappers, getters and setters. Short callee cases could mislead an Entropic Decision Algorithm since the callee could have only different tokens compared to the caller. We hypothesise that the entropic decision can be used if the callee and the caller have comparable sizes. The goal of the Size Decision Algorithm is not to detect very long functions, which are poor programming practices [14], but rather functions of relatively similar sizes. The Decision Algorithm initially uses the size filter and then passes the Candidate Paths for entropic evaluation.

Entropy Decision
The Decision Algorithm uses entropic values to determine the relevance of the functions in a Candidate Path. Its goal is to differentiate between essential functions and those that may be performing less important tasks. This is done by

assessing how much new information each function adds to the path. We use basic, joint, and conditional entropy in the entropic value calculations.

Entropy measures the diversity of tokens within a function. It is calculated using the formula $H(f_n) = -\sum_{i=1}^{n} t_i * log_2 t_i$, where t_i represents the token frequencies. In our context, we model each function f_n by its token distribution extracted from its code, where tokens represent syntactic elements such as keywords, operators, or identifiers.

Joint Entropy expands upon basic entropy by measuring the combined diversity of tokens when considering two functions together. The formula is $H(f_n, f_m) = -\sum_{i=1}^{n} \sum_{i=1}^{m} t_i * t_j * log_2(t_i * t_j)$, where tokens from two functions f_n and f_m are considered simultaneously. Conditional entropy quantifies how much additional information a function adds when another function is already known. It is calculated based on the basic and joint entropy using the chain rule formula $H(f_n | f_m) = H(f_n, f_m) - H(f_n)$.

In a Candidate Path, the Decision Algorithm computes the entropic metric by calculating the difference between conditional entropies across consecutive functions. For a path $f_1 \rightarrow f_2 \rightarrow f_3 \xrightarrow{s} f_4$, we assess how much new information f_4 adds compared to f_3 by computing: $H_{path} = H(f_4 | f_3, f_2) - H(f_3 | f_2, f_1)$. We use two functions to contextualise a call; using one would lead to fluctuations in the conditional entropy, in case the sizes of the caller and callee are imbalanced. Based on the entropic value, there are three distinct interpretations: similar entropic values, negative values and positive values.

Similar entropic values mean that both the dynamic average and the conditional entropy of the static edge have similar values. This means that the callee is comparable in size with the rest of the functions and shares a consistent amount of tokens. In other words, the callee performs instructions similar to those of the rest of the functions from the Candidate Path. In this case, we hypothesise that an integration test should also test the static function.

A negative entropic value shows that the callee is more diverse and possibly larger than the functions from the rest of the path. We continue the hypothesis by affirming that more diverse functions are desired to be tested in integration tests since they perform new instructions compared to the rest of the path.

A large entropic value shows that the static conditional entropy has a significantly smaller value. This can indicate one of two aspects about the static callee. One aspect is that the callee has a very small number of tokens, and in general that the callee can be considered a wrapper for other functions. The other aspect is that the same tokens are used in the statically selected function. This means that the callee provides utility functionalities for the existing objects. Part of our hypothesis is also that large entropic values indicate functions of lesser importance for the tested path. Thus, the Entropic Decision Algorithm will mark such paths as *fringe* cases, while the rest will be marked *core*.

Table 1. Shows the benchmark's details: the high-level overview of projects, their Natural Call Graphs representation, the number of integration tests.

Name	Stars	LOC	Static NCGs		Integration Tests
			Nodes	Edges	
Conan	6.6K	108K	3,458	1,932	2,043
Faust	6.5K	46K	2,662	1,676	1,081
Docker-API	6.1K	21K	738	1,242	402
Pex	2.2K	449K	1,800	5,110	288
Strawberryfields	683	32K	2,607	1,853	133
iSort	5.6K	23K	349	269	23
Emcee	1.3K	370K	155	82	19
Tox	3.2K	260K	517	5,770	9
RxPY	4.4K	39K	2,995	444	3
Sockeye	1.2K	15K	785	3,450	3

Special Method Filter

Python contains a set of special 'Dunder' methods for built-in data types and classes [2]. Some examples of such methods are: `__cmp__`, `__get__`, `__next__`, `__main__` and many others. In Candidate Paths, such methods will rarely provide any relevant instruction with respect to the path. Thus, this filter ensures that Candidate Paths where the static caller is a special method are marked by the Decision Algorithm as *fringe*. This will aid the tool avoid in marking cases as false positive and provide the users the chance to inspect more relevant *core* cases.

4   Evaluation

This section provides insights into the performance and utility of our approach by addressing the following research questions:

RQ_1. To what extent do the size and popularity of Python open-source projects influence the quality of their integration tests? (Sect. 4.1)

RQ_2. To what extent can the tool's performance be improved using different configurations of the Decision Algorithm: a size decision, an entropic decision, or a combination of both? (Sect. 4.3)

RQ_3. Can the tool distinguish between *core* and *fringe* cases? (Section 4.4)

RQ_4. Are the statically selected functions important to *core* paths? (Sect. 4.5)

RQ_1 aims to assess how integration testing relates to a project's size and popularity to determine if an integration testing tool is necessary. **RQ_2** investigates whether an entropic decision alone is sufficient for identifying *core* cases and whether considering function size can aid in identifying *fringe* functions.

Table 2. Shows the Dynamic NCGs built on the integration tests, the distribution of
the Candidate Paths and of the *Core* and *Fringe* cases from the Ground Truth.

Name	Integration Tests	Dynamic NCGs		Candidate Paths			Ground Truth	
		Nodes	Edges	Total	Unique	Unique Untested	*Core Cases*	*Fringe Cases*
Conan	2,043	19,531	19,869	1,659	778	649	490	159
Faust	1,081	1,512	1,800	312	26	26	4	22
Docker-API	402	14,843	19,474	2,630	159	121	18	103
Pex	288	14,492	16,406	1,363	90	78	45	33
Strawberryfields	133	7,170	7,682	3,725	244	194	137	57
iSort	23	1,240	1,336	470	37	22	6	16
Emcee	19	348	343	19	10	9	5	4
Tox	9	269	301	50	10	10	7	3
RxPY	3	219	308	87	59	58	7	51
Sockeye	3	719	989	177	95	67	26	41
Totals:	4,004	60,343	68,508	10,465	1,508	1,234	745	489

RQ$_2$'s goal is to determine the optimal configuration based on a sample dataset
consisting of 10% of the data.**RQ$_3$** evaluates the performance of our approach on
the remaining 90% of the data for practical use in software development. **RQ$_4$**
aims to generate insights about the nature of the *core* functions.

4.1   Benchmark

To answer **RQ$_1$**, we constructed a benchmark of ten open-source Python projects
listed in Table 1. The selection process for these projects considered two main
factors. The first factor was that the projects had a set of integration tests that
could be successfully executed. The second factor considered was the popularity
and the size of the project. The selection was made based on a sorted list of the
most starred projects. Six projects are relatively small, between 10K and 50K
lines of code, while the remaining four are larger, ranging from 108K to 449K
lines of code.

We generated a Static NCG for each project in the benchmark. The general
trend observed is that a project's size somewhat correlates with the number
of functions and function calls. However, there are some irregularities, such as
Strawberryfields, which has only 32K lines of code but 2,607 functions and 1,853
edges. This is because Strawberryfields is written in an object-oriented style
and it prioritises efficiency and portability, which requires a heavy reliance on
overloading and inner functions. Interestingly, Table 1 shows that the number of
stars or the size of a project does not necessarily correlate with the number of
integration tests. This highlights the need for tools to identify which parts of a
program have been missed in integration testing.

Table 3. Shows the Precision, Recall, Accuracy and F1-score when the tool marks cases as *fringe* on different levels on the sampled dataset. Left side shows performance for size, while right side shows for entropic level.

Size Level	Precision	Recall	Accuracy	F1-score	Entropy Level	Precision	Recall	Accuracy	F1-score
∅	0.67	1.0	0.68	0.81	∅	0.67	1.0	0.67	0.80
[0, 5)	**0.76**	**0.99**	**0.78**	**0.86**	[3.5, ∞)	0.68	0.96	0.73	0.82
[0, 10)	0.76	0.83	0.71	0.79	[2.8, ∞)	0.72	0.94	0.75	0.83
[0, 20)	0.79	0.71	0.68	0.75	**[2.6, ∞)**	**0.74**	**0.94**	**0.76**	**0.84**
[0, 50)	0.80	0.40	0.53	0.53	[2.4, ∞)	0.73	0.92	0.75	0.83
[0, 100)	0.82	0.28	0.48	0.41	[1.0, ∞)	0.73	0.63	0.63	0.69
[0, 150)	0.75	0.11	0.38	0.19	[0.0, ∞)	0.72	0.17	0.39	0.31

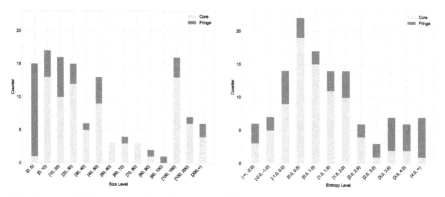

(a) *Core* and *fringe* cases filtered on size.   (b) *Core* and *fringe* cases filtered on entropy.

Fig. 3. Distribution of *core* and *fringe* cases on the sampled dataset.

4.2 Establishing Ground Truth

Table 2 shows the distribution of core and fringe cases generated from the benchmark. We used 4,004 integration tests to generate Dynamic NCGs. Our tool found 10,465 Candidate Paths by analysing the Static and Dynamic NCGs. We reduced the number of Candidate Paths to 1,234 by removing exact duplicates and paths that had already been tested. To establish the ground truth, each case in the final dataset was labelled as either *core* or *fringe*.

During the labelling process, three raters were involved. Two were male PhD students residing in the UK, with 4 and 8 years of programming experience. The third rater was a male software testing engineer residing in Romania with three years and testing experience. The raters were granted access to the source code for each case and were tasked with evaluating the importance of an untested function to the rest of the tested functions within a candidate path.

Out of the 1,234 cases, the raters have marked 777, 755 and 776 cases as being *core*. The ground truth consists of 786 *core* and 448 *fringe* cases, representing 64% and 36% of the candidate paths, respectively. We computed the level of

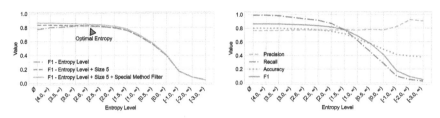

(a) Comparison of F1-scores at different en-(b) Evaluation metrics for the optimal config-
tropic levels   uration.

Fig. 4. Tool's performance under different settings on the testing set.

agreement using Cohen's Kappa coefficient for each pair of raters, resulting in
the values $0.80, 0.83$ and 0.89. These high agreement values indicate a substantial
level of consensus among the raters. Based on the ground truth, we sample a set
of 10% of the data to optimise the size and entropic Decision Algorithm. Then,
we evaluate the tool's performance using the rest of the ground truth.

4.3   Optimal Configuration for Decision Algorithm

The first step is to understand if the relationship between the sizes of the callee
and the caller can influence the decision process of the cases. We hypothesise in
Sect. 3.4 that a small sized callee would provide little insight into the entropic
decision, which could significantly increase false positives. For this reason, Fig. 3a
presents the distribution of *core* and *fringe* cases from the sampled dataset. It
can be noticed that there are a large number of *fringe* cases in the low size levels.
As the callee's size increases, the number of *core* cases also grows. Cases with
a very small callee also translate into fewer operations performed by the callee.
In most of these cases, the callees were either utility functions, logging functions
or functions to initialise objects. Since a high proportion of grouped *fringe* cases
can be seen, we compute and present in Table 3 the precision, recall, accuracy
and F1-score for all levels. The F1-score hits the peak at a value of 0.86, where
$[0, 5)$ is selected as the size limit for deciding *core* and *fringe* cases. This means
the tool would automatically mark each case as a *fringe* where the callee's size
is proportionally smaller than 5% of the caller.

Our hypothesis from Sect. 3.4 suggests that callee-caller candidates with similar entropy values translate into cases where the callee performs *core* actions
with respect to the caller. To ensure the validity of the hypothesis, the sampled dataset is analysed from an entropic perspective. Again, Fig. 3b presents
the distribution of cases. Compared to the size distribution, most entropic levels
contain a slightly higher number of *core* cases compared to *fringe* cases. However, the exception levels are when the entropic levels are high and the *fringe*
cases become predominant. The goal of the entropic decision is to filter out cases
where the callee is very different from the callee. This can be noticed from the
larger number of *fringe* cases at the high entropic levels. The metrics computed

for all entropic levels are presented in Table 3. Choosing the entropic level at 2.6 makes the F1-score reach the highest value of 0.84. The tool uses this entropic level to mark cases as *fringe* where the entropic value is higher than 2.6.

4.4   Optimal Configuration Over Ground Truth

Based on the sampled dataset, the size and entropic levels are $[0, 5)$ and $[2.6, \infty)$. To evaluate that these levels can be used in tools for software development, an evaluation of the performance of the tool is performed on the remaining 90% of the data. Figure 4a presents the comparison of the F1-score between three different settings of the tool over the ground truth: only entropic, entropic with size, and entropic with size along with Special Method Filter (presented in Sect. 3.4). The plots reinforce that the entropic level $[2.6, \infty)$ can be selected accurately since the tool nearly reaches the peak performance. In addition, it can be noticed that the optimal configuration of $[0, 5)$ for size, $[2.6, \infty)$ for conditional entropy with Special Method Filter performs with 4% in precision, and 4% in accuracy better compared to the rest of the settings. Thus, the performance of the tool is presented in Fig. 4b. **RQ₃** is answered positively since the tool achieves a 0.78 precision, a 0.94 recall, a 0.79 accuracy and a 0.85 F1-score.

4.5   Qualitative Analysis

To answer **RQ₄**, we present one *core* case in addition to the motivating example from Sect. 2.1. Additionally, we present two fringe cases, one identified based on entropic difference and the other based on the size difference.

Case I Core. Figure 5 presents a *core* case collected from Strawberryfields. *test_parameters_ with_operation* belongs to file *test_parameters_integration.py*, and the calls from the path can be found in *bosonicbackend/backend.py*. Function `run_prog` runs a Strawberryfields program using the bosonic backend. Then, `init_circuit` starts to instantiate the photonic quantum circuit by initialising the `weights`, `means` and `covs` depending on the different classes of quantum states, such as Cat, Fock or Gaussian. Based on the candidate path, the program enters the Cat state through the function `prepare_cat` from Listing 3 . The target of this function is to compute the arrays of weights, means and covariances. It can be seen from Lines 5, 10 and 12 that there are multiple ways to compute the arrays based on different conditions. The untested function `prepare_cat_real_rep` is called by `prepare_cat` on Line 12. This callee is presented in Listing 4 and continues `prepare_cat`'s objective by computing the arrays if it is a real-valued state. Lines 4–6 provide a brief overview of the mathematical operations performed by `prepare_cat_real_rep` to calculate `weights`, `means` and `covs`. This case is marked as *core* by the tool due to its entropic difference of 0.02. The strong similarity between the tokens of both functions, as evident in Listing 3 and Listing 4 , is also indicated by the entropic difference. Since `prepare_cat` is tested and it shares a similar objective with `prepare_cat_real_rep` (both computing the `weights`, `means` and `covs`), it should be encouraged to also test function `prepare_cat_real_rep`.

```
1 def prepare_cat(self, a, theta, p, representation, ampl_cutoff, D):
2
3   ...
4   # Case alpha = 0, prepare vacuum
5   if np.isclose(a, 0):
6     weights = np.array([1], dtype=complex)
7     means = np.array([[0, 0]], dtype=complex)
8     covs = np.array([0.5 * self.circuit.hbar * ... ])
9     return weights, means, covs
10  if representation == "complex":
11    return weights, means, covs
12  return self.prepare_cat_real_rep(a, theta, p, ampl_cutoff, D)
```

Listing 3: Caller of the untested function

```
1 def prepare_cat_real_rep(self, a, theta, p, ampl_cutoff, D):
2
3   ...
4   weights = np.cos(phi) * even_terms * ...
5   means = norm * np.concatenate(weights_real, weights)
6   cov = np.array([0.5 * hbar, 0], [0, (E * v) / ...
7   ...
8   return weights, means, cov
```

Listing 4: Untested function

Fig. 5. *Core*case from Strawberryfields library. Path is formed from functions: run_prog, init_circuit, prepare_cat and prepare_cat_real_rep. Function prepare_cat_real_rep computes a set of arrays as a continuation of prepare_cat due to specific conditions.

Case II*Fringe based on Entropic Difference.* Figure 6 presents a *core* case from *Sockeye. test_seq_copy* belongs to file *test_seq _copy_int.py* and the functions are from files: *translate.py* and *inference.py*. The first function, read_and_translate, reads input and initiates the translation process by calling the next node in the candidate path. translate.translate starts recording the time for logging purposes and starts the actual translation process using Translator.translate. Listing 5 shows a brief part of function Translator.translate. This function is 125 lines long and it uses a model to translate the input received. When the results output is combined, it will call the untested function, as shown in Lines 3–6 from Listing 5 ._remove_target_prefix_tokens presented in Listing 6 removes a number of elements from the beginning of target_ids and returns the modified list. Although _remove_target_prefix_tokens is used twice in Translator.translate, offering code reduction and reusability benefits, it has little value for the functions from the candidate path. The tool marks this case as *fringe* to its entropic difference of 3.27, surpassing the entropic level of 2.6. The entropic difference is high due to the extensive actions performed by Translator.translate and the token similarity across functions.

Case III *Fringe based on Size Difference.* A *fringe* case from Docker-Py is presented in Fig. 7. *test_run_with_error* belongs to file *models_containers_ test.py* and the calls are from: *models/containers.py* and *types/containers.py*. Function create is used to create a container without starting it. Then _create_ container_args takes user arguments and transforms them into container arguments. Inside _create_container_args, a HostConfig object is created which triggers a call to HostConfig.__init__. Part of the initialisation function is presented in Listing 7 . This function validates the inputs received and sets the values as the fields of the HostConfig object. In case the input

```
1 def translate(self, trans_inputs: List[TranslatorInput], fill_up_batches: bool = True)
      -> List[TranslatorOutput]:
2
3   if num_target_prefix_tokens > 0 and ...:
4     translation.target_ids = \
5     _remove_target_prefix_tokens(translation.target_ids,
6     translation.target_ids, num_target_prefix_tokens)
```

Listing 5: Caller of the untested function

```
1 def _remove_target_prefix_tokens(target_ids, num_target_prefix_tokens)
2
3   starting_idx = min(len(target_ids), num_target_prefix_tokens)
4   return target_ids[starting_idx:]
```

Listing 6: Untested function

Fig. 6. *Fringe* case due to large entropic difference from Sockeye library. The tested functions collected for this case are: read_and_translate, translate.translate and Translator.translate. Function _remove_target_prefix_tokens removes a specific number of elements from the beginning of a list.

```
1 def __init__(self, version, ...):
2   if userns_mode != "host":
3     raise host_config_value_error(
4       "userns_mode", userns_mode)
5   self['UsernsMode'] = userns_mode
```

Listing 7: Caller of the untested function

```
1 def host_config_value_error(param, param_value):
2   error_msg ='Invalid value for {0} param:{1}'
3   return ValueError(error_msg.format(param, param_value))
```

Listing 8: Untested function

Fig. 7. *Fringe* case due to small size difference from Docker-PY library. The path is: create, _create_container_args, HostConfig.__init__ and host_config_value_error. Function host_config_value_error generates the error message if the parameter's value is wrong.

is not as expected, host_config_value_ error is called (Lines 3–4). As Listing 8 shows, the function host_config_value_error generates the error message based on the parameter and its mismatched value. While host_config_value_error improves code reusability, it offers little value from testing it. Our tool marks this path as *fringe* since the Decision Algorithm detects that the callee is too small compared to the caller.

5   Threats to Validity

Internal Threats. The tool is subject to two possible internal threats. First threat appears in the generation of the Static NCG from the tool generating the call graph. PyCG achieved a high precision of 99.2%, with an adequate recall of 69.9% [20]. While the tool correctly identifies instances of function calls, there will be some functions that PyCG will not identify. Inherently, our Static NCG will miss these edges. The goal of our work is not to improve on PyCG, but rather to generate NCGs to suggest missed functions for integration testing.

On the other hand, the construction of the Dynamic NCGs is exposed to a different threat. We utilise Python Trace to track the execution of functions. The output consists of partial qualified names that are matched with fully qualified names using regular expression matching. This approach is consistent, but functions with identical names in the same namespace may not be matched correctly.

External Threats. Ideally, the natural language channel should harmonise with code instructions. Our tool relies on the relation between the natural language tokens and code instructions to identify the callee's relevance to the caller. However, there will be cases when the natural language is generic or carelessly chosen. Such cases likely become false positives due to the nature of our approach. The users of our tool can inspect *fringe* cases and sometimes identify names carelessly selected, which can provide refactoring and renaming opportunities.

Our approach may face limitations when dealing with modules that perform highly isolated or self-contained tasks. The relevance of cross-module functions cannot always be inferred from the relationships with adjacent functions. In these cases, entropic information may fail to indicate its importance. While reasoning over call sequences provides a valuable approach, the tool will mark false positives when the connections between functions are weak or unrelated to the main task.

6   Related Work

This section presents the founding notions of dual-channel research and approaches of dual-channel in testing.

Dual-Channel Research. Natural language channel information and its potential benefits in software engineering tasks have been studied for many years. Due to a lack of validation that similar names represent the same thing, Anquetil and Lethbridge defined reliable naming conventions and provided a system along with a set of conditions to assess the efficiency of naming conventions [1]. Caprile and Tonella extended their analysis by examining the lexical, syntactical, and semantic structure of the identifiers [3]. The authors present many potential areas where natural language information could be used, such as program maintainability, program analysis and name recommendations. In fact, they developed a tool to provide more meaningful names for methods [4].

While natural language information has been used for many years, dual-channel research was born based on the *naturalness* property [10]. Hindle et al. built an n-gram language model to harvest and interpret the repetitive patterns as statistical properties. The model was used for code completion as a plugin for Eclipse IDE. Next, Tu et al. added that code is also *localised*, which means that code is locally repetitive [23]. The authors proved that these local repetitions appear at the file level. Extended n-gram model with a "cache" to capture the local patterns has accuracy increased by 9.4%. The *naturalness* and *localness* properties paved the way for the dual-channel research area.

Casalnuovo et al. formalised that source code is formed using two communication channels [5]. First is the algorithmic channel, which represents all the instructions that the computer executes. The second channel is represented by the natural language channel, which represents the identifiers and comments used in the code. The role of the second channel is to present the purpose of the code in a human-friendly format. Dual-channel research represents solutions that leverage the connection between the two channels and it has been recently used to improve various software engineering tasks [8,16,17,19]. Our work shows that the *localness* property between caller-callee relationships can be used to construct NCGs and identify missed functions for integration testing.

Dual-Channel Solutions in Testing. Some testing areas benefit from using dual-channel approaches, such as test prioritisation and generation. Quicker identification of failing tests has been achieved by selecting tests based on the similarity computed between code and natural language information [9,15]. In test generation, models generate assert statements based on the patterns between functions and their tests [11,24]. While our work does not directly compare, we drew inspiration for our methodology. The biggest challenges for dual-channel approaches are finding the suitable intermediate representation and determining the granularity level to capture patterns. In our work, we combined these ideas by constructing NCGs and omitting comments from the function's tokens. We also use the similarity between functions to identify *core* or *fringe* functions.

7   Conclusion

This work shows that the relationship between functions can be extracted and used to create new program representations like NCGs. We demonstrate how such representation can aid various software engineering tasks by developing an approach to detect functions missed in integration testing. Our tool achieved an accuracy of 78% with a recall of 94%. However, it could perform even better on projects with clear and established coding and testing guidelines.

The techniques used in this research are not restricted to Python or specific types of testing. While the outcomes may vary, this work can be extended for unit testing or to support any programming language. One prospect would be to examine how testing in different programming languages influences dual-channel approaches. We believe that novel representations including dual-channel information can be used to guide future program analysis techniques. Although such work may be challenging, it may have the potential to enhance the state of program analysis substantially.

References

1. Anquetil, N., Lethbridge, T.C.: Assessing the relevance of identifier names in a legacy software system. In: Conference of the Centre for Advanced Studies on Collaborative Research (1998)
2. Beazley, D.M.: Python Essential Reference, 3rd edn. Sams, USA (2006)
3. Caprile, B., Tonella, P.: Nomen est omen: analyzing the language of function identifiers. In: Sixth Working Conference on Reverse Engineering (Cat. No.PR00303), pp. 112–122 (1999)
4. Caprile, B., Tonella, P.: Restructuring program identifier names. In: Proceedings 2000 International Conference on Software Maintenance, pp. 97–107 (2000)

5. Casalnuovo, C., Barr, E.T., Dash, S.K., Devanbu, P., Morgan, E.: A theory of dual channel constraints. In: Proceedings of the ACM/IEEE 42nd International Conference on Software Engineering: New Ideas and Emerging Results, pp. 25–28. ICSE-NIER 2020, Association for Computing Machinery, New York, NY, USA (2020). https://doi.org/10.1145/3377816.3381720

6. Conan: Conan: A python package manager (2015). https://docs.conan.io/en/latest/howtos/other_languages_package_manager/python.html. Accessed 16 Feb 2023

7. Cover, T.M., Thomas, J.A.: Entropy, Relative Entropy, and Mutual Information, vol. 2, pp. 13–55. Wiley, Hoboken (2005). https://doi.org/10.1002/047174882X.ch2

8. Dash, S.K., Allamanis, M., Barr, E.T.: Refinym: using names to refine types. In: Proceedings of the 2018 26th ACM Joint Meeting on European Software Engineering Conference and Symposium on the Foundations of Software Engineering, pp. 107–117. ESEC/FSE 2018, Association for Computing Machinery, New York (2018). https://doi.org/10.1145/3236024.3236042

9. Greca, R., Miranda, B., Gligoric, M., Bertolino, A.: Comparing and combining file-based selection and similarity-based prioritization towards regression test orchestration. In: 2022 IEEE/ACM International Conference on Automation of Software Test (AST), pp. 115–125 (2022). https://doi.org/10.1145/3524481.3527223

10. Hindle, A., Barr, E.T., Su, Z., Gabel, M., Devanbu, P.: On the naturalness of software. In: Proceedings of the 34th International Conference on Software Engineering, pp. 837–847. ICSE 2012, IEEE Press (2012)

11. Kampmann, A., Havrikov, N., Soremekun, E.O., Zeller, A.: When does my program do this? Learning circumstances of software behavior. In: Proceedings of the 28th ACM Joint Meeting on European Software Engineering Conference and Symposium on the Foundations of Software Engineering, pp. 1228–1239. ESEC/FSE 2020, Association for Computing Machinery, New York (2020). https://doi.org/10.1145/3368089.3409687

12. Krekel, H., Team, P.D.: Pytest - testing framework (2003). https://pytest.org. Accessed 03 Ma 2023

13. Martin, D., Rooksby, J., Rouncefield, M., Sommerville, I.: 'good' organisational reasons for 'bad' software testing: an ethnographic study of testing in a small software company. In: Proceedings of the 29th International Conference on Software Engineering. ICSE 2007, pp. 602–611. IEEE Computer Society, USA (2007). https://doi.org/10.1109/ICSE.2007.1

14. Martin, R.C.: Clean Code: A Handbook of Agile Software Craftsmanship. Pearson Education (2009)

15. Miranda, B., Cruciani, E., Verdecchia, R., Bertolino, A.: Fast approaches to scalable similarity-based test case prioritization. In: Proceedings of the 40th International Conference on Software Engineering ICSE 2018, pp. 222–232. Association for Computing Machinery, New York (2018). https://doi.org/10.1145/3180155.3180210

16. Partachi, P.P., Dash, S.K., Allamanis, M., Barr, E.T.: Flexeme: untangling commits using lexical flows. In: Proceedings of the 28th ACM Joint Meeting on European Software Engineering Conference and Symposium on the Foundations of Software Engineering ESEC/FSE 2020, pp. 63–74. Association for Computing Machinery, New York (2020)

17. Pârtachi, P.P., Dash, S.K., Treude, C., Barr, E.T.: Posit: Simultaneously tagging natural and programming languages. In: Proceedings of the ACM/IEEE 42nd International Conference on Software Engineering ICSE 2020, pp. 1348–1358.

Association for Computing Machinery, New York (2020). https://doi.org/10.1145/3377811.3380440

18. Pellerin, J., Team, N.D.: Nose - testing framework (2010). https://pypi.org/project/nose/. Accessed 03 Mar 2023

19. Petrescu, C.C., Smith, S., Giavrimis, R., Dash, S.K.: Do names echo semantics? A large-scale study of identifiers used in c++'s named casts. J. Syst. Softw. **202**, 111693 (2023). https://doi.org/10.1016/j.jss.2023.111693

20. Salis, V., Sotiropoulos, T., Louridas, P., Spinellis, D., Mitropoulos, D.: PYCG: practical call graph generation in python. In: 2021 IEEE/ACM 43rd International Conference on Software Engineering (ICSE), pp. 1646–1657 (2021)

21. Team, P.D.: Trace - python module to trace program's execution (1991). https://docs.python.org/3/library/trace.html. Accessed 03 Mar 2023

22. Tox: Tox - automation project (2010). https://tox.wiki/en/latest/index.html. Accessed 16 Feb 2023

23. Tu, Z., Su, Z., Devanbu, P.: On the localness of software. In: Proceedings of the 22nd ACM SIGSOFT International Symposium on Foundations of Software Engineering FSE 2014, pp. 269–280. Association for Computing Machinery, New York (2014). https://doi.org/10.1145/2635868.2635875

24. Watson, C., Tufano, M., Moran, K., Bavota, G., Poshyvanyk, D.: On learning meaningful assert statements for unit test cases. In: Proceedings of the ACM/IEEE 42nd International Conference on Software Engineering ICSE 2020, pp. 1398–1409. Association for Computing Machinery, New York (2020). https://doi.org/10.1145/3377811.3380429

Extending a Flakiness Score for System-Level Tests

Joanna Kisaakye[1,2]($\boxtimes$) (ID), Mutlu Beyazıt[1,2](ID), and Serge Demeyer[1,2](ID)

[1] Universiteit Antwerpen, Antwerp, Belgium
{joanna.kisaakye,mutlu.beyazit,serge.demeyer}@uantwerpen.be
[2] Flanders Make vzw, Kortrijk, Belgium

Abstract. Flaky tests (i.e. automated tests with a non-deterministic test outcome) undermine the trustworthiness of today's DevOps build-pipelines, and recent research has investigated ways to detect or even remove flaky tests. In contrast, others proclaim that test engineers should "Assume all Tests Are Flaky" because, in today's build-pipelines, one can never fully control all components of the system under test. Test engineers then capture the randomness of test results via what is called a *flakiness score*. In this paper, we extend an existing flakiness score to deal with system-level tests. We illustrate, via simulated test outcomes, how this refined score can support three different strategies for dealing with flaky tests—(i) Rerun, (ii) Fix and (iii) Monitor.

Keywords: DevOps · Flaky Tests · Flakiness Score

1 Introduction

DevOps is defined by Bass et al. as "*a set of practices intended to reduce the time between committing a change to a system and the change being placed into normal production, while ensuring high quality*" [2]. The combination of these practices is embedded in a fully automated build-pipeline. Such a build-pipeline is driven by a series of automated tests that scrutinise every code change.

Flaky tests (i.e. automated tests with a nondeterministic test outcome) undermine the trustworthiness of such a build-pipeline. Studies have shown that flakiness, when neglected, can lead to developer stress, and waste of time and resources, ultimately compromising product quality [12,21,25]. Consequently, various existing studies offer different solutions —both automated and manual— to detect or even remove flaky tests [4,7,8,18,29,31].

In contrast, others proclaim that test engineers should "Assume all Tests Are Flaky" [3,13]. Indeed, many data centric systems have evolved from monolithic architectures to micro-service architectures [5]. Build-pipelines therefore rely on a distributed test execution environment where some aspects of the system configuration are inherently out of the test engineers control. For embedded systems, the build-pipeline distinguishes between model-in-the-loop, software-in-the-loop

© IFIP International Federation for Information Processing 2025
Published by Springer Nature Switzerland AG 2025
H. D. Menéndez et al. (Eds.): ICTSS 2024, LNCS 15383, pp. 292–312, 2025.
https://doi.org/10.1007/978-3-031-80889-0_20

and hardware-in-the-loop [27]. There as well, the various system configurations induce a certain degree of uncertainty with respect to the real-time behaviour.

Adopting an "Assume all Tests Are Flaky" perspective, test engineers consider a test as having a probabilistic outcome (the range $[0 \ldots 1]$ in favour of a particular test outcome) instead of deterministic one (only one of $\{pass, fail\}$) and capture the randomness of test outcomes via what is known as a *flakiness score*. Several authors proposed such flakiness scores including Gao et al. [10], Kowalczyk et al. [16] and Rehman et al. [22]. Intuitive versions of such flakiness scores are already incorporated into continuous integration environments such as Jenkins and CircleCI. Of particular interest for our work are the formulae proposed by Kowalczyk et al., who quantify flakiness within a single version by means of *"Entropy"* and *"Flip rate"* [16]. To aggregate scores over versions and time, they compute unweighted and weighted averages.

1.1   Requirements for a System-Level Flakiness Score

In order to replicate the work of Kowalczyk et al., we approached a series of industrial companies whom we know suffered from flaky tests. Via a series of focus groups, we identified what would be needed to adopt a flakiness score in the build-pipeline.

Most importantly, the test engineers stated that such a flakiness score would be most appropriate for higher-level tests (such as integration tests and system tests) since nondeterministic outcomes at the unit test level are not tolerated. With the focus on higher-level tests, the focus groups also contested the simplistic *{pass, fail}* outcome status. Modern test management systems have more elaborate categories of test outcomes: *{pass, fail, error, skipped, blocked, incomplete, inconclusive, deferred}* to name but a few. Another issue that was raised—especially for embedded systems— was dealing with multiple system configurations to cope with the varying hardware upon which the system is deployed.

Finally, the focus groups identified three possible strategies to deal with flaky tests. We elaborate on each of them below.

(i) **Rerun.** The most intuitive strategy is to rerun a flaky test a few times, in the hope that it will pass eventually. A flakiness score then provides a systematic way of establishing how often one must rerun the test. Thus, a probabilistic score of 0.25 for test outcome *pass*, (and conversely 0.75 for *fail*) implies that we expect the test to fail 3 out of 4 times. If we rerun the test 8 times, we should obtain at least 2 *pass* test outcomes to proceed with the build.

(ii) **Fix.** Some test engineers are on a mission to remove the root cause of the flaky test as they are a serious impediment to an agile way of working. Plotting the flakiness score over the version history would show sudden increases after suspicious commits, which would allow test engineers to narrow the search for the source of the problem.

(iii) **Monitor.** Other test engineers confirm that —especially for system tests— they must accept a certain degree of nondeterminism. They wish for a dashboard showing the health status of the build-pipeline, with trends showing whether the flakiness scores increase or decrease. The team can then make informed decisions on the situation during sprint retrospectives.

In this paper, we investigate how to extend the flakiness score proposed by Kowalczyk et al. to deal with system-level tests with four different test outcomes *{pass, fail, error, skipped}* and with varying test configurations. We illustrate, by means of a simulation involving 1200 test cases, with artificially induced random outcomes, how this refined score can support three different strategies for dealing with flaky tests—(i) Rerun, (ii) Fix and (iii) Monitor.

The remainder of this paper is organised as follows. Section 2 gives an overview of the research on dealing with flaky tests, including the various flakiness scores reported today. Section 3 describes the original flakiness score, which we extended in Sect. 4. Section 5 describes how we simulated different test scenarios, which naturally leads to Sect. 6 reporting and interpreting the results from our requirements. Section 7 enumerates the threats to validity to conclude the paper in Sect. 8.

2 Related Work

In the survey by Habchi et al., participants affirm that flaky tests waste developer time by necessitating the investigation of false alerts and the communication of flaky tests across teams, an action that will be more costly as the teams grow in size [12]. In addition, they point out that flaky tests disrupt their continuous integration processes in proportion to the release frequency. They are particularly costly for critical releases such as hot fixes and negatively affect adherence to software testing practices within teams. Ultimately, Habchi et al. find that flakiness affects system reliability and can disguise bugs. The review of Tahir et al. corroborates the findings by Habchi et al. It shows that the problem has also been discussed at length in the grey literature by several developers from reputed software providers including Spotify, Microsoft, Salesforce, Uber, Facebook and Google [25].

Therefore, it is only reasonable to expect that a lot of research has looked into ways to detect, classify and fix the causes of test flakiness. The seminal work by Luo et al. is one of the first attempts to classify the causes of flakiness. The categories included async wait, concurrency, test order dependency, resource leak, network, time, IO, randomness, floating point operators and unordered collections [18]. These categories are expanded by Eck et al. to include too restrictive range, test case timeouts, test suite timeouts, and platform dependency [8].

Following the work to categorise flakiness causes, several attempts to detect and fix flaky tests automatically have also been proposed including: DeFlaker, by Bell et al. [4], FLEX, by Dutta et al. [7], iDFlakies, by Lam et al. [17], iFixFlakies, [24], iPFlakies, by Wang et al. [29], NonDex by Gyori et al. [11], and DexFix, by Zhang et al. [31]. For all these, evaluation involves either the application of the

Rerun strategy or contact with the developers of the applications under study via pull requests.

With such a variety of causes, some still unknown, there have been several calls to embrace flakiness and work with the knowledge and management of a certain known level of flakiness within a test suite [13,19,20]. Gao et al. pioneered the concept of quantifying flakiness as a function of the stability of the coverage, variants and graphical user interface state [10]. They utilise the notion of *entropy* to ascertain how external factors could affect the repeatability of system user-interface tests. Kowalczyk et al. build upon this and prior work to model flakiness according to the patterns of test results [16]. In their work, they introduce the concept of a *flip rate* as an additional factor, beside *entropy*, for the flakiness within a version. To study the trend of test outcomes across versions and time, they introduce two different ways to aggregate the flakiness score of a test based on simple averages and exponentially weighted averages. Their work is similar to the intuitive implementations available in continuous integration tools such as CircleCI and Jenkins.

Previous research has shown the value of establishing a flakiness score in order to adopt an "Assume all Tests Are Flaky" approach. The work from Kowalczyk et al. is especially relevant because it considers flakiness within and across versions and was evaluated using industrial datasets. Moreover, it also provides an algorithm for generating an artificial dataset against which further studies can be evaluated, without the need for an existing bug database. However, to the best of our knowledge, work on flakiness (i) only considers two possible test outcomes *{pass, fail}*; (ii) neglects the configuration of the system under test; (iii) disregards the actual use cases for a flakiness score. As such, it is worthwhile to investigate how the flakiness score by Kowalczyk et al. can deal with the Requirements for a System-Level Flakiness Score as established in Section 1.1.

3   Original Flakiness Score

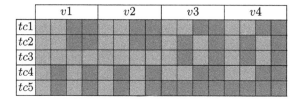

Fig. 1. Running Example with 4 versions and 5 test cases

To explain the key components of the original flakiness score by Kowalczyk et al., we use Fig. 1 as a running example. Thus, their definition of a flaky test is a test that manifests both pass (depicted as green cells in Fig. 1) and fail (depicted as red cells in Fig. 1) test outcomes. For example, all the test cases in Fig. 1 are flaky in one or more of the versions depicted.

Versions. The central concept to the model introduced by Kowalczyk et al. is a version. A version can be composed of several factors such as components of the software under test, test code, flags, configurations and infrastructure [16]. A change in any of the constituents of a version triggers the creation of a new version. For practical purposes, a version corresponds to the complete system under test as it is pushed in the build-pipeline.

In Fig. 1, we see the result of tests executed against four versions, $v1, v2, v3, v4$. Each cell of the table represents one test run outcome, r, within that configuration.

Test History. The next important concept is the history of recorded test outcomes across the different versions. Within an automated test environment, the total set of test run outcomes for a single test, tc, is expressed as the set:

$$R = (r_{v_1,tc_1}, \ldots, r_{v_1,tc_x}, r_{v_2,tc_{x+1}}, \ldots, r_{v_k,tc_l}) \tag{1}$$

From this, we can extract the subset $R_{v,*}$, which comprises the total outcomes for that test for a single version, v:

$$R_{v,*} = (r_{v,tc_1}, \ldots, r_{v,tc_m}) \tag{2}$$

In Fig. 1, the test history shows stable outcomes for test $tc3$ in versions $v1$ and $v2$, but flaky outcomes in versions $v3$ and $v4$.

Flakiness Scores Within a Version. The flakiness scores within a single version are then defined as functions $f : R_{v,*} \longrightarrow [0,1]$ that map a given test history, of length H, to a value between 0 and 1 that indicates the level of flakiness of a test. Kowalczyk et al. defined two different scores, one based on *entropy* and one on *flip rate*.

Entropy. The uncertainty of a test's result within a version is computed using Formula 3, where $p(i)$ is the probability of outcome i based on the set of outcomes $R_{v,*}$. Kowalczyk et al. only consider two unique outcomes, pass and fail, $\{P, F\}$, therefore the value of this metric falls between $[0,1]$, and $\log_2 p(i)$ is treated as 0 when $p(i) = 0$.

$$entropy(R_{v,*}) = -\sum_{i \in (P,F)} p(i) \log_2 p(i) \tag{3}$$

For example, test case $tc3$ has an *entropy* score of 0 in version $v1$, since $p(P) = 1, p(F) = 0$, and 1 in version $v3$, since $p(P) = 0.5, p(F) = 0.5$, in Fig. 1. Note that test case $tc1$ also has an entropy score of 1 in version $v3$ because it also has $p(P) = 0.5, p(F) = 0.5$. This shows the need for a score that can distinguish a slightly flaky test, $tc1$ in $v3$, from a flakier test, $tc3$ in $v3$.

Flip Rate. To distinguish the variation in flakiness, the concept of a *flip*, a transition from one test outcome to another is adopted. The *flip rate* is calculated using Formula 4, in which *numFlips* is the sum of transitions $P \longrightarrow F$ and $F \longrightarrow P$, and *numPossibleFlips* is the total number of possible transitions.

$$flipRate(R_{v,*}) = \frac{numFlips(R_{v,*})}{numPossibleFlips(R_{v,*})} \tag{4}$$

According to the running example, test case *tc3* has a *flip rate* of 0 in version *v1*, and 1 in version *v3*, because it flips on every transition in Fig. 1. However, test case *tc1* has a flip rate of 0.33 in version *v3* because it only flips once out of the three possible transitions.

Flakiness over Versions. For trend analysis, it is imperative to quantify flakiness of a test over versions. This flakiness is aggregated in two ways.

The first is the unweighted flakiness score, U, which is the average flakiness score, f, over the number of versions included, $|V_{t-H}^t|$, when a particular length of time, H, is considered, Formula 5.

$$U_H(R) = \sum_{v \in V_{t-H}^t} \frac{f(R_{v,*})}{|V_{t-H}^t|} \tag{5}$$

f for each version is computed using either *entropy* or *flip rate*. For example, using *flip rate*, the unweighted flakiness score of *tc2*, for the entire history depicted in Fig. 1, is 0.67, from $[0.33, 0.33, 1, 1]$. And, using *entropy*, it is 1 from $[1, 1, 1, 1]$.

The second aggregation is a weighted average, W, based on the concept of exponential moving averages, and assigns more weight to recent values, Formula 6, [14].

$$Y_n = \lambda x_n + (1 - \lambda)Y_{n-1} \tag{6}$$

The weighted flakiness score for the current time step, Y_n, is computed as the sum of the weighted flakiness of the runs in the current window, x_n, and the lesser weighted flakiness score of the previous time step, Y_{n-1}. The weights in W are λ and $(1 - \lambda)$, and they place more emphasis on recent values of x_n. The size of the windows is denoted by period (P). The discrete time step of a window, n, is computed as $n = \lceil t/P \rceil$, in which t is the current time representation. To compute the aggregate flakiness of the current window, x_n, we use Formula 7:

$$x_n = \sum_{v \in V_{(n-1)P}^{nP}} \frac{f(R_{v,*})}{|V_{(n-1)P}^{nP}|} \tag{7}$$

To obtain the normalised value, Z_n, necessary for trend analysis, we perform the normalisation visible in Formula 8.

$$W_{\lambda,P}(R, n) = Z_n = \frac{Y_n}{\lambda \sum_{i=0}^{n-1}(1 - \lambda)^i} \tag{8}$$

In our example, if we split the history into 4 separate windows, each window corresponding to a version, we get a period length of 1. If we adapt a λ of 0.1, the values in the denominator are $[0.1, 0.19, 0.271, 0.3439]$.

Using *entropy*, the weighted flakiness score of $tc2$ for the entire history is 1, with Y_n values $[0.1, 0.19, 0.271, 0.3439]$. Using *flip rate*, the weighted flakiness score of $tc2$, for the entire history, is 0.7 with Y_n values $[0.033, 0.0627, 0.15643, 0.240787]$.

4   Extended Flakiness Score

In this paper, we extend the flakiness score proposed by Kowalczyk et al. to deal with system-level tests with four different test outcomes *{pass, fail, error, skipped}* and varying test configurations. Figure 2 illustrates the four different test outcomes considered and the possible transitions that may manifest between these outcomes. Note that this drastically changes the concept of a flip used in Eq. 4. We now need to consider all possible arrows between the outcomes, except self-transitions because these are desirable.

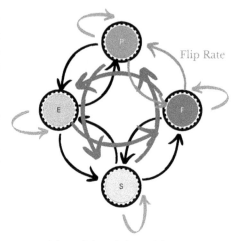

(P)ass, (F)ail, (E)rror, (S)kipped

Fig. 2. Four Different Test Outcomes

To enrich our running example, consider Fig. 3 (our original example) and Fig. 4. Both depict test histories against two different test configurations; where the first corresponds with a model-in-the-loop set-up (hence only *{pass, fail}* outcomes), and the second with a hardware-in-the-loop configuration (hence extra *{error, skipped}* outcomes). We base our interpretation of the test configurations the strategies to deal with flakiness: *Rerun, Fix* and *Monitor*.

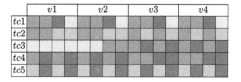

Fig. 3. Configuration 1 (model-in-the-loop)

Fig. 4. Configuration 2 (hardware-in-the-loop)

Flaky Behaviours. There are 5 different behaviours depicted in Fig. 3. $tc1$ is manifesting a constant rate of flakiness; a good example where the *Monitor* strategy would flag this case as normal. And, given the weighted and unweighted averages, we can quantify that $tc1$ passes on average half of the time so we need to rerun at least two times. $tc2$ suffers from an increasing rate of flakiness; the *Monitor* strategy should identify this as a candidate for further investigation. $tc3$ shows a sudden increase of flakiness, a prime candidate for the *Fix* strategy. $tc4$ shows a decreasing rate of flakiness which may occur after partial *Fix* of a flakiness root cause. Finally, $tc5$ shows the sudden disappearance of flakiness, an outcome that should be expected once a *Fix* is applied.

These behaviours are different in Fig. 4. $tc1$ is still manifesting a constant rate of flakiness; however, it is fluctuating between 3 outcomes. The weighted and unweighted averages estimate a pass outcome half of the time so we need to rerun at least two times with one pass result to accept the test. $tc2$ is manifesting an increasing rate of flakiness, but now with an error outcome. $tc3$ transitions from the skip outcome to the pass outcome before altering between pass and fail. $tc4$ has the same behaviour in both test configurations. $tc5$ constantly flips between the error and fail outcomes. The variety of outcomes present in Fig. 4 and the differences in flakiness behaviours between the two test configurations necessitates the investigation of particular transitions.

Transition Rate. To observe the rate of individual transitions, we define an additional way to quantify flakiness within a version, *transition rate*. For a particular pair of test outcomes, such as pass and fail, $\{P, F\}$, we can define the *transition rate*, T, as the number of times we observe transition, $P \longrightarrow F$, divided by the number of possible transitions or flips, Formula 9.

$$T(R_{v,*,\{P,F\}}) = \frac{numTransitions(R_{v,*,\{P,F\}})}{numTotalTransitions(R_{v,*})} \tag{9}$$

This definition of flakiness offers the chance to perform more fine-grained analysis concerning test transitions between particular test outcomes, and allows the consideration of a wider set of outcomes. For example, considering test case $tc1$, we see that it has a constant *transition rate* of 0.33 for transition $P \longrightarrow F$, and 0 for all other transitions in test configuration 1. However, in test configuration 2, it has an additional transition rate of 0.33 for transition $F \longrightarrow S$ for all versions. Therefore, if we sum up the transition rates for all possible transitions separately, we can observe that test case $tc1$ is flakier in test configuration 2. This can not be observed with only *flip rate*. Similarly, for test cases $tc2$, $tc3$ and $tc5$, we are unable to observe the true nature of flakiness with only *flip rate* and *entropy*.

To get the *flip rate* defined by Kowalczyk et al., we sum the *transition rate* for the transition $P \longrightarrow F$ to that of $F \longrightarrow P$ as in Formula 10. *flip rate* is therefore equivalent to the *dual transition rate*, DT.

$$flipRate(R_{v,*}) = DT(R_{v,*,\{P,F\}}) = T(R_{v,*,\{P,F\}}) + T(R_{v,*,\{F,P\}}) \tag{10}$$

The flakiness of a version can then be expressed as the *multi-transition rate*, MT, which is the sum of all *transition rate* values for all transitions.

$$MT(R_{v,*}) = DT(R_{v,*,\{P,F\}}) + DT(R_{v,*,\{P,E\}}) + DT(R_{v,*,\{P,S\}}) + \\ DT(R_{v,*,\{F,E\}}) + DT(R_{v,*,\{F,S\}}) + DT(R_{v,*,\{E,S\}}) \quad (11)$$

Accordingly, test case *tc2* in our running example has the same *multi-transition rate* value in both test configurations, 1 and 2. However, it manifests with different transitions, $P \longrightarrow F$ and $F \longrightarrow P$ in 1, and $P \longrightarrow E$ and $E \longrightarrow P$ in 2, which discrepancy should motivate a decision to assign time to address the cause for this flakiness sooner than later.

5   Simulation Set-Up

To investigate whether the refined score can support three different strategies for dealing with flaky tests, we perform a quantitative evaluation driven by two research questions.

- **RQ1:** *Replication.* Can we reproduce the original findings?
  - **Motivation.** While extending the model, we must ensure that we still make similar observations as the original.
  - **Approach.** We generate the same simulations as in the original study and compare our results. We verify whether the same values for H and λ emerge as the best. Next, we determine the performance of the formula, and verify whether they are comparable by calculating Spearman's correlation coefficient, Bonferroni corrected p-values and the mean squared error.
- **RQ2:** *Trend Analysis.* Can the extended flakiness model support the three different strategies for dealing with flaky tests ((i) Rerun, (ii) Fix and (iii) Monitor)?
  - **Motivation.** The extended model should address the Requirements for a System-Level Flakiness Score, as described in Sect. 1.1.
  - **Approach.** We expand the simulations, explicitly representing six possible behaviours a particular flakiness manifestation may exhibit, (i) Increasing, (ii) Decreasing, (iii) Sporadic, (iv) Constant, (v) Sudden_Increase, and (vi) Sudden_Flat_Line. Afterwards, we verify whether the formulae in the extended model are capable of distinguishing the different behaviours by observing their trends.

Just as the original study, we use a simulation involving 1200 test cases, with artificially induced random outcomes. Simulated data are ideal for early exploratory analysis as we can ensure that the data actually incorporates the phenomena we are investigating. We generate 2 different artificial datasets. The first is based on the algorithm provided by Kowalczyk et al., for which only two test outcomes are simulated. The second includes all the test outcomes depicted in Fig. 2, and incorporates six possible behaviours that may be captured by a flakiness score trend analysis from a flakiness manifestation. Our test generator scripts are provided as part of the replication package [15].

Artificial Dataset (A1). Our first dataset allows us to verify the replicability of the work of Kowalczyk et al., and compare our refinements, presented in Sect. 4, to their formulae, presented in Sect. 3. We used their algorithm to generate this artificial dataset. However, we assign start times to the generated versions which represent points in time when a version factor changed and a new version was created. This allows us to obtain a progression of versions run over time, in which the first version is run on the first day, the last on the last day, with the rest evenly spaced in between. To do this, in our test generator, we calculate the delay between the times when progressive versions should start running by dividing the specified number of days by the versions that need to be generated.

Dataset A1 is created using the same parameters as the original by Kowalczyk et al. Therefore, it has 96 flaky tests and 24 non-flaky tests. It simulates 120 tests run for 267 versions with a history length, H, of 64 days. The probability of tests with a fault is 0.45, the p_fault values distributed among those tests range from $[0.0005, 0.04]$. The probability of flaky tests is 0.8. The p_flake values for the flaky tests are uniformly distributed, and monotonically increasing from the first test to the last, within $(0, 1]$.

Artificial Dataset (A2). Our second dataset represents more complicated situations, all the test outcomes depicted in Fig. 2 are present. We incorporate test histories representing six possible behaviours of a flakiness manifestation, (i) Increasing, (ii) Decreasing, (iii) Sporadic, (iv) Constant, (v) Sudden_Increase, and (vi) Sudden_Flat_Line. The sets of tests and versions are generated in the same way as the first dataset. Each test is assigned a p_fault value in the range $[0.0005, 0.04]$ and an initial p_flake value within $(0, 1]$.

Since we simulate different behaviours, we perform the version sampling first, in which we compute the amount of change (δ) that will be applied for each version based on the behaviour assigned to the test. For the increasing and decreasing behaviours, this change is the distance from the upper bound (1) and lower bound (0), divided by the number of versions respectively. For sudden changes, it is 90% of the distance from the upper bound, if it is an increase, and the negative of the initial p_flake if it is a flat line. In this case, we randomly select the version at which the change should occur. After computing the change, we sample the binomial distribution generated using the tests p_fault, assign a verdict to the version sample, assign an updated p_flake to the version sample and select possible outcomes based on the actual verdict of the version.

We generate all the runs based on the version samples. To ascertain whether a run is flaky, we rely on the updated p_flake of the version sample, and, if so, flip the result based on the previous runs and the possible test outcomes. Note that we assume that a test can also alter when no fault is present.

Dataset A2 has 960 flaky tests and 240 non-flaky tests. Of the 960 flaky tests, each of the six possible behaviours —(i) Increasing, (ii) Decreasing, (iii) Sporadic, (iv) Constant, (v) Sudden_Increase, and (vi) Sudden_Flat_Line— are assigned 160 tests. Of the 960 flaky tests, 320 flaky tests alter between 2 outcomes, 320 between 3 and 320 between 4. We simulate 1200 tests run for 267 versions with a history length, H, of 64 days. The probability of tests with a fault remains the same, 0.45, with p_fault in the range $[0.0005, 0.04]$. The probability of flaky tests is also the same, 0.8, with monotonically increasing initial p_flake values within $(0, 1]$.

6   Simulations Results

This section presents the quantitative evaluation driven by two research questions (RQ1: *Replication*—RQ2: *Trend Analysis*) against the artificial datasets, A1 and A2.

6.1   RQ1: *Replication*

Procedure and Metrics. To confirm the performance of the formulae described in this work was comparable to the performance originally proposed by Kowalczyk et al., we compared the effects of the parameters, H, the history length, λ, the decay coefficient, and f, version flakiness function, on the performance of each aggregate formula, U and W.

Like the original study, for the unweighted models, we searched for the best H between values $[1, 64]$ with search steps of 2^i and i between $[0-6]$. Once settled on the most suitable history length, we searched for the best decay coefficient λ between $[0.1, 0.6]$ with steps of 0.1. For this study, the period, P, remained constant at 24 h.

To evaluate performance, we also measured identification and ranking accuracy, as defined in the original study [16]. Identification accuracy, the ability of each model to identify test flakiness, was computed by dividing the sum of true positives, tests with a score above 0, with an original p_flake value above 0, and true negatives, tests with a score equal to 0, with an original p_flake value equal to 0, by the total number of tests. Ranking accuracy, the models ability to quantify and rank flaky tests, was measured by computing the Spearman's correlation coefficient and Bonferroni corrected p-values of the correlation between the ranks assigned by the models and the original rank ascertained by ordering tests according to their original p_flake values. When computing identification accuracy, we also computed precision, recall and F1-score. As a measure of the proximity of the score to the underlying probability, we computed the mean squared error between the individual aggregate test scores and the actual p_flake.

A final consideration for our replication, that was not considered in the original study, is the *Perspective*. One could employ the scores and study flakiness score trends with a prospective perspective, starting with day 1's test execution data and increasing the amount of test execution data included in the score computation gradually until day 64, or with a retrospective perspective, starting with day 64's test execution data and increasing the amount of test execution data included in the score computation in the reverse direction. We expected the two trend analyses to mirror each other and collected data to prove or disprove this hypothesis.

Results. Table 1 shows an overview of the best performing parameters in both perspectives for the unweighted average flakiness score. It shows that *flip rate* and *dual transition rate* have identical performance as expected. It also confirms the superiority of *flip rate* over *entropy* as a measure for flakiness within a single version; one of the findings of the original study. We also found that *transition rate*, calculated for a single transition of interest, performs better than *entropy*. For all the simulations, we only considered the transition $P \longrightarrow F$; therefore, the performance in this case shows that *transition rate* is a promising alternative for close inspection of a test's flakiness for a particular version. A length of 64 days was optimal for both perspectives of inspection; however, in both cases, accuracy dropped below 1 only when H was 1. After a merged grid search across formulae and perspectives, in which all metrics had equal weight, we found that, apart from 64 days, the next best history lengths were 32 days when working retrospectively, that is the latest 32 days of data, and 16 to 32 days when working prospectively, that is the earliest 16 to 32 days of data. The correlation was strong and significant, and the mean squared error remained below 0.1 for all these lengths and perspectives.

Table 1. Best f and H values for unweighted flakiness score, Formula 5, U.

f	H	λ	Accuracy	Precision	Recall	F1	Spearman	Bonferroni	MSE
				Retrospective					
DTR	64	-	1.000	1.000	1.000	1.000	0.999	$1.232e - 149$	0.006
E	32	-	1.000	1.000	1.000	1.000	0.989	$2.674e - 97$	0.052
FR	64	-	1.000	1.000	1.000	1.000	0.999	$1.232e - 149$	0.006
TR	16	-	1.000	1.000	1.000	1.000	0.999	$5.989e - 120$	0.055
				Prospective					
DTR	64	-	1.000	1.000	1.000	1.000	0.999	$1.232e - 149$	0.006
E	64	-	1.000	1.000	1.000	1.000	0.989	$9.268e - 97$	0.051
FR	64	-	1.000	1.000	1.000	1.000	0.999	$1.232e - 149$	0.006
TR	64	-	1.000	1.000	1.000	1.000	0.998	$1.114e - 142$	0.062

f = Version Flakiness Formula H = History Length   MSE = Mean Squared Error
DTR = Dual Transition Rate E = Entropy FR = Flip Rate TR = Transition Rate

After computing weighted scores for a history length of 64 days, the most performant λ was 0.1. The best performing estimator of a versions flakiness was once again *flip rate*, with a correlation of 0.998, significance of $1.852e - 136$ and mean squared error of 0.008, followed by *transition rate*, with a correlation of 0.997, significance of $1.655e - 128$ and mean squared error of 0.059. Unlike the unweighted average, for which differences were observed when different perspectives were used to increase the window, there were no differences for weighted averages. This is expected since the full length of history was used for both perspectives.

> **RQ1:** *Replication.* When generating the same simulations as the original study, we are able to reproduce the findings of Kowalczyk et al. *Flip rate* and *dual transition rate* have identical performance, and we confirm their superiority over *entropy*, as a measure for flakiness within a single version. We also found *transition rate* a better model of flakiness within a version than *entropy*.

6.2 RQ2: *Trend Analysis*

Procedure and Metrics. For the quantitative evaluation against the artificial dataset A2, we implemented a few alterations to the procedure and metrics described in Sect. 6.1. First of all, considering all versions, we computed the average Fréchet distance between the curves of the original p_flake values and the corresponding aggregate flakiness score values, the curves U and W. Fréchet distance measures the similarity of curves in a metric space by taking into account the location and ordering of the points along the curves [9,26]. By calculating the Fréchet distance, we estimate how closely changes in the underlying manifestation's behaviour are reflected by the trend of flakiness scores. A small average Fréchet distance indicates a scoring formula that adapts quickly to changes, while a larger distance indicates the opposite. Secondly, to observe the power of the proposed scores under different conditions, we analysed the performance metrics over the injected flakiness behaviours and number of test outcomes present.

Table 2. Best *Perspective*, f and H values, after a merged grid search, for unweighted flakiness, U.

B	O	Perspective	f	H	Accuracy	F1	Spearman	Bonferroni	MSE	Fréchet
I	2	R	MTR	32	1.000	1.000	0.981	3.242e-37	0.021	0.206
	3	R, P	MTR	64	1.000	1.000	0.995	4.263e-57	0.048	0.279
	4	R, P	MTR	64	1.000	1.000	0.996	2.522e-44	0.056	0.304
D	2	P	MTR	16	1.000	1.000	0.996	7.003e-62	0.286	0.212
	3	P	MTR	32	1.000	1.000	0.992	4.024e-37	0.304	0.281
	4	P	MTR	32	1.000	1.000	0.998	3.806e-58	0.316	0.311
S	2	R	MTR	1	1.000	1.000	0.454	0.095	0.061	0.364
	3	R	MTR	2	1.000	1.000	0.252	1.000	0.068	0.471
	4	R	MTR	1	1.000	1.000	0.620	2.02e-4	0.059	0.383
C	2	R, P	MTR	64	1.000	1.000	0.998	9.503e-59	0.008	0.191
	3	R, P	MTR	64	1.000	1.000	0.996	5.284e-55	0.014	0.230
	4	R, P	MTR	64	1.000	1.000	0.998	3.635e-65	0.014	0.243
SI	2	R	MTR	2	1.000	1.000	0.619	1.685e-04	0.011	0.127
	3	P	MTR	1	1.000	1.000	0.942	4.507e-23	0.164	0.262
	4	R	MTR	8	1.000	1.000	0.751	4.483e-09	0.007	0.094
SF	2	R, P	TR	64	1.000	1.000	0.000	0.000	0.003	0.494
	3	R, P	TR	64	1.000	1.000	0.000	0.000	0.002	0.501
	4	R, P	TR	64	1.000	1.000	0.000	0.000	0.002	0.524

B = Flakiness Behaviour   O = Possible Number of Outcomes   I = Increasing   D = Decreasing
SI = Sudden_Increase   SF = Sudden_Flat_Line   S = Sporadic   C = Constant
MTR = Multi-Transition Rate   R = Retrospective   P = Prospective

Results. Table 2 shows an overview of the best performing parameters across both perspectives for the unweighted average flakiness score split by behaviour and number of outcomes. Table 3 shows an overview of the performance when exponential weighted averages are computed.

In the tables, we see perfect accuracy and F1 score, which was true for the majority of the cases, because these metrics have a simple definition for the purpose of indicating flakiness presence. We now focus on correlation, mean squared error and Fréchet distance which are better estimators of the severity of the underlying flakiness.

Table 3. Best *Perspective(Pers.)*, f, H and λ values, after a merged grid search, for weighted flakiness, Formula 8, W.

B	O	Pers.	f	H	λ	Accuracy	F1	Spearman	Bonferroni	MSE	Fréchet
I	2	P	MTR	32	0.1	1.000	1.000	0.989	2.084e-43	0.097	0.169
	3	P	MTR	32	0.2	1.000	1.000	0.975	3.213e-37	0.038	0.185
	4	R, P	MTR	64	0.1	1.000	1.000	0.980	1.736e-29	0.008	0.225
D	2	P	MTR	8	0.1	1.000	1.000	0.995	1.102e-59	0.245	0.146
	3	R	FR	16	0.1	1.000	1.000	0.884	3.119e-13	0.001	0.113
	4	R	TR	32	0.1	1.000	1.000	0.891	7.019e-17	4.46e-4	0.205
S	2	R	MTR	1	0.1 − 0.6	1.000	1.000	0.454	0.095	0.061	0.208
	3	R	MTR	2	0.6	1.000	1.000	0.268	1.000	0.066	0.308
	4	R	MTR	1	0.3, 0.5, 0.6	1.000	1.000	0.620	2.02e-4	0.059	0.207
C	2	P	MTR	16	0.1	1.000	1.000	0.995	5.902e-48	0.005	0.159
	3	P	MTR	32	0.1	1.000	1.000	0.997	2.410e-57	0.015	0.183
	4	P	MTR	8	0.1	1.000	1.000	0.990	5.057e-44	0.007	0.182
SI	2	R	MTR	2	0.3	1.000	1.000	0.621	1.550e-04	0.011	0.099
	3	P	MTR	1	0.1 − 0.6	1.000	1.000	0.942	4.507e-23	0.164	0.171
	4	R	MTR	8	0.2	1.000	1.000	0.736	1.669e-08	0.009	0.119
SF	2	R, P	E	64	0.6	1.000	1.000	0.000000	0.000000	0.002	0.350
	3	R, P	TR	64	0.6	1.000	1.000	0.000000	0.000000	5.3e-5	0.510
	4	R, P	FR	64	0.6	1.000	1.000	0.000000	0.000000	1.72e-4	0.488

Looking at each behaviour separately, we examined the most appropriate combination of perspective, formula, history length and λ, as the combination at which we observed the highest and most significant correlation, least mean squared error, and least Fréchet distance, in all outcome situations;

1. **Tests with gradually increasing flakiness:** A *multi-transition rate* based unweighted average, computed retrospectively with 32 days of data, performed best when there were only 2 outcomes. As the outcomes increased, a *multi-transition rate* based score, computed with 64 days of data, in which case both perspectives performed the same, proved best. In general, *multi-transition rate* and *entropy* performed better than *flip rate* and *transition rate* when computing unweighted averages. Computing the exponentially weighted average led to slightly worse correlation but better lower

error and Fréchet distance. The best scores were obtained by computing a *multi-transition rate* based score prospectively with 32 to 64 days of history and λ values of 0.1 or 0.2.

2. **Tests with gradually decreasing flakiness:** A *multi-transition rate* based unweighted score with a history length of 16 to 32 days, computed prospectively, performed the best for these tests. In this situation, *multi-transition rate* and *entropy* also performed better than *flip rate* and *transition rate*, when computing unweighted averages, for history lengths of 8 to 64 days. While a prospectively computed *multi-transition rate* based score, for a history length of 8 days, performed best when there were more than 2 outcomes, *flip rate* and *transition rate* based scores performed slightly better. In all outcomes situations however a *multi-transition rate* computed prospectively for 8 days with a λ value of 0.1 or 0.2 consistently ranked near the top of the list.

3. **Tests with sporadic flakiness:** For these tests, it was better to work retrospectively and compute an unweighted average based on history lengths of 1 to 2 days because all formulae revealed a score with the lower error and Fréchet distance in that setting. In addition, *multi-transition rate* had the least of these two metrics. This situation remained the same when computing exponentially weighted averages. For these scores, *multi-transition rate* based scores with a history length of 1 day were consistently among the best.

4. **Tests with constant flakiness:** For these tests, the most performant formula was *multi-transition rate* regardless of whether one was computing an unweighted or a weighted average. History lengths varied between 8 to 64 days. The performance of *entropy* was slightly better than that of *flip rate* as well, regardless of the number of outcomes. When computing a weighted average, *multi-transition rate* based scores with 8 to 32 days of data resulted in generally slightly better performance, especially with λ values of 0.1 or 0.2.

5. **Tests with sudden increases in their rate of flakiness:** When computing an unweighted average, we observed that using a prospective window *multi-transition rate* based score with 1 to 16 days of data performed better in general. Again, *entropy* proved more responsive than *flip rate* and *transition rate* When computing a weighted average, short history lengths of 1 or 2 days led to better performance when the number of outcomes was 2 or 3 and *multi-transition rate* was used as the version flakiness function. With four outcomes lengths of 8 or 16 days paired with λ values of 0.2 or 0.3 performed slightly better.

6. **Tests with sudden flat-lines in their rate of flakiness:** In this case, correlation was not relevant since the final p_flake was 0 for all tests. This is the one situation in which *transition rate* and *flip rate* based scores fared better than *entropy* and *multi-transition rate* based scores, when computing unweighted averages. The best performance was achieved with longer lengths of history such as 16 to 64 days. A length of 64 days, paired with a λ value of 0.6, consistently resulted in the best performance when computing weighted averages. *entropy*, *flip rate* and *transition rate* generally fared better than *multi-transition rate*.

In general, when analysed separately, all formulae experienced some degradation in performance as the number of outcomes increased. This degradation was more apparent for unweighted than weighted flakiness scores.

The question remains, how to identify the situation which applies to a particular test, and which formulae serve best for this purpose. Figure 5 shows samples of curves generated from the trend of exponentially weighted flakiness scores over time against the trend of original p_flake values, as originally sampled, for a test with suddenly increasing flakiness. We compare the two extreme decay coefficients, 0.1, the smoother curves, and 0.6, the jagged curves, and plot the confidence as an area plot within the graph. This figure demonstrates the responsiveness of *entropy* and *multi-transition rate* over *flip rate* and *transition rate*. Considering that the original p_flake values are fixed while the flakiness scores are based off samples, we can conclude that *entropy* and *multi-transition rate* offer acceptable estimations of the underlying behaviour. Thus changes observed in these trends, though delayed, will definitely illuminate situations of interest which would indicate the application of one of the strategies put forth in Sect. 1.1. We observe the impact of the decay coefficient on the trend portrayed by the flakiness score, with 0.1 shown to be the most smoothing option. This implies that what may appear as a slight rise in the flakiness score may actually be masking a larger issue.

We also observe, by looking at the trend of confidence values depicted by the area plot, versions for which the confidence, which is based on the number of test runs included in the flakiness score computation, dips. These are instances at which we do not have enough evidence. These should prompt an adjustment in the number of reruns if using the Rerun strategy to investigate a certain flakiness manifestation.

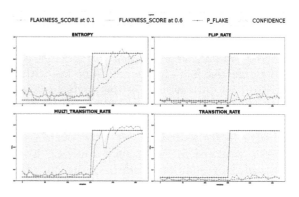

Fig. 5. Test with a suddenly increasing p_flake

Finally, when we studied the curves for the full set of tests, we observed that if the nature of flakiness is highly changeable, relying on test outcomes alone will not be sufficient. These curve comparison plots are provided as part of our replication package [15].

RQ2: *Trend Analysis.* Considering the requirements put forth in Section 1.1, our results show that including all the outcomes of a test, *multi-transition rate*, grants us the best estimate of the nature of the underlying flakiness in the majority of situations. The (i) Rerun strategy is supported by studying the trend of confidence based on the number of test runs included in the flakiness score computation. Places where (ii) Fixes are needed are best identified using short lengths of history retrospectively as it is best for detecting sudden increases. However, to verify the effect of a (ii) Fix, (i.e. a sudden flat line), one may rely on simpler defined scores and higher λ values if sufficient data has been collected. Considering the (iii) Monitor strategy, constant or gradually changing flakiness, is best observed prospectively with exponentially moving averages.

7   Threats to Validity

As with all empirical research, we identify the factors that may jeopardise the validity of our results and the actions we took to reduce or alleviate the risk. Consistent with the guidelines for case studies research (see [23, 30]), we organise them into four categories.

Construct Validity: Do we measure what was intended? As a purely data-oriented comparison of the ability of different formulae to estimate an unknown underlying distribution, the first issue lies with the dataset. With no access to the artificial dataset used in the study by Kowalczyk et al., we implemented their algorithm and mitigated this risk by verifying the proportions of flaky and faulty tests to normal tests used in their study. These proportions remain the same in the second dataset. The second issue is the metrics. We utilise the metrics proposed in the original study by Kowalczyk et al. We mitigate the risk added by additional metrics using only those that are applied alongside the original metrics or have been studied for the particular use case. For one thing, precision, recall and F1 score are often analysed alongside accuracy, [1, 6]. For another, Fréchet distance and its application to curve comparison has been studied at length by Tao et al. [26], and mean squared error and its application as a fitness function by Urbanek et al. [28].

Internal Validity: Are there unknown factors which might affect the outcome of the analyses? For some of the calculations, we rely on third party software implementations such as the Spearman's correlation by SciPy[1], which is a peer-reviewed work. The other third-party library is a Python 3.* implementation of Fréchet distance by Denaxas and Pikoula[2] based on the original definition by Eiter and Mannila [9]. In addition, the generation of the datasets relies heavily on random sampling. To mitigate this risk, we provide the entire dataset on

---

[1] https://scipy.org.
[2] https://github.com/spiros/discrete_frechet.

which this work is based alongside the dataset generators in our replication package [15], we expect similar results from other technologies.

External Validity: To what extent is it possible to generalise the findings? Each flakiness manifestation is different and the true underlying distribution is difficult to determine. To mitigate this risk, we split up the dataset and simulate different types of flakiness behaviour, thus adding variety to the dataset. The formulae noted in this work are designed to be generalisable to any test process with any set of outcomes.

Reliability: Are the results dependent on the tools? To address this risk, we use platform independent programming languages, Python and Java, to implement all tools used in this work, and provide the versions of Python plugins used. While there may be some variation implementation of the logic of operations, we expect similar results from the formulae should the implementation languages and operating systems differ.

8 Conclusion

In this paper, we investigate how to extend the flakiness score proposed by Kowalczyk et al. to deal with system-level tests with four different test outcomes *{pass, fail, error, skipped}*, and varying test configurations. We illustrate, by means of a simulation involving 1200 test cases with artificially induced random outcomes, how this refined score can support three different strategies for dealing with flaky tests—(i) Rerun, (ii) Fix and (iii) Monitor. We conclude that the extended score using *multi-transition rate* allows us to recognise gradual and sudden changes in test histories. We find that *entropy* is responsive even in situations when there are more outcomes to consider. When using an exponentially weighted average, a decay coefficient of 0.6 applies less smoothing and changes in flakiness behaviour are more apparent.

As such, we make the following contributions:

- We present an extended model and formulae for quantifying flakiness.
- We compare the extended model with the original and are able to reproduce the findings of Kowalczyk et al.
- We present evidence that the extended model can deal with more test outcomes than the default *{pass, fail}*.
- We create a new artificial dataset representing six possible behaviours for a flakiness manifestation (i) Increasing, (ii) Decreasing, (iii) Sporadic, (iv) Constant, (v) Sudden_Increase, and (vi) Sudden_Flat_Line.
- We demonstrate with this dataset that the extended flakiness score permits to recognise gradual and sudden changes in the underlying test flakiness.

Acknowledgments. This work is supported by the Research Foundation Flanders (FWO) via the BaseCamp Zero Project under Grant number S000323N.

References

1. Ahmad, A.: An evaluation of machine learning methods for predicting flaky tests. In: 27th Asia-Pacific Software Engineering Conference (APSEC 2020) Singapore (virtual), December 1, 2020, vol. 2767, pp. 37–46. CEUR-WS (2020)
2. Bass, L., Weber, I., Zhu, L.: DevOps: A Software Architect's Perspective. Addison-Wesley Longman Publishing Co., Inc (2015)
3. Bell, J., Briand, L., Harman, M., Marinov, D., Eldh, S.: Discussion Panel. In: Proceedings of 1st International Flaky Tests Workshop 2024 (FTW 2024) (2024)
4. Bell, J., Legunsen, O., Hilton, M., Eloussi, L., Yung, T., Marinov, D.: DeFlaker: automatically detecting flaky tests. In: 2018 IEEE/ACM 40th International Conference on Software Engineering (ICSE), pp. 433–444 (2018). https://doi.org/10.1145/3180155.3180164
5. De Lauretis, L.: From monolithic architecture to microservices architecture. In: 2019 IEEE International Symposium on Software Reliability Engineering Workshops (ISSREW), pp. 93–96 (2019). https://doi.org/10.1109/ISSREW.2019.00050
6. Di Nucci, D., Palomba, F., Tamburri, D.A., Serebrenik, A., De Lucia, A.: Detecting code smells using machine learning techniques: are we there yet? In: 2018 IEEE 25th International Conference on Software Analysis, Evolution and Reengineering (SANER), pp. 612–621 (2018). https://doi.org/10.1109/SANER.2018.8330266
7. Dutta, S., Shi, A., Misailovic, S.: FLEX: fixing flaky tests in machine learning projects by updating assertion bounds. In: Proceedings of the 29th ACM Joint Meeting on European Software Engineering Conference and Symposium on the Foundations of Software Engineering, p. 603–614. ESEC/FSE 2021, Association for Computing Machinery, NY, USA (2021). https://doi.org/10.1145/3468264.3468615
8. Eck, M., Palomba, F., Castelluccio, M., Bacchelli, A.: Understanding flaky tests: the developer's perspective. In: Proceedings of the 2019 27th ACM Joint Meeting on European Software Engineering Conference and Symposium on the Foundations of Software Engineering, pp. 830–840. ESEC/FSE 2019, Association for Computing Machinery, NY, USA (2019). https://doi.org/10.1145/3338906.3338945
9. Eiter, T., Mannila, H.: Computing discrete Fréchet distance. Technical report Christian Doppler Laboratory for Expert Systems (1994)
10. Gao, Z., Liang, Y., Cohen, M.B., Memon, A.M., Wang, Z.: Making system user interactive tests repeatable: when and what should we control? In: 2015 IEEE/ACM 37th IEEE International Conference on Software Engineering, vol. 1, pp. 55–65 (2015). https://doi.org/10.1109/ICSE.2015.28
11. Gyori, A., Lambeth, B., Shi, A., Legunsen, O., Marinov, D.: NonDex: a tool for detecting and debugging wrong assumptions on java API specifications. In: Proceedings of the 2016 24th ACM SIGSOFT International Symposium on Foundations of Software Engineering, pp. 993–997. FSE 2016, Association for Computing Machinery, NY, USA (2016). https://doi.org/10.1145/2950290.2983932
12. Habchi, S., Haben, G., Papadakis, M., Cordy, M., Traon, Y.: A qualitative study on the sources, impacts, and mitigation strategies of flaky tests. In: 2022 IEEE Conference on Software Testing, Verification and Validation (ICST), pp. 244–255. IEEE Computer Society, CA, USA (2022). https://doi.org/10.1109/ICST53961.2022.00034
13. Harman, M., O'Hearn, P.: From start-ups to scale-ups: opportunities and open problems for static and dynamic program analysis. In: 2018 IEEE 18th International Working Conference on Source Code Analysis and Manipulation (SCAM), pp. 1–23 (2018). https://doi.org/10.1109/SCAM.2018.00009

14. Holt, C.C.: Forecasting seasonals and trends by exponentially weighted moving averages. Int. J. Forecast. **20**(1), 5–10 (2004). https://doi.org/10.1016/j.ijforecast.2003.09.015
15. Kisaakye, J., Beyazıt, M., Demeyer, S.: Extending a Flakiness Score for System Level Tests (Replication Package) (2024). https://doi.org/10.5281/zenodo.13272415
16. Kowalczyk, E., Nair, K., Gao, Z., Silberstein, L., Long, T., Memon, A.: Modeling and ranking flaky tests at apple. In: 2020 IEEE/ACM 42nd International Conference on Software Engineering: Software Engineering in Practice (ICSE-SEIP), pp. 110–119 (2020). https://doi.org/10.1145/3377813.3381370
17. Lam, W., Oei, R., Shi, A., Marinov, D., Xie, T.: iDFlakies: a framework for detecting and partially classifying flaky tests. In: 2019 12th IEEE Conference on Software Testing, Validation and Verification (ICST), pp. 312–322 (2019). https://doi.org/10.1109/ICST.2019.00038
18. Luo, Q., Hariri, F., Eloussi, L., Marinov, D.: An empirical analysis of flaky tests. In: Proceedings of the 22nd ACM SIGSOFT International Symposium on Foundations of Software Engineering, pp. 643–653. FSE 2014, Association for Computing Machinery, NY, USA (2014). https://doi.org/10.1145/2635868.2635920
19. Machalica, M., Samylkin, A., Porth, M., Chandra, S.: Predictive test selection. In: 2019 IEEE/ACM 41st International Conference on Software Engineering: Software Engineering in Practice (ICSE-SEIP), pp. 91–100. IEEE (2019). https://doi.org/10.1109/ICSE-SEIP.2019.00018
20. Micco, J.: Flaky Tests at Google and How We Mitigate Them. https://testing.googleblog.com/2016/05/flaky-tests-at-google-and-how-we.html
21. Presler-Marshall, K., Horton, E., Heckman, S., Stolee, K.: Wait, wait. no, tell me. analyzing selenium configuration effects on test flakiness. In: 2019 IEEE/ACM 14th International Workshop on Automation of Software Test (AST), pp. 7–13 (2019). https://doi.org/10.1109/AST.2019.000-1
22. Rehman, M.H.U., Rigby, P.C.: Quantifying no-fault-found test failures to prioritize inspection of flaky tests at ericsson. In: Proceedings of the 29th ACM Joint Meeting on European Software Engineering Conference and Symposium on the Foundations of Software Engineering, pp. 1371–1380. ESEC/FSE 2021, Association for Computing Machinery, NY, USA (2021). https://doi.org/10.1145/3468264.3473930
23. Runeson, P., Höst, M.: Guidelines for conducting and reporting case study research in software engineering. Empirical Softw. Eng. **14**(2), 131–164 (2009). https://doi.org/10.1007/s10664-008-9102-8
24. Shi, A., Lam, W., Oei, R., Xie, T., Marinov, D.: iFixFlakies: a framework for automatically fixing order-dependent flaky tests. In: Proceedings of the 2019 27th ACM Joint Meeting on European Software Engineering Conference and Symposium on the Foundations of Software Engineering, pp. 545–555. ESEC/FSE 2019, Association for Computing Machinery, NY, USA (2019). https://doi.org/10.1145/3338906.3338925
25. Tahir, A., Rasheed, S., Dietrich, J., Hashemi, N., Zhang, L.: Test flakiness' causes, detection, impact and responses: a multivocal review. J. Syst. Softw. **206**, 111837 (2023). https://doi.org/10.1016/j.jss.2023.111837
26. Tao, Y., et al.: A comparative analysis of trajectory similarity measures. GIScience Remote Sens. **58**(5), 643–669 (2021). https://doi.org/10.1080/15481603.2021.1908927

27. Tibba, G., Malz, C., Stoermer, C., Nagarajan, N., Zhang, L., Chakraborty, S.: Testing automotive embedded systems under X-in-the-loop setups. In: 2016 IEEE/ACM International Conference on Computer-Aided Design (ICCAD), pp. 1—8 (2016). https://doi.org/10.1145/2966986.2980076

28. Urbanek, T., Prokopova, Z., Silhavy, R., Vesela, V.: Prediction accuracy measurements as a fitness function for software effort estimation. Springerplus 4(1), 1–17 (2015). https://doi.org/10.1186/s40064-015-1555-9

29. Wang, R., Chen, Y., Lam, W.: ipFlakies: a framework for detecting and fixing python order-dependent flaky tests. In: 2022 IEEE/ACM 44th International Conference on Software Engineering: Companion Proceedings (ICSE-Companion), pp. 120–124 (2022). https://doi.org/10.1145/3510454.3516846

30. Yin, R.K.: Case Study Research: Design and Methods, 3rd edn. Sage Publications, Thousand Oaks (2002)

31. Zhang, P., Jiang, Y., Wei, A., Stodden, V., Marinov, D., Shi, A.: Domain-specific fixes for flaky tests with wrong assumptions on underdetermined specifications. In: 2021 IEEE/ACM 43rd International Conference on Software Engineering (ICSE), pp. 50–61 (2021). https://doi.org/10.1109/ICSE43902.2021.00018

Advancements in Testing Methodologies

Autonomous Driving System Testing: Traffic Density Does Matter

Guannan Lou$^{(\boxtimes)}$ ⓘ, Donghwan Shin ⓘ, Neil Walkinshaw ⓘ,
and Robert M. Hierons ⓘ

The University of Sheffield, Sheffield S10 2TN, UK
{glou1,D.Shin,N.Walkinshaw,R.Hierons}@sheffield.ac.uk

Abstract. In recent years, the rapid development of deep neural networks and their application technologies has propelled autonomous driving systems (ADS) towards commercialisation. However, due to the high safety requirements of ADSs, ensuring their safety and reliability remains a critical challenge in software engineering. Existing testing methods focus on simple driving scenarios with few traffic participants, neglecting the impact of high traffic density on ADS driving performance. This paper presents an empirical study exploring how traffic density affects ADS behaviour. We developed a testing framework using two open-source ADSs to generate scenarios with varying traffic densities in a high-fidelity simulator. Our results indicate that changes in traffic density significantly affect ADS performance. Different traffic densities reveal various types of safety violations and help identify potential design flaws in ADSs. This study highlights the importance of considering traffic density in ADS testing and contributes to a better understanding of ADS performance under different traffic conditions.

Keywords: Software Engineering · Test Generation · Machine Learning · Autonomous Driving System

1 Introduction

In recent years, with the rapid development of deep neural networks and the progressive exploration of their applications, autonomous driving systems (ADS) have begun their journey toward commercialisation. Fully autonomous driving, which eliminates the need for a driver, has transitioned from laboratory testing to real-world implementation. According to data from the California Department of Motor Vehicles, over the past three years, more than 30 autonomous driving companies have conducted over 14 million miles of tests with more than 3,000 autonomous driving vehicles in California [11]. Some of these companies have already begun offering services such as autonomous driving taxis and buses [18]. Despite the considerable advancements in autonomous driving technology, reports of fatal accidents caused by errors in ADSs continue to emerge [23]. Ensuring the safety of ADSs and identifying such potential issues remain critical challenges for the widespread adoption of autonomous driving technology.

ⓒ IFIP International Federation for Information Processing 2025
Published by Springer Nature Switzerland AG 2025
H. D. Menéndez et al. (Eds.): ICTSS 2024, LNCS 15383, pp. 315–331, 2025.
https://doi.org/10.1007/978-3-031-80889-0_21

Considering the risk and cost involved in field testing, simulation-based ADS testing [1,6,9,10,16,17,24,34] has been widely studied recently. Using simulators to replicate the driving environment and the interactions between the ADS and its surroundings can identify a broader range of errors. The simulator updates the driving environment based on the ADS's driving operations and evaluates its performance by detecting specific types of violations. However, the involvement of simulators increases the complexity and duration of online testing, making it challenging to explore more complex driving scenarios. Current ADS testing methods often concentrate on simple driving scenarios involving three or fewer other vehicles. In contrast, real-world driving scenarios, especially in congested traffic, exhibit significant differences in terms of vehicle quantity, speed, and spacing between vehicles.

While the differences between congested traffic scenarios and simpler ones are apparent, the effect of different traffic densities on fault detection is still unclear. For example, can high traffic density reveal different types of safety violations? Do intermediate traffic densities between congested and simple scenarios differently affect ADS behaviour? Answering these questions will help us better understand the necessity of testing in congested traffic conditions.

Therefore, in this paper, we describe an empirical study to explore the impact of traffic density on ADS behaviour. Our research aims to answer the following questions

RQ1: Does traffic density affect ADS performance?
RQ2: Is it sufficient to test at the highest or lowest traffic densities?

To address these questions, we used two open-source ADSs, TCP [32] and Inter-Fuser [29], designed for real-world autonomous driving. For the online testing of these ADSs, we developed a testing framework capable of generating driving scenarios with varying traffic densities. This framework leverages a high-fidelity, physics-based autonomous vehicle simulator and integrates these ADSs into the testing environment. The framework allows us to configure maps, weather conditions, and infrastructure, as well as adjust the initial conditions of the ADSs and other traffic participants within the driving scenarios. We conducted statistical analyses on the collected data to provide answers to the research questions.

In summary, this paper makes a significant contribution by:

1. presenting the first empirical study comparing ADS behaviour under different traffic densities;
2. confirming ADSs perform differently with different traffic densities;
3. finding that certain violations are more likely to occur at traffic densities that are neither the highest nor the lowest;
4. publishing all experimental materials, including simulator-generated data, to support the replication of our study.[1]

The remainder of this paper is organised as follows. Section 2 details the empirical design, including the verification process and metrics. Section 3

---

[1] https://github.com/GuannanLou/Congested-ADS-Testing.

presents the results of the empirical evaluation. Section 4 discusses additional findings beyond the primary research questions. Section 5 discusses related work. Finally, Sect. 6 provides the conclusion of the paper.

2 Experiment Design

To evaluate the effect of traffic density on ADS testing, we divide it into 2 research questions:

RQ1: Does traffic density affect ADS performance?
RQ2: Is it sufficient to test at the highest or lowest traffic densities?

RQ1 examines whether the performance of ADS significantly depends on traffic density. Although high-density traffic environments could raise ADS issues, such as deadlock, current ADS testing methodologies have not properly investigated how to evaluate ADS performance in such conditions. Therefore, it is necessary to check whether there are differences in ADS performance across various traffic densities.

RQ2 explores whether the performance exhibits a consistent monotonic trend as traffic density increases. If so, focusing on the highest and lowest-density traffic scenarios would be sufficient. Otherwise, not only the extreme traffic environments but also the interim ones would be necessary. RQ2 will answer to this question.

To validate RQ1 and RQ2, we constructed five sets of driving scenarios, identical except for the traffic flow. We incrementally increased the traffic density in these scenarios from no other vehicles (level 0) to high traffic density (level 4). We then ran two state-of-the-art ADSs on these scenario sets and recorded their driving performance. Following previous studies [3], we used the Mann-Whitney U test to determine if there were significant differences in driving performance among the five sets and evaluated the magnitude of these differences using the Vargha-Delaney A_{12} effect size.

To answer RQ1, we primarily investigate whether the Mann-Whitney U test results for driving performance between scenarios with no other vehicles (level 0) and high traffic density (level 4) are significant, and we use the Vargha-Delaney A_{12} effect size to determine if driving performance exhibits a specific trend with changes in traffic density. In RQ2, we examine the distinctions between traffic density levels 1 to 3 and extreme traffic densities (levels 0 and 4), using the Vargha-Delaney A_{12} effect size to analyse whether there are anomalous increases or decreases in driving performance as traffic density decreases.

2.1 Experimental Subjects

Simulator. CARLA [12] is chosen as the simulator in this study, considering its realistic simulation capabilities and its previous use in challenges to evaluating the driving performance of ADSs in realistic street view [7]. It provides a complete set of pre-designed urban environments, including city layouts, various

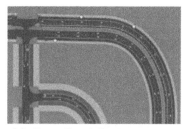

(a) Curve Road Section, r_{curve} (b) Straight Road Section, $r_{straight}$

Fig. 1. Demonstrations for 2 road sections in use.

vehicle types, buildings, pedestrians, road signs, etc. CARLA supports flexible sensor suite settings and various environmental conditions, including weather and time of day. In addition, it also provides a series of signal inputs for training driving strategies, such as GPS coordinates, speed, and acceleration, as well as detailed data on collisions and other violations.

ADS. We used two ADSs, TCP [32] and InterFuser [29], the two best ADSs on the CARLA autonomous driving leaderboard [7] at the time of starting the experiments. TCP [32] is an end-to-end ADS based on a single forward-facing visual input. InterFuser [29] incorporates additional point cloud inputs and multi-angle visual inputs to achieve a comprehensive understanding of the driving scenario. InterFuser's perception module generates a safety-oriented map, offering information about surrounding objects and traffic signs to predict the future movements of other traffic participants and plan the driving trajectory accordingly.

Driving Scenario Set. Following previous work [2,27], Town03 from CARLA was used to select the global scenario, which features a small city scene with various road sections, including roundabouts, crossings, and tunnels. Town03 includes traffic lights, vehicles, and pothole patches.

To ensure the results are generalised, the experiment is conducted on two road sections from Town03. The first road section, r_{curve}, depicted in Fig. 1(a), includes a left-turn road and requires 50 s for both ADSs to complete at a speed limit of 5 m/s without any interference. This scenario involves lane keeping, with vehicles parked by the road and two lanes in each direction. To simulate real traffic, other vehicles can be generated on all lanes. The second road section, $r_{straight}$, shown in Fig. 1(b), consists of two straight roads joined by a crossing with traffic lights and takes 25 s for both ADSs to complete. This straight-driving scenario involves driving through the crossing, with two lanes in each direction.

To provide more scenarios, the initial states of the scenario set were varied. Following [22], 11 features in the scenario vector were used to control weather conditions and the starting and ending positions of the ego-vehicle, which is the

Table 1. Features in the scenario vector to control the the driving scenario.

Category	Feature	Type	Lowest Value	Highest Value
Weather	cloudiness	float	0–0.5: sunny day	1: complete overcast
	precipitation	float	0–0.5: no rain	1: heavy rain
	precipitation deposits	float	0–0.5: no puddles start on the road	1: road covered by rain
	wetness	float	0–0.5: dry road	1: fully wet road
	wind intensity	float	0–0.5: clam	1: strong wind
	fog density	float	0–0.5: no fog	1: heavy fog
	fog falloff	float	0: fog starts in the sky	1: fog starts on the road
	sun azimuth angle	float	0: arbitrary North	1: corresponding South
	sun altitude angle	float	0: midday	1: midnight
Ego vehicle position	start offset	float	0: no offset	1: 50 m offset on the start point along the lane
	end offset	float	0: no offset	1: 50 m offset on the end point along the lane

vehicle controlled by the ADS. Details are listed in the Table 1. Each feature was normalised within the range of 0 to 1. To simplify the scenario, the initial speeds of the ego-vehicle and other vehicles were fixed. Also, weather-related values of 0 to 0.5 were considered to be no change.

In the driving scenario set for simulation and testing, each driving scenario's features were randomly sampled. To make fair comparisons, the set was kept consistent across all road sections and ADSs.

2.2 Methodology

To answer RQ1 and RQ2, we follow the four steps for each ADS: (1) traffic flow generation, (2) scenario execution, (3) performance evaluation and (4) significance testing.

Traffic Flow Generation. This step introduces traffic flows to simulate environments at five distinct traffic density levels, ranging from level 4 to level 0. Specifically, vehicle spacing is determined based on the desired traffic density, with level 4 to 1 having average vehicle distances, d_{avg}, of 7, 14, 21, and 28 m, respectively. Level 0 implies an absence of other vehicles in the scenario. To mimic real traffic, each vehicle's initial position is adjusted randomly within a range of $\pm t$, where the threshold t ensures that each vehicle would not come too close to others in the initial state and cause collisions. t is computed as follows:

$$t = (d_{avg} - l_{max})/2 \tag{1}$$

where l_{max} is the maximum vehicle length from the vehicle blueprint library, which is set to 5 m. Figure 2 demonstrated lane congestion at 5 traffic density levels. Following the traffic generation process in the CARLA challenge [7], the simulator dynamically managed the trajectories of other vehicles during tests to

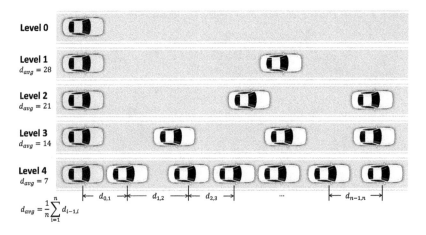

Fig. 2. Traffic density level

ensure their interactions with the environment and maintain their traffic rule compliance. The generated traffic flow was then added to the driving scenario set. To make fair comparisons, the scenario features in the driving scenario set were kept consistent under different traffic densities.

Scenario Execution. To execute generated driving scenario sets, the simulator is used to assess the ADS's performance in the given scenario set. The simulator transforms each scenario into a stream of real-time sensor signals, including camera and LiDAR signals, and relays these to the ADS being tested. The ADS processes the sensor signal stream using its perception and path-planning algorithms to generate vehicle control commands. The simulator then uses these commands to control the ADS's movement within the simulated driving scenario. During the execution of these tests, the simulator continuously records driving data, such as speed, trajectory, and distance to other vehicles. Upon completion of the tests, the recorded data will be used for the performance evaluation. Considering that on the two road sections, without interventions from other vehicles, the two ADSs require 50 s and 25 s respectively to complete the test, we set a timeout of 120 s for each scenario execution. This ensures that a normally performing ADS has sufficient time to complete the test.

Performance Evaluation. This step analyses the recorded driving data to assess critical aspects such as safety and comfort. In this study, six distinct performance metrics, according to the previous work [16,22], were employed: *Running Red Light, Route Completion, Collision, Outside Lane, Largest Acceleration,* and *Largest Braking.* The last two metrics aim to evaluate the driving quality in terms of comfort. Below we detail the equation for each metric in the form of $f(s, v_e)$ where s refers to a driving scenario from the driving scenario set and v_e refers to the ADS being evaluated. All metrics are normalised on a scale from 0 (i.e., failure) to 1 (i.e., safe).

Running Red Light, $f_{red}(s, v_e)$, aims to catch the ADS running a red light. When the ADS runs a red light, then f_{red} should be 0, otherwise f_{red} is 1.

$$f_{red}(s, v_e) = \begin{cases} 1 & not\ happens \\ 0 & happens \end{cases} \tag{2}$$

Route Completion, $f_r(s, v_e)$, evaluates the ability of an ADS to finish the route. There are k waypoints in the test route, and the ego-vehicle passed k_{pass} waypoints.

$$f_r(s, v_e) = \frac{k_{pass}}{k} \tag{3}$$

Collision, $f_c(s, v_e)$, evaluates the ability of an ADS to avoid collisions. There are n vehicles in the testing scenario, and v_i is the i-th vehicle. The testing scenario contains τ time frames, and d_t is the Euclidean distance between two vehicles at the time frame t.

$$f_c(s, v_e) = \min_{t=0}^{\tau} \min_{i=1}^{n} d_t(v_e, v_i) \tag{4}$$

Outside Lane, $f_o(s, v_e)$, evaluates the ability of an ADS to follow the lane and is the global farthest distance between the ego-vehicle and its closest waypoint w_i at timestamp t among all N waypoints in the oracle route.

$$f_o(s, v_e) = \max_{t=0}^{\tau} \min_{i=1}^{n} d_t(v_e, w_i) \tag{5}$$

Largest Acceleration, $f_{la}(s, v_e)$, gives the motion sickness by using the maximum acceleration among all timestamp T to evaluate the extent of motion sickness caused by an ADS. a_{t,v_e} is the acceleration of the vehicle v_e at the timestamp t.

$$f_{la}(s, v_e) = \max_{t=0}^{\tau} a_{t,v_e} \tag{6}$$

Largest Braking, $f_{lb}(s, v_e)$, is the maximum braking among all timestamps and evaluates the extent of motion sickness caused by the braking of the ADS. b_{t,v_e} is the braking of the vehicle v_e at the timestamp t.

$$f_{lb}(s, v_e) = \max_{t=0}^{\tau} b_{t,v_e} \tag{7}$$

Significance Testing. Following the previous study [3], the driving scenario set includes 30 driving scenarios to ensure the validity of subsequent hypothesis testing. Tests were conducted on 2 road sections across 5 traffic density levels, evaluating 2 ADSs separately in each scenario. A test case refers to a one-time execution for an ADS on a driving scenario with the selected road section and generated traffic. Each test case was repeated 3 times.

Then the distribution of ADSs' performance under different traffic densities was summarized. Statistical tests were also used to examine the differences between these distributions. Following previous work [3], given that the distribution of ADS performance metrics is non-normal, the Mann-Whitney U test was employed to determine if the performance metrics under varying traffic densities originate from the same distribution. The Vargha-Delaney A_{12} effect size was used to quantify the effect size of the Mann-Whitney U test.

2.3   Threats to Validity

Current research focuses on defining and discussing the necessity of testing congested scenarios within the context of ADS evaluation. Complex scenarios involving traffic interactions, such as auxiliary roads merging into main roads under congested conditions, roundabouts, and multi-directional traffic flows, have not been addressed in this paper. Nonetheless, results of tests on basic turning and straight road segments have demonstrated the presence of unique anomalies in congested scenarios.

3   Evaluation Result

Experiment Settings. The experiment consisted of executing 1800 test cases (30 cases for 2 ADSs on 2 road sections under 5 traffic density levels for 3 times execution). Experiments were run on an Ubuntu machine with RTX-3090 GPU.

Performance Summarisation. Figure 3 illustrates how six performance metrics for ADSs evolve in response to varying traffic densities on two road sections, depicted across six subplots, each dedicated to a specific metric. Within each subplot, pairs of ADSs and road sections are represented by five vertically arranged bars, corresponding to traffic density levels from 4 (top) to 0 (bottom). The colour gradient in each bar, transitioning from red to blue, indicates the level of risk associated with each performance metric, where red denotes higher risk and blue denotes lower risk. The length of each coloured segment within the bars reflects its proportion relative to the total number of test cases examined.

Using the top bar in the second column of the first row in Fig. 3 as an example, it depicts the distribution of the *Collision* metric for TCP during 90 test cases under density level 4 (extremely congested traffic) on the r_{curve}. The dark red colour indicates that collisions occurred in about 70% of the test cases.

From a broader perspective, the influence of traffic density on certain performance metrics of ADS on specific road sections can be seen in Fig. 3. For instance, in the metrics of *Route Completion*, *Collision*, and *Outside Lane* of TCP on the r_{curve}, there is a noticeable decline in the proportion of dangerous test cases as the traffic density level decreases. Conversely, for metrics like *Running Red Light*, the traffic density does not significantly alter their distribution. Therefore, statistical tests are necessary to rigorously establish whether traffic density impacts the distribution of these performance metrics.

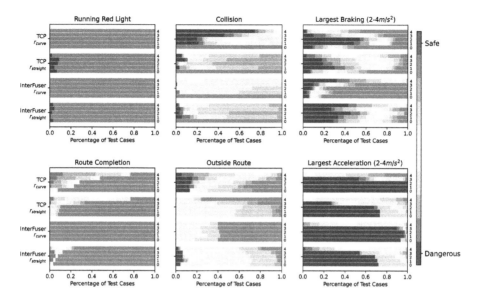

Fig. 3. ADS Performance under different traffic densities (density level 4 to 0, from top to bottom).

Significance Test on Performance's Differences. As depicted in Fig. 4, we conducted validation for each pair of density levels regarding performance metrics. Figure 4 comprises 24 subfigures, organised into four rows and six columns. The rows correspond to different combinations of ADS and road sections, while the columns represent various performance metrics. Each subfigure displays a 5×5 matrix where each cell contains the result from the Mann-Whitney U test and Vargha-Delaney A_{12} effect size, comparing performance metric data between the column and row conditions under the specified traffic density. All cells with $*$ refers to significant differences of the Mann-Whitney U test Below each matrix, a numerical value indicates the proportion of cells within the lower triangular portion of the matrix that are statistically significant. The cell colours range from blue to white to red, corresponding to Vargha-Delaney A_{12} effect sizes from 0 to 0.5 to 1. Dark blue indicates that the performance metric is significantly more hazardous at the traffic density on the vertical axis compared to that on the horizontal axis, while dark red indicates the opposite. White indicates no significant difference between the two.

For example, for the subfigure in the first row and second column of Fig. 4, the red colour of the cell in the first row and second column of the subfigure indicated that the proportion of dangerous $RouteCompletion$ for TCP on the r_{curve} at density level 4 was higher than at density level 3. The $* * *$ symbol signifies that this difference was highly significant. The 90% below the cell mean that out of 10 comparisons, 9 demonstrate statistical significance.

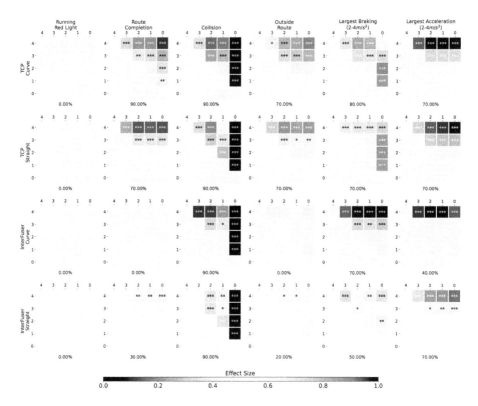

Fig. 4. Vargha-Delaney A_{12} effect size for ADS performance under different traffic densities. The $*$ marks refer to the significance for Mann-Whitney U test for ADS performance under different traffic densities ($*$: $p < 0.05$, $**$: $p < 0.01$, $***$: $p < 0.001$).

3.1 RQ1: Does Traffic Density Affect ADS Performance?

Overall, according to Fig. 4, except for the *Running Red Light*, most subgraphs display a high proportion of cells showing significant differences, indicating that traffic density has a substantial impact on performance metrics. For instance, 90% of cells are significant regarding the *Collision* performance metric for TCP on two road sections, reflecting marked performance disparities across varying traffic densities. The test of *Running Red Light*, which measures an autonomous driving system's ability to detect and stop at a red light, should not be affected by traffic density. This is supported by the absence of significant cells in this category in Fig. 4, which aligns with common understanding.

Notably, two distinct patterns are evident across the subgraphs in Fig. 4. For example, on the r_{curve}, TCP's *Largest Acceleration* shows concentrated dark cells at higher traffic densities (levels 4 and 3), showing monotonic relations between traffic density and ADSs' dangerous cases. This pattern is evident in 10 subgraphs. Conversely, on the $r_{straight}$, TCP's *Largest Braking* exhibits dark red cells at the lowest traffic density (level 0), indicating that ADS's dangerous cases increase with the decrease of traffic density, but decrease on the lowest traffic density. 5 subgraphs exhibit this pattern. In particular, 2 of the subgraphs concurrently exhibit both identified patterns.

Furthermore, the influence of traffic density levels on TCP and InterFuser varies. Specifically, for the *Largest Braking* metric, InterFuser has more dangerous cases under high-density traffic, while TCP is safer when traffic density goes high. According to Fig. 3, TCP's *Largest Braking* metric, at traffic density levels 4 and 0, indicating high density and no other vehicles, respectively, demonstrates safer performance. However, as traffic density decreases but remains above zero, the incidence of dangerous test cases markedly increases. In contrast, the number of dangerous test cases for InterFuser gradually decreases as the traffic density level declines.

These differences are attributable to the distinct driving strategies and path-following capabilities of each ADS. InterFuser, with more aggressive driving behaviour and closer following distances, is prone to hard braking on straight roads under high traffic conditions. On the other hand, TCP, with weaker path-following ability, tends to veer out of lanes and come too close to other vehicles. This problem becomes more pronounced as traffic density decreases and the gap between vehicles widens, particularly on curved road segments at density levels 2 and 1, where dangerous test cases are more frequent.

Result 1

Changing traffic density substantially influences the performance of ADSs. Moreover, the manner and magnitude of the influence differ between TCP and InterFuser.

3.2 RQ2: Is it Sufficient to Test at the Highest or Lowest Traffic Densities?

As illustrated in RQ1, Fig. 3 shows a linear relationship for performance metrics such as *Largest Acceleration* and *Route Completion* for the two ADS as traffic density decreases. However, some performance metrics exhibit a trend where they initially become more hazardous and then safer. This is evident in the *Largest Braking* of TCP in two road sections and the *Outside Lane* of InterFuser on the $r_{straight}$.

For TCP, low traffic density allows for a greater distance from the vehicle ahead and higher *Largest Acceleration*, leading to momentarily higher speeds. This necessitates more frequent hard braking to maintain a stable distance from the preceding vehicle. In high traffic density, the reduced distance to the vehicle ahead results in smoother driving and lower *Largest Braking*. Consequently, the number of TCP test cases that violate the *Largest Braking* limit is highest at density levels 2 and 1, rather than levels 4 and 0.

Regarding InterFuser's *OutsideRoute* metric, its superior road-following ability prevents violations on the r_{curve}, making it unaffected by traffic density. However, on the $r_{straight}$, the more sensitive perception system causes false alarms, leading to unnecessary emergency lane changes. This type of violation is described in Sect. 4.1. Under high-density traffic, InterFuser cannot perform emergency avoidance, limiting the number of failed cases in the *OutsideRoute* metric. At density level 1, increased vehicle spacing facilitates emergency manoeuvres, increasing failed cases. As density decreases further, fewer surrounding objects lead to fewer false alarms, reducing failed cases. This suggests that extreme value analysis may not be suitable for autonomous driving tests involving varying traffic densities.

Result 2

Testing exclusively in scenarios of either excessively high or low traffic densities may be inadequate for autonomous driving assessments. Certain types of violations tend to occur more frequently in scenarios characterised by moderate traffic densities.

---

4   Additional Findings

Through the investigation of the research questions in Sect. 3, it was evident that traffic density influences the performance of an ADS, highlighting the necessity of testing ADS performance under varying traffic densities.

During the analysis of ADS performance across different traffic densities, several anomalies were observed. InterFuser showed a significant increase in high-*Collision*-risk test cases and an unusually high rate of *Route Completion* failures in low-density traffic. A detailed manual investigation of these test cases revealed 3 additional findings. These findings underscore the results of RQs and highlight the importance of considering traffic density when analysing ADS errors.

4.1   InterFuser's Emergency Lane Changing

On the $r_{straight}$, InterFuser is vulnerable to incorrect collision detection, leading to unnecessary emergency lane changes. InterFuser utilises a multi-sensor fusion strategy for input construction, enhancing its robustness compared to TCP, particularly under extreme weather conditions. However, this complexity also heightens the likelihood of recognition errors. On the $r_{straight}$, an erroneous recognition from a single frame causes InterFuser to anticipate an imminent collision, prompting a lane change as a preventive manoeuvre. During such lane changes, InterFuser sometimes overlooks the traffic conditions in the adjacent lanes, which leads to collisions with other vehicles. These incidents represented 9 out of 14 collision-related violations recorded for InterFuser on the $r_{straight}$.

Notably, with a decrease in traffic density levels, the occurrence of this type of violation initially increases from 7, reaches a maximum of 15 at level 1, and then decreases to 8 at level 0. The marked rise in incidents at level 1 compared to level 0 suggests that an increased number of vehicles in the driving environment may lead to this error being triggered more frequently. Furthermore, higher traffic densities, by reducing the gaps between vehicles, tend to restrict the opportunities for such lane-changing manoeuvres.

This finding supports RQ2, indicating that certain violations are more likely at moderate traffic densities, rather than at the highest or lowest levels.

4.2   TCP's Overly Cautious Driving Habits

While ADS deadlock due to complex traffic interactions under high-density traffic is acknowledged in some ADS development literature [15,19], it is rarely discussed in ADS testing studies. However, our experiments show more pronounced deadlock issues in TCP. Compared to InterFuser, TCP demonstrates a more cautious driving strategy in two key areas.

Firstly, on the $r_{straight}$, TCP consistently maintains a separation exceeding two vehicle lengths from the car ahead, even during stops at intersections. This is generally unnecessary in urban environments. As a result, TCP tends to move slowly in high traffic densities, failing to complete the tests within the designated times. Specifically, TCP's rates of failure to complete tests without collisions were 14 out of 82 at traffic density level 4 and 62 out of 85 at level 5. In contrast, InterFuser recorded substantially lower non-completion rates of 4 out of 86 and 17 out of 88 at the same levels. Considering the potential for congestion in crossings and delays at traffic signals under high traffic conditions, InterFuser's performance is deemed acceptable; however, TCP requires further optimisation to handle such high-density traffic scenarios efficiently. Secondly, on the r_{curve}, as the distance between TCP ego-vehicle and vehicles in adjacent lanes decreases, TCP is prone to be influenced by neighbouring lane traffic. When approaching vehicles in other lanes, TCP prefers to decelerate and stop rather than adjust its travel direction, which can lead to the deadlock.

These findings support the results of RQ1, indicating that higher traffic density increases the likelihood of certain violations occurring.

4.3   Sudden Overtaking

During the experiments, we noticed similar collisions not attributable to the ADS. Thus, in the experiment, test cases with this kind of violation were removed. This collision type is illustrated in Fig. 5. Specifically, on the r_{curve}, if there was sufficient distance between the ego-vehicle and the vehicle ahead at the start of the test, vehicles in the right lane could attempt to cut in. Both ADS models tested, TCP and InterFuser, failed to adequately anticipate this manoeuvre, frequently resulting in collisions.

In the 450 test scenarios under various traffic densities, TCP and InterFuser experienced 25 and 38 such incidents, respectively. The highest incidence rate occurred at the lowest traffic density level, with TCP and InterFuser recording 20 and 33 incidents respectively. The occurrence of these incidents significantly decreased at higher traffic densities, with both models recording only 5 incidents at traffic density 2 and none at higher densities due to closer vehicle spacing.

Current traffic regulations grant ADS the right of way in these scenarios, meaning it's not responsible for collisions. However, for safety, ADS should decelerate to minimise potential harm to passengers.

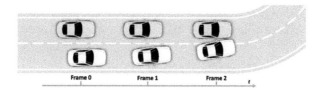

Fig. 5. Suddenly overtaking collision violations. Yellow vehicle is the ego-vehicle. (Color figure online)

This finding also supports the result of RQ2, indicating that certain violations are more likely to occur at traffic density level 1 rather than at level 0 or 4.

5 Related Work

ADS Testing. When testing ADSs, two primary challenges arise: managing the complexity of systems that incorporate neural networks and the difficulty of exhaustively generating test cases for all potential inputs. Current work [26, 30] views the ADS as a black box, employing meta-heuristic search techniques such as genetic algorithms and simulated annealing to explore the parameter space, prioritising the identification of challenging test cases. Most studies in this area concentrate on specific characteristics of driving scenarios, such as the initial positions and speeds of certain traffic participants [1,6,24,34], while conforming to fixed road configurations and predetermined vehicle paths. Some studies change road structures to test the ability of an ADS to follow the road [14, 31], while the complex interactions with the traffic flow is not concerned.

AV-Fuzzer [24], a prominent SBT framework for ADS, characterises driving scenarios by vectorizing the driving behaviours of traffic participants and modifying these parameters to look for scenarios that are more likely to cause collisions within the Apollo system. AutoFuzz [34], a grammar-based fuzzer, leverages the API of the autonomous driving simulator to generate semantically and temporally valid complex scenarios. It optimises test inputs through an evolutionary search method constrained by neural networks to discover a wider range of unique traffic violations.

Notably, existing methods typically describe a traffic participant in the scenario using one or more dimensions. As the number of traffic participants increases, the search space expands significantly, leading to increased complexity in the search process. For instance, AV-Fuzzer scenarios involve only two other traffic participants, while AutoFuzz scenarios include up to four. Generating dense traffic scenarios with more than 20 traffic participants remains a challenge for current methodologies. This limitation hinders existing technologies from effectively capturing the unique anomalies that occur during congested scenarios, such as the overly cautious driving habits of TCP.

Congested Scenarios in ADS Design. Although automated driving technology has seen commercial deployment in certain areas in recent years, the uncertainty of traffic participants and complex vehicle interactions in congested scenarios, such as forced merging on ramps, remain significant challenges for automated driving systems. To navigate efficiently and safely in such environments, ADSs must understand the behaviours and intentions of other vehicles, perform dynamic reasoning, and engage in interactive motion planning. Current research primarily focuses on three methods: probabilistic reasoning [25,28], the artificial potential field method [4,33], and reinforcement learning [5,8,19,21] .

Probabilistic reasoning [25,28] uses dynamic Bayesian networks to model vehicle interactions. While effective in handling the uncertainty of driving behaviours, this approach struggles with complex bidirectional interactions in high-density traffic. The artificial potential field method [4,33] employs various functions to describe interactions among traffic participants uniformly. Despite its ability to integrate multiple environmental factors, the method faces challenges of the large factor dimensions and optimisation complexity in congested scenarios. Reinforcement learning [5,8,19,21] addresses adaptive interaction planning in dynamic environments through continuous interaction and learning of optimal strategies. However, the trial-and-error nature of reinforcement learning raises concerns about adherence to state constraints in uncertain scenarios, and issues related to its transferability also require attention [13,20].

Existing methods demonstrate that ADSs still have room for improvement in congested scenarios and provide reference scenarios for ADS testing.

6   Conclusion

In this study, we empirically investigated the impact of traffic density on the performance of Autonomous Driving Systems (ADS). Our results show that different traffic densities lead to various safety issues and design flaws. High traffic density worsened route completion and collision rates, while running red lights was unaffected. Intermediate densities posed unique challenges, emphasising the need for testing across various conditions.

The distinct behaviours of TCP and InterFuser emphasise the need for tailored testing strategies. TCP's conservative driving resulted in more failures in high-density traffic, whereas InterFuser's aggressive lane-changing increased collisions in lower-density environments. These findings highlight the complexity of real-world driving scenarios and the limitations of current testing methods, which often overlook high-density conditions. We advocate for more comprehensive and realistic testing frameworks to enhance ADS robustness and safety for public deployment.

Future research in this field is promising, particularly in exploring a wider range of congested scenarios to uncover additional anomalies. Further investigation is also needed into combining test generation methods to identify congested scenarios more likely to trigger abnormal ADS behavior.

References

1. Abdessalem, R.B., Nejati, S., Briand, L.C., Stifter, T.: Testing advanced driver assistance systems using multi-objective search and neural networks. In: Proceedings of ASE, pp. 63–74. ACM (2016)
2. Ang, J.W.D., Seow, C.K., Subramanian, K., Pranata, S.: Big data scenarios simulator for deep learning algorithm evaluation for autonomous vehicle. In: Proceedings of GLOBECOM, pp. 1–6. IEEE (2020)
3. Arcuri, A., Briand, L.C.: A hitchhiker's guide to statistical tests for assessing randomized algorithms in software engineering. Softw. Test. Verification Reliab. **24**(3), 219–250 (2014)
4. Basha, S.M., Ahmed, S.T., Al-Shammari, N.K.: A study on evaluating the performance of robot motion using gradient generalized artificial potential fields with obstacles. In: Proceedings of ICCIDM, pp. 113–125. Springer (2022)
5. Brito, B., Agarwal, A., Alonso-Mora, J.: Learning interaction-aware guidance for trajectory optimization in dense traffic scenarios. IEEE Trans. Intell. Transp. Syst. **23**(10), 18808–18821 (2022)
6. Calò, A., Arcaini, P., Ali, S., Hauer, F., Ishikawa, F.: Generating avoidable collision scenarios for testing autonomous driving systems. In: Proceedings of ICST, pp. 375–386. IEEE (2020)
7. CARLA: CARLA autonomous driving leaderboard. https://bit.ly/43W9FgQ (2023). Accessed 12 Oct 2023
8. Chen, J., Yuan, B., Tomizuka, M.: Model-free deep reinforcement learning for urban autonomous driving. In: Proceedings of ITSC, pp. 2765–2771. IEEE (2019)
9. Deng, Y., et al.: A declarative metamorphic testing framework for autonomous driving. IEEE Trans. Software Eng. **49**(4), 1964–1982 (2023)
10. Deng, Y., Zheng, X., Zhang, M., Lou, G., Zhang, T.: Scenario-based test reduction and prioritization for multi-module autonomous driving systems. In: Proceedings of ESEC/FSE, pp. 82–93. ACM (2022)
11. DMV: Autonomous vehicles (2024). https://bit.ly/3Lb1Vit. Accessed 10 June 2024
12. Dosovitskiy, A., Ros, G., Codevilla, F., López, A.M., Koltun, V.: CARLA: an open urban driving simulator. In: Proceedings of CoRL, vol. 78, pp. 1–16. PMLR (2017)
13. Fang, M., Li, Y., Cohn, T.: Learning how to active learn: a deep reinforcement learning approach. In: Proceedings of EMNLP, pp. 595–605. Association for Computational Linguistics (2017)
14. Gambi, A., Müller, M., Fraser, G.: Automatically testing self-driving cars with search-based procedural content generation. In: Zhang, D., Møller, A. (eds.) Proceedings of ISSTA 2019, pp. 318–328. ACM (2019)
15. Goto, T., Itaya, H., Hirakawa, T., Yamashita, T., Fujiyoshi, H.: Solving the deadlock problem with deep reinforcement learning using information from multiple vehicles. In: Proceedings of IV, pp. 1026–1032. IEEE (2022)
16. Haq, F.U., Shin, D., Briand, L.C.: Efficient online testing for DNN-enabled systems using surrogate-assisted and many-objective optimization. In: Proceedings of ICSE, pp. 811–822. ACM (2022)
17. Haq, F.U., Shin, D., Nejati, S., Briand, L.C.: Comparing offline and online testing of deep neural networks: an autonomous car case study. In: Proceedings of ICST, pp. 85–95. IEEE (2020)
18. Hawkins, A.J.: You can take a ride in a self-driving Lyft during CES (2018). https://bit.ly/4biHP0k. Accessed 10 Oct 2024

19. Hou, X., Gan, M., Wu, W., Wang, C., Ji, Y., Zhao, S.: Merging planning in dense traffic scenarios using interactive safe reinforcement learning. Knowl. Based Syst. **290**(1), 1–9 (2024)
20. Hou, X., Zhang, J., He, C., Li, C., Ji, Y., Han, J.: Crash mitigation controller for unavoidable T-bone collisions using reinforcement learning. ISA Trans. **130**(1), 629–654 (2022)
21. Hu, Y., Nakhaei, A., Tomizuka, M., Fujimura, K.: Interaction-aware decision making with adaptive strategies under merging scenarios. In: Proceedings of IROS, pp. 151–158. IEEE (2019)
22. Huai, Y., Almanee, S., Chen, Y., Wu, X., Chen, Q.A., Garcia, J.: scenoRITA: generating diverse, fully mutable, test scenarios for autonomous vehicle planning. IEEE Trans. Software Eng. **49**(10), 4656–4676 (2023)
23. Krisher, T.: 3 crashes, 3 deaths raise questions about Tesla's autopilot (2020). https://bit.ly/45yHvcq. Accessed 10 June 2024
24. Li, G., et al.: AV-FUZZER: finding safety violations in autonomous driving systems. In: Proceedings of ISSRE, pp. 25–36. IEEE (2020)
25. Li, K., Wang, X., Xu, Y., Wang, J.: Lane changing intention recognition based on speech recognition models. Transp. Res. Part C: Emerg. Technol. **69**(1), 497–514 (2016)
26. Lou, G., Deng, Y., Zheng, X., Zhang, M., Zhang, T.: Testing of autonomous driving systems: where are we and where should we go? In: Roychoudhury, A., Cadar, C., Kim, M. (eds.) Proceedings of ESEC/FSE, pp. 31–43. ACM (2022)
27. Lyssenko, M., Gladisch, C., Heinzemann, C., Woehrle, M., Triebel, R.: From evaluation to verification: Towards task-oriented relevance metrics for pedestrian detection in safety-critical domains. In: Proceedings of CVPR, pp. 38–45. IEEE (2021)
28. Ma, J., Xie, H., Song, K., Liu, H.: A Bayesian driver agent model for autonomous vehicles system based on knowledge-aware and real-time data. Sensors **21**(2), 331 (2021)
29. Shao, H., Wang, L., Chen, R., Li, H., Liu, Y.: Safety-enhanced autonomous driving using interpretable sensor fusion transformer. In: Proceedings of CoRL, vol. 205, pp. 726–737. PMLR (2022)
30. Tang, S., et al.: A survey on automated driving system testing: landscapes and trends. ACM Trans. Softw. Eng. Methodol. **32**(5), 124:1–124:62 (2023)
31. Tang, S., Zhang, Z., Zhou, J., Zhou, Y., Li, Y., Xue, Y.: Evoscenario: integrating road structures into critical scenario generation for autonomous driving system testing. In: Proceedings of ISSRE, pp. 309–320. IEEE (2023)
32. Wu, P., Jia, X., Chen, L., Yan, J., Li, H., Qiao, Y.: Trajectory-guided control prediction for end-to-end autonomous driving: a simple yet strong baseline. In: Proceedings of NeurIPS, vol. 35, pp. 6119–6132 (2022)
33. Xie, S., Hu, J., Bhowmick, P., Ding, Z., Arvin, F.: Distributed motion planning for safe autonomous vehicle overtaking via artificial potential field. IEEE Trans. Intell. Transp. Syst. **23**(11), 21531–21547 (2022)
34. Zhong, Z., Kaiser, G.E., Ray, B.: Neural network guided evolutionary fuzzing for finding traffic violations of autonomous vehicles. IEEE Trans. Softw. Eng. **49**(4), 1860–1875 (2023)

Annotation-Based Input Modeling for Combinatorial Testing

Markus Fugger[1], Manuel Leithner[2]($\boxtimes$) (iD), and Dimitris E. Simos[2] (iD)

[1] TU Wien, Wien, Austria
[2] SBA Research, Wien, Austria
{mleithner,dsimos}@sba-research.org

Abstract. Combinatorial testing (CT) is an efficient and effective black-box testing technology, combining mathematically guaranteed input space coverage with comparatively small test sets. However, it requires a current and complete model of all input parameters to a system under test (SUT), their respective value domains, and any constraints between parameters. This factor greatly hinders the adoption of CT in real-world development settings, as creating and maintaining an input parameter model requires signficant effort and is often not sufficiently integrated into relevant workflows in the face of software evolution. To alleviate this drawback, we propose an annotation-based method that aims to improve the locality of model information. It allows developers to define parameter values as well as constraints in immediate vicinity to function or method definitions, enabling them to incorporate modeling into their workflows with minimal overhead. Required oracles are implemented following a common structure and interface, permitting flexible evaluation of results while retaining low complexity for common cases. By incorporating the automated generation and execution of combinatorial test sets into continuous integration processes, our method streamlines the practical application of CT and thus aims to facilitate the industrial adoption of this high-assurance testing approach. A practical implementation targeting the Kotlin programming language serves as the basis for our evaluation, which verifies the applicability of our method when incorporated into an existing medium-sized codebase. At the same time, it offers directions for future work, including improvements regarding stateful testing in object-oriented languages.

Keywords: Combinatorial Testing · Input Parameter Model · Software Evolution · Source Code Annotations

1 Introduction

Testing is an integral part of any well-designed software development lifecycle (SDLC). Its primary purpose is to validate whether a software component functions correctly when confronted with a specific input. As the cost of fixing

© IFIP International Federation for Information Processing 2025
Published by Springer Nature Switzerland AG 2025
H. D. Menéndez et al. (Eds.): ICTSS 2024, LNCS 15383, pp. 332–348, 2025.
https://doi.org/10.1007/978-3-031-80889-0_22

bugs increases throughout the stages of development, testing should ideally be conducted as early and as comprehensively as possible.

In practice, many projects rely on manually written unit tests (which test a particular use case) or automated fuzzing. While the former is capable of exercising complex sequences of events, the coverage it provides is minuscule and uncommon or unexpected inputs might never be tested. Meanwhile, fuzzing aims to mutate inputs in order to increase coverage and identify faults. However, it is highly probabilistic and prone to shallow exploration of control flow, offering no guarantees regarding coverage.

Combinatorial testing (CT) is a black-box testing method that combines mathematically guaranteed coverage of the input space of a system under test (SUT) with a relatively small number of test cases [23]. It has been shown to be efficient and effective in a wide range of settings ranging from software conformance [24] and security [14] testing to hardware testing [21]. CT requires a model of the input space of the SUT, commonly referred to as an input parameter model (IPM), describing all available parameters, their value domains, and any constraints between them (for example, consider a method that accepts a boolean parameter indicating that a person is a child along with an integer parameter specifying the age; if the former parameter is true, the latter can only assume values between 0 and 18). However, in practical settings, an IPM is often not available. Economic pressure and the fast-paced environment facilitated by customer demands tend to make it difficult to introduce additional overhead including the creation and maintenance of such documentation.

The aim of this work is to minimize the effort required to define and update IPMs and test oracles and remove some of the most daunting barriers to the adoption of CT in practical SDLCs. We introduce an approach that utilizes source code annotations to define the value domains of method parameters as well as any applicable constraints. It further streamlines the creation of test harnesses and oracle definitions by offering a common interface that is flexible enough to support complex test setup/teardown scenarios. Finally, our method supports the automated generation and execution of test cases in continuous integration/deployment (CI/CD) environments. While our approach is applicable to most modern languages that feature constraint processing capabilities, our implementation is focused on Kotlin, an object oriented programming language that is currently recommended for Android development and interoperable with Java. In a case study based on a Sim City clone, we replace existing unit tests with CT equivalents using our presented methodology to evaluate its advantages and drawbacks.

The remainder of this work is structured as follows. Section 2 introduces CT and its underlying mathematical structures as well as source code annotations. Next, Sect. 3 outlines the most important related work focused on model definition with a particular focus on Kotlin and Java. Section 4 introduces our methodology and the steps required to apply it to real-world development workflows, followed by a case study (Sect. 5) that applies these processes to a medium-sized code base. Section 6 summarizes our contributions, outlines the most important results, and provides directions for future work.

2   Preliminaries

This section elaborates the concepts underlying our approach, beginning with CT and covering arrays before moving on to source code annotations.

2.1   Combinatorial Testing

The test target in CT – be it a function, program, piece of hardware or some other type of system – is called a system under test (SUT) [2, 23]. Its input parameters and their individual domains of values are defined in an input parameter model (IPM). Additional constraints may exclude specific combinations of values within the same test case. A test case assigns each parameter one particular value within its domain while respecting the given constraints. In practice, parameter values are often symbolic (e.g. "some negative value"), necessitating a translation step before the case is submitted to the SUT.

When a test case is submitted, an oracle decides if the SUT behaved correctly. The definition of correct behavior depends on the SUT as well as the goal of the testing process. The goal of traditional CT is to detect faults where either the behavior of the SUT deviates from predefined rules, while that of security-focused combinatorial security testing (CST) [14] is to identify vulnerabilities. In this variant the input model is not necessarily based on values accepted by the SUT, but rather on control characters, known token values, or other crafted input designed to modify the way input is processed by the SUT.

In addition to the IPM, a practitioner seeking to utilize CT must choose a parameter called *strength* t ($1 < t < k$, where k is the number of parameters in the IPM). This parameter controls the guaranteed level of input space coverage afforded by the discrete mathematical structure that underlies a combinatorial test set, which is called a multi-level covering array (MCA), a form of covering array (CA) that allows for non-uniform domain sizes. A $MCA(N; t, k, \{v_1, ..., v_k\})$ is an array with N rows, each corresponding to a single test case, and k columns, each representing one parameter. For every possible selection of t distinct parameters, all possible parameter-value combinations occur at least once in the MCA. Naturally, choosing a larger t leads to a larger array, since more parameter-value combinations need to be covered, but also results in better fault detection capabilities since more of the input space is covered. On the extreme end of this scale, an exhaustive test set (i.e. $t = k$) would cover all parameter-value combinations and, as long as the input model and oracle are correct, guarantee to identify all faults of the SUT. However, such a test set is commonly infeasible to execute. For example, for a SUT with 10 parameters, each of which can assume 10 distinct values, an exhaustive test set would contain 10^{10} test cases, while a combinatorial test set with strength $t = 6$ requires requires $1, 494, 326$ tests [7], a reduction of 99.985%. One may be sceptical regarding the fault detection capabilities of such arrays. NIST conducted multiple studies analyzing known bugs across different industries, in which they were unable to find interaction faults triggered by more than 6 parameters [24]. Some industries had no interaction fault with more than 4 parameters.

2.2   Source Code Annotations

The concept of annotations can be regarded as an extension of preprocessor directives available in programming languages such as C. In Java, they were introduced as part of J2SE 5.0 in 2004 [16] as a means of providing metadata information associated with classes and methods. Nowadays, annotations can be used in many different use cases [10,16,28,33] such as:

- **Compiler Directives.** Developers can use annotations to interact with the compiler. An example is @SuppressWarnings, which can be used to deactivate warnings such as those regarding deprecated functions.
- **File Generation.** In this use case, a developer decorates an element with an annotation for the purposes of generating additional files or classes. In this work, the @CTATest annotation generates a combinatorial test class.
- **Documentation.** With the use of the @Documented annotations, developers can signal that annotations should be documented by JavaDoc or other tools.
- **Logging and Testing.** Annotations can also be processed at runtime, which enables them to be used for logging or testing.
- **Configuration** Some libraries rely on annotations for configuration. For example, a storage framework might offer a @Entity annotation, which would mark a class as a database entity.

In Kotlin, an annotation can be defined by creating a class prefixed with the **annotation** keyword. An example is shown in Listing 1.1.

Listing 1.1. Annotation Declaration Example

```
@Target ( AnnotationTarget .CLASS,  AnnotationTarget .FUNCTION)
@Retention ( AnnotationRetention .SOURCE)
@Repeatable
annotation class Example(val metadata:  String )
```

Annotations can then be used to add metadata to a class or method by prefixing the annotation's name with the @ character as shown in Listing 1.2.

Listing 1.2. Annotation Usage Example

```
@Example ("meta") class Foo {
  @Example ("data")
  fun baz(foo: Int): Int {
    return 1
  }
}
```

Annotations have three additional properties: Target, retention and repeatability. While the target limits the scope of an annotation (e.g. by making it only applicable to classes), repeatability dictates whether the same annotation can be used on an element multiple times. Finally, retention defines whether annotations are present in binary code and if they can be accessed via reflection.

While annotations are widespread and have many uses, a handful of **limitations** remain [6] that influence the methodology presented in this work.

- **Limited granularity.** Annotations are not applicable in every context. Examples of components that can not be annotated in Kotlin include generic statements, expressions or method bodies.
- **Limited parameter types.** Annotation parameters are restricted to specific types; in Java, these are primitive values, strings, enums, classes, other annotations and arrays containing the preceding types.
- **Static values.** Values assigned to annotation parameters must be resolvable in a static context. This means that e.g. methods or properties resolved via reflection can not be used.

Annotations are acted upon by processors, which can be executed either at compile time utilizing an annotation processing API or at runtime using reflection [31]. The metadata and capabilities available to the two paradigms differ, although approaches that allow for hybrid solutions exist [30,31].

3   Related Work

We now move on to a discussion of related work. We first review works focused on model creation and evolution in model-based testing before moving on to existing testing approaches in Kotlin and Java.

3.1   Model Creation and Evolution in Model-Based Testing

The effort required to construct and maintain a suitable model of the SUT is often prohibitively high. To circumvent this issue, one work revolving around web application testing [3] employs a learning approach that requires the user to define possible actions (such as logging into a page). The method utilizes these primitives as building blocks for test cases which are used to learn a model of the SUT. Another work [13] seeks to combine exploratory testing (wherein a tester interacts with the SUT) with a background process that offers information and possibilities to mark important steps to the tester and transforms the resulting information into a description suitable for model-based testing.

While the previously mentioned works necessitate user interaction, Møller and Torp [27] propose a method for regression testing of JavaScript libraries. They utilize existing software that depends on the respective library; by analyzing the interactions between these software components, their technique constructs a model of the library's interface and uses it to generate regression tests for future library versions. Amalfitano et al. [1], meanwhile, attempt to automatically reverse engineer the GUI of a SUT to obtain a state machine model.

In contrast to the aforementioned works, which try to offer technical solutions to the challenge of model creation and maintenance, others seek to implement organisational processes. Entin et al. [12] propose a method based on usage models that starts at an early stage and involves developers as well as additional stakeholders. While the model is initially created by quality assurance experts, it is then refined through feedback iterations before being utilized for test generation. A similar idea that relies on UML diagrams as models [18] argues that they can be created early based on requirements and adjusted later in the process. Test generation is based on the refined UML diagrams. Another work [5] proposes to model a system by using given requirements and identifying uncertainties. During test execution, the framework observes the SUT and reports results back to the modeler, who can refine the model and add or remove uncertainties.

In the area of CT, Dalal et al. [9] introduce AETGSpec, a tool which aims to be easy to use without the need for extensive requirements. While it does not provide the same depth as other tools, the authors argue that it still offers the possibility to craft high quality test cases. Test execution is performed manually.

In contrast to our approach presented herein, none of these works aim to simultaneously solve the disconnect between the SUT and the associated model as well as enable automated test generation and execution.

3.2   SUT Model Definitions in Kotlin and Java

We now review existing methods to define a model of an SUT in various testing concepts. In JUnit [17], one of the most popular Java testing frameworks, methods representing tests (i.e. implementing unit tests) are marked using annotations. It is also possible to pass a list of parameter sets using an extended version of this annotation. Extensions allow for entire classes to be marked as tests [32] or testable using random inputs [29]. However, unlike the approach presented herein, the interface to the SUT (the method to be tested) is never defined through annotations, rendering automated generation of test cases infeasible.

In the context of web applications, most works rely on the Web Services Description Language (WSDL) [19, 26, 34]. While our approach could be extended toward this use case, it is currently out of scope.

The closest work to the approach presented herein views one class as a container that holds all information relevant for a test case, including the method under test, and provides annotations for setup and teardown tasks [4]. This is a very flexible technique that additionally enforces coherence between SUT and test harness, as changes to the interface of the former that are not reflected in the latter will lead to compile errors. The latter property does not hold for an alternative work [25] that references packages, classes and methods as strings.

4   Methodology

We now move on to a description of our methodology. We first outline the steps required to implement CT in practice [23] and the specifics of our approach:

1. **IPM definition.** The parameters of the SUT as well as their values and constraints are defined. In this work, this step is implemented by creating an input class containing all parameters to a particular SUT method and annotating its properties.

2. **CA generation.** In order to obtain a combinatorial test set, a CA is generated using the aforementioned model. Our work automates this step by passing extracted IPMs and the requested strength to an existing generator.
3. **Test set translation.** With each row of the CA representing a test case, most SUTs require a transformation step of symbolic values contained in the CA to their actual types such as integers, enumerations or objects. This work automates this step.
4. **Test set execution and oracle.** Submitting translated inputs to the SUT is often accompanied with setup and teardown steps. In this work, a wrapper method acting as a test harness and oracle is passed a reference to the SUT and the test cases. While the creation of the wrapper incurs manual work, it does not need adjustments until the interface or intended behavior of the SUT changes. The former will generally lead to compilation errors, while the latter will often be made evident by failing tests.

Figure 1 visualizes the components required to implement our approach. Entities marked in blue or purple must be created by developers, whereas those in green are automatically generated by our implementations marked in red.

4.1   Input Class

An input class represents all inputs to a particular SUT for one test case. It serves as a basis for translating CA rows to individual test cases as well as for the test harness passing these values to the SUT. Storing test inputs in objects separates test translation from execution, leading to cleaner code and more visibility of issues resulting from interface changes. An example is shown in Listing 1.3.

4.2   Annotations

Three types of annotations are used: Input parameter type annotations, which define the value domain of parameters; constraint annotations, which impose restrictions on generated tests; and the CTATest annotation that ties together the SUT method, the input class (which stores inputs corresponding to an individual test case), and the test harness.

Input Parameter Type Annotations. Based on the input parameter model formats offered by the popular CA generators

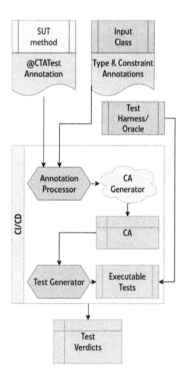

Fig. 1. Component overview. (Color figure online)

ACTS [36], CAgen [35] and PICT [8], three parameter types are used: Booleans, integers, and enumerations. Each can be utilized by decorating a property of the input class with the respective annotation.

- **CTABoolean:** This annotation defines a boolean parameter.
- **CTAInt:** This annotation defines an integer parameter. Additional parameters can be used to define integer domains:
    - **Range:** An integer range is defined using two parameters `from` and `to`.
    - **Value List:** Domains can be defined explicitly by using the `values` parameter and passing a list of integers.
- **CTAEnum:** This annotation defines an enumeration in one of two ways:
    - **Enum:** If the annotation is placed on an enum class, its available values are extracted automatically.
    - **Strings:** By annotating a string property and providing a `values` parameter, a set of strings can be defined. This gives developers more flexibility to define enumerations that are not necessarily reflected as an enum class.

Listing 1.3. Example input class

```
/**
 * Example enumeration with two values
 **/
enum class EnumExample {
  Value1 , Value2
}
/**
 * Constraints annotation
 * If the enum parameter equals ''Value1'', stringEnum can not be ''RED''.
 * If intRange equals 2, intValueList must be set to 4.
 */
@CTAConstraints(
  CTAIfConstraint("enum_$CTEQUALS_\"Value1\"_$CTIMPLIES_stringEnum_
      $CTNOTEQUALS_\"RED\""),
  CTAIfConstraint("intRange_$CTEQUALS_2_$CTIMPLIES_intValueList_
      $CTEQUALS_4"),
)
class ExampleClass {
  //Integer range
  @CTAInt(from = 0, to = 5)
  var intRange: Int = 1
  //Integer with discrete values
  @CTAInt(values = [0, 1, 2, 3, 4, 5])
  var intValueList: Int = 3
  //Boolean
  @CTABoolean
  var boolean: Boolean = false
  //Enumeration, see class above
  @CTAEnum
  var enum: EnumExample = EnumExample.Value1
  //String enumeration with three values
  @CTAEnum(values = ["RED", ''GREEN", ''YELLOW"])
  var stringEnum: String = ''RED"
}
```

Constraint Annotations. Constraints enforce restrictions on what values can be assigned to parameters within a test case based on a logical formula. Our constraint annotations are modeled after the features offered by ACTS [36], which supports the following operators (for technical reasons, our implementation uses alternative representations that do not correspond to Kotlin or Java operators):

- && The logical AND operator; written as $CTAND within an annotation.
- || The logical OR operator; represented by $CTOR.
- => An implication; written as $CTIMPLIES.
- ! Negation; represented by $CTNOT.
- == and != (equality and inequality), written as $CTEQUALS and $CTNOTEQUALS.

Fundamentally, the ACTS [36] documentation defines constraints as a conjunction of implications. These implications do not require a left-hand side (LHS); if there is no LHS, it is assumed to evaluate to true. In our work, the conjunction is represented as an annotation called **CTAConstraints** containing one or more **CTAIfConstraint** elements, each of which represents one implication as a string.

There are certain drawbacks associated with this approach. Ideally, one would directly reference classes and their members in constraints. This would allow for additional compile-time verification and thus prevent issues arising from simple developer mistakes. However, Kotlin and Java annotations do not allow for this design, as they require annotation parameters to be compile-time constants that can not reference external functions or dynamically modified values. Another approach would be to compose constraints from other annotations (e.g. representing a logical conjunction, disjunction, or other part of a logical formula). However, annotations in Kotlin cannot self-reference, which creates issues when trying to translate a formal grammar with self-referencing into an annotation format. As a result, the decision was made to use a simple string format.

The CTATest Annotation. Finally, we need to provide an annotation that connects the SUT with its input class and the test harness described below. The CTATest annotation is applied to the method under test and takes a test harness class as its first parameter, followed by a variable number of input classes. Listing 1.4 shows an example of annotating a SUT method called testingTestClasses() (in practice, this method would likely take some parameters).

Listing 1.4. Example usage of CTATest

```
@CTADebug
class CTATests {
    @CTATest(CTATestContainerImpl::class, TestClass::class)
    fun testingTestClasses() {}
}
```

4.3 Test Harness and Oracle

Tests in object oriented programming languages often require extensive setup and teardown procedures to set up required classes and their associated information. Additionally, the definition of correct behavior is strongly related to the individual SUT, requiring flexible handling of these steps. Based on these insights, our approach requires developers to implement a class that adheres to an interface **CTATestContainer** prescribing a single method as shown in Listing 1.5. This method must accept a reference to the SUT method as well as an array of input classes (in our current implementation, only one input class is accepted per test case). Semantically, the task of this method is to perform set-up steps, call the referenced method with the parameters provided by the input class, potentially execute a teardown procedure and finally evaluate the results of the SUT to return a test verdict as a boolean.

Listing 1.5. Interface for container class

```
interface CTATestContainer {
    fun oracle(methodToTest: KFunction<*>, inputs: Array<Any>): Boolean
}
```

4.4   Annotation Processor

The purpose of the annotation processor is to create an IPM suitable for CA generation and to pass on required information to the test generator that translates the resulting CA to executable tests. Two capabilities are of critical importance for this step: First, being able to scan source code and extract all annotations, and second, the ability to generate new code objects during processing. For the purposes of our work, we utilize the Kotlin Symbol Processing API (KSP) [15], the successor of the popular Kotlin Annotation Processing Tool (KAPT) [20]. KSP fulfills our requirements, is developed by Google and well-known in the Kotlin community, making it unlikely to be abandoned in the near future.

The annotation processor gathers all annotations described above and constructs an input file in ACTS [36] format. An example of such a file is shown in Listing 1.6.

Listing 1.6. Example ACTS input file

```
[System]
Name: TestClassCTTest
[Parameter]
boolean(boolean): true, false
enum(enum): Example1, Example2
numberWithArrayOfValues(int): 0, 1, 2, 3, 4, 5
numberWithRange(int): 0, 1, 2, 3, 4, 5
stringEnum(enum): RED, GREEN, YELLOW
[Constraint]
enum = ''Example1" => stringEnum != ''RED"
numberWithRange = 2 => numberWithArrayOfValues = 4
```

This ACTS file is then passed to a CA generator such as CAgen [35], along with a user-selected strength t, ultimately resulting in a CA being constructed. In the next step, the test generator reads in this file and transforms it to executable tests.

4.5   Test Generator

The task of the test generator is to transform the CA resulting from the previous step into a test set, which is a list of objects instantiating the input class described above. It additionally analyzes the imports required by the SUT as well as the input class, as these must be present for test execution to be possible. Finally, the test generator creates a source file based on a template, packaging the required imports and the test set along with a test method. The latter is decorated using a JUnit `ParameterizedTest` annotation [17] while defining the packaged test set as the object containing individual test cases. A simplified version of the resulting source file is shown in Listing 1.7.

Listing 1.7. Test executor template

```
<static imports e.g. jUnit, basic Kotlin functions>
<dynamic imports e.g. input class, container class>

class <class name> {
    @ParameterizedTest
    @MethodSource(<test case source>)
    fun testing<class name>(<inputs>) {
        <invoke oracle>
        <if oracle negative response -> fail test>
    }

    companion object {
        <test case source> = Stream.of(
            <invoking helper function with inputs of one test case>
            ...
        )
    <helper function which creates class with passed inputs>
    }
}
```

4.6 Continuous Integration and Deployment

Continuous integration (CI) is a concept whereby changes to source code – commonly tracked in a revision control system – are automatically compiled, tested and integrated into a common codebase. Continuous deployment (CD) goes beyond this step and additionally deploys the resulting objects, e.g. to a test or even live environment. One of the goals of our work is to automate combinatorial test set generation and execution within CI/CD pipelines. To this end, our processing components (i.e. the annotation processor and test generator) are driven by a CI/CD task implemented for the popular Gradle [11] build system.

A typical Gradle build involves compiling the codebase and, among other tasks, also running referenced test cases inside the test package. Crucially, KSP – which our annotation processor and test generator are built to use – also offers its own task via Gradle, which executes the compilation task alongside any defined processors. This results in solid support for continuous integration, as developers can decide to either simply run a full build, which would compile, invoke KSP, and run generated tests, or run specific steps as needed.

As mentioned in the previous section, our test generator uses a template to create JUnit 5 tests. JUnit is one of the most widespread testing frameworks in Java and Kotlin environments and well integrated into Gradle. By adding the folder that houses the generated test files to Gradle's test package, we ensure they are found and executed.

4.7   Limitations

A range of limitations remain to be resolved, some caused by architectural decisions or external dependencies, while others remain to be addressed by future
work.

- **Kotlin.** The choice of programming language for implementing our approach
  brings about a handful of limitations. Our Kotlin implementation is only
  applicable to projects written in Kotlin and currently only supports the Gradle build system. While an extension towards other build systems and CI/CD
  solutions is straightforward, changing the target programming language will
  likely require significant modifications.
    - **Version mismatches.** The SUT needs to build upon the same or a later
      Kotlin version as the library, a limitation imposed by the compiler itself.
    - **Annotations.** Kotlin has great support for annotations, allowing them
      to be used on classes, functions, and variables. However, as noted above,
      their parameters must be compile-time constants and annotations can not
      reference each other, preventing us from creating a more elegant interface
      for IPM definitions.
- **Oracle problem.** A common problem in testing is the difficulty of creating a
  correct oracle. In practice, identifying faulty behavior requires intimate knowledge of the SUT and may even require introspection of its state in addition
  to inputs and outputs. Automating this step is a topic of active research. Our
  approach makes no effort to absolve developers from implementing oracles.
- **State in object-oriented programming.** Object-oriented programming
  (OOP) organizes code around objects with data and behaviors. Setup procedures for a test case must bring the SUT method and all objects it accesses
  into a suitable state, a task that often proves challenging. It would be possible
  to extend our approach in order to include parameters representing the state
  in the IPM. Due to the added complexity, we leave this step as future work.
- **Class instantiation.** Like most object-oriented programming languages,
  Kotlin imposes accessibility restrictions on class members. During test execution, the input class needs to be instantiated and its properties assigned to
  the correct values. Currently, our implementation requires an input class to
  have an empty constructor and its properties to be reassignable.

5   Case Study

We now move on to a case study based on our Kotlin implementation[1]. We
apply our solution to an existing medium-sized codebase in order to evaluate its
applicability. As the focus of this experiment was the usability of our approach
in practice and not CT in general, we opted to set the strength $t = 3$ in all cases.

Our selection criteria for the codebase were as follows:

---

[1] Implementation available at https://github.com/sTeaKORE/cta.

1. The project must be implemented in Kotlin, with the project matching our Kotlin version, and incorporate Gradle.
2. It should be of medium size; we opted to search for projects with more than 10,000 lines of code, but less than one million. This criterion aims to ensure that the case study is representative, but does not incur the extensive effort required to familiarize oneself with very large codebases.
3. Limited external dependencies. Particularly in the context of Android, where Kotlin is the recommended language, a wide range of externally defined data structures is common, the instantiation of which can be rather complex.

Based on these criteria, we selected KotCity [22], a city simulator in the style of SimCity, as our evaluation target. We opted to focus on three existing unit tests and replace them with CT counterparts. These tests cover three fundamental methods in the context of city building simulations: Collision detection, path finding, and detecting potential building upgrades. An overview of the tests, the required number of parameters and constraints as well as the number of resulting tests is given in Table 1. Creating an annotation for a method took our tester (a user with basic knowledge of ACTS and advanced skills in Kotlin) around one minute per parameter and an additional three minutes per constraint; this was reported to be a partially iterative process based on considerations that arose during oracle creation, which was generally the most time-consuming task (up to an hour). Automated test generation and translation was completed in under five minutes while test execution remained under a minute in all instances.

Table 1. Evaluation Test Results

Test Name	Parameters	Constraints	Test Set Size
Collision	3	0	5766
Path Finding	6	6	2945
Upgrader	12	3	6128

5.1 Collision Detection

In KotCity, the playing field is a two-dimensional plane divided into fixed-size blocks. The player can execute commands on these blocks, including construction tasks that build a structure of a given type at this location. This can lead to collisions when attempting to place a structure. The existing unit test starts with an empty playing field of varying size, loads a JSON file containing different types of building, and tries to build two buildings in the same spot or too close to each other. Three parameters are defined in the file: A point made up of x and y coordinates and the name of the building type. We created an input class as shown in Listing 1.8 and wrote a test harness that implements the same behavior as the unit test. A total of 5766 test cases were created, an excerpt of which is contained in Listing 1.9. All test cases were executed successfully. Besides the difficulty of inferring the input format from a JSON file instead of relying on Kotlin classes, applying our approach was unproblematic.

Listing 1.8. Collision Test - Input class

```
class CollisionInputClass {
    @CTAEnum(values = ["slum1", ''slum2'',_''cheap_house", ''hotel"])
___var_buildingType:_String_=_''placeholder"
    @CTAInt(from = 0, to = 30)
    var x: Int = 0
    @CTAInt(from = 0, to = 30)
    var y: Int = 0
}
```

Listing 1.9. Collision Test - Sample test cases

```
slum1,0,30
slum2,1,0
cheap_house,0,0
```

5.2 Path Finding

Our second test revolves around the path finding algorithm implemented in the game. The SUT is a method that is given a point on the map and attempts to find a way out of the city using available roads. By analyzing the existing unit test, it was inferred that the SUT can only find a valid path if a road from one side of the city to the other exists on the map. The input class is shown in Listing 1.10. Three points are defined through a pair of coordinates each: Two make up the beginning and end of a road that is placed on the map during setup, while the third reflects the starting point that is passed to the SUT. Six constraints ensure that the road spans across the map and is not collapsed at a single point.

Listing 1.10. Path Finding Test - Input Class

```
@CTAConstraints(
    CTAIfConstraint("xRoadStart $CTEQUALS xRoadEnd $CTIMPLIES yRoadStart
        $CTNOTEQUALS yRoadEnd"),
    CTAIfConstraint("yRoadStart $CTEQUALS yRoadEnd $CTIMPLIES xRoadStart
        $CTNOTEQUALS xRoadEnd"),
    CTAIfConstraint("xRoadStart $CTEQUALS 0 $CTIMPLIES xRoadEnd
        $CTNOTEQUALS 0"),
    CTAIfConstraint("yRoadStart $CTEQUALS 0 $CTIMPLIES yRoadEnd
        $CTNOTEQUALS 0"),
    CTAIfConstraint("xRoadStart $CTEQUALS 30 $CTIMPLIES xRoadEnd
        $CTNOTEQUALS 30"),
    CTAIfConstraint("yRoadStart $CTEQUALS 30 $CTIMPLIES yRoadEnd
        $CTNOTEQUALS 30"),
)
class PathfindingInputClass {
    @CTAInt(from = 0, to = 30)
    var xStart: Int = 0
    @CTAInt(from = 0, to = 30)
    var yStart: Int = 0
    @CTAInt(values = [0, 15, 30])
    var xRoadStart: Int = 0
    @CTAInt(values = [0, 15, 30])
```

```
    var yRoadStart: Int = 0
    @CTAInt(values = [0, 15, 30])
    var xRoadEnd: Int = 0
    @CTAInt(values = [0, 15, 30])
    var yRoadEnd: Int = 0
}
```

The resulting CA contains 2945 test cases. While the creation of the input class was straightforward, implementing a correct oracle proved challenging. Our initial assumption was that any road present on the map would allow the path finding algorithm to succeed; however, we later learned that it requires a road to be within three blocks of its starting point. Additionally, path finding currently does not handle diagonal roads. Modifying our oracle to take these limitations into account allowed it to return a correct verdict and led to all tests passing.

5.3   Upgrade Eligibility Detection

The SUT of our third and last test is a method that detects buildings that are eligible for upgrades based on a parameter called goodwill. We modeled the coordinates, type, and goodwill of three buildings. Three constraints ensure that the positions do not overlap. Our test harness places the buildings on a map, calls the SUT and evaluates whether it correctly identifies buildings to upgrade. Contrary to our initial expectations, some structures natively start with higher upgrade levels and the SUT – in contrast to its documentation – only marks one building as eligible for upgrades, not three. After adjusting the oracle, all 6128 test cases resulting from generating a CA passed successfully.

6   Conclusion

This work presented an annotation-based approach to defining input parameter models for the purposes of combinatorial testing of methods in object-oriented programming languages. It aims to ease the adoption of CT by increasing the proximity between code and model, streamlining the task of model creation and maintenance. Changes to the interface of the SUT result in compilation errors and are thus easily identifiable. Our approach requires the manual creation of an input class and a combined test harness/oracle class. The remaining steps, including covering array generation, translation to test cases and their execution, are automated and can be easily integrated into existing CI/CD pipelines.

Our case study demonstrated the applicability of our approach to existing codebases. At the same time, a number of limitations are yet to be addressed, some resulting from implementation details such as the choice of language, while others arise from unresolved issues in the field of combinatorial testing.

Acknowledgments. SBA Research (SBA-K1) is a COMET Centre within the COMET – Competence Centers for Excellent Technologies Programme and funded by BMK, BMAW, and the federal state of Vienna. COMET is managed by FFG.

Disclosure of Interests. The authors have no competing interests to declare that are relevant to the content of this article.

References

1. Amalfitano, D., Fasolino, A.R., Tramontana, P., Ta, B.D., Memon, A.M.: MobiGU-ITAR: automated model-based testing of mobile apps. IEEE Softw. **32**(5), 53–59 (2014)
2. Ammann, P., Offutt, J.: Introduction to Software Testing. Cambridge University Press, Cambridge (2016)
3. Bainczyk, A., Schieweck, A., Steffen, B., Howar, F.: Model-based testing without models: the todomvc case study. ModelEd, TestEd, TrustEd: Essays Dedicated to Ed Brinksma on the Occasion of His 60th Birthday, pp. 125–144 (2017)
4. Basso, F.P., Oliveira, T.C., Farias, K.: Extending junit 4 with java annotations and reflection to test variant model transformation assets. In: Proceedings of the 29th Annual ACM Symposium on Applied Computing, pp. 1601–1608 (2014)
5. Camilli, M., Bellettini, C., Gargantini, A., Scandurra, P.: Online model-based testing under uncertainty. In: 2018 IEEE 29th International Symposium on Software Reliability Engineering (ISSRE), pp. 36–46. IEEE (2018)
6. Cazzola, W., Vacchi, E.: @ java: Bringing a richer annotation model to java. Comput. Lang. Syst. Struct. **40**(1), 2–18 (2014)
7. Colbourn, C.J.: Covering array tables for t=2,3,4,5,6 (2008)
8. Czerwonka, J.: Pairwise testing in the real world: practical extensions to test-case scenarios. In: Proceedings of 24th Pacific Northwest Software Quality Conference, Citeseer, pp. 419–430. Citeseer (2006)
9. Dalal, S.R., et al.: Model-based testing in practice. In: Proceedings of the 21st International Conference on Software Engineering, pp. 285–294 (1999)
10. Darwin, I.: Annabot: A static verifier for java annotation usage. Adv. Softw. Eng. **2010** (2009)
11. Davis, A.L.: Gradle. Learning Groovy 3: Java-Based Dynamic Scripting, pp. 105–114 (2019)
12. Entin, V., Winder, M., Zhang, B., Claus, A.: A process to increase the model quality in the context of model-based testing. In: 2015 IEEE Eighth International Conference on Software Testing, Verification and Validation Workshops (ICSTW), pp. 1–7. IEEE (2015)
13. Frajták, K., Bures, M., Jelinek, I.: Model-based testing and exploratory testing: Is synergy possible? In: 2016 6th International Conference on IT Convergence and Security (ICITCS), pp. 1–6. IEEE (2016)
14. Garn, B., Lang, D.S., Leithner, M., Kuhn, D.R., Kacker, R., Simos, D.E.: Combinatorially XSSing Web Application Firewalls (2021)
15. Google: Ksp- kotlin symbol processing api (2021). https://kotlinlang.org/docs/ksp-overview.html
16. Gosling, J., Joy, B., Steele, G., Bracha, G.: The Java Language Specification, 3rd Edn. Addison-Wesley Professional (2005)
17. Gulati, S., Sharma, R.: Java unit testing with junit 5. Java Unit Testing with JUnit (2017)
18. Hasling, B., Goetz, H., Beetz, K.: Model based testing of system requirements using uml use case models. In: 2008 1st International Conference on Software Testing, Verification, and Validation, pp. 367–376. IEEE (2008)
19. Heckel, R., Lohmann, M.: Towards contract-based testing of web services. Electron. Notes Theoret. Comput. Sci. **116**, 145–156 (2005)
20. Jetbrains: Kotlin annotation processing tool (2017). https://kotlinlang.org/docs/kapt.html

⌐. Kampel, L., Kitsos, P., Simos, D.E.: Locating hardware trojans using combinatorial testing for cryptographic circuits. IEEE Access **10**, 18787–18806 (2022). https://doi.org/10.1109/ACCESS.2022.3151378
22. kotcity: City simulation written in kotlin (2018). https://github.com/kotcity/kotcity
23. Kuhn, D.R., Bryce, R., Duan, F., Ghandehari, L.S., Lei, Y., Kacker, R.N.: Combinatorial Testing: Theory and Practice, Advances in Computers, vol. 99 (2015)
24. Kuhn, R., Lei, Y., Kacker, R.: Practical combinatorial testing: beyond pairwise. IT Prof. **10**(3), 19–23 (2008)
25. Marschall, P.: Detecting the methods under test in java. Bachelor thesis (2005)
26. Martin, E., Basu, S., Xie, T.: Automated testing and response analysis of web services. In: IEEE International Conference on Web Services (ICWS 2007), pp. 647–654. IEEE (2007)
27. Møller, A., Torp, M.T.: Model-based testing of breaking changes in node. JS libraries. In: Proceedings of the 2019 27th ACM Joint Meeting on European Software Engineering Conference and Symposium on the Foundations of Software Engineering, pp. 409–419 (2019)
28. Noguera, C., Duchien, L.: Annotation framework validation using domain models. In: Schieferdecker, I., Hartman, A. (eds.) ECMDA-FA 2008. LNCS, vol. 5095, pp. 48–62. Springer, Heidelberg (2008). https://doi.org/10.1007/978-3-540-69100-6_4
29. Pacheco, C., Ernst, M.: Randoop: feedback-directed random testing for java. In: Companion to the 22nd ACM SIGPLAN Conference on Object-oriented Programming Systems and Applications Companion, pp. 815–816 (2007)
30. Pawlak, R.: Spoon: compile-time annotation processing for middleware. IEEE Distrib. Syst. Online **7**(11), 1–1 (2006)
31. Pigula, P., Nosal, M.: Unified compile-time and runtime java annotation processing. In: 2015 Federated Conference on Computer Science and Information Systems (FedCSIS), pp. 965–975. IEEE (2015)
32. Proulx, V.K., Jossey, W.: Unit test support for java via reflection and annotations. In: Proceedings of the 7th International Conference on Principles and Practice of Programming in Java, pp. 49–56 (2009)
33. Rocha, H., Valente, M.T.: How annotations are used in java: an empirical study. In: SEKE, pp. 426–431 (2011)
34. Tsai, W.T., Paul, R., Wang, Y., Fan, C., Wang, D.: Extending WSDL to facilitate web services testing. In: 7th IEEE International Symposium on High Assurance Systems Engineering, 2002. Proceedings, pp. 171–172. IEEE (2002)
35. Wagner, M., Kleine, K., Simos, D.E., Kuhn, R., Kacker, R.: Cagen: a fast combinatorial test generation tool with support for constraints and higher-index arrays. In: 2020 IEEE International Conference on Software Testing, Verification and Validation Workshops (ICSTW), pp. 191–200. IEEE (2020)
36. Yu, L., Lei, Y., Kacker, R.N., Kuhn, D.R.: Acts: a combinatorial test generation tool. In: 2013 IEEE Sixth International Conference on Software Testing, Verification and Validation, pp. 370–375. IEEE (2013)

Author Index

A

Augusto, Cristian   239

B

Barnard, Pepita   217
Bautista, John Robert   217
Berger, Christian   114
Bertolino, Antonia   239
Beyazıt, Mutlu   292
Butler, Alexis   275

C

Cabrero-Daniel, Beatriz   114
Cezar Petrescu, Constantin   275
Corpaci, Luiza   3

D

Dakhama, Aidan   169, 217
Dall'Anese, Daniele   159
de la Riva, Claudio   239
del Castillo, Miguel Herencia García   210
Demeyer, Serge   292
Dona, Malsha Ashani Mahawatta   114

E

Erol, Hande   46

F

Farahi, Arya   217
Feldt, Robert   30
Foulefack, Rosmaël Zidane Lekeufack   95, 159
Freimanis, Andris   30
Fugger, Markus   332

G

García, Ekaitz Arriola   210
García, Ricardo Moya   210
González de Diego, Ángela   63
Gross, Dennis   23

H

Hierons, Robert M.   315

I

Iglesias, Guillermo   210

K

Kampel, Ludwig   3
Khoee, Arsham Gholamzadeh   30
Kisaakye, Joanna   292
Knight, Simon   193
Knoblauch, Dorian   256
Kumar Dash, Santanu   275

L

Laos, Kazim   217
Leithner, Manuel   332
Lekeufack Foulefack, Rosmaël Zidane   131
Liu, Anqi   217
Lou, Guannan   315

M

Mallinger, Kevin   3
Marchetto, Alessandro   95, 131, 159
Mazón, Manuel Jesús Cerezo   210
Menéndez, Héctor D.   169, 185, 217
Morán, Jesús   239

P

Parthasarathy, Dhasarathy   30
Prikler, Liliana Marie   79, 151

R

Raubitzek, Sebastian   3
Rhodin, Patrick Andersson   30

S

Shin, Donghwan   315
Shrestha, Abhishek   256
Simos, Dimitris E.   3, 332

H. D. Menéndez et al. (Eds.): ICTSS 2024, LNCS 15383, pp. 349–350, 2025.
https://doi.org/10.1007/978-3-031-80889-0

6

23

..l, Guillermo   185

Tuya, Javier   239

V

Vecellio Reane, Martina   159

W

Wagner, Michael   3

Wainwright, Katie   193

Walkinshaw, Neil   315

Webb, Helena   193

Wingfield, Laura R.   193

Wotawa, Franz   63, 79, 151

Y

Yu, Yinan   30, 114

www.ingramcontent.com/pod-product-compliance
Lightning Source LLC
Chambersburg PA
CBHW050510100225
21662CB00007B/89